QUEER(ING) RUSSIAN ART

REALISM, REVOLUTION, PERFORMANCE

Myths and Taboos in Russian Culture

QUEER(ING) RUSSIAN ART

REALISM, REVOLUTION, PERFORMANCE

Edited by Brian James Baer and Yevgeniy Fiks

Myths and Taboos in Russian Culture

This book is supported in part by The Amie and Tony James Gallery/Center for the Humanities, CUNY Graduate Center.

Library of Congress Cataloging-in-Publication Data

Names: Baer, Brian James, editor. | Fiks, Yevgeniy, editor.
Title: Queer(ing) Russian art : realism, revolution, performance / edited by Brian James Baer and Yevgeniy Fiks.
Description: Boston : Academic Studies Press, 2023. | Series: Myths and taboos in Russian culture | Includes bibliographical references.
Identifiers: LCCN 2023018642 (print) | LCCN 2023018643 (ebook) | ISBN 9798887192512 (hardback) | ISBN 9798887192529 (adobe pdf) | ISBN 9798887192536 (epub)
Subjects: LCSH: Sex and art. | Homosexuality in art. | Sexual minorities in art. | Art and society--Russia (Federation) | Art and society--Soviet Union.
Classification: LCC N72.S49 Q34 2023 (print) | LCC N72.S49 (ebook) | DDC 700/.4538--dc23/eng/20230523
LC record available at https://lccn.loc.gov/2023018642
LC ebook record available at https://lccn.loc.gov/2023018643

Paperback 2025

ISBN 9798897830978 (paperback)
ISBN 9798887192529 (adobe pdf)
ISBN 9798887192536 (epub)

Book design by Lapiz Digital Services.
Cover design by Ivan Grave.
On the cover: Georgii Liubarskii, *Everything under the Red Banner* (1924), poster.

Published by Academic Studies Press
press@academicstudiespress.com
www.academicstudiespress.com

Contents

Acknowledgments

A number of people were instrumental in making this volume a reality. Generous support from Katherine Carl, curator of the James Gallery and deputy director of the Center for the Humanities at the Graduate Center of City University of New York, helped get this project off the ground and provided the funds necessary to compensate the translators, Aleksei Grinenko, Ryan Green, and Innokenty Grekov, who played such a crucial role in this project. A warm thank you to Vitaliy Chernetsky, who made the initial introduction to Oleh Kotsyuba, the acquisitions editor at Academic Studies Press, who then enthusiastically supported the project, and to Tim McCarthy, without whose generosity and solidarity Yevgeniy Fiks's contribution to this volume, "Soviet Union, July 1991," would not have been possible. We are also very grateful to the anonymous reviewers of this project, whose detailed comments and suggestions contributed greatly to the final product. Last, but definitely not least, we owe an incredible debt of gratitude to Helena Goscilo whose meticulous copyediting and encyclopedic knowledge of Russian visual arts (and not just Russian) were invaluable as we finalized the introduction. That being said, any remaining errors or infelicities are ours alone.

Note on Transliteration

With Russian-language sources, the Library of Congress transliteration system was used without diacritical marks to render proper names, titles, and quoted passages. Where there is an established English spelling of a name, however, that established spelling was used, e.g., Eisenstein, instead of Eizenshtein, Tchaikovsky, instead of Chaikovskii, Meyerhold, instead of Meierkhol'd, and Walter Nouvel, instead of Val'ter Nouvel'.

Introduction

Brian James Baer and Yevgeniy Fiks

While the topic of queer sexuality in Russia has been investigated for decades now by scholars working in the fields of sociology, history, literary studies, and musicology, it has yet to be studied in any comprehensive or systematic way by those working in the visual arts.[1] In fact, with the notable exception of a cluster of articles on Neoacademism published in the journal *Russian Review* in 2019 and Allison Leigh's *Picturing Russia's Men: Masculinity and Modernity in Nineteenth-Century Painting* (2020), it has been largely ignored.[2] *Queer(ing) Russian Art: Realism, Revolution, Performance* is meant to fill this lacuna by providing a platform for new scholarship that connects Russian art with queerness in a variety of ways. Working from different theoretical and disciplinary perspectives, the contributors expose and explore the queer imagery and sensibilities in works of Russian visual art and beneath the surface of conventional histories of Russian art.

In its approach, the volume stands at the intersection of Visual Studies and Queer Studies. In regard to Visual Studies, we follow Valerie A. Kivelson and Joan Neuberger (2008, 2), who differentiate the field from art history "in its emphasis on seeing as an embedded social practice," while aligning it with Cultural Studies "in its attention to the shifting, fragmentary, culturally and individually specific responses to visual objects." From Queer Studies, we take queer to mean "the post-structuralist figure of identity as a constellation of multiple and unstable positions" (Jagose 1996, 3), or, as conceived by Richard Meyer (2019, 7), "a site of sexual meaning and symbolic investment under continual negotiation both by those who name themselves as gay or lesbian and by those who do not." The act of queering therefore constitutes for us an analytical mode that "dramatize[s] incoherencies in the allegedly stable relations between chromosomal sex, gender and sexual desire" (Jagose 1996, 3).

That being said, we do not wish to suggest that queerness exists *only* in the eye of the beholder—that *there is no there there*—as doing so risks playing into the hands of those who would render queer individuals invisible. Validating a queer approach to art, often critiqued as biased or minoritarian, therefore entails exposing the traditional reluctance of art historians, curators, and dealers to "see" queerness in art and artists as itself highly subjective. That reluctance is by no means only evident in Russian art history or in studies of art before the twentieth century.[3] Andy Warhol, for example, was advised in the 1980s to be less "swish" in order to appeal to a broader market of art buyers, and his sexuality was not discussed in any serious way by art historians until the early 1990s (see Doyle, Flatley and Munoz 1993). Even today, popular representations of Leonardo da Vinci focus on possible romantic relationships with women.[4] As Jonathan Jones remarks in *The Guardian* (March 26, 2021): "It's as if Leonardo's homosexuality is incompatible with the universality of his art."[5]

Thanks to the work of historical recovery by scholars such as Dan Healey (2001), Francesca Stella (2015), and Ira Roldugina (2016a and 2016b), no one today can deny that there were queers and queer subcultures throughout Russia—in Russian cities and Soviet prisons, but also in Russia's rural communities. The publication of the diaries of the queer writer Mikhail Kuzmin (1998, 2000, and 2009) and, more recently, of the artist Konstantin Somov (2017), in complete, unexpurgated, and annotated editions, attests to this fact, as does Andrei Poznanskii's scrupulously researched two-volume biography of the composer Pyotr Tchaikovsky (2009). These works challenge traditional stereotypes of artistic homosexuals as "tortured," in the case of Tchaikovsky or as "very gentle and modest," in the case of Somov (Nina Berbereva qtd. in El'shevskaia 2003, 13). At the same time, this volume is not in the business of "outing" Russian artists; its interest lies in the conditions that allow for the production, circulation, and reception of queer art above and beyond the sexual orientation of the artist, although not excluding it. Our dual task therefore involves acknowledging both the ontological status of queers in Russia and the epistemological power of queering.

To that end, our volume adopts a very broad understanding of queer as including any experience or performance of nonnormative gender and sexuality, and of queering as any intervention that exposes, challenges, or subverts dominant heteronormative assumptions, beliefs, and practices. The relative nature of the designation nonnormative is especially important when studying gender and sexuality across languages and cultures because it acknowledges that what is considered queer today may not have been considered queer in another time and place, and vice versa. Accordingly, we hope to avoid imposing a Western minoritarian model of homosexuality as well as Western models of queerness onto other cultures in ways that would erase the distinct contexts of queer representation there, on the one hand, or limit our study to gay-identified artists, on the other.

And so, the volume's focus on queerness seeks to offer an alternative to the exclusive and discriminatory identitarian politics of ethno-nationalists while also avoiding a minoritarian discourse of tolerance. To that end, we posit queerness as residing both in objects and in ways of seeing and in the unpredictable relationship between the two, celebrating "the polymorphous and polyvocal notability of the homoerotic in visual production" (Smalls 1996, 26). This also opens up a dual reading of the title, as not only queering art per se, but also queering what it means to frame art as Russian, given the complex multicultural reality of imperial Tsarist, Soviet, and post-Soviet Russian culture.

That being said, the volume is informed by critical perspectives on culture that arose in the multicultural imperial space of "Russian" culture, specifically Lotmanian semiotics, with its view of the unpredictability of cultural change that results from the constant repurposing and reaccentuating of material from that culture's semiotic reservoir—a model that overlaps in interesting ways with Judith Butler's notion of performativity—and of Bakhtinian views on language, which stress the historicity and social embeddedness of words and other linguistic and cultural forms, imbuing the practice of artistic citation with queer, polyglossic potential. In adopting analytical approaches associated both with Russian/Soviet culture and the West and by bringing together a group of scholars working both in Russia and abroad, the volume hopes to avoid the persistent postcolonial dynamic by which enlightened Western scholars "explain" Russian culture to Russians. (Indeed, we should not ignore the fact that market censorship in the West has exerted significant constraints on queer artists, as discussed above). The past thirty years, since the fall of communism, have seen increasing international exchange and cooperation across the Humanities so that new generations of researchers now regularly reference and critically engage with a shared body of theoretical works, archival material, and empirical studies on the subjects of gender and queer sexuality, which lends this volume a coherence of approach and terminology despite the fact that more than half of the authors wrote their chapters in Russian. And so, we must also acknowledge the enormous contribution of translators to this project and hope that this volume will set a standard for more collaborative and egalitarian cross-cultural and cross-lingual scholarship. Translation no doubt added a layer of complexity, but it also provided an opportunity for dialogue and debate among the authors, translators, and editors that greatly enriched the project.

A Time for Queering

There could be, perhaps, no more apt time for a book on this subject. Queer scholarship and lived experience are under attack in countries across the world in the face of nationalist revivals that involve stoking bigotry in support of a far-right agenda based on "traditional family values." In Russia, this was highlighted by the passage in 2013 of a federal law banning "homosexual propaganda," which has led paradoxically to widespread public discussion of queer sexuality and to the designation of age restrictions on all sorts of cultural products, alerting readers to their "queer" content. (Recent editions of Merezhkovskii's *Resurrected Gods*, for example, now carry a +16 designation on the cover, and the unexpurgated diaries of artist Konstantin Somov, a +18 designation.) However, as Roman Utkin (2021, 8) rightly notes, "While homophobic and transphobic legislative actions serve political agendas and are largely symbolic for much of the population, they directly affect queer and trans Russian citizens."[6] Indeed, as Alexander Kondakov and Evgeny Shtorn (2021) have documented, the legislation has resulted in increasing violence against queer Russians (see also Kondakov 2017).

More troubling in the realm of culture than the mandatory age designations, which may do as much to entice readers as they do to repel them, is the government's attempt to erase Russia's queer history. Consider the biopic of the composer Pyotr Tchaikovsky directed by film and theater director Kirill Serebrennikov, with a script by Iurii Arabov, which was in progress during the very public debates over homosexual propaganda before the passage of the federal law mentioned above (see Bullock 2018). Fearing the fate of the film was in danger, the scriptwriter gave an interview to the newspaper *Izvestiia*, in which he stated, without equivocation: "There is nothing to suggest that Tchaikovskii was a homosexual. Only philistines think that. There's no need for cinema to show what philistines believe" (qtd. in Bullock 2018, 53). He then went further, declaring the topic of homosexuality itself to lie "outside the sphere of art," which not only renders the queerness of artists irrelevant but also contradicts traditional Russian associations of homosexuality with spirituality, artistic refinement, and creativity (see Baer 2009). And so, in the present climate, the production and dissemination of queer knowledge and queer ways of seeing has assumed considerable political urgency.

The conservative-authoritarian turn in Russian politics since 2012, which led to the 2013 federal law banning homosexual propaganda, has had a pronounced effect on the visual arts in Russia. Although the construal of art and artists as enemies began shortly after Putin's rise to power (see Erofeev 2018), it was following the appointment of Vladimir Medinskii as Minister of Culture in 2012 that "culture was defined as the spiritual experience of the country and the 'collection of moral and ethical values' that was to be handed on to future generations" (Jonson 2018b, 49). As Lena Jonson (2018b, 49) explains: "The major task was to fortify patriotism and national pride through the education system (school curricula, history textbooks), the media and cultural outputs (film, theatre, the visual arts, etc.)." This cultural policy was pursued in the realm of art in an especially heavy-handed, top-down manner, which involved appointing conservatives to head major art institutions, closing or merging museum spaces and galleries, and funding only exhibitions that aligned with the government's increasingly narrow aesthetic, favoring "a more traditional, figurative, decorative and optimistic art" with broad popular appeal (Jonson 2018b, 51).

It is perhaps no surprise then that the promotion of such art has led to the rehabilitation of official Soviet art, which is being accomplished largely by depoliticizing it, another way to forgive and forget the authoritarian violence of Stalinism. Consider the recent Deineka/Samokhvalov exhibition in St. Petersburg, which was "imagined as a soccer match between two major Soviet painters from rival cities" (Pinkham 2020, 47) and which, predictably, did not display Deineka's haunting wartime paintings and drawings discussed by Gleb Napreenko in chapter 5 of this volume. And those who visit the Stalinist Exhibition of Achievements of the National Economy in Moscow today will be serenaded over the loudspeakers by international pop music, such as Michael Bublé's jazzy version of the Spiderman theme song. Such Putin-era repackaging of Soviet art is clearly meant to evacuate any political content from these works in order to paper over the violent discontinuities in twentieth-century Russian history with a kitschy banality. For example, the reviewer of the Deineka/Samokhvalov exhibition for the *New York Review of Books* declared, "It was gimmicky but cute, and it successfully conveyed the idea that the exhibition wasn't a dry academic exercise but a popular event. Nearly a century on, socialist realism can finally be fun" (Pinkham 2020, 47). Such a statement is strikingly at odds with those of the contemporary Russian artists interviewed by Lena Jonson and Andrei Erofeev in their 2018 volume *Russia: Art, Resistance and the Conservative-Authoritarian Zeitgeist*, who warn, "serious shifts are taking place as art has become used for the glamorous framing of various commercial or other events and that a trend of harmless, decorative and shallow art is taking over. In this way, contemporary art is losing its critical and reflective qualities while at the same time becoming more visible in society" (Jonson 2018a, 10). To be clear, our purpose in queering Russian art is not to make Socialist Realism and its Putin-era reincarnations fun.

This volume also appears in the wake of important revisionist histories of Soviet culture, which have helped fashion a new critical language "that does not reduce the description of socialist reality to dichotomies of the official and the unofficial, the state and the people, and to moral judgements shaped within cold war ideologies" (Yurchak 2005, 9). Those revisionist histories highlight the complex and often unpredictable workings of both official Soviet culture and the independent and underground movements that existed alongside it, as well as the very dynamic culture located in between the "activists" and the "dissidents," as Alexei Yurchak describes them, namely, the diehard supporters of the Soviet state and its diehard opponents.

Now liberated from the reductive binaries of the Cold War, art historians too have been undertaking a profound rethinking of artistic movements, in particular, modernism, which was arguably the most politicized artistic mode in the postwar era and is today studied as "a world phenomenon" (Hayot and Walkowitz 2016, 1). In the West, this rethinking has led to an expansion of the term to include artists such as Derain and Balthus, whose naturalism had previously excluded them (see Perl 2017), while in the Soviet Union, features of modernism have been traced in canonical works of Socialist Realism (see Babich 2017). Moreover, the fact that Soviet artists often looked for new directions and inspiration from their past, in particular, the creative explosion that marked the early post-Revolutionary period, and from the local reception of non-Russian art, should caution against reading acts of artistic resistance or critique in the Soviet Union or in contemporary Russia as a desire for Western political, economic, or cultural forms. While acknowledging its transnational dimension, the politics of queer performance in the field of pre-Soviet, Soviet and post-Soviet art must be addressed in its own terms.

Structure of the Volume

The overarching theme of the volume is Russia's engagement with what Whitney Davis theorizes as "queer beauty," referring to the repertoire of homoerotic artistic works from ancient Greece and Rome. Regular engagements with that artistic legacy from the Renaissance through Neoclassical revivals to today underscore the enduring relevance of these ancient Greek and Roman motifs and styles and guarantee the continued circulation of queer beauty in cultures throughout the Occident and beyond. Russia's engagement with queer beauty began in the eighteenth century, following Peter the Great's turn toward Western Europe, which led to the widespread adoption of Western European artistic forms and subjects and the largescale collecting of Western art. This volume traces an arc stretching from Russia's embrace of Neoclassicism in the eighteenth century to the adoption of a federal law banning homosexual propaganda in 2013.

The first section, titled Theoretical Framings, offers an overview of queer art and of queer approaches to viewing art that challenge a minoritarian understanding of queer art as art made exclusively by and for queer-identified individuals. The chapter explores Russia's engagement with the queer beauty of ancient art, which, while offering opportunities for queer artists and viewers, cannot be reduced to some mimetic rendering of queer desire. Certain logics underlying the production of artistic forms in early modern and modern Europe, such as allegory and citation, offer alternative sources for the production and circulation of nonnormative representations of gender and sexuality, other than mimesis.

The second and largest section of the volume traces pre-Soviet, Soviet, and Post-Soviet engagements with queer beauty, by both artists and art historians. This section opens with Olga Khoroshilova's study of cross-dressing in eighteenth-century elite culture. Documenting its ubiquity in practice while noting the scarcity of direct visual testimony, Khoroshilova notes the mismatch between the reality of the practice and its presence in the visual archive of the time; representations of cross dressing occurred most frequently in mediated form—through allegorical representations. The second chapter by Nikolai Ivanov explores the Russian, then Soviet reception of Aleksandr Ivanov's series of nude paintings of young boys. Informed by the author's diaries and correspondence with friends in which the artist discusses his romantic attachments, Ivanov opens an interpretive space—queer in its ultimate unresolvability—between a critical position predicated on the total autonomy of the artistic realm, which denies (or ignores) the artist's homosexual desire, and a critical position that sees painting as a more or less direct expression of the artist's inner life, according to which Ivanov's nudes would confirm his pederastic orientation. Chapter 3, by Brian James Baer, explores Konstantin Somov's engagement with queer beauty, mediated by eighteenth-century libertine culture and seventeenth-century Commedia dell 'Arte. The chapter demonstrates how a consideration of the artist's queer project of representing nonreproductive sexuality can lead to a reevaluation of his oeuvre, as well as its relationship to modernism. The subject of Gleb Napreenko's chapter explores one of the most popular practitioners of Socialist Realism, Alexander Deineka, whose work was profoundly shaped by the neoclassicism of the Soviet 1930s. Napreenko, however, focuses on the uncanny in Deineka's wartime works, exposing trauma as a moral and aesthetic problem for Soviet art of the time. In the next chapter, "Carnivalesque Carnality: The Queer Potential of Sergei Eisenstein's Homoerotic Drawings," Ada Ackerman explores the explicitly homoerotic drawings of Soviet director Sergei Eisenstein as part of a broader engagement with queer beauty throughout his cinematic oeuvre and in his memoirs.

Yelena Kalinsky's "Moscow Conceptualism's Erotic Objects" is the first of four chapters to deal with queer beauty in the context of late Soviet and early post-Soviet culture. Kalinsky focuses on Moscow Conceptualist Vadim Zakharov's work, which has never before been discussed from the standpoint of sexuality or gender. The following three chapters, Andrei Khlobystin's "A Russian Schizorevolution? Observations on the New Academy of Fine Arts and Queer Issues in the Late 1980s and Early 1990s," Maria Engström's "Queering Socialist Realism: The Case of Georgy Guryanov," and Helena Goscilo's "The Lure of Implied Transgression as Revolutionary Retrospective: The Illicit as *la Belleza* in Bella Matveeva's Art," look at the work of the New Academy artistic collective founded by Timur Novikov. Their ambivalent—parodic?—relationship to queer beauty and to citations of queer beauty in official Soviet art reflected broader trends in the Russian art world exploring artistic positionings outside the Cold War binaries of official/dissident and East/West. The New Academy artists combined representational styles associated with Socialist Realism with a decorative performativity more typical of the prerevolutionary and immediate postrevolutionary period. Unlike revolutionary art, however, which thoroughly blended art and politics, their radical stylistic eclecticism, along with the strong homoerotic component, appeared as a rejection of "political" art or of the very possibility of political art.

The last two chapters in this section deal with post-Soviet performances of queer beauty. Andrey Shental's chapter "Sexual and Gender Dissent in a Bipolar World," examines two Petersburg Russian artists, Georgy Guryanov and Vladislav Mamyshev-Monroe, who recycle, reaccentuate, and reprogram canonical works of art and historical figures in a variety of ways, while Roman Osminkin's study of queer artist Babi Badalov, highlights how Badalov's post-Soviet, diasporic, "non-Russian" queerness informs his art and his understanding of his "place" in the world.

The final section of the volume contains two works of conceptual art with queer thematics, followed by three critical statements by Russian art historians on the current state of queer art and art history in Russia, ending with three interviews with contemporary queer artists, all addressing notions of translation, understood very broadly as movement between different media, disciplines, and cultures that has the effect of decentering knowledge and queering artistic experience. Georgy Mamedov and Oksana Shatalova's chapter makes use of "archival" materials to create a fictional narrative of a Brezhnev-era project to recapture and reimagine the ideals of revolutionary passion and idealism in the Kollontai Commune in 1970s Frunze. The next chapter by Yevgeniy Fiks reimagines a conference of various Russian and American queers that took place in Moscow and Leningrad in 1991 (and 2015), with 1991 representing a liminal, utopian moment in Russian culture when everything seemed possible, and with 2015 representing something quite different. Told in the voices of the various participants, Fiks highlights the conflicting agendas and overlapping desires that marked the "birth" of a gay rights movement in Russia.

The first of the art historical essays, by Viktoria Smirnova-Maizel, discusses Polina Zaslavskaya's exhibition *Material Evidence,* which consists of a series of illustrations based on investigations into the murders of members of Russia's LGBTQ community. The exhibition questions the basic premises of realism by representing objects that might appear to be the epitome of realism: pieces of evidence. But, of course, material evidence is only the trace of an event that will be subjected to interpretation in court, and the exhibition itself, while documenting the fact of violence against Russian queers, begs the viewer to confront the interpretive question of why this is happening. The next essay, Seroe Fioletovoe's "Battle over Names: Radical Queer on the Russian Activist Art Scene," discusses the radicalization of queer artists under Putin, who seek to reclaim the mantle of revolution in the context of Russia's increasingly "conservative-authoritarian Zeitgeist" (Jonson and Erofeev 2018). Seroe Fioletovoe situates queer artistic activism formally and politically in the broader context of Putin-era Russian radical actionism in public space. Nadia Plungian's "Queer in the Land of the Bolsheviks or the Archeology of Dissent" draws historical (dis)connections between early Soviet artistic and social practices and Putin-era discourse on nonnormative sexuality and gender identity.

This section ends with interviews with three contemporary "queer" artists, filmmaker Masha Godovannaya, writer and photographer Slava Mogutin, and artist Yevgeniy Fiks, each of whom understands the queerness of their work in quite specific ways, informed by their experience growing up in the Soviet Union and post-Soviet Russia and their experience of emigration. Rather than offering a minoritizing view of queer artists, these interviews in fact "disseminate" the notion of queerness, while also suggesting provocative overlaps and commonalities, underscoring the fact that queerness is shaped by one's life experience and the broader sociopolitical and intellectual context but is not determined by them.

Conclusion

Since the adoption of the "gay propaganda law" in 2013, Russian society has seen an unprecedented increase in public discussion of nonconforming sexuality and gender identities, both in mass media and in cultural production. A new generation of artists addressing queerness in their work has emerged since 2013 in numbers unthinkable in the first two post-Soviet decades: Hagra, Shifra Kazhdan, German Lavrovsky, Yulia Tsvetkova, Nikita Zhukovskiy, Boris Konakov, Alexander Obrazumov, Polina Muzyka, and Dima Fedorov, among others. There are also many works from Russia's past that could be productively reinterpreted through a queer lens. And so, we do not pretend that this volume is in any way comprehensive. Rather, it represents a first step not only in creating a history of queer Russian art and artists but also, following feminist art historian Griselda Pollock, in imagining queer interventions in art histories.[7]

Notes

1 The word sexuality, let alone homosexuality, does not appear in the index of Bown and Taylor's 1993 *Art of the Soviets*, Kivelson and Neuberger's 2008 *Picturing Russia*, or Blakesley's 2016 *The Russian Canvas: Painting in Imperial Russian, 1757–1881*. In a recent issue of *Russian Review* dedicated to visual studies, the word queer appears only twice, but those two instances are worth mentioning. One is by Oksana Bulgakowa (2022, 637), author of an important biography of Soviet director and film theorist Sergei Eisenstein: "How can we study the transformations of the past and of today without transgressing disciplines, without fearing that we have chosen the 'wrong' subject, and without the habitual reversion to ritual incantations about the specter of ideology? How can we do so by bypassing sociology, psychology, deconstruction, feminism and queer theory, structuralism and post-structuralism, and semiotics?" The other is by Vlad Strukov (2022, 630–631), who uses the term metaphorically: "My colleagues working on visual, media, or digital culture are not fully included in the field. They occupy a position of 'queer scholars,' always working on the margin of discourse and challenging the normative position of the field." This volume attempts to move queerness from the margins to the very center of the study of modern (that is, post-Winckelmann) art and art history.

2 The two English-language volumes dedicated to the topic of eroticism in Russian art, Flegon's 1976 *Eroticism in Russian Art* and Petrova's 2007 *Venus sovietica*, are both "dedicated to the beauty of the female body" (Flegon 1976, 11), but from a distinctly heterosexual male perspective. A notable exception in that regard is the 1997 volume *Muzhskoe telo v istorii kul'tury*, by post-Soviet Russia's leading sexologist, Igor Kon; although not dedicated to Russian art alone, this volume includes a number of queer works by Russian artists.

3 As James Smalls (1996, 23) argues, "In general, there has always been a tendency in dealing with the art of this period to dissipate or derail challenging questions of sexuality into alternate terrains of investigation that do not threaten a status-quo structure of heterosexuality." That same year, however, saw the publication of a special issue of *Art Journal* 55 (4) entitled: *We're Here: Gay and Lesbian in Art and Art History.*

4 A recent Amazon prime series on the life of Leonardo da Vinci, *Amazing Leonardo* (2019), directed by Jesus Garces Lambert and starring straight actor Aidan Turner, from the BBC Poldark series, has been criticized for focusing on a fictional relationship between the artist and a woman, Caterina de Cremona. While the series acknowledges da Vinci's homosexuality, the central role of de Cremona is based on a Romantic myth that was given credence by one modern biographer, Charles Nicholl, who justified his decision with the claim that da Vinci "can't have painted female nudes without experiencing heterosexual love."

5 Such attitudes reflect what James Smalls (1996, 25) describes as "a queer-wary legacy of sidestepping the issue." Our project therefore seeks to contribute to Smalls' call for "a more pointed acknowledgment and earnest reassessment of how and to what end expressions of same-sex sexualities and desire operate in an on visual production" (26).

6 At the same time, we must avoid re-drawing simplistic maps that would separate a "backward" Russia from an "enlightened" West. Indeed, one need only consider the role of U.S. religious groups in formulating the Russian law banning gay propaganda (see Moss 2021), as well as the many laws being formulated and passed today in the U.S. banning transgender individuals from participating in sports according to their chosen gender, to remind oneself of the transnational dimension of contemporary homophobia.

7 As Pollock (1988, 17) put it, "We no longer think of a feminist art history but a feminist intervention in the histories of art."

References

Babich, Roman, ed. 2017. *Modernizm bez manifesta. Tom II. Russkoe iskusstvo 1920–1950.* Moscow: ABCdesign.

Baer, Brian James. 2009. *Other Russias: Homosexuality and the Crisis of Post-Soviet Identity.* New York: Palgrave Macmillan.

Blakesley, Rosalind P. 2016. *The Russian Canvas: Painting in Imperial Russia, 1757–1881.* New Haven: Yale University Press.

Bulgakowa, Oksana. 2022. "The Slavic Soul and Visual Culture Studies: A Marriage of Inconvenience?" *Russian Review* 81 (4): 635–638.

Bullock, Philip Ross. 2018. "'That's Not the Only Reason We Love Him': Tchaikovskii Reception in Post-Soviet Russia." *Slavic Review* 77 (1): 53–76.

Erofeev, Andrei. 2018. "Culture as the Enemy: Contemporary Russian Art under the Authoritarian Regime." In *Russia—Art, Resistance, and the Conservative-Authoritarian Zeitgeist,* edited by Lena Jonson and Andrei Erofeev, 127–133. London: Routledge.

Flegon, Alec. 1976. *Eroticism in Russian Art.* London: Flegon Press.

Hayot, Erik and Rebecca L. Walkowitz. 2016. Introduction to *A New Vocabulary for Global Modernism*, edited by Eric Hayot and Rebecca L. Walkowitz, 1–10. New York: Columbia University Press.

Jagose, Annamarie. 1996. *Queer Theory: An Introduction.* New York: New York University Press.

Jones, Jonathan. 2021. "Leonardo, Ladies' Man: Why Can't We Accept That Da Vinci Was Gay?" *The Guardian* (March 26). https://www.theguardian.com/artanddesign/2021/mar/26/garków-aidan-turner-amazon-prime-video-series-gay.

Jonson, Lena. 2018a. *Russia—Art, Resistance, and the Conservative-Authoritarian Zeitgeist,* edited by Lena Jonson and Andrei Erofeev. London: Routledge.

Jonson, Lena. 2018b. "The New Conservative Cultural Policy and Visual Art." In *Russia—Art, Resistance, and the Conservative-Authoritarian Zeitgeist,* edited by Lena Jonson and Andrei Erofeev, 48–64. London: Routledge.

Kivelson, Valerie A. and Joan Neuberger. 2008. "Seeing into Being: An Introduction." In *Picturing Russia: Explorations in Visual Culture,* edited by Valerie A. Kivelson, and Joan Neuberger, 1–11. New Haven: Yale University Press.

Kon, Igor. 2003. *Muzhskoe telo v istorii kul'tury.* Moscow: Slovo.

Kondakov, Alexander. 2017. *Prestupleniia na pochve nenavisti protiv LGBT v Rossii.* St. Petersburg: Tsentr Nezavisimykh Sotsiologicheskikh Issledovanii.

Kondakov, Alexander and Evgeny Shtorn. 2021. "Sex, Alcohol, and Soul: Violent Reactions to Coming Out after the 'Gay Propaganda' Law in Russia." In "Illegal Queerness: Russian Culture and Society in the Age of the 'Gay Propaganda' Law." Special issue, *Russian Review* 80 (January): 37–55.

Leigh, Allison. 2020. *Picturing Russia's Men: Masculinity and Modernity in Nineteenth-Century Painting.* London: Bloomsbury Visual Arts.

Meyer, Richard. 2019. Preface to *Art & Queer Culture,* 2nd ed., edited by Catherine Lord and Richard Meyer, 7–10. London: Phaidon.

Moss, Kevin. 2021. "Russia's Queer Science, or How Anti-LGBT Scholarship is Made." In "Illegal Queerness: Russian Culture and Society in the Age of the 'Gay Propaganda' Law." Special issue, *Russian Review* 80 (January): 17–36.

Pinkham, Sophia. 2020. "Realists of the Soviet Fantasy." *The New York Review of Books* LXVII (8): 47–49.

Pollock, Griselda. 1988. "Feminist Interventions in the Histories of Art." In *Vision and Difference: Femininity, Feminism the Histories of Art.* London: Routledge.

Smalls, James. 1996. "Making Trouble for Art History: The Queer Case of Girodet." *Art Journal* 55(4): 20–27.

Strukov, Vlad. 2022. "On the Margin of Discourse?" *Russian Review* 81(4): 629–631.

Utkin, Roman. 2021. Introduction to "Illegal Queerness: Russian Culture and Society in the Age of the 'Gay Propaganda' Law." Special issue, *Russian Review* 80 (January): 7–16.

Yurchak, Alexei. 2005. *Everything Was Forever, Until It Was No More: The Last Soviet Generation.* Princeton: Princeton University Press.

Part One

Theoretical Framings

Chapter 1

Between Semiotics and Phenomenology: The Problem of Queer Beauty

Brian James Baer

"Resolve our doubts, Master," he said, turning toward Leonardo, "is it Bacchus or a hermaphrodite?"

"Neither the one nor the other, Your Majesty," said Leonardo, blushing as if he were guilty of something. "It is John the Baptist."[1]

"John the Baptist? This can't be! Excuse me, but what are you saying?"

This mixture of the sacred and the profane seemed blasphemous to him, but at the same time pleasing. He then decided that he shouldn't lend it any significance: Who knows what can get into the mind of a painter?

—Dmitry Merezhkovskii,
Voskreschie bogi [*Resurrected gods*]
([1900] 1906: 776–777)[2]

A small room; on the sill of the window opening onto the garden, there were flowers: tea roses, begonias, geraniums; over the commode there were photos: [my host] as a child, friends, Michelangelo's David . . .

—Mikhail Kuzmin,
Diary, September 6, 1906

Art historian Whitney Davis places the problem of "queer beauty" at the very center of western art history, at least since eighteenth-century Neoclassicism, when the writings of Johann Winckelmann canonized ancient Greek sculpture as an aesthetic ideal in terms of both form and content. Winckelmann's "invention of antiquity" (Harloe 2013), however, was deeply influenced by his own homosexuality. As Davis (2010, 43) comments, "Winckelmann's Platonizing tendency was not—it was quite specifically not—the suppression of pederastic love. It was the normalization of pederastic love." While Winkelmann's writings would become enormously influential for artists and art historians, as well as writers and philosophers, the homoerotic ideals of ancient Greek and Roman art he espoused "could not be adopted in just the same way" in post-Enlightenment Europe, given "the widespread prohibition of nonstandard sexuality (in particular homosexuality)" (ibid., 10). As a result, queer beauty became a problem that began to be addressed in works of aesthetic theory and art history, both overtly (for example, Schopenhauer's addendum on homosexuality in the 1858 edition of *The World as Will and Representation*, John Addington Symonds's "Problem of Greek Ethics" (1873), and Freud's 1910 psychobiography of Leonardo da Vinci), and covertly, through omission, abstraction, euphemism, and misrecognition.[3]

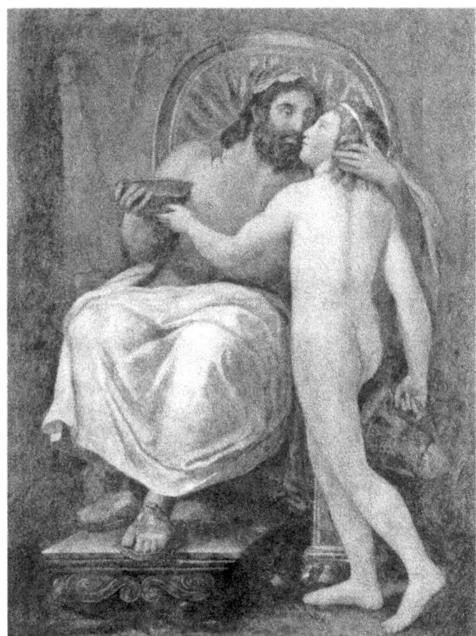

FIGURE 1. Anton Raphael Mengs and Giacomo Casanova, *Jupiter and Ganymede* (1758), fresco on canvas. Galleria Nazionale d'Arte Antica, Rome

Indeed, Winkelmann's own interpretation of ancient Greek and Roman art was fraught with projection and misrecognition. Consider the fresco on canvas by the Italian artists Anton Raphael Mengs and Giacomo Casanova, titled *Jupiter and Ganymede*. It was created to fool the German art historian, who took it for an authentic work, confirming his view of the centrality of same-sex desire in ancient Greek and Roman art (see fig. 1).

Winckelmann's idealization of the queer beauty of ancient Greek and Roman art was built on another misrecognition, namely, that ancient sculptures were originally unpainted, contributing to "the myth of whiteness in classical sculpture" (Talbot 2018).

At the same time, the idealization of queer beauty *as* beauty, Davis argues, "leaves itself open to queering in its own turn" (49), which involves "forcibly (re)introducing into the overlay what has been eliminated or excluded—beauty queered" (46–47). Beginning in the nineteenth century, the de-idealization of (queer) beauty, or the refusal to abstract or misrecognize a work's homoerotic energy, offered a discursive opportunity for proto-gay liberationists, such as Walter Pater, John Addington Symonds, and Elisar von Kupffer—and, as I discuss in chapter 11, the Russian artist Konstantin Somov—to compel "acknowledgement of the diversity and depth—the empirical range and causal primacy—of human erotic instincts and motivations, including nonstandard and nonnormative ones" (ibid., 6–7).

With this in mind, the project of queer(ing) Russian art will be pursued below along three related and at times intersecting axes. Axis one traces the historical engagement on the part of Russian artists and art historians with the queer beauty of ancient Greek and Roman art and of the Italian Renaissance art inspired by it. Axis two theorizes the inherent queerness of the visual arts, focusing on the historicity of styles and motifs and the semiotic practices of allegory, citation, and differentiation, which trouble the relationship between "naturalistic truth and pictorial truth" (Perl 2017, 10) and produce queer imagery, that is, images that go against the grain of dominant or official representations of gender and sexuality.[4] Axis three explores the "viewer's share" in interpreting works of art, with special attention paid to the queer(ing) gaze, which challenges "the presumption of a heterosexual gaze" that has long characterized art historical writings and opens art history to what Mieke Bal (1999, 1–8) has theorized as "preposterous history."[5]

A Queer History of Russian Art, or Queer Beauty in Russian Contexts

In 1900, the writer and religious philosopher Dmitrii Merezhkovskii published a novel about the Italian artist Leonardo da Vinci, titled *Resurrected Gods*, which deals quite overtly not only with the problem of queer beauty but also with Russia's distinct engagement with it: alongside the life of da Vinci, Merezhkovskii includes the story of Evtikhii, a Russian icon painter from Uglich who visits Italy as part of a diplomatic mission. The novel was quickly translated into several

European languages, including German, which allowed Freud to cite it in support of his diagnosis of da Vinci as a latent homosexual.[6] While Merezhkovskii portrays the libertine French king, François I, as amused by da Vinci's merging of Christian and pagan, sacred and profane, and male and female in his painting of St. John the Baptist, as expressed in the epigraph above, Evtikhii is deeply troubled by it: "Evtikhii felt both fear and surprise upon realizing that in these familiar and beloved images from the Uglich Psalter, which he had known since childhood and that seemed sacred to him, there were seductive Hellenic evil spirits" (Merezhkovskii 1906, 769). Queer beauty had found its way into Russian art.[7]

Evtikhii's surprise is entirely justified insofar as Russian art was dominated by the Russian Orthodox Church until the eighteenth century. In fact, before the reign of Peter the Great in all of Russia there was only one publishing house, administered by the Church, and it was forbidden to paint nudes until the late eighteenth century. Moreover, unlike Roman Catholicism, the Eastern Orthodox Church forbade statuary as idolatrous, thus foreclosing any engagement with the queer beauty of ancient sculpture, as occurred in religious statuary during the Italian Renaissance. Central to Orthodox worship was the icon, or the representation of a religious figure or figures painted on wood by monks and nuns. Intended to provide the worshipper with a "window to heaven," traditional icons deemphasize the physical features of their subjects, who, except for some ascetics, are portrayed fully clothed.[8] And so, there was not and could not have been anything akin to Il Sodoma's *St. Sebastian* in Russia before the late eighteenth century.

That being said, Renaissance humanism did have some effect on the visual arts in Russia. In 1557, Ivan III convened a religious council, or Stoglav, which issued a decree expanding the range of subjects allowed in Russian painting. In addition to religious subjects, Russian artists were now allowed to portray tsars and historical figures. Those paintings, often done on wood, were referred to as *parsunas* and marked the emergence of portrait painting in Russia, which would come to dominate Russian secular art in the eighteenth century (see chapter 2 in this volume). It also contributed to the religious schism that took place in the sixteenth century.

Such institutional prohibitions, however, should not be taken as a "reflection" of Russian social reality, which was by no means puritanical (see Heller 1989, 10–13). In fact, there are many historical accounts by both foreign and domestic observers of a vibrant sexual and erotic culture among various social classes in Russia. In addition, imperial Russia had a rich and colorfully bawdy folk culture tradition as well as a highly developed culture of obscenity, or *mat*. That being said, Eduard Fuchs includes no Russian works before the twentieth century in his *History of Erotic Art* (1904), except for a sixteenth century Russian woodcut of naked women in a *bania*, or bathhouse. Therefore, one could conclude, "The difference is in the publicity or lack of publicity in dealing with sexual topics" (Flegon 1976, 7), not in their existence. For this reason, Russian culture is often characterized as bifurcated, split between a "chaste" high culture and an obscene popular culture (see Kon 1997; Lalo 2011), without a well-developed erotic or libertine culture that might have mediated between the two (see Nivat 1989; Lalo 2011)—at least not until the early twentieth century.

Sustained Russian engagement with ancient Greek and Roman art and the art of the Renaissance began in the eighteenth century when Russian artists were sent by Peter the Great to Italy and Holland to study western art, and, in 1757, under Tsarina Elizabeth I, the Russian Imperial Academy of Fine Arts was established.[9] The academy promoted neoclassical style and techniques, along with the privileging of the male nude, and sent its students to various European capitals for further study.[10] Originally housed in the Shuvalov Palace—Ivan Shuvalov was a founder of the Academy, as well as of the Imperial Moscow University—a new building was commissioned by Catherine the Great in 1764. That neoclassical edifice, situated on the banks of the Neva, was completed twenty-five years later. And so, while Russia's engagement with queer beauty was belated, Russia's

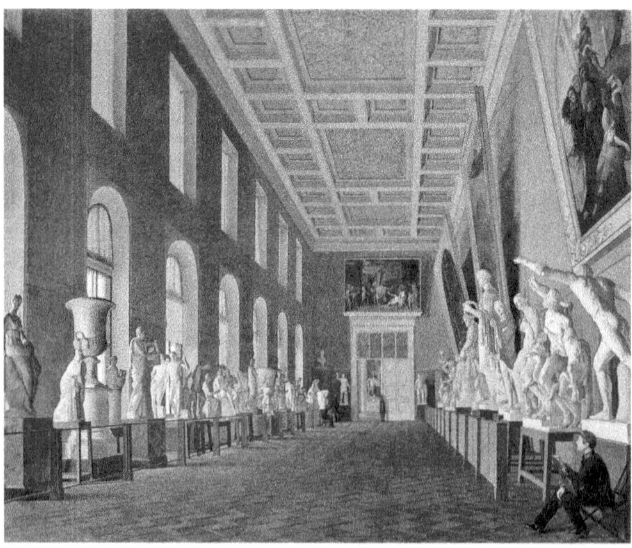

FIGURE 2. Grigorii Karpovich Mikhailov, *Second Antique Gallery in the Academy of Arts* (1836), oil on canvas. The State Russian Museum, St. Petersburg

rulers appeared intent on making up for lost time. The acquisition of western art, including ancient Greek and Roman sculpture, occurred on a massive scale, as depicted in G. K. Mikhailov's *Second Antique Gallery in the Academy of Arts* (*Vtoraia antichnaia gallereia v Akademii khudozhestv,* 1836) (see fig. 2) and Valery Jacobi's *Inauguration of the Academy of Arts, July 7, 1765* (*Inauguratsiia Imperatskoi Akademii khudozhestv 7 iulia 1765 goda,* 1889).

Under Catherine the Great, the ban on depicting nudes was lifted, and Catherine's enormous collection of western European art would become the basis of the collection of the Hermitage Museum. This period also saw the first Russian translations of modern art history, in particular, the writings of Johann Winckelmann.[11] Indeed, the homoerotic fragment in which Winckelmann posits the Apollo Belvedere as an aesthetic ideal circulated widely as a fragment. Some of the Russian translators played down or eliminated the homoeroticism of the passage, while others boldly rendered it. As Konstantin Lappo-Danilevsky (2013, 250) notes, "Chekalevskii was not frightened by the hint of homoeroticism, which he translated without the slightest embarrassment: '. . . and those lips were essentially the same as the ones that excited the passion of the handsome Branchus'"—the shepherd Branchus was a lover of the god Apollo, who endowed him with the gift of prophesy.

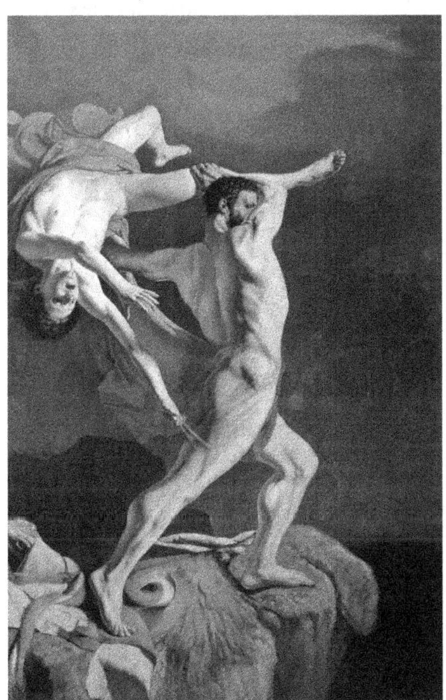

FIGURE 3. Pavel Sorokin, *Hercules and Lichas* (1849), oil on canvas. Odesa Art Museum, Odesa

As a result, queer beauty entered Russian art not only in depictions of mythological subjects, such as Pavel Semyonovich Sorokin's *Hercules and Lichas* (*Gerkules i Likhas,* 1849) (fig. 3), but also in Christian-themed works, such as Sorokin's *The First Christian Martyrs under Prince Vladimir* (*Pervye khristianskie mucheniki pri kniaze Vladmire,* 1886) (see fig. 4) and Aleksandr Ivanov's religious paintings (see chapter 3 in this volume),

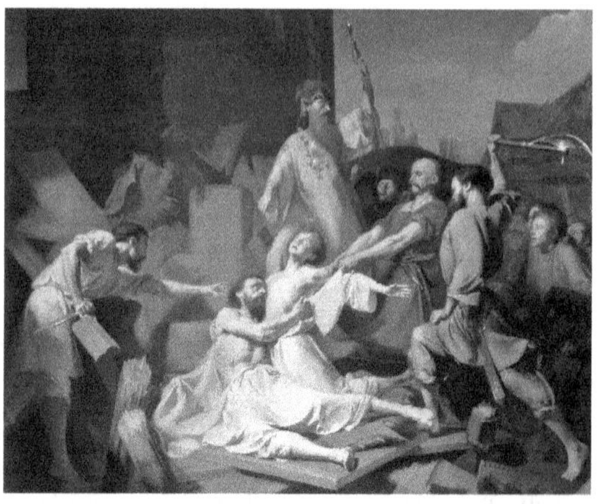

Figure 4. Pavel Sorokin,
The First Christian Martyrs (1886), oil on canvas.
The State Tretyakov Gallery, Moscow

as well as in works on Russian historical subjects, such as Evgraf Sorokin's *Yan Usmovets Stops a Bull* (*Ian Usmovets ostanavlivaet byka,* 1849) (see fig. 5). Of course, the violence of the imagery may be intended to foreclose an erotic reading.

Aleksandar Flaker (1989, 91), therefore, is not entirely correct when he argues, "Even Romanticism did not lift the prohibitions imposed on sexuality, which weighed especially heavily on Russian art—which had few representations of nude bodies." More just and nuanced is the observation by Michel Niqueux (1989, 94): "With centuries of delay, the Russian nude has not undergone the aestheticization of the Renaissance or of Renoir. Regarding the nude, what interested Tatlin was its sculptural volume (*Nude,* 1913), and what restrained Kustodiev was the banal, everyday context in the form of his *Beauty* (*Krasavitsa,* 1915) or of the voluminous figure ironically titled *The Russian Venus* (*Russkaia Venera,* 1925–26)." That being said, Russia's belated engagement with the nude has perhaps made it especially vulnerable to the charge of being a foreign import and a threat to aesthetic and religious transcendence. Consider Prince Myshkin's reaction to viewing Hans Holbein the Younger's

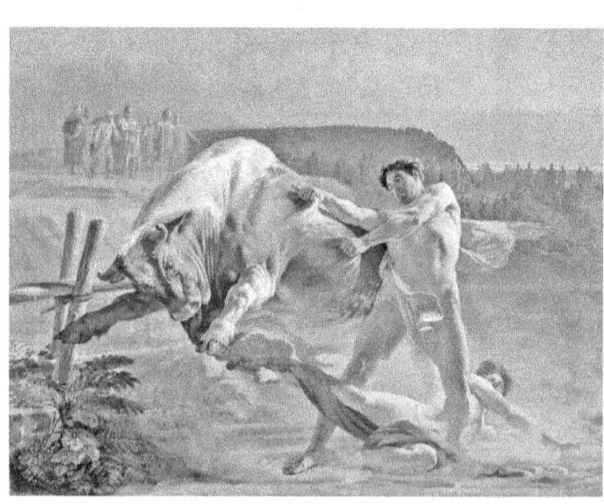

Figure 5. Evgraf Sorokin,
Yan Usmovets Stops a Bull (1849), oil on canvas.
Far East Museum of Art, Khabarovsk

The Body of Dead Christ in the Tomb (1521) in Dostoevsky's *The Idiot*, "Why, a man's faith might be ruined by looking at that picture!"

This tradition of reticence has arguably had a stronger effect on Russian art history than on Russian art itself. As Igor Kon (2003, 322) notes, "The problem of the naked male body in Russian art has for many years been unaddressed by Russian art historians. The only Russian article on nudity in representational art that I have been able to find is Luk'ianov (1995), and that makes no mention of male bodies. This prudery has historical roots" (Kon 2003, 322). Indeed, the first complete Russian translation of Winckelmann's magnum opus, *The History of Art*, appeared only in 1888. As recently as 2005, the blurb for a collected volume on the body in Russian culture could still claim: "While everything, or almost everything is known about the Russian soul, the Russian body remains a *terra incognita* in the scholarly realm" (Kabakova and Kont 2005).

The split between high and low culture began to close in the early twentieth century, during the period known as the Silver Age, as symbolized by such erotic masterpieces as Aleksei Remizov's *What Is Tobacco* (*Chto est' tabak*, 1910), with illustrations by Konstantin Somov, *Le livre de la Marquise* (1914–1918), a collection of French erotic writings in poetry and prose, also illustrated by Konstantin Somov, and Mikhail Kuzmin's *Covered Pictures* (*Zanaveshennye kartinki*, 1920), with illustrations by Vladimir Milashevskii. (Note the central role of queer Russians—Somov and Kuzmin—in this cultural project; and so, it is not surprising that Alexei Lalo would use an illustration by Somov for the cover of his 2011 *Libertinage in Russian Culture and Literature.*) This was a time when erotic art went mainstream, as evident in the beautifully bound Russian translation of Eduard Fuchs's *Illustrated History of Erotic Art* (1908). It was also a time when art—and specifically the question of queer beauty—was being addressed in literary works, ranging from fictional biographies of queer artists, such as Akim Volynskii's *Leonardo da Vinci* (1900) and Dmitry Merezhkovskii's *Resurrected Gods: Leonardo da Vinci* (1900), to novels featuring artists and works of art, such as Mikhail Kuzmin's *Wings* (1906) and Lidiia Zinovieva-Gannibal's *Thirty-three Abominations* (1907), which present same-sex desire as an aesthetic problem (see chapter 3 in this volume). Queer beauty became a topic of heated debate at this time. As the philosopher and journalist Vasilii Rozanov wrote in reference to Kuzmin's *Wings*: "Hadrian and Antinous would probably throw up from the disgusting bathhouse attendant Boris and his bathhouse adventures, can it be that the ancients liked *that*?!" (qtd. in Bershtein 2011, 80).

While works of erotic visual art would continue to be produced throughout the twenties, their subject matter was emphatically heterosexual (see, for example, the drawings of Ivan Efimov). After the Revolution, artistic works with overt homosexual thematics were produced mostly by émigrés, such as Konstantin Somov and Pavel Tchelitchew, and by Sergei Eisenstein, while abroad (see chapter 6 in this volume). Russian art criticism began to address the subject of queer beauty in the decade before and after the Bolshevik Revolution, but the Soviet state under Stalin instituted a virtual moratorium on any discussion of same sex desire or behavior, leading even scholars of ancient Greece and Rome either to deny the existence of homosexuality, as in the official Soviet treatment of Sappho, or to resort to coy euphemisms, such as *eti spetsificheskie otnosheniia*, 'those particular relationships' (Kon 1997, 355). This had a deleterious effect on Russian art history. (See chapters 1 and 2 in this volume.) So, while Russian artists were quick to engage with queer artistic styles, motifs, and modes following the lifting of censorship restrictions in the years preceding and following the fall of the Soviet Union, it took art historians a while to catch up. For example, in the catalogue for the exhibition *Towards the Tenth Anniversary of Neoacademism. 1989–1999*, art historian Ekaterina Andreeva spoke of the "androgyny and autoeroticism" of the artists, terms that could have appeared in a review from the pre-revolutionary Silver Age. Only in the catalogue for the twentieth anniversary show was she able to describe their work as "erotic provocations" (2015, 28)—aimed not exclusively at themselves (as in autoeroticism) but at their viewers. Many Russian art historians remain reluctant to engage with the sexuality of queer artists, dismissing it as vulgar biographism, reductive identity politics (see El'shevskaia 2003, 13–14), or as simply "unnecessary" (Berezovskaia 2016, 4).

The puritanism of Stalinist culture existed alongside its promotion of athleticism and bodily vitality, which resulted in various (ultimately futile) attempts to foreclose the erotic potential of naked and near naked bodies. (Note that a new translation of Winckelmann's *History of Art* was published by Academia Press in 1935, a reflection of the neoclassicism of that decade.) It is important, however, not to conflate the early Soviet years with High Stalinism, as the twenties were a time of extraordinary artistic diversity; avant-garde movements flourished as artists attempted to live out the iconoclastic spirit of the Revolution. At that time, abortion was legal, homosexuality was not mentioned in the first Soviet criminal code, and an unusually liberal sexual culture emerged among Soviet youth. Even nudism, which was popularized in the Silver Age, took on a symbolic resonance after the Revolution, "when the first Soviet Nudists organized Evenings of the Denuded Body in Moscow in 1922, declaring that nudity was the truly democratic form of dress" (Bowlt 1996, 46). In the realm of culture, Russian translations of Freud appeared in the early twenties, and 1927 saw the first Russian translation of André Gide's *L'Immoraliste.* Tales of sexual and gender liberation in the Soviet Union attracted western observers, such as the Belgian anarchist Jean Marestan, the Austrian psychiatrist Wilhelm Reich, the queer Swiss journalist Ella Maillart, and the queer French writer André Gide.[12] Not all of them, however, were pleased by what they witnessed. Gide would return to France quite disenchanted, and Reich warned that the Soviets' ban on homosexuality and abortion foretold the demise of the Revolution.

Following Stalin's consolidation of power, all artistic activity came under state control, independent artistic collectives were disbanded, and Socialist Realism was declared the official aesthetic policy, which was described at the Soviet Pavilion at the 1939 World's Fair in Paris as "the truthful portrayal of life in the Land of the Soviets," a truthfulness that was guaranteed by "the simplicity and plastic clarity of the pictorial language of Soviet paintings, sculpture and graphic art" (Anon 1993, 8). This celebration of immediacy and transparency downplayed if not denied the mediating influence of the artist, even the most "realist" of whom necessarily applies "procedures of selection and combination of material, adoption of specific and limited viewpoints, and so forth," not to mention "the mediating role played by reception" (Kenez and Shepherd 1998, 42, 41).

While featuring an abundance of strong youthful bodies, works of Socialist Realism were remarkably chaste, typically "de-eroticized and idealized as an integral part of a bucolic landscape—the Socialist Garden of Eden" (Goscilo 2006, 254). Heroic male and female figures during the period of High Stalinism typically gaze upward into the "bright future," almost never directly at each other, even when, or perhaps especially when, completely nude, as in Matvei Manizer's sculpture *Youth. In a Country of Joy and Happiness* (*Iunost'. V strane radosti i schast'ia*, 1946)—and this was so despite the regime's promotion of heterosexual reproduction, which it did both negatively, through laws outlawing homosexuality and abortion, and positively, through campaigns to promote and reward childbirth. (For more on Soviet pronatalist policies, see Hoffman 2000).

The nude would reappear in the 1940s as a symbol of the Soviet victory in the World War II, producing some particularly ambivalent works, such as Deineka's *After the Battle* (*Posle boya*, 1944) (see fig. 6).

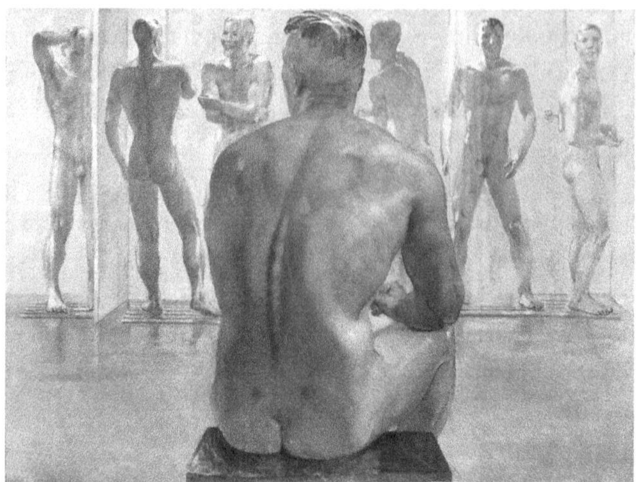

FIGURE 6. Alexander Deineka, *After the Battle* (1944), oil on canvas. Kursk Art Gallery, named after A. A. Deineka, Kursk; © 2023 Estate of Alexander Deineka / UPRAVIS, Moscow / ARS, NY)

The painting features several naked young men showering together, smiling, and laughing "as if after a football match" (Simpson 2004a, 117)—suggesting that the physical and mental trauma of war could be simply washed away. Their bodies are perfect, glistening in the water of the shower; there is no hint of injury. But the front of the painting is dominated by the back of another young naked soldier, interrupting the visual field and blocking the viewer's perspective. The tilt of the young man's head suggests that he is not looking straight forward, but off to the side, approximating the pose of Rodin's *Thinker*. The solitary soldier on the far right is the only one who takes notice of him, directing a concerned glance at his seated comrade, whose expression cannot be seen by the viewer, intimating the intensity of his traumatic experience but also the strictures of official Soviet art of the Stalinist period, which left little room for doubt, ambivalence, or anguish.[13]

While the Thaw following Stalin's death saw growing experimentation and eclecticism in Soviet art and a return of figures looking with a gaze fixed directly at the viewer—see, for example, Viktor Popkov's *Builders of Bratsk* (*Stroiteli Bratska*, 1960) or Geli Korzhev's *Traces of War* (*Sledy voini*, 1963–64)—erotic/sexual subject matter remained relatively rare in officially approved art. It began to emerge in the seventies and eighties, and not only among independent and underground artists. People's Artist of the Soviet Union and a member of the Soviet Academy of Arts Evsei Moiseenko's works, for example, combined stylistic experimentation with scenes of idyllic homosocial bonding in paintings such as *Boys* (*Mal'chiki*, 1975) and *August* (*Avgust*, 1975–80).

The combination of stylistic eclecticism with overt homoeroticism in Russian art really took off in late Perestroika and in the early post-Soviet period. During that time, eroticism and sexuality became such prominent features in Russian art that Thomas Campbell (2007, 68) proposed the emergence of a "homo-device" in the visual arts, including film (see Graham 2001 and Alaniz 2003 and on the Necrorealists). The function of that device, in Campbell's view, had more to do with positioning oneself or one's art on the post-Soviet market than it did with expressing one's "true" sexuality. As Campbell (2007, 69–70) argues:

> The homo-device is thus also a tool used by the artists to advance their own careers, an instrument for forging public personae that irritate a homophobic domestic audience while eliciting sympathy, curiosity, and patronage from homophilic artistic *cognoscenti* in the west. The homo-device is a means of creating an artistic brand name. At the same time, it undermines the ways that identity—cultural, social, sexual or historical—is construed today.

Timur Novikov's series of works dedicated to Oscar Wilde represents all these aspects of the homo-device, while not ruling out that Novikov's art was also an expression of his queer sexuality.[14]

The New Academy artists of the late Soviet and early post-Soviet periods celebrated the queer beauty not only of classical art but also of Soviet citations of classical art (as discussed in chapters 8, 9, 10, and 11 in this volume). While depictions of the perfect male form appeared in the paintings of the New Academists, photographers at that time were busy de-idealizing the Soviet body, highlighting the gap between the Grecian ideal promoted by official Soviet culture and the actual bodies that had endured the reality of Soviet socialism. Such de-idealization is evident in the work of queer artists, such as Slava Mogutin and Vladislav Mamyshev-Monroe, and non-queer artists, such as Ukrainian photographers Boris Mikhailov, Arsen Savadov, and Oleksandr Kharchenko (see Simpson 2004a).

Under Putin, an increasingly ambivalent relationship toward queer beauty emerged long before the open antagonism symbolized by the 2013 ban on homosexual propaganda. Consider Aleksandr Sokurov's 2002 film *Russian Ark*, in which the queer French aristocrat and author of *La Russie. 1939*, Marquis de Custine wanders through the Winter Palace, now the Hermitage Museum. Commenting on works of art, mostly of western European origin, which in many cases were acquired by Catherine the Great, Custine interacts with a disembodied Russian narrator. One might have expected Custine to pay special attention to the many works of queer beauty in Catherine's collection, but instead Sokurov portrays Custine as a devout Catholic and a heterosexual. He is upset that paintings on religious themes are hung side by side with paintings on pagan themes, echoing Evtikhii's alarm at finding Hellenic "spirits" in Russian icons. In the actual travelogue, however, Custine complains that too many paintings are hung on a single wall, *not* that sacred paintings are hung alongside profane ones.

Although Custine's homosexuality was a well-known fact at the time he traveled to Russia, it is not alluded to in Sokurov's film. In fact, all the works of art he stops to admire feature distinctly heterosexual subject matter; he dances with a woman in front of Rembrandt's *Danae* (1636/1647), and in the sculpture gallery, he walks uninterested past several statues of male nudes, eventually stopping to admire Antonio Canova's Neoclassical sculpture of the three graces (1817), crying out: "This is the true heir to the ancient masters." Custine also mentions that his mother, a sculptress, had almost married Canova, who in fact never married and produced some of the most homoerotic sculptures in all of Western art, such as *Endymion* (1822) and *Theseus and the Minotaur* (1782). In Sokurov's film, the cosmopolitan queer traveler and critic of despotism, as well as Neoclassical Russian architecture, becomes not only a rather provincial, heterosexual Catholic, but also an apologist for autocracy—"I was wrong to criticize your tsars—all this beauty and opulence—even if they were all tyrants"—foreshadowing perhaps the overt political assault on queer beauty that would come to characterize official Putin-era culture after 2011.

The Unpredictable Queerness of Art, Part 1: Homosexuality as Sign

Understanding the semiotics of queer beauty requires that we acknowledge, first, that homosexuality is a sign, and as a sign it can be and has been deployed to various ends. In the Renaissance, for example, the charge of sodomy was used by western travelers to *other* Russia, casting it as primitive and wild (see Olearius 1967, 142; Cross 1971, 70–71), a charge that was also leveled against the indigenous peoples of the Americas by western explorers and colonizers (Todorov 1984, 150). Artistic styles and motifs are also signs, capable of signifying beyond the work of art itself. In fact, one of the enduring contributions of Winckelmann's writings on art history is the connection he draws between Greek sculpture and Athenian democracy. Certainly, Catherine the Great's embrace of Neoclassical art was meant to lend visual support to her liberal agenda, ennobling it, and portraying her as enlightened. The semiotic connection between Neoclassical art (as signifier) and liberal politics (as signified) is, however, arbitrary, as illustrated by the fact that Catherine remained committed to Neoclassicism even after her authoritarian turn, following the Pugachev Revolt.

In that regard, it is interesting to note that the Marquis de Custine included a good deal of art criticism in his travelogue, *La Russia. 1839*. Alongside a condemnation of Russian autocracy—as the story goes, Custine traveled to Russia as a monarchist and left a constitutionalist—is an equally damning critique of Russian Neoclassical art and architecture. Clearly following the lead of Jean-Jacques Rousseau who in *The Social Contract* critiqued Peter the Great as possessing only an "imitative genius" as opposed to "true genius," Custine condemns Russian Neoclassicism as an imitation of an imitation: "The too celebrated statue of Peter the Great, placed on its rock by the Empress Catherine, first attracted my attention. The equestrian figure is neither antique nor modern; it is a Roman of the time of Louis XV. To aid in supporting the horse, an enormous serpent has been placed at his feet; which is an ill-conceived idea, serving only to betray the impotence of the artist" (1989, 92). Under the influence of Winckelmann, Custine's art criticism combines a Neoclassical appreciation of timeless form with a Romantic appreciation of the influence of geography. Winckelmann's claim that Northern climes were not conducive to reproducing "Greek Taste" (1765, 2) is evident in Custine's comment regarding Russia: "The air of this country is unfavorable to the finer arts. Productions that spring spontaneously elsewhere, will only grow in the hot house. Russian art will never be a hardy plant" (103). But Custine goes further, claiming that Russia's topography and climate are ill-suited even to the viewing of classical art: "The Russians, who flatter themselves they are reproducing the wonders of antiquity, and who, in reality, are only caricaturing them, raise their soi-disant Grecian and Roman structures in immense fields, where they are almost lost to the eye" (153) and elsewhere: "What are Rembrandt, Correggio, Michael Angelo, and Raphael, in a dark room? The north has doubtless its own kind of beauty, but it is still a palace without light" (584). The self-identified "imperial traveler" found Russian Neoclassicism enraging: "Such parodies of Greece and Italy, *minus* the marble and the sun, are, it must be allowed, calculated to revive all my anger" (313). He would come to associate those debased Neoclassical forms with political despotism.

Homosexuality and art were also notably entangled during the Cold War, when homosexuality was used by each of the superpowers against the other.

In some cases, homosexuality was associated with specific forms of art—consider Soviet Premier Nikita Khrushchev's pronouncement after touring an exhibit of modern art: "Abstraktsionisty—pidorasy," or "Abstract artists are faggots." In other cases, homosexuality was entangled with more general questions of representation. Consider American academic Nathan Leites's Cold War study, sponsored by the Rand Corporation and the United States Air Force, which found traces of "repressed homosexual desire" in the writings of leading Bolsheviks and pre-Soviet Russian intellectuals. Weaponizing the post-War fascination with psychoanalysis—see Dagmar Herzog's *Cold War Freud* (2016)—Leites produced two studies, *The Operational Code of the Politburo* (1951) and *A Study of Bolshevism* (1955). Summarizing the latter book in the conservative journal *Commentary*, the Cold Warrior Daniel Bell (1955, online) writes: "Two principal drives, according to Leites, explain Russian intellectual character. These are a preoccupation with death and latent passive homosexual impulses." Bell then goes on to reassure his readers, "During the early truce talks in Korea, American negotiators, headed by Admiral Joy, were equipped with [Leites's] slim book"—providing them with an "operational code" to decipher an adversary that was now construed as triply inscrutable to the "average" American, as Asian, communist, and homosexual.

Homosexuality was viewed, however, not only as an external threat to the US. Imagined in terms of effeminate men and masculine women, homosexuality represented the total collapse of difference in a society that was doubling down on segregation: of Blacks and Whites, and of the sexes, as evident in women's fashion and the glorification of the nuclear family, with a working dad and a stay-at-home mom. Especially threatening in that social context was the capacity of the homosexual to pass, leading to the association of homosexuals with espionage. In 1950, a Senate subcommittee issued a report declaring homosexuality to be a national security threat; as a result, homosexuals were expelled from the US State Department in increasing numbers throughout the decade (see Johnson 2004). Referred to by Republican Senator Everett Dirksen as "lavender lads," homosexuals would become targets of the House Un-American Activities Committee, led by Senator Joe McCarthy. Many gay writers and artists in the US found themselves at this time either ignored by the left as apolitical or demonized by the right as existential threats to the American way of life, now defined in opposition to a godless (and, according to Leites, homosexual) Russia. As Robert J. Corber (1997, 1) notes in his *Homosexuality in Cold War America*: "In the 1950s, even supposedly progressive critics denied the importance of gay male writers, claiming that their criticisms of postwar American society were insufficiently political."

Controlling the production and the interpretation of visual imagery, however, is no easy task, as Madina Tlostanova (2018, 23) suggests: "Art is metaphorical by definition and therefore slips more easily out of power's grip." But such a pronouncement is too general and ahistorical for this project, which seeks to embed interpretations within specific local and transnational contexts. To that end, Norman Bryson's semiotic history of western painting models a deeply historical interpretation not only of styles and motifs but also of modes of semiosis by focusing on the shifting relationship between denotative and connotative meaning. To do this, he applies key concepts from Peircean semiotics, namely, icon, index, and symbol, to represent different semiotic modes. Insofar as the monosemous index points directly to its denotative meaning—"like an arrow, a Peircean index, it directs our gaze" (Bal 2004, 67)—it reduces the act of interpretation to a moment of recognition; the polysemous symbol, on the other hand, attracts connotative meanings; less codified than indices and more arbitrary than Peircean icons, symbols are most open to interpretation: "They are subject to fluctuation according to change within context; the meanings of the codes of connotation, by contrast with the codes of iconology, are therefore both non-explicit and polysemic" (Bryson 1983, 71).

Bryson uses early Byzantine religious stencils as an example of art in which the denotative function dominates: the highly stylized depictions of religious subjects clearly index Scriptural narratives or theological concepts. While in Western Europe, the addition of seemingly extraneous connotational values in religious art of the late medieval and early Renaissance contributed to creating a "reality effect" that sought to guarantee the truth of the denotative values, the addition of more realistic, less iconic elements also introduced a tension between denotation and connotation, between transcendent, codified Truth and individual interpretation.[15] The connotative meaning(s) of the symbol could interfere with or interrupt the functioning of the index; in Wittgenstein's terms, the "shaping of the sign," or its perception, may profoundly complicate the "handling of the sign," its interpretation, which occurs in what Wittgenstein refers to as "a queer kind of medium, the mind" (Wittgenstein 1958, 3).

The tension between connotative and denotative meaning in western art emerged perhaps most problematically in depictions of the body as more realistic representations transformed religious icons into potential objects of desire. Indeed, the virile naked body of Il Sodoma's *St. Sebastian* not only invites a desirous glance that threatens to disrupt if not altogether derail the spiritual gaze, it also confuses religious and physical ecstasy, and invites the queer viewer to replace a religious index (the arrows signifying his martyrdom) with a sexual symbol (the arrows signifying bodily penetration).[16] Indeed, the protagonist in Japanese author Yukio Mishima's *Confession of a Mask* experiences his first orgasm while gazing at a reproduction of Guido Reni's *Saint Sebastian*: "That day, the instant I looked upon the picture, my entire being trembled with some pagan joy. My blood soared up; my loins swelled as though in wrath" (1995, 288).

The threat posed by the intrusion of the connotative on the denotative has been experienced perhaps most acutely in the traditionally Orthodox countries of Eastern Europe, provoking Byzantine Iconoclasm in the eighth and ninth centuries, the prohibition on nudes up to the eighteenth century, the campaign against formalism in the arts in the Soviet Union under Stalin, and most recently in Vladimir Putin's refusal to say the name of the group Pussy Riot out loud, let alone translate the name into Russian—the monologic autocrat's embarrassment in the face of polysemy.[17] But, as Bryson (2004, 3) remarks, "However coherent or persuasive a given interpretation may be, there will inevitably be a remainder not acted upon, a 'reserve' of details that escape the interpretive act."

In homophobic contexts, that reserve of details may constitute the queer potential of a work of art. Consider Roland Barthes's (1977, 54) notion of *obtuse meaning*, which he juxtaposes to informational and symbolic meaning, defining it as "the third, the 'one too many', the supplement that my intellection cannot succeed in absorbing." Barthes introduces this concept in his analysis of a still from Sergei Eisenstein's film *Ivan the Terrible* depicting a scene in which "two supernumeraries are raining down gold on the young czar's head" (53). What Barthes does not say aloud and perhaps could not say aloud at that time is that there is something distinctly queer about this obtuse, third meaning: "a certain compactness of the courtiers' make-up, thick and insistent for the one, smooth and distinguished for the other; the former's 'stupid' nose, the latter's finely traced eyebrows, his lank blondness, his faded, pale complexion, the affected flatness of his hairstyles suggestive of a wig, the touching-up with chalky foundation talc, with face powder" (53). These traits, Barthes argues, "possess a theatrical individuality" that "exceeds the copy of the referential motif [and] compels an interrogative reading" (53).[18]

For the queer viewer, such details, as well as other traces of queer beauty, function as what Barthes (1981, 26) describes in relation to photography as a *punctum*, which "will break (or punctuate) the *studium*," which he defines as "that very wide field of unconcerned desire, of various interest, of inconsequential taste: I like / I do not like" (26). Barthes's description takes on an erotic valence when he acknowledges that the punctum—which can also mean "sting, speck, cut, little hole" (27)—does not just penetrate the studium; it penetrates the viewer: "this element which rises from the scene, shoots out of it like an arrow, and pierces me." The eroticism of the description intensifies: "A photograph's punctum is that accident which pricks me (but also bruises me, is poignant to me)" (27). The obtuse meaning generated by Eisenstein's supernumeraries in *Ivan the Terrible,* a film characterized by "complex and intense crossings of gender lines" (LaValley 2001, 57), could be considered a punctum, but one that does not only pierce the viewer but also hails them as queer.[19]

Or consider the following scene in Merezhkovskii's fictional biography of Leonardo da Vinci, in which the Russian icon painter Evtikhii opens his copy of the Uglich Psalter of 1485, from which he had learned to read as a child. But now, after having spent time in Italy as part of a diplomatic mission during which he was exposed to western art and had the opportunity to meet Leonardo da Vinci, Evtikhii can no longer view the illustrations in his Russian psalter as he previously had, as innocent: "Now, having seen so many ancient sculptures in the palaces and museums of Venice, Rome, and Florence, these images, with which he was familiar since childhood, suddenly took on new meaning for him" (Merezhkovskii 1906, 768). He now perceives in the religious imagery of his psalter references to ancient figures and myths:

> By what miracle had the gods expelled from Olympus, after so many wanderings and transformations, through the brush of an old Russian master, working from an even older Byzantine original, reached the city of Uglich? Distorted by the barbarian artist, they appeared awkward, timid, as though ashamed of their nakedness, among the stern prophets and ascetics—they looked half frozen, rigid from the cold of the Hyperborean night. At the same time, somewhere, in the bend of the elbow, in the turn of the neck, in the curve of the hip, there shimmered the last reflection of an ancient allure. (768–9).[20]

That queer co-presence of styles and motifs is discussed by John Addington Symonds in regard to a classicist depiction of Fortitude (c. 1260) on the pulpit of the cathedral of Pisa, sculpted by Nicola Pisano. The muscular, naked figure, believed to have been modelled on an ancient Roman sculpture of Hippolytus, stands at odds with its setting, leading Symonds to imagine how "monks leaning from Pisano's pulpit preached the sinfulness of natural pleasure to women whose eyes were fixed on the adolescent beauty of an athlete" (qtd. in Davis 2010, 118). Of course, women were not the only ones prone to such distraction, as the homosexual Symonds was no doubt aware.

The Unpredictable Queerness of Art, Part 2: Beyond Mimesis

This section explores the distinct semiotic practices of allegory, citation, and differentiation, which trouble, albeit in somewhat different ways, the relationship between "naturalistic truth and pictorial truth" (Perl 2017, 10) by rejecting mimesis, resulting in nonnormative or queer representations of gender and sexuality, on the one hand, and enabling if not encouraging queer readings of visual representations, on the other.

Allegory

One of the most significant generators of non-mimetic representational art is allegory. As "a representation of an abstract or spiritual meaning through concrete or material forms" (Webster's 1996, 55), visual allegory has historically been closely associated with religious and political ideology, which helps explain its centrality in Soviet art. As Wolfgang Holz (1993, 73) notes, "It can be argued that the most striking semiotic strategy in Socialist Realist art is the principle of allegory—a cultural category that originates in antiquity." Allegory worked to actualize Soviet ideology, making it real for a population that was overwhelmingly peasant (reactionary according to Marxist teaching) and illiterate (hence, difficult to enlighten). As Holz elaborates: "One critic has suggested that allegory again became dominant in Socialist Realism because of the traditional affinity of allegories with ideology in general, and more particularly because of the role of Soviet art in social planning, which tended to move art away from the hallowed ideas of individual 'insight' and 'expression'" (73).

At the same time, the ubiquity of allegory may seem curious in a country that strove for transparency in art, as expressed in the introductory text for the Soviet pavilion at the 1939 World's Fair, quoted above. While one might argue that an allegory fixes meaning more firmly, that is, the relationship between the signifier and the signified in an allegory is less arbitrary than in a Saussurian sign or a Peircean symbol (allegories are typically categorized as Saussurian symbols or Peircean icons), Mieke Bal (2004, 71) points out, "Allegory demonstrates the fundamentally polysemous nature of signs. If images and stories can mean something entirely outside themselves, then, one would think, there are no limits, no constraints." Marina Warner (1985, xix) makes a similar point in her monumental study of allegory, arguing that the trope possesses "a double intention: to tell something which conveys one meaning but which also says something else." As a result, "irony and enigma are among its constituents."

Indeed, the relationship of allegorical representations to material reality (hence, any claim they might have to realism) is twice attenuated—first, by the fact that the subject of allegory is typically an abstract notion or quality and, second, by the fact that the gender of an allegorical figure is often determined by the grammatical gender of the concept that is allegorized, and so is arbitrary. As Roman Jakobson notes in his seminal essay "On Linguistic Concepts of Translation": "Even such a category as grammatical gender, often cited as merely formal, plays a great role in the mythological attitudes of a speech community. [. . .] Ways of personifying or metaphorically interpreting inanimate nouns are prompted by their gender" (1959, 237).[21] Note, for example, one of the best-known allegorical representations in modern western art—Eugène Delacroix's *Liberty Leading the People* (1830), in which a fearless, bare-chested Liberty leads revolutionaries across the barricades. It is certainly no coincidence that Liberty is depicted as a woman, for in French *liberté* is grammatically feminine, as is the Statue of Liberty, which was a gift to the United States from France and is often referred to as Lady Liberty. This is also why France is symbolized by Marianne, as France, too, is grammatically feminine, and why Justice is allegorized as a blindfolded woman carrying a scale. (The word justice in Latin is feminine).

The symbolic capital of allegorical figures may, however, have little to do with their actual social or political capital, and in fact may be diametrically opposed to it. As Warner makes clear in her discussion of female allegories, the central assumption "that an abstract concept—liberty, justice or victory—can be appropriately expressed by a female figure, remains in force today, and it is rarely challenged, although few people think that women have special claims on liberty, or victory, or justice" (1985, 17). Or consider the fact that the so-called Indian head penny was first minted in the US in 1859, just eight years after the passage of the Indian Appropriations Act, which consigned indigenous tribes to reservations. The penny features the profile of a Caucasian woman (Columbia, perhaps) wearing a traditional Indian headdress as a symbol of liberty.[22] At the same time, the linguistic determination of the sex of the allegorical figure must accommodate the qualities allegorized, leading to queer representations, that is, representations that defy the reigning gender stereotypes of the day. Delacroix's Liberty, for example, towers over the male figures in the painting, creating a tension "between the connotations of maternal tenderness and Amazonian zeal" (Warner 1985, xxii). This also explains the girth of the mother confronting a Nazi officer in Sergey Gerasimov's *The Mother of a Partisan* (*Mat' partizana*, 1943), suggesting that she is to be read as an allegory of Rodina-Mat', or the Motherland.[23]

The representation of relationships between concepts also results in queer pairings, such as Baroque depictions of the union of Justice and Peace, both grammatically feminine in Latin, featuring two beautiful maidens gazing lovingly at each other or even locked in an embrace. (See, for example, Rosalba Carriera's 1726 *An Allegory of Justice and Peace*; Pompeo Batoni's c1745 *Peace and Justice*; Corrado Giaquinto's 1753-1754 *Allegory of Justice and Peace*; and Theodor van Thulden's 1649 *Allegory of Peace and Justice after the Thirty Years War*.) Such allegorical unions were especially popular in the Soviet Union. Unlike the baroque depictions of Justice and Peace, however, early Soviet allegories were very often male and were typically portrayed not alone but in same-sex pairs represented in a variety of affectionate poses, allegorizing *soiuz* (union), which is grammatically masculine, and *tovarishchestvo*, or comradeship, conceived at the time as male-male bonding, or "men without women," as Eliot Borenstein (2001) describes the motif in early Soviet literature. In fact, the tradition of gendering comradeship or solidarity as fraternal unions was established already in the nineteenth century in leftist trade union circles. (The word brotherhood in fact remains in the official names of many labor unions today.) Proust also invoked fraternal unions to reference homosexuals: "A freemasonry far more extensive, more effective and less suspected than that of the Lodges," suggesting the tenuous nature of the boundary emerging at that time between homosociality and homosexuality (1982, 268).

The need to portray these unions as egalitarian and working class dictated that the two male figures be either shirtless or unadorned, as in Vera Ermolaeva's cover for a 1918 chapbook of Russian translations of Whitman's *Pioneers! O Pioneers!* featuring two simply dressed men embracing (see Murray 2019).[24] In the early Soviet period, the male-male allegory often represented collaboration in a common cause, whether it be to defend the nascent Soviet Russian Republic, as in a 1919 poster for the Red Army, with two male figures looking outward to face the enemy, or in the 1919 cover of *Red Petrograd* (*Krasnyi Petrograd*), featuring two shirtless workers smelting steel. A more erotic component emerges in these male-male allegories in the early twenties, as in the 1924 poster for the Union of

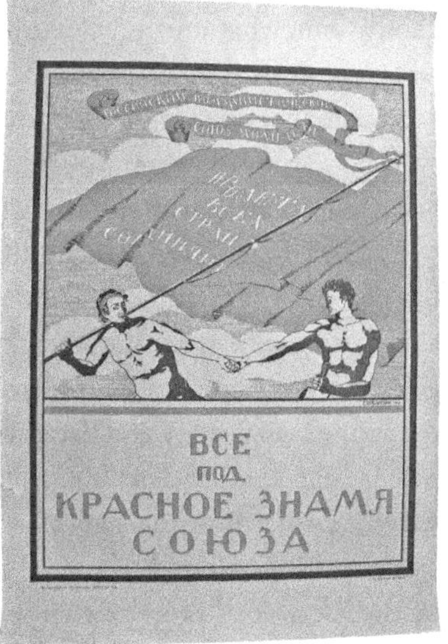

FIGURE 7. Georgii Liubarskii, *Everyone under the Red Banner of Union* (1924), poster. Private Collection

Communist Youth by Georgii Liubarskii titled *Everyone under the Red Banner of Union* (*Vse pod krasnoe znamia soiuza*), featuring two muscular, shirtless young men joining hands and gazing into each other's eyes under an enormous red flag bearing the slogan: "Proletarians of all countries unite!" (fig. 7). Liubarskii also created the logo of a muscular, semi-nude Greek for the publishing house Academia (see fig. 8).

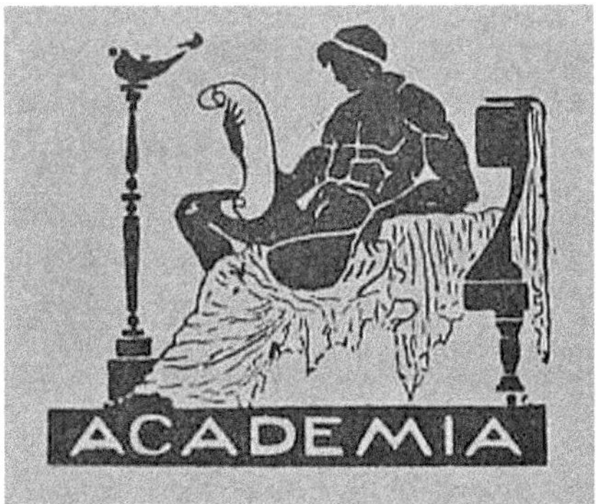

FIGURE 8. Georgii Liubarskii, Logo for the Publishing House *Academia* (1923). Private Collection

There emerged at this time other subsets of the male-male allegory adapted to address specific political or ideological needs, as, for example, the 1924 three-ruble note with a drawing of two recumbent men. One is a peasant, and the other a worker; the head of the former rests

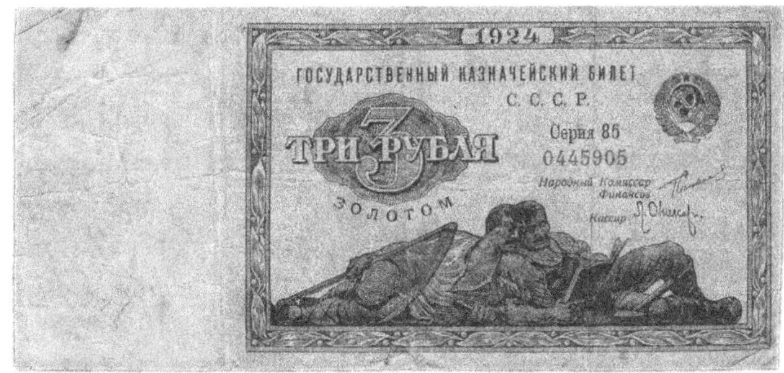

FIGURE 9. Soviet three ruble note (1924). Private Collection

gently, somewhat dreamily, on the latter's shoulder while they look together at a book (fig. 9).

Such allegories were the product of a government initiative described as "smychka" (meaning 'union' or 'linking'), which sought to bring together workers and peasants—who were construed as natural antagonists in Marxist philosophy. Such images served to mystify the conditions in early Soviet Russia (where the peasantry far outnumbered the proletariat) that made it especially unfavorable to communist revolution.[25] (The fact that the worker holds the book suggests that he is nonetheless the vehicle of the other's enlightenment.) The need to reunite civil society and the army after years of war was expressed in the 1921 poster *Long Live the Communist International!* (*Da zdravstvuet kommunisticheskii international!*) featuring two men standing together, both clutching a flagpole carrying a massive red banner. The necessity of distinguishing the male figure on the left as an allegory of civil society from the male figure on the right, who is clearly marked as a soldier (he is wearing a helmet and has a very stern expression on his face), leads the artist to depict the former's civilian dress as exaggeratedly flowing and blousy and his hair as long and tousled, producing a rather queer pairing (see fig. 10). This is a good example of a case in which the representational requirements of the allegory, the need to distinguish the two men, generate queer imagery or imagery that is vulnerable to a queer reading.

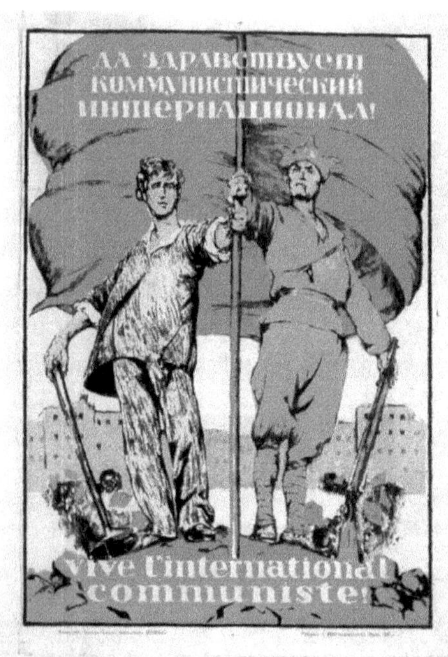

FIGURE 10. Artist unknown, *Long Live Communist International!* (1921), poster. Private Collection

Another subset of male-male allegory evolved to represent the multiethnic Soviet Union, comprising various ethnicity-based republics—often referred to as *bratskie narody,* or 'brotherly nations'—as in V. B. Koretskii, K. K. Ivanov, O. M. Savostiuk,

B. A. Uspenskii's *Together Forever!* (*Naveki-vmeste!*, 1954), with a Russian and Ukrainian standing side by side looking forward; each of the male figures supports an illustrated placard with one hand while the figure on the right holds a spear upright behind the back of the figure on the left in an quasi-embrace.

While many allegories of the multinational Soviet Union were populated by groups of individuals, both male and female, representing all the republics, the poster by Koretskii, Ivanov, Savostiuk, and B. A. Uspenskii is meant to underscore the "special" relationship between Russia and Ukraine. This propagandistic allegory was extended to the fraternal nations of the Eastern bloc as captured in the now famous photograph of Soviet Premier Leonid Brezhnev kissing East German Premier Erich Honecker on the lips, a traditional Russian greeting that is imbued here with political resonance.

Needless to say, erotic parodic readings of these allegories exploded in the late Soviet and early post-Soviet periods. One of the more notable examples is the Leningrad-based artist Dmitrii Vrubel's *Fraternal Kiss* (*Bratskii potselui*, 1990), which appropriates the Brezhnev-Honecker photograph, blown up and posted, strategically, on a remaining section of the Berlin wall. Above the image is the following text in Russian: "Gospodi! Pomogi mne vyzhit'" [Lord! Help me survive], and beneath the image, "sredi etoi smertnoi liubvi" [amid this deadly love]. The entire sentence is presented at the very bottom in German. Another well-known example is the photograph *Era of Clemency* (*Era miloserdiia*, 2004) created by the Russian artists Viacheslav Mizin and Aleksandr Shaburov, known as Sinie nosy, 'blue noses,' featuring two policemen kissing in a birch forest. A parodic element is introduced by intensifying the erotic component—they are necking—and by violating the traditional terms of the allegory, which dictate the cooperation of two men in a project, united in solidarity. Instead, we have two police officers in an unabashedly intimate posture; the sameness of the same-sex couple could be said to mark the symbolic death of one of the most productive Soviet allegories. It is certainly no coincidence that official images of the current Russian president show him sometimes shirtless, but always alone, while erotic parodic versions of the allegory continue to circulate to signify unholy unions—as the one with Putin and Trump kissing à la Brezhnev and Honecker.[26] The context, however, has changed.

Of course, the promotion of more traditional gender relations that took place in the mid-1930s, following Stalin's consolidation of power, led to the increasing prominence of heterosexual unions in Soviet allegories, such as Vera Mukhina's iconic statue, *The Worker and the Kolkhoz Woman* (*Rabochii i kolkhoznitsa*), which was created for the 1937 World's Fair in Paris and now stands at the entrance to the Exhibition of Achievements of the National Economy in Moscow. These allegories play on traditional gender stereotypes, with the female figure typically representing agriculture, hence fertility and reproduction, and the male figure representing industry, hence power and construction, "despite the large proportion of women among industrial workers" (Clark 1993, 43).[27] As Helena Goscilo and Andrea Lanoux (2006, 13–15) point out, the fact that women are typically depicted as smaller and slightly behind the male figures construes women as temporally and socio-politically less progressive. Those associations are driven home with the help of attributes: the women are often depicted holding shafts or bushels of wheat and the men, power tools, as in the countless images from the 1930s of the hero of Soviet labor Aleksei Stakhanov, holding a rather phallic drill. The phallic connotations of the drill are driven home in Sarra Lebedeva's solo sculpture *Miner* (*Shakhter*, 1937), in which a bare-chested young man, legs astride, holds a standing drill that extends from his crotch to the ground.

Heterosexual unions, unsurprisingly, are represented as far less egalitarian than male-male bonds. As Victoria Bonnell (1993, 140) notes in regard to representations of peasant women: "Before the 1930s, [they] seldom, if ever appeared alone in political posters but nearly always in a relationship of contiguity to other, more positive social categories." (The same was true of World War II posters.) Moreover, the male figure is almost always placed above or ahead the female, even in works created by female artists, such as Mukhina's *The Worker and the Kolkhoz Woman*. And, unlike the dreamy romanticism of the early male-male depictions, these hetero couples rarely look at or touch each other; they typically gaze outward toward their "bright future." This dynamic holds true even when both figures are located in the countryside, as in Igor' Savchenko's 1934 film *The Accordion* (*Garmon'*). In one sequence, the husband and wife are shown in a field, he in the foreground and much taller than the wife. The discrepancy reflects the Soviet valorization of size as an indicator of political power and significance. She balances a sheaf of wheat in front of her while the husband holds a six-foot scythe upright by his side.

Citation

Another non-mimetic mode of representational visual imagery is citation, referring not to "reality" but to other artistic styles or motifs. For the Soviets, citation was used quite intentionally to "establish the origins, pedigree and legitimacy" of the new Soviet state (Reid 1993, 175). Indeed, Soviet culture under Stalin was in many ways a culture of citation, with books in all fields introduced by obligatory references to Marx, Engels, Lenin, and Stalin, a phenomenon brilliantly satirized by Tatyana Tolstaya in her novel *Slynx* (*Kys'*, 2000).[28] The fact that the aesthetic program of Socialist Realism was implemented not through detailed programmatic statements but by citing exemplars (see Clark 1984), one could argue, made all subsequent works profoundly citational in nature.

This was also the case in Soviet art. While Socialist Realist art has been discussed as having a dual temporal focus, depicting the Soviet present while also imagining its future (Bassin 2008, 214),[29] its aesthetic orientation toward the past as expressed in the slogan *ucheba u klassikov*, 'learn from the classics,' in particular "the triad Greece-Rome-Renaissance" (Paperny 2011, 19), made it virtually impossible to avoid citing, consciously or not, the queer archive of ancient art. As the architect Ivan Fomin put it in 1933, "Taking classical art as my foundation, I must look at it as raw material, and with a bold and firm hand redraw it with a certain new style that is in keeping with our new revolutionary epoch" (qtd. in Selivanova 2017, 23). The Soviets, therefore, went to great lengths to regulate the practice of artistic and literary citation to contain the unpredictable, even subversive potential of citationality, which, like irony, may challenge "the possibility of an essential truth or a singular gaze" (Horne and Lewis 1996, 7). Official genealogies of Socialist Realism, therefore, sought to limit artistic citation to the naturalist works of the Russian *peredvizhniki* artists of the 1860s and to a restricted number of canonical works of representational art.

Controlling citational practices and the interpretation of citations, however, is no easy task. On a semantic level, citation forecloses the possibility of equivalence—a "cited" sign can never mean the same as the initial sign. As Mieke Bal (2004, 69) explains, "The concept of intertextuality [her term for citationality], indifferent as it is to authorial intention, implies that the adopted sign necessarily comes imbued with meaning. This meaning may have been changed, but the new meaning that replaces it will carry the trace of its predecessor." Every citation transforms the original sign either by enhancing its value or, in the case of parodic citation, by decreasing it, and by placing it into a new social, artistic context. Indeed, even in transnational movements that are built on a common cultural reservoir, such as Neoclassicism in eighteenth-century Europe and the Americas, citational practices will nonetheless "arise and develop within the entirely distinct logic and system of coordinates" of the individual countries involved (Selivanova 2017, 26). In addition, the endless iterability of citations leads to the historical accumulation or layering of citations, complicating the very question of origins.[30] Consider, for example, a post-Soviet citation (Georgy Guryanov's paintings, discussed in chapter 8) of a Soviet citation (Avram Room's 1936 film *A Stern Young Man*) of a Renaissance citation (Michelangelo's David) of the queer beauty of the ancient Greeks. What we have here is "a multi-layering of meanings which always lets the previous meaning continue, as in a geological formation, saying the opposite without giving up the contrary" (Barthes 1977, 58), necessarily troubling the aspirational monologism of official Soviet culture. Moreover, citations raise unique extra-semantic questions, such as: Who is citing the utterance and to what end? What audience is constituted through the recognition of an utterance or a sign as a citation? And how does this new historical and cultural context alter the possible interpretation of the citation?

At the same time, the very historicity of artistic forms and motifs and the various ways they can be re-accented or queered through citation by both artists and viewers—via eroticization, parody, and eclecticism, and in various combinations thereof—make citationality an especially productive site of queer subversion. Indeed, citation has been studied as a characteristic feature of camp talk, a mode of expression that emerged in modern gay subcultures (see Harvey 2002), where acts of citation were more performative than declarative—although citations, one could argue, always have a strong performative dimension, establishing the erudition of the speaker or the ideological correctness of their utterance. Moreover, citationality can have a dual function—to screen queer content by invoking respectable artistic forebears while cuing queer viewers to that very content. Take, for instance, Duncan Grant's mural *Bathing* (1911), created for the student dining hall at the Borough Polytechnic in London and now housed at the Tate Gallery. Among the athletic nude male bathers is a figure posed in such a way as to clearly reference Michelangelo. For some, the reference to the Renaissance master might dignify the content of the painting, shielding it from the erotic gaze, while for the queer viewer who knows something about Michelangelo's sexuality, the citation is an invitation to eroticize the entire painting (see Pilcher 2017, 29). Or consider the subversive use of citation in Yevgeniy Fiks's project *Pleshkas of Russian Art*. Fiks purchased several catalogues for the large-scale Guggenheim Museum's monumental *RUSSIA!* exhibition. He then created several pages of text on pieces of translucent paper containing quotes from Simon Karlinsky, Dan Healey, and other scholars documenting the existence of queer culture in Russia, which was completely ignored in the official catalogue. Fiks then inserted the pages in the catalogue in the appropriate sections. He returned to the Guggenheim bookshop and clandestinely slipped his "revised" catalogues among the "normal" *RUSSIA!* versions on sale. Consequently, some people bought Fiks's catalogue from the Guggenheim bookshop and probably only discovered the inserts once they got home.

Erotic Citation

The queer potential of citation is perhaps nowhere more evident than in references to ancient Greek and Roman cultures, which have played such a major role in Neoclassical and Neo-Hellenist movements throughout Europe, from the Renaissance on and reemerging in the Stalinist culture of the 1930s, as discussed by Katerina Clark in *Moscow, The Fourth Rome* (2011). Indeed, some of the leading artists of Socialist Realist painting, such as Deineka and Ivan Fomin, openly acknowledged their indebtedness to ancient Greek art (see Goscilo 2017, 55; Selivanova 2017). Among the semiotic material available from the classical reservoir were images of varying degrees of queerness, ranging from beautiful youths and idealized athletic male bodies to intense male attachments, and even overt homoerotic relationships, featuring, for example, Hadrian and Antinous, Hercules and Ioläus, Apollo and Hyacinth, Pan and Daphnis, and Zeus and Ganymede, among others. The first two pairs were historical figures while the following three were mythological.[31]

According to the myth of Zeus and Ganymede, the Greek god became enamored of a beautiful youth and so assumed the form of an eagle in order to carry the boy back with him to Olympus. One might say that the Renaissance renderings of Zeus in the guise of an eagle was meant to blunt the homoerotics of the encounter—ancient Greek portrayals as well as more recent ones depict Zeus in human form (see Hupperts 2006, 30 and Beurdeley 1997, 52)—until one looks at Michelangelo's drawing in which an enormous eagle, wings outstretched, is posed behind the naked Ganymede, clutching his legs with his talons as he lifts him off the ground. Incidentally, Michelangelo gifted the drawing to the young Tommaso de' Cavalieri, who is believed to have been "the great love of the painter-sculptor-architect's long and often solitary life" and to whom he dedicated dozens of love poems (Saslow 2018, 12). Contrast this to Rembrandt's *Abduction of Ganymede* (1631), "in which the eagle's inflamed lasciviousness is contrasted to the expression of fear and disgust on the face of Ganymede, who is portrayed not as the mythological youth, but as a child"—a painting Pushkin described as "strange" (Lotman 2019, 169). The point, therefore, is not that all the artists who depicted these queer subjects were queer—indeed, they may have been commissioned to paint them—but that queer artists, like Michelangelo and Grant, had the opportunity to exploit an accepted, even respected repertoire of queer motifs and themes, not only to eroticize them but also to intensify their pathos.[32]

Historically, queer artists and viewers have been able to occupy "official" artistic images and tropes simply through repeated acts of erotic citation, which occurred with Saint Sebastian, who in the Renaissance was transformed into a ravishing, muscular youth pierced by arrows, often with an enigmatic look of ecstasy on his face. The appropriation of St. Sebastian as a queer icon was aided, of course, by the fact that one of the most famous depictions of the saint was done by the Italian artist Giovanni Bazzi, known as Il Sodoma, or the Sodomite. Writers and artists in the late nineteenth and early twentieth century gave new life to the image of St. Sebastian, exploiting and amplifying the queer pathos of the beautiful martyr.[33] The image of St. Sebastian appears in the 1990s in the work of Natalia Kamenetskaia (see her Digital St. Sebastian) in a way that fulfills both a citational and a differentiating function, begging the question of whether such citations are a "restructuring of the past" or an "invention of the future" (Kuraev 1993, 13).

In some cases, queer images were able to circulate in official Soviet culture because the regime was unaware of or actively denied queer interpretations of the image—as occurred with Sappho, whom Soviet scholars and translators, such as Vikentii Veresaev, insisted was not a lesbian. The ambiguity of citational practices also allows the artist both to appropriate the cultural capital of the referenced artist or work while also attenuating any responsibility for the image, as director Sergei Eisenstein does when naming one of his homoerotic sketches *Greek Philosophy* and another *L'Amour que n'ose pas dire son nom* (The love that dare not speak its name); in both instances homosexuality is located outside Russia and the images are attributed to others. As a citational gesture, such naming is deeply ambivalent—is he inscribing these queer figures in a foreign genealogy or inscribing himself in an international genealogy of queer artists?

There is no doubt Soviet censors were aware of the queering power of erotic citation as evidenced in objections to the original poster for the 1933 film *Hot Blood* (*Goriachiaia krov'*), by Anatolii Bel'skii, which appears to be a sexualized citation of the Russian painter Kuzma Petrov-Vodkin's classic 1912 painting *Bathing the Red Horse* (*Kupanie krasnogo konia*). The poster features a naked soldier, his eyes aglow and wearing a somewhat demonic grin, riding a sorrel-colored

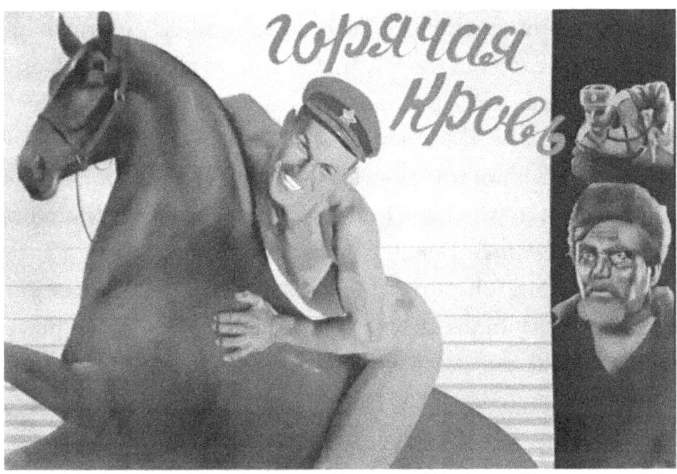

FIGURE 11. Anatolii Bel'skii, Poster for the film *Hot Blood* (c. 1932). Private Collection

horse bareback (see fig. 11). The revised poster features the same soldier, fully clothed and now standing in front of his horse, wearing a more wholesome smile.

A more acceptable citation of Petrov-Vodkin's work appears in Arkadii Plastov's 1938 *Bathing Horses* (*Kupanie konei*), which seeks to eliminate any hint of sexual desire. Unlike Petrov-Vodkin's youth, who gazes directly into the eyes of the viewer, these boys frolic in a kind of Edenic bliss, wholly oblivious to their nakedness or to the viewer's presence. While this artistic conceit of the boys' sexual innocence would allow subsequent portrayals of naked youth in Soviet art, one cannot prevent the queer viewer from looking beyond that conceit by seeing Plastov's painting as a citation of far more openly queer and libidinous works. This is also the case with Petr Konchalovskii's painting *Red Army Cavalry Bathing* (*Kupaniie krasnoi konnitsy*, 1928) featuring five naked men. Unlike Plastov's youths, four of the adult men in Konchalovskii's are depicted facing the viewer. Is the level of unselfconscious exposure meant to guarantee their heterosexuality? Who can say?

Parodic (and Erotic-Parodic) Citation

While artists can exploit citation for queer purposes, as Michelangelo did with Ganymede, viewers, too, can draw queer references, that is, references or citations that rely on the historicity of artistic forms and motifs to provoke parodic and erotic-parodic interpretations. Such erotic-parodic queerings of Socialist Realism became common in the Sots Art of Komar and Melamid, especially in their Nostalgic Socialist Realism series (1982–1983). The series includes *The Origin of Socialist Realism,* featuring a beautiful bare-breasted muse leaning over and caressing Stalin's chin, while the leader appears wholly uninterested; *Stalin in front of the Mirror,* in which the leader gazes with evident pleasure at his own reflection; and *What Is to Be Done?,* featuring two adolescent boys. The older and taller one puts his arm fully around the shoulders of the younger one, pulling him close, and points into the distance. The younger boy's glance, however, does not exactly follow the trajectory of the older boy's finger; his sidewards glance imbues the painting's title, which is written clearly on the cover of the book in the younger boy's arms, with sexual connotations. This double citation, in the title of the painting and on the book depicted in the painting, reflects the dual origin of the phrase: it is the title of Nikolai Chernyshevsky's progressive novel of the late nineteenth century and of a seminal work by Lenin, which intentionally cites Chernyshevsky. Far less coy is the queering of Socialist Realism in Vladimir Sorokin's postmodern fiction, most notoriously in his novel *Blue Lard* (*Goluboe salo,* 1999), which features, among other things, a sodomitic relationship between Stalin and Khrushchev. (Incidentally, the word *goluboi* in Soviet slang was used to refer to homosexuals, a calque perhaps from the French phrase "l'amour bleu.") Such erotic-parodic citation is also characteristic of the camp performances of Mamyshev-Monroe.

Eclectic Citation

In the 1970s, during the so-called period of Stagnation under Brezhnev, eclectic citational practices, associated in the West with postmodernism, emerged among younger Soviet artists. The artistic eclecticism of that time was, according to Susan Reid, a harbinger of the fall of the Soviet Union, challenging the direct patrilinear citation practices of official Soviet art, opening up a range of potential interpretations, and inviting the viewer to take a more active role in the process of interpretation. This eclecticism, however, did not only subvert the monologism of official discourse, deterritorializing it, in Yurchak's (2005) formulation; it also introduced a sense of relativism into the culture, which undermined basic notions of sincerity, truth, and faith, while allowing increasingly jaded, nonconformist individuals to "pass" as Soviet subjects by citing hollowed-out platitudes. As Reid (1993, 173) explains:

> In everyday life skill in dissembling and double-voicing were essential strategies for social survival and advancement. In this situation, the existence of a sincere self which might be fully present in art or any other public form was questionable. This was fertile ground for the embrace of Bakhtinian concepts. The 'masquerade of styles' in 'permitted' painting of the age of stagnation parallels the phenomenon of the *personazhnyi avtor*, the use of an assumed persona style and voice, which is an essential element of non-conformist culture in Moscow in the seventies and eighties.

In a sense, it was not so much the individual images or styles cited that were problematic, although artists of the time did seek to expand the citational reservoir, but the multiplicity of styles. Such eclectic citational practices risked undercutting the authoritative discourse on art, in particular, official claims of transparency and truth, by "draw[ing] attention to the 'artificiality of art'" and creating "a surplus of meaning" that "resists containment by official ideology" (Reid 1993, 171). Such eclectic citational practices, one could say, queer the relationship between "naturalistic truth and pictorial truth" (Perl 2017, 10). Consider, for example, in Erik Bulatov's *Sky Sea* (*Nebo More*, 1984), in which the artist superimposes the words "sea" and "sky" over a sunny, realistically portrayed landscape, suggesting that visual codes are no less mediating and mediated than verbal ones. This was worrying to Soviet critics in the Brezhnev era, who "objected that art history was coming between young artists and the study of contemporary reality" (171). Of course, not all stylistic eclecticism is queer or ambiguous. In fact, eclecticism in the work of Dmitrii Zhilinskii, is used to rehabilitate Soviet masculinity by giving it a "human face," while in the work of the late Soviet and early post-Soviet artist Ilya Glazunov, it is used to create a nationalist fantasy of an enduring Russian identity. (For more on this expansive view of Russian culture, with its imperial implications, see Kalinin 2018.)

With the fall of communism, which began with Perestroika, the authoritative discourse that had organized Soviet culture collapsed, unleashing the historically new and highly unstable citational practices that combined irony and seriousness, mockery and admiration, iconoclasm and nostalgic adoration, refusing "to accept any boundary between [them]" (Yurchak 2005, 242). As Nikolai Gusev, leader of the Leningrad rock band *Strannye igry* [Strange games], put it, "Balancing between irony and genuine fascination is what has always interested me most. I want to avoid the situation, where my stuff could be interpreted 'straight', unambiguously" (qtd. in Yurchak 2005, 238). The queer founder of the New

Academists, Timur Novikov, developed a kind of eclectic citational practice that could be considered camp, or *stiob*, insofar as it punctures artistic pieties on all sides while assuming a pose of absolute piety, as in his *Apollo Standing on a Black Square* (*Apollon, popirauchii Chernii kvadrat*, 1991), *Apollo, Hyacinth, and Cyparissus* (*Apollon, Giazint i Kiparis*,1990), or the group project *Passiones Luci* (1995), an illustrated version of Apuleius's *Golden Ass*. In fact, the very title of his collective, the New Academy, can be considered a layered citation, invoking at one and the same time Plato's Academy, as well as the Renaissance Humanists' New Academy, and perhaps even the Academia publishing house, founded in Petrograd in the 1920s, which produced high quality translations of a very cosmopolitan assortment of works, including the complete works of Plato (1921-1938) and André Gide's *L'Immoraliste* (1927).

The queering effect of eclectic citation is perhaps nowhere more evident than in the cross-dressing of the performance artist Vladislav Mamyshev-Monroe. If we were to analyze his imitation of Marilyn Monroe by itself, it might appear as a homage to Russia's "imaginary West" in all its surface glamour. When juxtaposed to Mamyshev-Monroe's other iconic character, Adolf Hitler, however, Monroe becomes part of a deeply disturbing portrayal of a schizophrenic twentieth century: "Splitting the consciousness of the planet's population, Hitlerism and Monrology operate to this day" (Mamyshev 2002, 235). An eclecticism that might seem shocking to a Western viewer is a somewhat "natural" product of Soviet culture, in which both Monroe and Hitler were "suppressed in Soviet ideology" (Mamyshev 2002, 237) as the defining others of communist political and social values, each possessing a dangerous, libidinous allure.

At one moment, Mamyshev-Monroe's eclecticism appears to take to its parodic limit the traditional view of the Russian as a "universal man," capable of embodying and synthesizing all aspects of world culture. This position was articulated perhaps most fully by Dostoevsky at the dedication of the Pushkin monument in Moscow in 1888, and echoes of it persisted in the discourse of Soviet universalism and are evident in the conservative-authoritarian rhetoric of contemporary Russia (see Kalinin 2018). The next moment, however, Mamyshev-Monroe appears as a manifestation of a postmodern universe where multiple identity positions swirl about, ungrounded. We see both tendencies expressed in his artistic manifesto "Where the Heck Am I? Where Are My Things?" subtitled: "The stable mobility and the mobile stability of Vladislav Mamyshev's objective subjectivism":

> It is difficult to write about oneself in the third person and it is even more difficult to write about myself in the first or in the second person. But am I writing about myself? "Who am I? Where am I? How the heck did I get here and where are my things?" – these are the questions which I have had to ask myself since I took on this difficult task—to put the universe in myself. (Mamyshev 2002, 234)

That being said, the contingency of this "local" reading of Western history by no means negates its relevance outside of Russia. In fact, it is that very contingency, or the alternative cultural logic that produces it, that makes possible readings that are utterly unthinkable in other local cultures, such as the US. Perhaps only today, thanks to the Black Lives Matter movement, are people willing and able to see the cult of Monroe as symbolic of a post-war reassertion of Whiteness that replaced the violent state apparatus of Nazi Germany with the seductive ideological apparatus of Hollywood. Moreover, the idea that Mamyshev is not your grandmother's Monroe—nor is he your grandmother's drag queen—is further underscored by his willingness to replay the iconic scene of the actress standing atop a subway grate while fully exposing his male genitalia, transforming his body into "an instrument of critical practice" (Piotrowski 2002, 226).

Differentiation

The semiotic function of differentiation, as described by Susan Gal and Judith T. Irvine operates as follows: "The contrasting qualities in the signs are 'found' or projected onto the contrasting phenomena that the signs are taken to index. In other words, a sign in this case is defined by what it is not, as opposed to what it is. The specific qualities presumed to be in contrast depend on the ideologies—background knowledge, interests, and projects—that social actors bring to the scene of comparison" (2019, 19). If in cultures marked by deep ruptures or explosions, to use Lotman's term, the citational function in art assumes special importance, then so, too, does the differentiating function, but to opposite ends. While the former functions to reestablish genealogies, the latter functions to create and enforce differences, marking the birth of a new culture or social order. That being said, the functions may overlap, especially when citationality is used queerly; for example, does a parodic citation actually fulfill a more differentiating function than a citational one? Or consider the citations of Oscar Wilde in the work of the post-Soviet New Academy artist Timur Novikov, which serve both to establish a genealogical connection to pre-Soviet Silver Age culture and to differentiate his representational art from Socialist Realism by celebrating precisely the kind of formal experimentation, exaggerated decorative ornamentation, and self-indulgent narcissistic individualism that had been anathematized by the Soviets as formalist.

There are several moments in the history of modern Russia when depictions of same-sex desire have assumed a distinctly differentiating function, typically following the sudden lifting of censorship restrictions on representations of sex and sexuality, among other things. This is not surprising, perhaps, given the strong association of sexual openness and freedom (including freedom from procreation) with modernity, making these representations symbolic of the "modern" world, for better or worse (see Engelstein 1992; Bershtein 2018, 146–153). When representations of homoeroticism and homosexuality fulfill such a differentiating function, their meaning easily becomes overdetermined.

One especially striking example of the differentiating function of artistic representations of sex and sexuality occurred after the First Workers' Revolution of 1905, which saw a relaxation of press censorship. That period ushered in Russia's first gay- and lesbian-themed novels: Mikhail Kuzmin's *Wings* (*Kryl'ia*, 1906) and Lidiia Zinovieva-Gannibal's *Thirty Three Abominations* (*Tridtsat'-tri uroda*, 1907); the first book-length Russian treatise on homosexuality, Vasilii Rozanov's *People of the Moonlight* (*Liudi lunnogo sveta*, 1911); the homoerotic poetry of Mikhail Kuzmin and Nikolai Kliuev; and the Russian translation of the complete collected works of Oscar Wilde (1912). In the realm of the visual arts, this period witnessed a boom in nudes, which lasted well into the first decade of the Soviet Union, as well as the appearance of the greatest works of erotic art in all Russian history, mentioned above. Depictions of queer sexuality at that time served to differentiate contemporary Russian culture from the more conservative and moralizing culture of the late nineteenth-century.[34]

The Bolshevik Revolution, of course, represented another abrupt turning point in Russian culture, but not in terms of homosexuality or, at least, not initially. While such is the case, the Soviet state's attempt to distance itself from the bourgeois culture of imperial Russia, in particular, the "sexual ambivalence that lies at the heart of Russian masculinity at the end of the tsarist era" (McReynolds 2008, 133), urged the masculinization of Soviet culture. This made things increasingly uncomfortable for some Soviet queers over the course of the twenties and definitively so following Stalin's consolidation of power in the thirties. Stalin's establishment of official heteronormativity was expressed in the criminalization of male homosexuality and abortion in 1934. The Soviet Union under

Stalin would become extremely puritanical in regard to all things sexual, although it did permit rather overt displays of masculine virility, as in Vasily Iakovlev's enormous portrait of General Zhukov on a rearing stallion trampling captured Nazi flags. Depicted from below, the horse's genitalia are quite prominently displayed.

In terms of the differentiating function, the 1930s represented a particular challenge, for Soviet art had to distinguish itself not only from Western bourgeois art but also from German fascist art, which, like Soviet art of that time, was feeding from the same conceptual/cultural trough of ancient Greek and Roman art and modern eugenics. This phenomenon was of particular concern in regard to the legitimation of nudes, requiring that Soviet works of art display "a perceived lack of eroticism and a distance from 'fascist' eugenical concerns" (Simpson 2004b, 113).

The differentiating function of artistic styles reached an unprecedented global dimension in the post-World War II period, when the binaries of the Cold War, consolidated through government interventions, exerted an enormous influence on the art world. As John Curley (2018, 13) notes, "Ideology has always guided the interpretation of images, but perhaps never yet on the Cold War's systematic, global scale." Abstraction in the post-war period became associated from the Western perspective (and with covert financial support from the US government) with the "Western" values of freedom and individualism. "The view that abstract art was synonymous with democracy," was even expressed by the conservative US president, Dwight D. Eisenhower, who declared modern art to be "a pillar of democracy" (Saunders 2013, 226; 228). From the Soviet side, however, abstract art was associated, at least in official discourse, with egoism, opacity, elitism—and homosexuality, as discussed above. Representational art, on the other hand, became associated on both sides of the Iron Curtain with communism, which in the Soviet Union meant communal values, egalitarianism, and accessibility to the masses, while in the West, that association signified authoritarianism and creative sterility.

Cold War polarization would shape not only the official style and subject matter for artists and art historians on both sides of the Iron Curtain but also the modes of resistance and protest. For example, rather than turn to abstraction, which was associated with the West, many Russian underground and dissident artists critiqued realism from the inside, through pastiche and parody, as in the work of the Moscow Conceptualists and later in the work of the Petersburg New Academy artists.[35] On the other hand, a number of gay identified artists in the

West, such as Paul Cadmus and David Hockney, were embracing representational art.

By the late 1980s, however, Western queer art had become defined by identity politics and a mandate for openness and directness, which loosely followed the trajectory of progressive (mostly left-wing) Western art that, not unlike the Soviet model, was perceived as privileging content over form. Western artists whose work was influenced by the culture wars of the 1980s and the HIV/AIDS crisis, such as David Wojnarowicz, Keith Haring, and Nan Goldin, appeared among the last specimens of "Cold War art," right before the collapse of the Soviet Union (see Lord and Meyer 2019, 147–186). This queerly coincided with the opening of late-Soviet and early post-Soviet society to the issue of (homo)sexuality and queerness, especially after the decriminalization of male homosexuality in 1993. Western queer activist art, however, appeared too foreign for most queer Russian artists, who had come from a different political and historical context; they would forge their own distinct engagement with queer beauty.

The late-Soviet and early post-Soviet period in Russia was marked by the relatively sudden lifting of censorship restrictions, which made possible the unprecedented appearance of sexually explicit works of literature, art, and film, up to an including pornography. As Paul Goldsmith (1999, 318) comments, "The collapse of communism brought with it many small revolutions and changes, not the least of which was the appearance of large-scale commercial pornography." In that context, styles and subject matter banned by the Soviets assumed a clear differentiating function, distinguishing post-Soviet culture from its prudish, largely asexual predecessor. As Renee Baigell and Matthew Baigell (2001, 10) note, "Official Soviet art policy inhibited the making of images of the nude body for its own sake," and so "with democracy, controls were completely lifted, and painting of the nude body became in and of itself an act of freedom." This was especially true of representations of queer sexuality, which were often employed as a metonym for sexuality in general or for the open discussion of sexuality, making the "meaning" of queer sexuality at that time, as in the Silver Age, overdetermined and leading to the emergence of the homo-device, discussed above.

The Queer(ing) Gaze: From Disinterested to Embodied

The aesthetic gaze as theorized by Kant in the Enlightenment was characterized as both disinterested and abstracted: "He treats aesthetic judgements as universal in terms of (the supposed universality of disinterested subjective feelings of) pleasure" (Margolis 1995, 9). The disinterested Kantian gaze is evident in artist portraits of the time. Consider, for example, the many portraits of the Italian Neoclassical sculptor Antonio Canova. In one pastel by Hugh Douglas Hamilton, titled *Antonio Canova in His Studio with Henry Tresham and a Plaster Model for Cupid and Psyche* (1788–91), Canova and his friend are calmly discussing a model of Cupid and Psyche that stands right beside them; the two mythological figures are horizontal, locked in an amorous embrace, while the artists are turned away from the sculpture, calmly engaged in a conversation. In *Portrait of Antonio Canova* (1815), by Angelica Kauffman, Canova is standing next to a plaster model of a naked Hercules, and in *Portrait of Antonio Canova in his Studio Completing the La Touche "Amorino,"* circa 1793, by Domenico Conti, he is standing beside a life-size figure of a naked Amorino on a pedestal. In both portraits, Canova gazes out at the viewer with an expression of placid indifference on his face.

By the end of the nineteenth century, however, such disinterestedness had been thoroughly rejected, at least by artists themselves. Works of art and works of literature about art at this time regularly presented art as erotically charged, and that erotic charge was typically heterosexual. Consider *The Kreutzer Sonata* (1901), an oil painting on canvas by René-Xavier Prinet, inspired by Leo Tolstoy's 1889 novella of the same title. The painting features a male violinist and a female pianist who are so overcome with desire as they perform Beethoven's composition for violin and piano dedicated to Rudolph Kreutzer that they interrupt their performance to kiss. And then there are the erotic drawings of Mihály Zichy, a Hungarian artist who occupied the position of court painter under Tsar Alexander II, Tsar Alexander III, and Tsar Nicholas II. Three of the drawings in the extant collection of twelve feature a male artist making passionate love to his female subject. Such scenes were also common in literary works of the time. Consider Anatole France's novel *Le Lys rouge*, in which the protagonists, Countess Thérèse Martin-Bellème and the Jacques Dechartre, fall in love and kiss for the first time while viewing a painting of the Virgin Mary by Angelico in a museum in Florence, Italy. Notably, Dechartre is a sculptor, while the countess's previous lover, Robert Le Ménil, "had no appreciation of painting" (France 1898, 146).

Art historians, however, were slow to abandon Kantian disinterestedness.[36] As Norman Bryson (2004, 7) notes: "Film studies recognized that viewers brought to their experience of visual culture much more than iconographical knowledge—the ability to distinguish between a Nativity and a Pietà, or to identify particular saints and their whole history of having been socialized according to the specificities of gender and sexuality. Art history's grasp of spectatorship lacked this dimension almost entirely." While traditional art history saw perspectivalism as an unqualified achievement of western art, Bryson argued that it was predicated on the elimination of "the diachronic movement of deixis," which situates the artist and viewing subject in space and time rather than abstracting their position. In this way, perspectivalism "creates, or at least seeks to create, a synchronic instant of viewing that will eclipse the body, and the glance, in an infinitely extended Gaze of the image as pure idea: the image as *eidolon*" (94). In a later essay, Bryson (2004, 5) connects the Gaze with the third person discourse of traditional art history, its "rhetoric of professional impersonality," which obscures the fact that "even the most 'historicist' account of a work of art is rooted in an encounter with the work in the present."

Outside the field of art history, the gaze has been the subject of intense theorization across disciplines for much of the twentieth century as part of a broad critique of the bourgeois liberal subject and its claims of unity and autonomy. One of the most influential conceptualizations of the gaze was that of the French psychoanalyst Jacques Lacan, who described the child's first viewing of herself in a mirror as marking the subject's entry into the Symbolic Order, the realm of language and the law, which he presents as an alienating subjection.[37] Michel Foucault historicized the gaze by positing it as central to the construction of the modern subject. According to Foucault (1977), the modern subject is constructed through subjection to a disembodied disciplinary gaze, symbolized by the panopticon. Norman Bryson applied this to the visual arts, tracing the duality of modern subjectivity in the development of perspective in western painting. While perspective ostensibly conflates the viewer's vantage point with that of the artist, the single vanishing point, Bryson (106) argues, "marks the installation within the painting of a principle of radical alterity, since its gaze returns that of the viewer as its own object: something is looking at my looking: a gaze whose position I can never occupy." And so, for Bryson, the Gaze describes "a transcendent point of vision that has discarded the body of labour and exists only as disembodied *punctum*"—transforming the subject into an object.

Laura Mulvey (1975) introduced a gender dimension to the visual field with her concept of "the male gaze," which she uses to describe the visual field of Hollywood films in which the male characters watch while the female characters are watched.[38] Such a visual field reflects and reproduces a hegemonic masculinity by associating maleness with activity and agency, and femininity with languorous subjection, or passivity. While Mulvey's work has been justly criticized for its failure to conceptualize agency for female or queer viewers other than submitting to or colluding with the heterosexual masculine gaze (Kaplan 1990) or to complicate the male gaze by recognizing the "coercive aspect of identification" involved in the construction of masculinity (Bryson 1994, 231),[39] it is largely accepted today that "the body and its genderedness are continually implicated in the act of looking" (Bal 2004, 86). Postcolonial scholars, such as Frantz Fanon, have contributed to the theorization of the racialized gaze, which exercises an ocular violence effecting "the disintegration of identity in the face of the white man's gaze" (Mitchell 1997, 219).

While acknowledging that the visual field is never innocent or uninhabited, that it is always shot through with vectors of power, W. J. T. Mitchell (1997, 231) observes: "The visual exchanges across the boundaries of race and gender are never reducible to the dialectics of master and slave, subject and subject, much less subject and object." There is room for resistance. Today, the concept of the queer or queering gaze is often used to refer either to queer artists and cinematographers who attempt to create an alternative visual field to the white, heteronormative, patriarchal, and imperialist one described by Mulvey and Fanon, or to works of art and film that resist being easily read and categorized within a binary heteronormative logic.

Based on these various models of the visual field, a counter-hegemonic approach to visual arts would assume a fully embodied and socially situated gaze, grounded in the ultimate "undecidability of aesthetic experience" (Bishop 2012, 27) and "the uncanny phenomenology of visual culture" (Mitchell 1997, 218). Or as W. J. T Mitchell (1997, 221) put it, "The desires of pictures are not just those of signs signaling other signs, but of bodies calling to bodies." In line with that thinking, Mieke Bal (2004, 42) describes perception as "a psychosomatic process, strongly dependent, for example, on the position of the perceiving body in relation to the perceived object," and Madina Tlostanova (2018, 22) asserts, "Art in its visual, verbal and synthetic forms remains a crucial intersection of being and knowledge."

As an alternative to the abstracted, hegemonic Gaze, Bryson puts forward the Glance, which "proposes desire, proposes the body, in the durée of its practical activity" (122), often taking on the role of "saboteur, trickster" (121).[40] Bryson's Glance is fully embodied and socially situated: "Address[ing] vision in the durational temporality of the viewing subject; it does not seek to bracket out the process of viewing, nor in its own techniques does it exclude the traces of the body of labour" (Bryson 1983, 94). For Bryson, this recuperation of deixis opens up the possibility of a materialist art history, one that fully acknowledges and validates not only what Gombrich refers to as "the beholder's share," but also the particular share of those beholders marked by racial, gender or sexual otherness, whose "double consciousness" (see DuBois 1897; Winkler 1993) represents a distinct site from which to "see through"—by that, I mean to critique and de-naturalize the totalizing, binary logic structuring the hegemonic Gaze and to expose "what occlusions and repressions occur in the visual field, when the latter is understood as centered on the third person, not only in art history or in curatorial practice, but in the conceptual models we use to think through questions of power in vision, questions of the gaze" (Bryson 2004, 5).

In a similar way, Lena Jonson uses Jacques Rancière's notion of the "distribution of the sensible" to theorize the visual field in Putin-era Russia following the conservative-authoritarian shift that took place around 2012. This concept is especially useful in conceptualizing the relationship between art, politics, and society as it "extends aesthetics beyond the strict realm of art to include the conceptual coordinates and modes of visibility operative in the political domain" (Rancière 2006, 82). In that model, the hegemonic gaze "produces a system of self-evident facts of perception based on the set horizons and modalities of what is visible and audible as well as what can be said, thought, made or done" (2006: 85), which Rancière refers to as consensus. To the extent that dissensus refers to "everything that questions and challenges [consensus]" (Jonson 2018a, 9), it corresponds to Bryson's Glance and to Davis's concept of beauty queered. As Jonson (2018a, 10) glosses it, "Dissensus in art takes place as a hidden or indirect dispute over the framework of what is given but does not mean the existence of open conflict. Instead, this art withdraws from ready-made conditions of meaning and refuses to create any alternative frames of discourse for art practice." Queering, therefore, may be considered a form of dissensus, and as such, a way of carving out a space between what Maria Engström and Vlad Strukov theorize as "visuality" versus "visibility." For Engström and Strukov, queer visuality has been "appropriated by the [Russian] government, disabling queer visibility and disempowering LGBTQ communities in their struggle for civil rights."[41]

The impossibility of ultimately controlling the semantic remainder (or surplus) of symbols and the productivity and mobility of the queer glance constitute the queer potential of art and the possibility of creating alternatives to the hegemonic disciplinary force field of the Gaze. Understood in this way, Bryson's glance has much in common with Bakhtin's notion of the "sideward glance." Within the social life of language that exists in the gap between Saussure's langue (language as system) and parole (individual utterance), Bakhtin's sideward glance acknowledges the "double-voiced," often citational nature of most discourse, construing monologism as the exception to the norm, an ultimately futile but also potentially violent attempt to eliminate or control the inherent polyphony of human discourse. This does not, however, keep authoritarians from trying. Lev Gudkov's (2016, online) argument that Putin-era propaganda seeks to establish a *sistemnyi kliuch,* or systemic key, construes this disciplinary project as an attempt to control the polysemy of symbols by transforming them into indices and by condemning alternative interpretations as false. Hence, the new seriousness in official Russian culture, "where everything, including art, is understood literally" (Jonson 2018a, 12).

This also helps to explain the special animus directed at "gay propaganda" in Putin-era Russia. In their capacity to "pass" as straight, gay people are an especially unruly sign (see Baer 2016). As Bryson (2004, 22) remarks: "For the operator of homosexual discourse there is something hallucinatory and uncanny about the mode of the stigma's appearance. Unlike comparable markers of, for example, race and gender, the homosexual stigma has the diabolical property of being able to disappear, like a message written in invisible ink: the homosexual can *pass,* can melt into the crowd." The appearance of homosexuality in Russian mass media following the lifting of censorship restrictions in the late eighties and the legalization of homosexuality in 1993 was perceived as a semiotic problem. As Vladimir Zhirinovskii and Vladimir Iurovitskii complained in their 1996 *The ABCs of Sex,* homosexuals had destroyed the word *goluboi* by making it polysemous, turning it into what Lee Edelman (1993) theorized as a homograph. (Meaning 'light blue,' *goluboi* was also a slang term for gay.) Hence the appearance of works of Russian pop psychology dedicated to decoding the behavior of gay people, to making homosexuality legible. As Dilia Enikeeva (2003, 143) argues in her *Gei i lesbianki* [Gays and lesbians], only 15 percent of gays "act like women" and so are obviously homosexual. Nonetheless, she assures her readers, "there are several nuances, by which one can determine whether someone is gay," nuances produced by the mismatch between the gay person's "behavioral sex and biological sex" (143).

One of the most important of those nuances is the *osobyi vzgliad* (particular glance) of the gay man. In a homophobic visual field, the gay glance could be seen as functionally equivalent to the vanishing point in Renaissance perspectivalism—"mark[ing] the installation within the painting of a principle of radical alterity, since its gaze returns that of the viewer as its own object" (Bryson 1983, 106). But this is not a third-person object. As Bryson (2004, 23) argues elsewhere, "The moment when the stigmatizer thinks he sees the sign of infamy is accordingly perilous in the extreme, for in recognizing these oblique clues and indices the stigmatizer has left the universe of third-person discourse, with its taxonomic certainties and hygienic distance from danger, and has entered the forbidden zone of homoerotic intimacy."

Against the backdrop of a transparent realism or of a monologic literalism, the hallucinatory presence of homosexuality troubles meaning making on both an ontological and an epistemological level. We see evidence of this in Yevgeniy Fiks's interview with Slava Mogutin, when Mogutin recounts how as a youth he found queerness in the works of Soviet artists like Deineka, or conversely, when Soviet viewers detected homosexuality in the portraits of Konstantin Somov, despite the best efforts of the Soviet curators to conceal the artist's sexuality and to omit works of overt homosexual content from the exhibitions that took place in the USSR in the 1970s (see Golubev 2019, 13).

Conclusion: Preposterous Histories of Russian Art

This focus on the semiotic remainder in works of art ("obtuse meaning") and on modes of semiosis not grounded in mimesis, modes that expose the mismatch between "naturalistic truth and pictorial truth," has the potential to transform art history from an act of abstract decoding to one of embodied performance. As Bryson (2014, 3) remarks, "Rather than being a 'relay' conveying an intention from artist to viewer, the work is thus the occasion for a performance in the field of its meaning—where no single performance is capable of actualizing or totalizing all of the work's semantic potential." From that perspective, one might imagine an art history that incorporates the queer(ing) gaze to generate alternative, non-patrilineal aesthetic genealogies, an art history that would reject the very logic of succession in favor of an unresolvable simultaneity and copresence, one that dares to read works of art against the grain of official culture and in provocative regroupings, which may challenge what Serguei Oushakine (2022, 612) has recently described as "a default state where every new generation of visual scholars must find itself within the same limited set of seemingly eternal concepts."

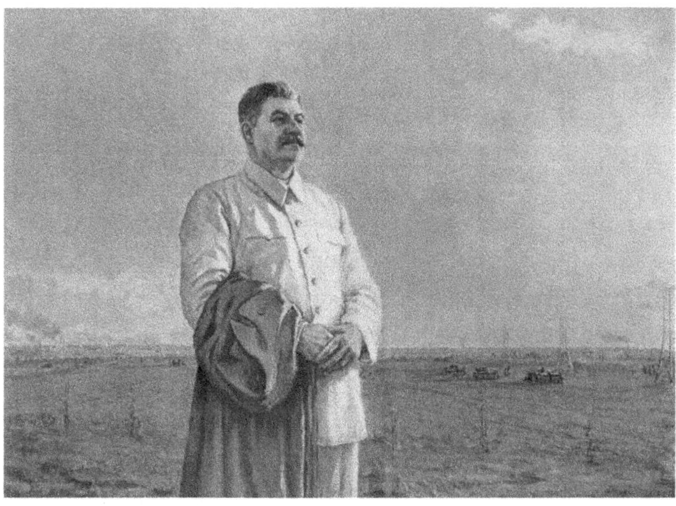

FIGURE 12. Fyodor Shurpin, *The Morning of Our Motherland* (1948). The State Tretyakov Gallery, Moscow

Consider, for example, a queer rereading of Fyodor Shurpin's classic Socialist Realist painting *The Morning of Our Motherland* (*Utro nashei Rodini*, 1948) (see fig. 12). In the painting Stalin, dressed in his unadorned white military uniform—in semiotic terms, virtually naked (see Lotman 2013, 120 on Stalin's dress)—stands motionless in a field facing the morning sun, which casts a warm glow over his face and torso. Bassin (2008, 217) notes a "palpable ambiguity" in the painting: "Stalin is a sun god, but being a sun god suggests a oneness and harmony with the sun, with the cosmos, and the natural world—the very same natural world that the Soviets were so single-mindedly striving to subjugate and reshape." But if we were to group this painting with Anne-Louis Girodet's Neoclassical *The Sleep of Endymion* (1791), then Stalin, "resplendent in his trademark white tunic, which brightly reflects the intensive sunshine of the dawn" (Bassin 2008, 215), can be read as a citation of Endymion, whose pale face and naked torso are bathed in the light of the moon. The light illuminating Endymion, whom James Smalls (1996, 20) describes as "a bewildering image of erotic contemplation of the male body," signals the approach of Selene, the moon goddess, who visits the sleeping youth every night to lie with him, ultimately bearing him fifty daughters. The similarity of their illuminated white bodies and the association of both these figures with fertility—Stalin is standing in the middle of a plowed field—connects these images in a way that queers Stalin, transforming him into a passive figure who is ravished. Indeed, if Stalin were a sun god, wouldn't he be emanating light rather than reflecting it, a fact that aligns him more closely with the moon than the sun—an association normally gendered as female (in one version of the myth, Selene gives birth only to daughters). The citation is not as farfetched as it might first appear when one considers that the myth of Endymion, popular with the Romantics, was given new life in Russian art of the Silver Age—see, for example, Nikolai Kalmakov's *Artemis and Sleeping Endymion* (*Artemida i spiashchii Endimion*, 1917) or Petrov-Vodkin's *Sleep* (*Son*, 1910)—further evidence of that period's fascination with alternative forms of masculinity, embodied in Vasilii Rozanov's concept of "people of the moonlight," a phrase he uses to describe "spiritual" homosexuals. But here, Endymion is re-sited within the "libidinal economy of Stalinism" (Baudin and Heller 1989, 130) to represent Stalin not only as powerful father but also as reproductive mother, a reciting made especially urgent by the unspeakable carnage of the Second World War and the purges that preceded it. In that sense, Stalin's glimmering white tunic can be compared with the broad white back of the showering soldier in Deineka's *After the Battle*—both surfaces act to screen the violence and death of Stalinism, with which Russia has yet to fully reckon. What would it mean then to read the title of Mamyshev-Monroe's dissertation, *This Is Not the Sun Rising—This Is Monrology Coming over for Coffee*? As a parodic citation of Shurpin's painting and as a rejection of the libidinal economy it represents?

If, as James Smalls contends in his 1996 essay "Making Trouble for Art History," "Art history constitutes itself as heterocentrist discourse through application of methodological paradigms designed to make and keep white masculinity and heterosexuality normative and hegemonic," then preposterous histories of art seek to validate alternative paradigms, built on nonhegemonic, embodied positions, from which we might expose "hitherto unexamined assumptions about meaning and the world," as well as "the ambiguity that results from the possible discrepancy between the object that is present and the statement that is made about it" (Bal 2004, 165).

Notes

1 Merezhkovskii uses the common Orthodox epithet, *predtecha*, or 'forerunner,' to refer to John, which presents him as a Peircean index, pointing to the coming of the Christ; indeed, he is often depicted with his index finger pointing upward.

2 All translations from the Russian are the author's unless otherwise indicated. By the way, the French King's final exclamation is rendered in Herbert Trench's 1902 English translation, *The Romance of Leonardo da Vinci*, as: "Everyone knows that painters have queer fancies!" (Merezhkovsky 1902, 445).

3 Regarding the ambivalent legacy of Winckelmann, James Smalls (1996, 24) writes, "It was the sublimation of Winckelmann's own homodesires in creating a history of art methodology that has encouraged or, more specifically, mandated, suppression of homoerotic desires in art history as we know it. [. . .] Surely the circumstances surrounding Winckelmann's murder by a young, roguish love interest and his status as the founding father of modern art history complicates matters." For more on the relationship between Winckelmann's sexuality and his aesthetics, see Potts 1994; for more on Winckelmann's death, see Mayer 1982, 167–174.

4 In popular discussions of art, representational art is often conflated with realism, an enduring effect perhaps of the Cold War binary of Abstract Expression and Socialist Realism, as Frances Stonor Saunders (2013, 229) suggests: "The Congress for Cultural Freedom's support for experimental, predominantly abstract painting over representational or realist aesthetics must be viewed in this context." I am making a distinction between the two by noting the connection between realism and mimesis, as imitation of reality, and representational art, which can be realist but is not necessarily so. I concentrate on those modes of visual semiosis that are representational but not mimetic, such as allegory, citation, and differentiation, discussed in greater detail below.

5 As James Smalls (1996, 23–24) argues, "Art history constitutes itself as heterocentrist discourse through application of methodological paradigms designed to make and keep white masculinity and heterosexuality normative and hegemonic."

6 In Trench's 1902 English translation of the novel, Evtikhii's plotline is omitted.

7 The British writer and art historian John Addington Symonds made a similar point about Renaissance art in regard to a painting of St. Sebastian by Il Sodoma, although his reaction was more positive than Evtikhii's: "This is a truly demonic picture in the fascination it exercises and the memory it leaves upon the mind. Part of its unanalyzable charm may be due to the bold thought of combining the beauty of a Greek Hylas with the Christian sentiment of martyrdom. Only the Renaissance could have produced a hybrid so successful, because so deeply felt" (1879, 501).

8 As Rosalind Blakesley (2016, 1) notes, "The long and venerable tradition of icon painting was thriving [in the first half of the nineteenth century] but, for Russians, icons were not works of art but sacred objects whose primary function was to enhance the act of devotion. With notable exceptions, icon painting remained anonymous, the individual playing little part in images that were intended to transport the view to a higher spiritual realm."

9 For a detailed history of the Academy and its practices, see Blakesley 2016, 11–31.

10 Figure studies of male nudes, known as *académies*, were a central part of instruction. As Allison Leigh (2020, 107) notes, "Exclusively male models would assume poses inspired by classical sculpture or those found in old master painting."

11 Blakesley (2016, 54) notes, that Petr Chekalevsky's *Discourse on the Free Arts with a Description of Several Works by Russian Artists* (1792) "included excerpts from Winckelmann's texts." But Winckelmann's aesthetics also permeated the Russian art world through his close friend Johann Friedrich Reiffenstein (1719–1793), who became head of the Academy after Shuvalov. "A famed collector and connoisseur of antiquities, confidant of Angelica Kauffmann and champion of Winckelmann," Reiffenstein had many connections in Italy, which "enabled young Russians to work in the studios of Kauffmann, Pompeo Batoni and other fashionable devotees of Winckelmann" (115).

12 Maillart published her travelogue *Parmi la jeunesse russe* in 1932 and Marestan published his *L'émancipation sexuelle en URSS* in 1936.

13 As such, the soldier's back in the forefront of the painting could be said to function in a way analogous to the distorted, highly elongated skull in Holbein's *The Ambassadors*. Not only does the skull undercut the celebration of material wealth presented in the rest of the picture, but it also has to be painted "in a (literally) quite different optic from everything else in the picture" lest it become "an object like everything else" (Berger 1977, 91). Similarly, Deineka's sitting soldier has to refuse visibility lest he be incorporated into the only available positions within Soviet ideology of the time: a loyal Soviet citizen or an enemy of the people. In turn, he blocks the viewer's line of vision, denying them the transparency and total visibility promised by the showering soldiers' unashamed nakedness. As such, he could be said to transform their nakedness into nudity.

14 For more on the New Academy, see the 2019 cluster of articles in *Russian Review*, by Julie Cassiday, Jonathan Brooks Platt, and Helena Goscilo (Vol. 78/April).

15 Denotation should not, however, be confused with "*pure* perception." As Bryson (1983, 61) explains, "The denotation of painting consists in its intersection with all the schemata of recognition (Nativity, Betrayal, Madonna Enthroned) codified in iconology: denotation results from those procedures of recognition which are governed by the iconographic codes."

16 For a comprehensive overview on the evolution of St. Sebastian as a queer icon, see Kaye (1996).

17 As reported in *Artnet*: "Vladimir Putin, apparently, won't refer to them at all. According to the trio, he has never actually said their name aloud" (Monro 2014, online). As Mieke Bal (2004, 71) says in regard to polysemy: "It has been convincingly argued that since viewers bring their own cultural baggage to images, there can be no such thing as a fixed, predetermined, or unified meaning. In fact, the very attempts to fix meaning furnish, among other things, the most convincing evidence for this view. [. . .] In such cases, the denial of polysemy goes together with the very practice of it."

18 For those familiar with Russian history of the time, the meaning may appear less obtuse. Not only did Western travelers to Russia in the sixteenth century point out what appeared to them to be rampant homosexuality, but Russians themselves leveled charges of homosexuality against their leaders, in particular Ivan the Terrible (Healey 2006, 111). In Joan Neuberger's reading of the film, those details connect Ivan's court with the more flamboyant and

effeminate members of the Polish court, as part of a "visual universe that both presents and complicates binary conceptions of self and other" (Neuberger 2008, 81).

19 For Mieke Bal (2004, 185), "the moving detail of the ear that sticks out through [Christ's] hair," functions as a Barthian punctum in Caravaggio's *Doubting Thomas* (1660–61), indicating that Christ's "human quality overrules his divine status in all respects." This prepares the ground for a homoerotic interpretation of Christ's wound which only becomes possible when viewed alongside Caravaggio's *Amor Vincet Omnia* (1662) and *Heavenly Amor Defeats Earthly Love* (1602–03), by Caravaggio's contemporary and rival Giovanni Baglione. In relating what she describes as a "twentieth-century art fiction that challenges and overcomes the bond between sexuality and abuse, stereotyping and power," Bal emphasizes the fact that "no expository agent can foresee, program, or totally preclude such visual experience. Some of this must simply be left to luck, intuition, and to the art itself" (186–187).

20 This is astonishingly similar to Bryson's description of Giotto's *The Betrayal*: "As we move from Duccio to Giotto, we witness something like an exponential expansion of the information the image furnishes. Nothing is there, in the discourse of scripture, to legitimate or claim that vast corpus of data concerning the position, in which is now an exactly articulated rotational space, of Christ, disciples, guard, nor the data concerning the individual appearance of attendant figures which the image relays through its multiple and free-standing portraits, nor the contingent detail of how, at a precise moment, the folds of cloak and tunic fell" (Bryson 1983, 59).

21 This fact is often missed or elided by Anglophone scholars as English does not have the category of grammatical gender. And so, when James Cracroft (2008, 140) describes an image of a woman on the reverse side of the Russian prerevolutionary five-hundred-ruble bill as a "female personification of imperial Russia," it might appear that the gender of this personification is arbitrary. It is not; the Russian word for Russia is grammatically feminine.

22 This is how the designer of the image, James B. Longacre, advocated for the design in a letter to Mint Director James Ross Snowden: "From the copper shores of Lake Superior, to the silver mountains of Potosi, from the Ojibwa to the Araucanian, the feathered tiara is as characteristic of the primitive races of our hemisphere, as the turban is of the Asiatic. Nor is there anything in its decorative character, repulsive to the association of Liberty . . . It is more appropriate than the Phrygian cap, the emblem rather of the emancipated slave, than of the independent freeman, of those who are able to say 'we were never in bondage to any man.' I regard then this emblem of America as a proper and well-defined portion of our national inheritance; and having now the opportunity of consecrating it as a memorial of Liberty, 'our Liberty,' American Liberty; why not use it? One more graceful can scarcely be devised. We have only to determine that it shall be appropriate, and all the world outside of us cannot wrest it from us" (Snow 2009, 25). This is perhaps the most spectacularly egregious act of cultural appropriation: using an Indian headdress as a symbol of liberty. The fact that it sits atop the head of a Caucasian woman underscores the extermination and resettlement that made this appropriation possible.

23 For more on the relationship between grammatical gender and Russian national identity, see Zaitseva 2006.

24 Whitman, by the way, was enormously popular in early twentieth century Russia; in fact, one of the great translators and promoters of Whitman in Russia was Kornei Chukovsky,

who as a sixteen-year-old adolescent bought a copy of *Leaves of Grass* from a sailor in Odessa. That being said, he never became popular among queer readers, as he did in England and the U.S., due no doubt to the fact that his translators removed much of the gender ambiguity and homoeroticism from Whitman's poetry by heterosexualizing the references (see Murray 2017, n.p.).

25 For more on smychka, see: https://www.encyclopedia.com/history/encyclopedias-almanacs-transcripts-and-maps/smychka.

26 The context, however, has changed, and such images are now rightly criticized as the basis of the humor is essentially homophobic. As Lee Hurley (2018, online) argues in *The Guardian*: "Trump and Putin, like so many others, may fear being gay but every time you joke that they are, you reinforce the validity of that fear, not only to them, but to the rest of society. Yes, you say, being gay is something to be ashamed of. If it wasn't, why would so many use it to make fun of people they hate so much." While the argument is certainly legitimate, and the danger of making homophobia fun is very real, Hurley seems unaware of the history of this allegory, which underscores the two leaders troubling relationship to the most authoritarian aspects of the Soviet state, such as Trump's use of "enemy of the people" in regard to journalists and Putin's justification of the mass violence of the Stalin era.

27 The proliferation of allegories of fecundity was perhaps to mask the failure of the Soviet collectivization of agriculture that took place from 1929–1933 under the first Five Year Plan, which resulted in large-scale famine.

28 The notion of the Soviet Union as a culture of citation was brilliantly satirized by Tatyana Tolstaya in her novel *Kys'* (2000), translated into English by Jamey Gambrell as *Slynx* (2003). The novel describes a dystopian society 200 years after a cataclysmic nuclear event referred to as the Blast that is ruled by a dictator who plagiarizes great works of Russian literature from the pre-Blast period. The society is divided into three groups: *prezhnie* (oldeners), educated people born before the Blast, *pererozhdentsy* (degenerators), uneducated people born before the Blast who are now covered in fur and walk on all fours, and the *golubchiks*, who were born after the Blast and carry a variety of mutations. Only the *prezhnie* recognize the actual sources of the dictator's citations. The novel traces the path to "enlightenment" of Benedikt Karpov, one of the *golubchiks*, who works as a scribe. After meeting the simple-minded leader, Fedor Kuz'mich, in person, Karpov begins to realize that he could not possibly be the author of the works Karpov has been copying.

29 The combination of realism and an orientation toward the future make Socialist Realist art into the communist analog of advertising in the capitalist world. As John Berger (1977, 130; emphasis added) notes, "Publicity images also belong to the moment in the sense that they must be continually renewed and made up-to-date. Yet they never speak of the present. Often they refer to the past and *always they speak of the future*." A bright future in the capitalist world is literally purchased through commodities while in the communist world it is achieved when the viewer buys into communist ideals. Bryson (1983, 160) associates Socialist Realism with neo-Byzantine stencils, describing Byzantium as "a regime less interested in purchase than in didactic communication of liturgy and sacred texts." But works of Socialist Realism did not have a strictly didactic function; they envisioned a seductive communist future, hence were more interested in purchase.

30 As Mieke Bal (2004, 67) comments: "Derrida's concept of dissemination is a powerful tool for breaking open the monolithic discourse of origins that appears to be the stronghold of the discipline, whether in iconography (origin of motifs), connoisseurship (origin of the work of art), or patronage studies (origin of the conception of the work)."

31 I mention the mythological source of these images as this also challenges the popular tendency to conflate assumptions regarding representational art with realism or naturalism. When the subject cited is mythological, then, as with allegory, the most "realistic" renderings are not of material reality at all. And so, while Roman Jakobson (1959, 232) is certainly correct in noting, "We never consumed ambrosia or nectar and have only a linguistic acquaintance with the words 'ambrosia,' 'nectar,' and 'gods'—the name of their mythical users; nonetheless, we understand these words and know in what contexts each of them may be used," depictions of ambrosia cannot be evaluated as more or less realistic to the extent that ambrosia does not exist in reality, only in artistic depictions.

32 Puff is right, of course, in stressing the interpretive ambiguity of these citations. As Puff (2006, 93) notes in regard to Ganymede: "Resurrected by Italian humanists, the myth of Ganymede once more became a subject widely treated by artists. Yes—as with much homoerotic art from the early modern period—representations of his abduction resist easy interpretation. Did the Ganymede story offer a justification for depicting languorously posed adolescents, did it offer an allegory of male homosexuality for an educated elite, or was it intended to depict the Neoplatonic theme of the soul ascending to heaven?"—or all of the above? For a more comprehensive discussion of the topic, see James Saslow's *Ganymede in the Renaissance: Homosexuality in Art and Society* (New Haven: Yale University Press, 1986).

33 See, for example, the poem "Sebastian-Martyr" (1887) by Grand Duke Konstantin Romanov, the five-act play *The Martyrdom of St. Sebastian* (1911) by Italian playwright Gabriele D'Annunzio, and sketches and films by Soviet director Sergei Eisenstein (see Bergan 1997, 23–24).

34 That period also represented a potential merging of Russia's elite and folk cultures, which were distinguished by their treatment of sex and sexuality. For centuries, Russian high art was dominated by the Russian Orthodox Church, which forbid religious statuary entirely (the Eastern Church has always considered statuary idolatrous) and the painting of nudes until the late eighteenth century.

35 The specific subversive approach to realism undertaken by the Moscow Conceptualists is described by Daniil Leiderman (2018, 165) as "shimmering (*mertsatel'nost'* or *mertsanie*)" a term he takes from Conceptual artist and writer Dmitrii Prigov (1999, 58–59), which Leiderman describes as "a strategic counter-ideology of principled tergiversation designed to prevent the consolidation of the authoritative voice within the artwork." In other words, while critical and subversive, it also seeks "to prevent or pre-empt the consolidation of an authoritative artistic voice or artwork" (Leiderman 2018, 165).

36 Margolis (1995, 10) make a similar point: "Hegel's concern with understanding art in terms of a historical culture hardly surfaces before his own intervention and, in the nineteenth and twentieth centuries (until very recently), has competed only weakly in English language aesthetics."

37 As Bryson (2014, 31) puts it, "From the moment when the child jubilantly assumes the mirror's image of himself, he condemns himself to a life of servitude." But Bryson goes on to argue that the scenario sketched out by Lacan assumes the existence of some anterior subject before the mirror stage from which the child can be alienated. And so, Bryson concludes, "the whole Lacanian vocabulary of *aliénation* and *méconnaisance* seems to have been imported from some other (Hegelian, Marxist) conceptual universe" (32).

38 On the importance of Mulvey's essay to art history, Bryson (2014, 6) comments, "The particular appeal of Mulvey's thinking to art historians lay partly in the feeling that here, at last, was what had been missing for a long time from the modern discipline, a theory of the view—and one that was deeply grounded in social history."

39 As Bryson (2004, 10) comments in regard to Mulvey's model: "But could the transaction never be female-to-female, that is, homosexual—or lesbian?"

40 On the trickster in contemporary Russian art, see Lipovetsky (2018).

41 For a description of their research project, see: http://queervisualculture.org/about/

References

Alaniz, José. 2003. "Necrorama: Spectacles of Death and Dying in Late/Post-Soviet Russian Culture." PhD thesis, University of California at Berkeley.

Andreeva, Ekaterina. 2016. "Dobavki v monrologiiu." In *Vladislav Mamyshev-Monro v vospominaniiakh sovremennikov,* edited by Elizaveta Berezovskaia, 7–11. Moscow: Moskovskii Muzei Sovremennogo Iskusstva.

Anonymous. 1993. "The Introductory Text to the Soviet Pavilion at the World's Fair, 1939." In *The Aesthetic Arsenal: Socialist Realism Under Stalin,* edited by Miranda Banks, 8–11. New York: Institute for Contemporary Art.

Babich, Roman, ed. 2017. *Modernizm bez manifesta. Tom II. Russkoe iskusstvo 1920–1950* Moscow: ABCdesign.

Baigell, Renee and Matthew Baigell. 2001. *Peeling Potatoes, Painting Pictures: Women Artists in Post-Soviet Russia, Estonia, and Latvia.* New Brunswick, New Jersey: The Jane Voorhees Zimmerli Art Museum and Rutgers University Press.

Bakhtin, Mikhail M. 1981. "Discourse in the Novel." In *The Dialogic Imagination. Four Essays,* edited by Michael Holquist and translated by Caryl Emerson and Michael Holquist, 259–422. Austin: University of Texas Press.

Bal, Mieke. 1999. *Quoting Caravaggio: Contemporary Art, Preposterous History.* Chicago: The University of Chicago Press.

———. 2004. *Looking in: The Art of Viewing.* London: Routledge.

Barthes, Roland. 1981. *Camera Lucida: Reflections on Photography.* Translated by Richard Howard. New York: Hill and Wang.

Bassin, Mark. 2008. "*The Morning of Our Motherland*: Fyodor Shurpin's Portrait of Stalin." In *Picturing Russia: Explorations in Visual Culture,* edited by Valerie A. Kivelson, and Joan Neuberger, 214–217. New Haven: Yale University Press.

Baudin, Antoine and Leonid Heller. 1989. "Le corps et ses images dans le réalisme socialiste." In *Amour et érotisme dans la littérature russe du XXe siècle: Actes du colloque de juin 1989, organisé par l'Université de Lausanne, avec le concours de la Fondations du 450ème anniversaire,* edited by Leonid Heller, 127–145. Bern: Peter Lang.

Bell, Daniel. 1955. "The Study of Man: Bolshevik Man, His Motivations." *Commentary* (February). Available at: https://www.commentarymagazine.com/articles/daniel-bell-2/the-study-of-man-bolshevik-man-his-motivations/. Last accessed May 21, 2021.

Bergan, Ronald. 1997. *Sergei Eisenstein: A Life in Conflict.* Woodstock, New York: The Overlook Press.

Berger, John. 1977. *Ways of Seeing.* Harmondsworth: Penguin Books.

Bershtein, Evgenii. 2018. "The Discourse of Sexual Pathology in Russian Modernism." In *Reframing Russian Modernism,* edited by Irina Shevelenko, 143–171. Madison: University of Wisconsin Press.

Beurdeley, Cecile. 1997. *L'Amour blue.* Translated by Michael Taylor. Fribourg: Evergreen.

Bishop, Claire. 2012. *Artificial Hells: Participatory Art and the Politics of Spectatorship.* London and New York: Verso.

Blakesley, Rosalind P. 2016. *The Russian Canvas: Painting in Imperial Russia, 1757–1881.* New Haven: Yale University Press.

Bonnell, Victoria. 1993. "The Peasant Woman in Stalinist Political Art of the 1930s." In *The Aesthetic Arsenal: Socialist Realism Under Stalin,* edited by Miranda Banks, 140–155. New York: Institute for Contemporary Art.

Borofski, Aleksandr. 1993. "Non-conformist Art in Leningrad." In *Art of the Soviets. Painting, Sculpture and Architecture in a One-Party State, 1917–1992,* edited by Matthew Cullerne Bown and Brandon Taylor, 196–204. Manchester: Manchester University Press.

Bowlt, John. 1996. "Body Beautiful: The Artistic Search for the Perfect Physique." In *Laboratory of Dreams: The Russian Avant-garde and Cultural Experiment,* edited by John E. Bowlt and Olga Matich, 37–58. Stanford: Stanford University Press.

Bryson, Norman. 1983. *Vision and Painting: The Logic of the Gaze.* New Haven: Yale University Press.

———. 1994. "Géricault and 'Masculinity.'" In *Visual Culture: Images and Interpretations,* edited by Norman Bryson, Michael Ann Holly, and Keith Moxey, 228–259. Hanover: Wesleyan University Press.

———. 2004. "Introduction: Art and Intersubjectivity." In *Looking in: The Art of Viewing,* by Mieke Bal, 1–39. London: Routledge.

Campbell, Thomas. 2007. "Homosexuality as Device: Necrorealism and Neoacademism." *Ante Projects* 5: 68–79.

Clark, Katerina. 1984. *The Soviet Novel.* Chicago: University of Chicago Press.

———. 2011. *Moscow, The Fourth Rome: Stalinism, Cosmopolitanism, and the Evolution of Soviet Culture, 1931–1941.* Cambridge: Harvard University Press.

Clark, Toby. 1993. "The 'New Man's' Body: A Motif in Early Soviet Culture." In *Art of the Soviets. Painting, Sculpture and Architecture in a One-Party State, 1917–1992,* edited by Matthew Cullerne Bown and Brandon Taylor, 33–50. Manchester: Manchester University Press.

Corber, Robert J. 1997. *Homosexuality in Cold War America: Resistance and the Crisis of Masculinity.* Durham: Duke University Press.

Cracroft, James. 2008. "Pictographs of Power: The 500-Ruble Note of 1912." In *Picturing Russia: Explorations in Visual Culture,* edited by Valerie A. Kivelson and Joan Neuberger, 139–141. New Haven: Yale University Press.

Cross, Anthony. 1971. *Russia under Western Eyes, 1517–1825.* New York: St. Martin's Press.

Curley, John J. 2018. *Global Art and the Cold War.* London: Laurence King Publishing.

Doyle, Jennifer, Jonathan Flatley and José Esteban Muñoz. 1993. Introduction to *Pop-out: Queer Warhol,* edited by Jennifer Doyle, Jonathan Flatley and José Esteban Muñoz, 1–19. Durham: Duke University Press.

DuBois, W.E.B. 1897. "The Strivings of the Negro People." *The Atlantic Monthly* (August): 194–197.

El'shevskaia, Galina. 2003. *Korotkaia kniga o Konstantine Somove.* Moscow: Novoe Literaturnoe Obozrenie.

Engelstein, Laura. 1992. *Keys to Happiness: Sex and the Search for Modernity in Fin-de-Siècle Russia.* Ithaca: Cornell University Press.

Enikeeva, Dilia. 2003. *Gei I lesbianki.* Moscow: Astrel'; ACT.

Erofeev, Andrei. 2018. "Culture as the Enemy: Contemporary Russian Art under the Authoritarian Regime." In *Russia—Art, Resistance, and the Conservative-Authoritarian Zeitgeist,* edited by Lena Jonson and Andrei Erofeev, 127–133. London: Routledge.

Fiks, Yevgeniy. 2012. *Pleshkas of Russian Art,* collection of the artist. New York.

Flaker. Aleksandar. 1989. "Avant-garde et érotisme." In *Amour et érotisme dans la littérature russe du XXe siècle: Actes du colloque de juin 1989, organisé par l'Université de Lausanne, avec le concours de la Fondations du 450ème anniversaire,* edited by Leonid Heller, 91–100. Bern: Peter Lang.

Flegon, Alec. 1976. *Eroticism in Russian Art.* London: Flegon Press.

Foucault, Michel. 1977. *Discipline and Punish.* Translated by Alan Sheridan. New York: Pantheon.

France, Anatole. 1898. *The Red Lily.* New York: Bretano's.

Gal, Susan and Judith T. Irvine. 2019. *Signs of Difference: Language and Ideology in Social Life.* Cambridge: Cambridge University Press.

Goldsmith, Paul W. 1999. *Pornography and Democratization: Legislating Obscenity in Post-Communist Russia.* Boulder: Westview Press.

Golubev, Pavel. 2019. *Konstantin Somov: Dama, snimaiushchaia masku.* Moscow: Novoe Literaturnoe Obozrenie.

Gombrich, E.H. 1960. *Art and Illusion: A Study in the Psychology of Pictorial Perception.* New York: Bollingen Foundation.

Goscilo, Helena. 2017. "Deineka's Heavenly Bodies: Space, Sports, and the Sacred." In *Russian Aviation, Space Flight, and Visual Culture,* edited by Vlad Strukov and Helena Goscilo, 53–88. London: Routledge.

Goscilo, Helena and Andrea Lanoux. 2006. "Introduction: Lost in the Myths." In *Gender and National Identity in Twentieth-century Russian Culture,* edited by Helena Goscilo and Andrea Lanoux, 3–29. DeKalb: Northern Illinois University Press.

Gudkov, Lev. 2016. "Sledy porazheniya: Pochemu effekt propagandy budet oshchushchatsya eshche dolgo', *Slon* (February 20). Available at: https:// slon.ru/ posts/ 64280. Reposted at www.levada.ru/ 2016/ 02/ 24/ sledy- porazheniya/ print/. Last accessed May 16, 2021.

Harloe, Katherine. 2013. *Winckelmann and the Invention of Antiquity: History and Aesthetics in the Age of Altertumswissenschaft.* Oxford: Oxford University Press.

Harvey, Keith. 2002. "Camp Talk and Citationality: A Queer Take on 'Authentic' and 'Represented' Utterance." *Journal of Pragmatics* 34: 1145–1165.

Healey, Dan. 2001. *Homosexual Desire in Revolutionary Russia. The Regulation of Sexual and Gender Dissent.* Chicago: University of Chicago Press, 2001.

Heller, Leonid. 1989. "Amour, érotisme, littérature russe: Réflexions en guise de preface." In *Amour et érotisme dans la littérature russe du XXe siècle: Actes du colloque de juin 1989, organisé par l'Université de Lausanne, avec le concours de la Fondations du 450ème anniversaire,* edited by Leonid Heller, 5–20. Bern: Peter Lang.

Hoffman, David L. 2000. "Mothers in the Motherland: Stalinist Pronatalism in its Pan-European Context." *Journal of Social History* 34(1): 35–54.

Holz, Wolfgang. 1993. "Allegory and Iconography in Socialist Realist Painting." In *Art of the Soviets. Painting, Sculpture and Architecture in a One-Party State, 1917–1992,* edited by Matthew Cullerne Bown and Brandon Taylor, 73–85. Manchester: Manchester University Press.

Horne, Peter and Reina Lewis. 1996. Introduction to *Outlooks: Lesbian and Gay Sexualities and Visual Cultures,* edited by Peter Horne and Reina Lewis, 1–9. London: Routledge.

Hupperts, Charles. 2006. "Homosexuality in Greece and Rome." In *Gay Life and Culture: A World History,* edited by Robert Aldrich, 29–55. New York: Universe Publishing.

Hurley, Lee. 2018. "An Image of Putin and Trump Kissing Isn't Funny. It's Homophobic." *The Guardian* (July 21). Available at: https://www.theguardian.com/commentisfree/2018/jul/21/trump-putin-kissing-homophobic-queer-joke.

Jagose, Annamarie 1996. *Queer Theory: An Introduction.* New York: New York University Press.

Jakobson, Roman. 1959. "On Linguistic Aspects of Translation." In *On Translation,* edited by R. A. Drawer, 232–239. Cambridge, MA: Harvard University Press.

Johnson, David K. 2004. *The Lavender Scare.* Chicago: The University of Chicago Press.

Jonson, Lena. 2018a. Introduction to *Russia—Art, Resistance, and the Conservative-Authoritarian Zeitgeist,* edited by Lena Jonson and Andrei Erofeev, 1–23. London: Routledge.

———. 2018b. "The New Conservative Cultural Policy and Visual Art." In *Russia—Art, Resistance, and the Conservative-Authoritarian Zeitgeist,* edited by Lena Jonson and Andrei Erofeev, 48–64. London: Routledge.

Kabakova, Galina and Fransis Kont, eds. 2005. *Telo v russkoi kul'ture: Sbornik statei.* Moscow: Novoe Literaturnoe Obozrenie.

Kalb, Judith. 2018. "Shifting Time-Frames and Metaphorical Spaces: Dmitry Merezhkovsky, Russian Modernism, and the Classical Past." In *Reframing Russian Modernism,* edited by Irina Shevelenko, 53–77. Madison: University of Wisconsin Press.

Kalinin, Ilya. 2018. "The 'Russian World': Genetically Modified Conservatism, or Why 'Russian Culture' Matters." In *Russia—Art, Resistance, and the Conservative-Authoritarian Zeitgeist,* edited by Lena Jonson and Andrei Erofeev, 27–47. London: Routledge.

Kaplan, E. Ann. 1990. "Is the Gaze Male?" In *Women and Film Both Sides of the Camera,* 23–35. London: Routledge.

Kaye, Richard A. 1996. "Losing His Religion: Saint Sebastian as Contemporary Gay Martyr." In *Outlooks: Lesbian and Gay Sexualities and Visual Cultures,* edited by Peter Horne and Reina Lewis, 86–105. London: Routledge.

Kenez, Peter and David Shepherd. 1998. "'Revolutionary' Models for High Literature: Resisting Poetics." In *Russian Cultural Studies: An Introduction,* edited by Catriona Kelly and David Shepherd, 21–55. Oxford: Oxford University Press.

Kivelson, Valerie A. and Joan Neuberger. 2008. "Seeing into Being: An Introduction." In *Picturing Russia: Explorations in Visual Culture,* edited by Valerie A. Kivelson, and Joan Neuberger, 1–11. New Haven: Yale University Press.

Kon, Igor'. 1997 *Seksual'naia kul'tura v Rossii. Klubnichka na berezke.* Moscow: O.G.I.

———. 2003. *Muzhskoe telo v istorii kul'tury.* Moscow: Slovo.

Kondakov, Alexander. 2017. *Prestupleniia na pochve nenavisti protiv LGBT v Rossii.* St. Petersburg: Tsentr Nezavisimykh Sotsiologicheskikh Issledovanii.

Kondakov, Alexander and Evgeny Shtorn. 2021. "Sex, Alcohol, and Soul: Violent Reactions to Coming Out after the 'Gay Propaganda' Law in Russia." In "Illegal Queerness: Russian Culture and Society in the Age of the 'Gay Propaganda' Law." Special issue, *Russian Review* 80 (January): 37–55.

Kuraev, Mikhail. 1993. "Perestroika: The Restructuring of the Past or the Invention of the Future." In *Late Soviet Culture. From Perestroika to Novostroika,* edited by Thomas Lahusen with Gene Kuperman, 13–20. Durham: Duke University Press.

Kuzmin, Mikhail. 1998. *Dnevnik 1934 goda,* edited by G.A. Morev. St. Petersburg: Izdatel'stvo Ivana Limbakha.

———. 2000. *Dnevnik 1905–1907,* edited by Nikolai Bogomolov and Sergei Shumikhin. St. Petersburg: Izdatel'stvo Ivana Limbakha.

———. 2009. *Dnevnik 1908–1915,* edited by Nikolai Bogomolov and Sergei Shumikhin. St. Petersburg: Izdatel'stvo Ivana Limbakha.

Lalo, Aleksei. 2011. *Libertinage in Russian Culture and Literature: A Bio-History of Sexualities at the Threshold of Modernity.* Leiden: Brill.

LaValley, Al. 2001. "Maintaining, Blurring, and Transcending Gender Lines in Eisenstein." In *Eisenstein at 100: A Reconsideration,* edited by Al LaValley and Barry P. Scherr 52–64. New Brunswick, NJ: Rutgers University Press.

Leiderman, Daniil. 2018. "The Strategy of Shimmering." *Russian Literature* 96–98: 51–76.

Leigh, Allison. 2020. *Picturing Russia's Men: Masculinity and Modernity in Nineteenth-Century Painting.* London: Bloomsbury Visual Arts.

Lipovetsky, Mark. 2018. "A Dilemma for the Contemporary Artist: The 'Revolutionary Pessimism' of Roman Osminkin." In *Russia—Art, Resistance, and the Conservative-Authoritarian Zeitgeist,* edited by Lena Jonson and Andrei Erofeev, 247–263. London: Routledge.

Lord, Catherine and Richard Meyer. 2019. *Art & Queer Culture,* 2nd ed. London: Phaidon.

Lotman, Juri. 2013. *The Unpredictable Workings of Culture.* Translated by Brian James Baer. Tallinn: Tallinn University Press.

———. "The Symbol in the System of Culture." In *Culture, Memory and History. Essays in Cultural Semiotics,* edited by Marek Tamm and translated by Brian James Baer, 161–173. London: Palgrave Macmillan.

Luk'ianov, Boris. 1995. "Zametki o nagote v iskusstve." *Khudozhnik* 1:6–13.

Mamyshev (Monroe-Hitler), Vladislav. 2002. "Where the Heck Am I? Where Are My Things?" In *Primary Documents: A Sourcebook for Eastern and Central European Art since the 1950s*, edited by Laura Hoptman and Tomáš Popiszyl, 234–241. New York: Museum of Modern Art.

Margolis, Joseph. 1995. "Aesthetic Attitude." In *Oxford Companion to Philosophy*, edited by Ted Honderich, 9-13. Oxford and New York: Oxford University Press.

Mayer, Hans. 1982. *Outsiders: A Study in Life and Letters.* Translated by Denis M. Sweet. Cambridge, MA.: MIT Press.

McReynolds, Louise. 2008. "Visualizing Masculinity: The Male Sex That Was Not One in Fin-de-Siècle Russia." In *Picturing Russia: Explorations in Visual Culture*, edited by Valerie A. Kivelson and Joan Neuberger, 133–138. New Haven: Yale University Press.

Merezhkovskiy, Dmitri. 1902. *The Romance of Leonardo da Vinci.* Translated by Herbert Trench. London: G.P. Putnam's Sons.

———. 1906. *Voskresshie bogi: Leonardo da Vinchi.* 3rd edition. St. Petersburg: M.V. Pirozhkov.

Meyer, Richard. 2019. Preface to *Art & Queer Culture*, 2nd ed., edited by Catherine Lord and Richard Meyer, 7–10. London: Phaidon.

Mitchell, W.J.T. 1997. "What Do Pictures Want? An Idea of Visual Culture." In *In Visible Touch: Modernism and Masculinity*, edited by Terry Smith, 215–232. Chicago: University of Chicago Press.

Monro, Cait. 2014. "Pussy Riot on Art, Activism, and Their Name's Hilarious Russian Translation." Artnet (November 3). Available at: https://news.artnet.com/art-world/pussy-riot-on-art-activism-and-their-names-hilarious-russian-translation-152590. Last accessed May16, 2021.

Munoz, Jose Esteban. 1999. *Disidentifications. Queers of Color and the Performance of Politics.* Minneapolis. University of Minnesota Press.

Murray, Nina. 2019. "Walt Whitman in Russia: Three Love Affairs." *The Public Domain Review.* Available at: https://publicdomainreview.org/essay/walt-whitman-in-russia-three-love-affairs. Last accessed February 18, 2021.

Neuberger, Joan. 2008. "Eisenstein's Cosmopolitan Kremlin: Drag Queens, Circus Clowns, Slugs, and Foreigners in *Ivan the Terrible.*" In Insiders and Outsiders in Russian Cinema, edited by Stephen M. Norris and Zara M. Torlone, 81–95. Bloomington: Indiana University Press.

Niqueux, Michel. 1989. "La critique marxiste face à l'éroticisme dan la littérature russe (1908-1928)." In *Amour et érotisme dans la littérature russe du XXe siècle: Actes du colloque de juin 1989, organisé par l'Université de Lausanne, avec le concours de la Fondations du 450ème anniversaire*, edited by Leonid Heller, 83–90. Bern: Peter Lang.

Nivat, Georges. 1989. "Le puritisme russe, pouquoi?" In *Amour et érotisme dans la littérature russe du XXe siècle: Actes du colloque de juin 1989, organisé par l'Université de Lausanne, avec le concours de la Fondations du 450ème anniversaire*, edited by Leonid Heller, 91–100. Bern: Peter Lang.

Olearius, Adam, 1967. *The Travels of Olearius in 17th-Century Russia*, edited and translated by S. Baron. Stanford: Stanford University Press.

Oushakine, Serguei. 2022. "Let's Sharpen Our Optic Nerves." *Russian Review* 81(4): 610–613.

Paperny, Vladimir. 2002. *Architecture in the Age of Stalin: Culture Two*. Translated by John Hill and Roann Barris. Cambridge: Cambridge University Press.

Perl, Jed. 2017. "Metaphysicians of Modernism." *The New York Review of Books* LXIV(13): 10–14.

Pilcher, Alex. 2017. *A Queer Little History of Art*. London: Tate Publishing.

Pinkham, Sophia. 2020. "Realists of the Soviet Fantasy." *The New York Review of Books* LXVII (8): 47–49.

Piotrowski, Piotr. 2002. "Male Artist's Body: National Identity vs. Identity Politics." In *Primary Documents: A Sourcebook for Eastern and Central European Art since the 1950s*, edited by Laura Hoptman and Tomáš Popiszyl, 225–233. New York: Museum of Modern Art.

Platt, Jonathan Brooks. 2018. "Wartime Intimacy: Zoya Kosmodemyanskaya and the Chto Delat School for Engaged Art." In *Russia—Art, Resistance, and the Conservative-Authoritarian Zeitgeist*, edited by Lena Jonson and Andrei Erofeev, 227–246. London: Routledge.

Pollock, Griselda. 1988. "Feminist Interventions in the Histories of Art." In *Vision and Difference: Femininity, Feminism the Histories of Art*. London: Routledge.

Potts, Alex. 1994. *Flesh and the Ideal: Winckelmann and the Origins of Art History*. New Haven: Yale University Press.

Poznanskii, Andrei. 2009. *Petr Chaikovskii. Biografiia*. 2 vols. St. Petersburg: Vita Nova.

Prigov, Dmitrii. 1999. "Shimmering." In *Slovar' terminov moskovskoi kontseptualnoi shkoly*, edited by Andrei Monastyrskii, 58–59. Moscow: Ad Marginem.

Proust, Marcel. 1982. *Remembrance of Things Past*. Vol. 2. Translated by C. K. Scott Moncrieff and Terence Kilmartin. New York: Vintage.

Puff, Helmut. 2006. "Early Modern Europe, 1400-1700." In *Gay Life and Culture: A World History*, edited by Robert Aldrich, 79–101. New York: Universe Publishing.

Reich, Wilhelm. 1936. *Die Sexualität im Kulturkampf*. Copenhagen: Sexpol-Verlag.

Reid, Susan. 1993. "'The 'Art of Memory': Retrospectivism in Soviet Painting of the Brezhnev Era." In *Art of the Soviets. Painting, Sculpture and Architecture in a One-Party State, 1917–1992*, edited by Matthew Cullerne Bown and Brandon Taylor, 161–187. Manchester: Manchester University Press.

Roldugina, Ira. 2016a. "Otkrytie seksual'nosti: Transgressiia sotsial'noi stikhii v seredine XVIII v. v Sankt Petersburg: po materialam Kalinkinskoi komissii (1750–1759). *Ab Imperio* 2: 29–69.

———. 2016b. "'Pochemu my takie liudi?': Rannesovetskie gomosekualy ot pervogo litsa. Novye istochniki po istorii gomoseksual'nykh identichnostei v Rossii." *Ab Imperio* 2: 183–216.

Saslow, James M. 2018. "Michelangelo's Gifts to Tommaso. Gay and Lesbian Review Worldwide." *Gay and Lesbian Review Worldwide* 25(3):12–15.

Saunders, Frances Stonor. 2013. *The Cultural Cold War: The CIA and the World of Arts and Letters*. New York: The New Press.

Selivanova, Aleksandra. 2017. "Sovetskaia antichnost'." In *Modernizm bez manifesta. Tom II. Russkoe iskusstvo 1920–1950*, edited by Roman Babich, 23–43. Moscow: ABCdesign.

Simpson, Pat. 2004a. "Peripheralising Patriarchy? Gender and Identity in Post-Soviet Art: A View from the West." *Oxford Art Journal* 27(3): 391–415.

———. 2004b. "The Nude in Soviet Socialist Realism: Eugenics and Images of the New Person in the 1920s–1940s." *Australian and New Zealand Journal of Art* 5(1):113–137.

Smalls, James. 1996. "Making Trouble for Art History: The Queer Case of Girodet." *Art Journal* 55(4): 20–27.

Snow, Richard. 2009. *A Guide Book of Flying Eagle and Indian Head Cents*. Atlanta: Whitman Publishing.

Somov, Konstantin. 2017. *Dnevnik 1917–1923*, edited by Pavel Golubev. Moscow: Dmitrii Sechin.

Stella, Francesca. 2015. *Lesbian Lives in Soviet and Post-Soviet Russia: Post/Socialism and Gendered Sexualities*. Houndmills: Palgrave Macmillan.

Symonds, John Addington. 1879. *Renaissance in Italy: The Fine Arts*. New York: Henry Holt and Company.

Talbot, Margaret. 2018. "*The Myth of Whiteness in Classical Sculpture." The New Yorker* (22 Oct). https://www.newyorker.com/magazine/2018/10/29/the-myth-of-whiteness-in-classical-sculpture. Last accessed 28 June 2023.

Tlostanova, Madina. 2018. *What Does It Mean to Be Post-Soviet? Decolonial Art from the Ruins of the Soviet Art*. Durham: Duke University Press.

Todorov, Tzvetan. 1984. *The Conquest of America: The Question of the Other*. Translated by Richard Howard. Norman: University of Oklahoma Press.

Utkin, Roman. 2021. Introduction to "Illegal Queerness: Russian Culture and Society in the Age of the 'Gay Propaganda' Law." Special issue, *Russian Review* 80 (January): 7–16.

Warner, Marina. 1985. *Monuments and Maidens: The Allegory of the Female Form*. Berkeley: University of California Press.

Winckelmann, Johann. 1765. *Reflections on the Painting and Sculpture of the Greeks: with Instructions for the Connoisseur and An Essay on Grace in Works of Art*, translated by Henry Fussell. London: A. Millar.

Winkler, John J. 1993. "Double Consciousness in Sappho's Lyrics." In *The Lesbian and Gay Studies Reader*, edited by Henry Abelov, Michèle Ainal Barale, and David Halperin, 577–594. London: Routledge.

Wittgenstein, Ludwig. 1958. *The Blue and Brown Books*. Oxford: Blackwell.

Yurchak, Alexei. 2005. *Everything Was Forever, Until It Was No More: The Last Soviet Generation*. Princeton: Princeton University Press.

Zaitseva, Valentina. 2006. "National, Cultural and Gender Identity in the Russian Language." In *Gender and National Identity in Twentieth-century Russian Culture*, edited by Helena Goscilo and Andrea Lanoux, 30–54. DeKalb: Northern Illinois University Press.

Part Two

Queer Beauty in Context

Chapter 2

"In Appearance, Both a Lad and Lass": Images of Androgyny in Eighteenth-Century Russian Art

Olga Khoroshilova

Images of androgynous figures have received little attention in Russian art history despite the proliferation of such images in Russian portrait painting, especially in the eighteenth century. During the period, androgyny was a common topic in Russia and other countries, appearing in literature and a number of visual art forms. In this chapter, I attempt to analyze the emergence and development of androgynous imagery in paintings, drawings, and jewelry pieces, ranging from the masculine-looking tsarina Minerva of the Petrine era to the masked balls of Catherine the Great's reign, when images of androgynous and cross-dressing figures were popularized in the theatrical and visual arts as well as in the secular rituals of court life.

Surprisingly, cross-dressing was already a topic of frequent discussion at the beginning of the eighteenth century, in the era of Peter I. The brawny, manly warrior virgin Minerva, one of the emperor's favorite mythological characters, became a doppelgänger for his spouse, Catherine. Following the precedent, Empresses Elizabeth Petrovna and Catherine the Great would, in turn, transform themselves into Minervas, acting as guardian angels of wars and warriors. Without so much as a blush, they would don guards' uniforms, show up astride prancing horses in front of regiments, and, in acts of unheard-of daring, attend masquerades in the guise of young male officers. The Russian empresses' enthusiasm for the Guards' uniform and other forms of drag catalyzed a cross-dressing trend in eighteenth-century Russian fashion. Ladies at court would sometimes present themselves in gentlemen's clothing, while gentlemen would appear in comic versions of women, resplendent in crinolines and gowns. Not surprisingly, it was during that period that a company of Amazons—female soldiers in formal military garb—appeared in Russia.[1]

Cross-dressing Empresses

The eighteenth century saw an efflorescence of cross-dressing not only in Russia but throughout Europe. At court, women took delight in dressing up as men, while men skillfully transformed themselves into women. The period's fashion, with its wigs, fake moles, and heaps of face powder, was conducive to this trend. Yet the popularity of cross-dressing in Russia was not only a product of European influences. The rise of cross-dressing was also closely linked to Peter I's reforms, which enabled women to play a more active role in government and court life.

Feofan Prokopovich's sermon at the coronation of Catherine by Peter I himself signaled this development, when he compared the tsar's wife, Catherine, to a host of tough heroines: "the Babylonian Semiramis, the Scythian Tamira, the Amazon Penfesileia, the Byzantine Elena, Pulkheria, and Evdoxia" (Wortman 1995, 74). With a characteristically Baroque eloquence, he extolled the virtues of "this great Heroine," Catherine, in words reminiscent of those ordinarily invoked by Peter's generals to describe their officers' most valiant feats: "[S]o strong in this respect that few men can compare to her, on campaigns, [in] bad weather, adversity, boiling heat, frigid weather, storms, hard crossings, noisy rooms and other such difficulties harmful to the health" (74).

Thus, the tsarina came to be regarded not as Peter I's subordinate but as his loyal co-ruler, endowed with some definitively masculine qualities. This image was further enhanced by some of Catherine's personal traits. For example, Friedrich-Wilhelm von Bergholz noted that not only was she an accomplished dancer but also a fine horse rider, that her character exemplified a harmonious unity between femininity and an almost masculine degree of prowess.

Over the course of the eighteenth century, the mythological Athena or Minerva emerged among Russian empresses. Athena was a virgin warrior and a guardian angel of war and warriors. Her primary attributes are a shield and a helmet. To imitate this antique goddess, the ruling Minervas of Russia wore military outfits, substituting dress uniforms for armor and a helmet. The first one to do so was Catherine, Peter I's wife and loyal supporter. The tsarina was known for bold outfits that lent her an androgynous air. The Persian campaign of 1722–1723 is a case in point. Catherine accompanied Peter to the scene of military maneuvers. During a period of extreme heat in Astrakhan, she shaved off her hair and wore a men's fur hat to avoid sunstroke. This bold gesture acquired a military connotation—centuries later, some Russian women would crop their hair or shave it off entirely, masquerading as men so they could fight on the front lines of World War I. Evidence suggests that the empress's wardrobe contained several sets of dress uniforms, which she would wear for military shows and other events: "Shortly before her death, as she appeared, as was her wont, in a colonel's uniform to review Leib-Guard troops, the Semyonovsky Regiment forming into an infantry square, a shot from an unidentified source passed her at a close distance, killing a Russian merchant" (Andreev 1869, 20).

Empress Anna Ioanovna also cultivated associations with Minerva and, upon ascension to the throne, became colonel first of the Preobrazhensky Leib-Guard Regiment and then of the Izmailovsky, Horse-Guard, and Cuirassier Regiments, also serving as captain of the Chevalier Guards and the Preobrazhensky bombardment unit. The empresses that followed her, Elizabeth I and Catherine II, or Catherine the Great, were even more frequently compared to Minerva, and the image of Empress Minerva was circulated by portrait painters and medal makers. For instance, in 1767, following an order by Catherine the Great, Johann Georg Waechter created a medal commemorating Catherine's ascension to the throne. He adorned the front side of the medal with a right-facing silhouette of the empress's head and shoulders, the empress wearing armor and a helmet adorned with a clipped feather plume, or hackle, deliberately styled after the Roman Minerva. The empress was immensely pleased by the portrait.

Russian painters, sculptors, graphic artists, and even grand duchesses (for example, Maria Feodorovna, the wife of the future Russian emperor Paul I) also depicted the empress as a smiling yet stern virgin warrior in a helmet and mail. Soon enough, European masters, including miniaturists, were copying these portraits. Among the most well-known are the copies made on the basis of Maria Fedorovna's cameo by James Tassie—his beautiful copies can be found in many European collections. Thus, when shopping for buttons for a men's kaftan in Paris, one could reportedly find ones bearing the image of Catherine as Minerva.

Yet Elizabeth I outdid her female predecessors in terms of military and other forms of cross-dressing. In that, she was representative of her time. Among mid- and late-eighteenth-century European women, wearing men's attire was a fairly common practice. Face powder and masks were their flesh and blood, and deception their lifestyle. Sometimes the tsarina would appear at a masquerade resplendent in a men's kaftan and culottes, the crowd at court skillfully pretending not to recognize Her Majesty. Grand Duchess Ekaterina Alekseevna (the future Catherine II) was among those who witnessed these transformations. Quietly observing the masculine-acting Elizabeth, she noted her graceful movements, light step, her elegance and gallantry, in other words, all that constituted the image of a true gentleman at the time. Her *Papers* (*Zapiski*) contain a description of a 1744 masquerade where Elizabeth made an appearance in a man's costume and, after a deftly performed minuet, marched up to Catherine. "I allowed myself to tell her," Catherine II reminisces, "that it was women's luck that she was not a man and that a portrait of her habited thus might drive many women to distraction. She liked what I conveyed to her out of the fullness of my heart and responded in kind, telling me graciously that if she were a man, I would be the one to receive an apple from her" (Catherine II 1907, 310).[2]

Ekaterina Alekseevna may have seen the empress wearing the exact costume that was painted by Louis Caravaque in the mid-1740s. It is no wonder she mystified her contemporaries with her masquerade costume and wig, which may have been made by the court tailor Iohann Eck, who, despite being flooded with requests from the empress, adapted to her pace and temperament and delivered all her orders without delay.

If we are to believe historian Kazimir Valishevsky, Elizabeth's extravagant wardrobe (nearly fifteen thousand dresses!) included stylized military outfits: "Elizabeth attended [masquerades] dressed in men's costumes—now a French musketeer, now a Cossack hetman, now a Dutch sailor" (Valishevskii 1911, 81). She also owned real military dress coats. Elizabeth was especially fond of the dark green field officer uniform of the Preobrazhensky Leib-Guard Regiment. It is in this uniform that she was painted by Georg Grooth in the famous 1743 portrait, titled *Portrait of Elizaveta Petrovna on a Stallion with a Negro Footboy*. In the portrait, she is wearing a hat with a galloon and a white hackle, boots with cuffs, a scarf with tassels, a green coat, culottes, and a kaftan, decorated with a double row of golden galloon, as mandated for field officers. It is a very accurate depiction of the Preobrazhensky Leib-Guard Regiment uniform circa 1742.

Grooth's portrait and the uniform itself are a token of the empress's affection for the so-called Leib-Guard campaigners, the tall and brawny Grenadiers who carried out a coup d'état in 1741 for the benefit of the "Petrine daughter." The tsarina would not forget the favor—the Leib-Guard campaigners basked in the monarch's generosity during her reign and, in the end, seemed to lose all vestige of restraint, which led to their periodic arrest "for impertinence."

The tsarina would put on a Guards' uniform for the army holidays, looking sharp in a galloon-trimmed coat and tall boots, astride a noble steed. The officers and soldiers admired their empress, which she used to her advantage. Dress uniforms, tailored to perfection in keeping with the decreed standards, reinforced a sense of solidarity among the Guards, which bonded the troops to the empress and, consequently, forestalled any thoughts of uprising.

Of the few items from her abundant military wardrobe to have survived, one of the most elegant pieces, is a Grenadier cap, made of black leather with gilded appliqués in a rococo style. It was made in 1755 to celebrate the anniversary of her ascension to the throne. In order to remember those who had helped her, the empress invited her loyal, well-fed Leib-Guard campaigners to the palace and attended the festivities wearing the Preobrazhensky Regiment uniform and this charming Grenadier cap. Interestingly enough, it was patterned on a snuff box. Made in 1741–1742, it bears a close resemblance to the Grenadier cap in that it was also made of leather and gilded silver.

The Grand Duchess Ekaterina Alekseevna (Catherine II), who also loved military style, fully embraced Elizabeth's approach. She learned to use the uniform for governing and even surpassed the "Petrine daughter" by turning Leib-Guard gear and formal dress into a means of political propaganda. Like Elizabeth, the Grand Duchess dabbled in masculine attire. In the 1750s, she would sometimes go hunting dressed "from head to toe in men's clothes." Still more frequent were her appearances in a fashionable, formfitting Amazon's suit: a coat with lapels, a vest, and a wide skirt with a long slit, well-suited for horseback riding. Catherine left a description of one of those outfits: "Knowing that the empress [Elizabeth] does not like me riding astride, like a man, I requested an English lady's saddle, put on an English Amazon suit made of very expensive fabric, sky blue and silver, decorated with crystal buttons, which could easily pass for diamonds. My black hat was trimmed with a string of diamonds" (Catherine II 1907, 303). Georg Grooth painted the Grand Duchess in such an outfit (see *Grand Duchess Catherine in a Hunting Outfit*, from the 1740s). There is a good copy of one of his portraits, made by Kirill Golovachevsky, at the art museum of the Kadriorg Palace in Tallinn, Estonia. It is an appropriate location for the painting as Ekaterina Alekseevna went hunting in the forests of "Catherine's Valley" (Kadriorg/Katharinental).

The Grand Duchess's wardrobe boasted several sets of men's clothes, designed for court masquerades, but not only. Sometimes Catherine would put them on "to have a moment of fun and frivolity." Such was the case on December 17, 1752, when she, dressed as a man, escaped from the Winter Palace with Lev Naryshkin.

Another visual record of the monarch's cross-dressing is a miniature in the collection of the State Tretyakov Gallery that is attributed to Iohann Stenglin. It is believed to have been made in 1762, but the miniature may in fact date back to the early or mid-1750s if one considers Catherine's attire. What she has on is not an Amazon suit, but a proper dress uniform, represented in minute detail, with all the decorative trimmings, the protocols for which Stenglin seemed to know very well. Blue cloth, lemon-yellow overlay, with silver buttons—it is the uniform of the Grand Duchess's Golstein infantry unit, which Catherine headed from 1751 to 1762. This unit visited the royal residence of Oranienbaum in the first half of the 1750s. And it well may be that the miniature was made during one of the visits, since the Grand Duchess would greet her regiment wearing the appropriate uniform with a ribbon—and discernible on her chest is the star and ribbon of St. Catherine's order. On this occasion, the Grand Duchess decided to forego the culottes and tall boots in favor of a skirt made of thick silvery silk, perhaps the very one she would wear with the Amazon caftan when hunting.

Yet perhaps the most famous portrait of Catherine in men's clothes was painted by Vigilius Eriksen in the 1760s (the Hermitage, St. Petersburg). In the portrait, titled *Catherine II in a Leib-guard Uniform on Horseback,* Eriksen presents the tsarina wearing the costume in which she had led the coup d'état of 1762. The identity of the person who lent this outfit to her is wellknown. On June 28, 1762, while staying at the Summer Palace, Catherine was getting ready to march to Oranienbaum in order to depose Peter III. She decided that the mission called for a dress coat, which she then borrowed from Alexander Talyzin, a Leib-Guard officer of the Semyonovsky Regiment. It was a kaftan of the 1756–1761 style—single-breasted, decorated with a golden galloon, a turndown collar, and brass buttons along the sides, cuffs, and pocket flaps. This was a common dress coat for a low-ranking officer, made from plain cloth, with no extra pomp, and everything was in keeping with the Guards' regulations.

She constructed her look from readily available articles of clothing. The culottes must have come from her own "masculine" wardrobe, since Talyzin's tiny ones would probably not have fit. The hat—if we are to believe Eriksen's portrait—was not in line with the Semyonovsky uniform either, as it was missing the characteristic golden tassels. According to legend, Catherine furnished her sword with a constable's lanyard, which had been gifted to her by Grigory Potemkin, who served in the Horse Guards Regiment. Incidentally, this helps explain the empress's affection for horse-guardsmen, over whom she presided as colonel and chief. She always enjoyed wearing this regiment's uniform.

Yet it was not the dress coat and the sword that came to symbolize the initiation of the coup d'état but rather the order of St. Andrew ribbon, which (according to Ekaterina Dashkova's account) Catherine literally snatched out of Count Panin's hands, leaving him flabbergasted, and tacked onto her kaftan in a slapdash fashion. The hat decorated with oak branches, the dress coat, the ribbon, and the tall boots created the appearance of someone other than Peter III's humble wife. She transformed herself into an avenging empress. Catherine, a born political strategist, was conscious of the psychological effect that military dress had on people. The dress coat was a powerful garment that conveyed serious intentions with more eloquence than a ball gown or an ermine cape. It intimidated by displaying authority and strength. The newly made empress sought not only to win over Peter III's opponents but also to intimidate his supporters.

He or She?

Russian people have traditionally admired power and worshipped those who held it. It is not surprising then that the Russian empresses' fondness for men's attire and military uniforms—their cross-dressing antics—set a trend for noble women at court. The first to follow their lead was Ekaterina Dashkova. Embroiled in the coup d'état of 1762, she decided to wear men's clothes to avoid being recognized on the street as one of the conspirators. On June 27, she summoned a tailor, ordered him to make her an outfit, and spent the rest of the day clad in a men's overcoat while awaiting her new garments. However, as night fell, she learned, to her chagrin, that the tailor had failed to complete the order. When Catherine II received the support of the Leib Guards on June 28, the princess had no further need to disguise herself as a man. The danger had passed, and Dashkova hastened to rejoin the newly installed empress. Together, these two brave women changed into uniforms, which better befitted the occasion. Catherine put on Talyzin's dress coat, while Dashkova donned a Preobrazhensky officer's kaftan, which she had borrowed from Mikhail Pushkin.

The princess was, no doubt, thoroughly delighted with this look as well as the effect it produced on other people. In her diaries, she recounts with evident pleasure the degree of surprise that her "appearance occasioned among these reverend senators, none of whom recognized me in my military disguise, being easily conceived by the empress, she informed them who I was." She looked like "a boy in military uniform, who had intruded into their sanctuary, and had with so little deference whispered in the ear of majesty" (Bradford 1840, 83).

The princess was in no hurry to part with the uniform and, following the coup d'état, continued to wear a Preobrazhensky officer's kaftan for several more days. Describing a meeting during which the empress decorated her with the ribbon of St. Catherine, the princess writes, "I kissed her hand in acknowledgement. So here I was, dressed in uniform, with a ribbon across my shoulder without its star, a spur upon one heel, and looking like a boy of fifteen years of age" (Bradford 1840, 97–8).

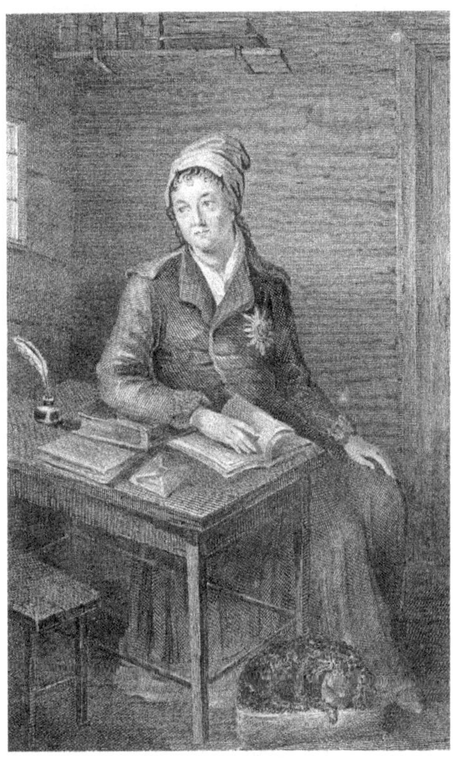

Figure 1. Artist unknown, *Princess Ekaterina Romanovna Dashkova in Old Age* (1840), engraving. Collection of Olga Khoroshilova

Dashkova had dabbled in cross-dressing before the coup. A letter from the Grand Duchess Ekaterina Alekseevna circa early 1762 mentions this: "Between five and six o'clock I am going to Ekaterinhoff. I am going to change there as I do not wish to be seen passing through town in men's attire. For this reason, I decline to take you [Ekaterina Dashkova] in my carriage and advise you to go directly there, lest this truly remarkable horse rider should be mistaken for my suitor" (Lopukhin 1992, 116). Unfortunately, there are no known portraits of Dashkova in men's attire or military uniform. During a later period, however, engraved portraits were made for which the princess, now in her fifties, sat in a "sensible" English riding coat quite like a man's (see fig. 1).

It must have been due to her fondness for the formal, somewhat masculine English style that some of Dashkova's contemporaries accused her of looking like a man and even called her a "hermaphrodite." As Charles Masson describes her: "The Princess Dashkof, that 'Tomyris talking French,' masculine in her tastes, her gait and her exploits, was still more so in her titles and her functions of *director* of the Academy of Sciences and *president* of the Russian Academy. It is well known that she long solicited Catherine to appoint her colonel of the guards, a post in which she would undoubtedly have acquitted herself better than most of those by whom it was held" (Masson 1895, 311). As Count Louis Philippe de Ségur commented, "It was through a whimsical accident of nature that [she] was born a woman" (Ogarkov 1893). And even the poet Gavrila Derzhavin, the princess's protégé, unable to contain his creative bile, scribbled a quatrain:

> She was companion to Astraea
> When she from heaven came
> To mount the throne;
> And now she is Apollo. (Derzhavin 1866, 350)[3]

Incidentally, literary scholar Afanasii Bychkov found another, much more biting version of Derzhavin's verse: "In appearance: / Both a lad and lass."[4]

The select few individuals whom Dashkova considered friends commented on her masculine turn of mind and character. Martha Wilmot, for instance, wrote: "Everything about her—from speech to dress—everything is original [. . .]. She was born to be a minister or a commander, her place is at the helm of government." Contrary to Wilmot, Alexander Herzen made a case to his readers that "E. R. Dashkova was born a woman and remained a woman all her life" (Gertsen 1985, 210). But the Russian liberal's words fell on deaf ears. The prevailing popular image of Dashkova would remain that of a somewhat crude, intelligent woman who had masculine ways.

It is likely due to this and other reasons that Princess Dashkova has been routinely identified with portraits of "unknown" Russian women in military uniform resembling handsome young men. Such was the case with a portrait in Moscow's State History Museum. It depicts a hale young woman with round, pink cheeks, wearing a man's wig, a necktie, a dress coat with embroidery, and the star and ribbon of the Order of St. Catherine. The writing on the back would seem to leave no doubt as to who was depicted: "La Princesse Dachkoff, née Worontsoff, amie de l'Imperatrice Catherine." Research has established, however, that the painting was made much later, in the nineteenth century. Yet the provenance of the portrait (from the collection of Prince Semyon Mikhailovich Vorontsov), as well as the image of a woman clad in uniform, seemed to sustain the hypothesis that this was Princess Dashkova. But this hypothesis was erroneous.

The color of the jerkin and the shape of the galloon suggest the Cuirassier Regiment. Yet Ekaterina Dashkova could only have worn the Leib-Cuirassier uniform after July 24, 1762, when her spouse was made vice colonel of this regiment by the colonel herself, Empress Catherine II. The Leib-Cuirassier uniform during Peter III's reign did not look like the one in the portrait—officers would wear kaftans lined with green cloth and golden galloons. The jerkin of the lady in the portrait, however, is clearly outfitted with silver galloons over dark blue cloth.

In any case, Princess Dashkova adored military uniforms and the way she looked in them. Recounting the coup of 1762, she would talk frequently about how wonderful she looked in uniform and how she fooled everyone with her boyish appearance. Had she in fact worn this foppish Cuirassier jerkin and sat for a portrait in it, she would inevitably have written about it in her diaries or mentioned it somewhere in a letter. And it would no doubt have showed up in discussions among her contemporaries, who seized on every opportunity to gossip about her "masculinity." Yet no such testimony or court anecdote exists. The round-faced young woman of the portrait is not Princess Dashkova, and her identity remains a mystery.

Empresses Elizabeth and Catherine, who loved cross-dressing and did not for a moment consider concealing this "petit péché," or peccadillo, from those around them, even prompted the ladies at court to experiment with their appearances. Some of them, in imitation of the mischievous tsarinas, would attend masquerades in the guise of pomaded, refined young men wearing what was, in part, men's costumes. And like the empresses, they were likely to catch the eye of other women who were deceived by their appearance.

In fact, they continue to deceive to this day, especially when it comes to gullible museum curators, who, bewildered by the cross-dressing, compose hilarious explanatory notes. For example, there is a curious portrait dating back to the early 1770s that is titled *The Portrait of an Unknown Man in a Tricorn* and is located at the State Tretyakov Gallery. It was included in the latest exhibition of paintings by Fyodor Rokotov, which was held at the Tretyakov Gallery in 2016. The note below stated that the young man had been painted over a woman's portrait (the sitter possibly being Olimpiada Balbekova), her face left untouched by the artist. And yet, this odd fact seems to have been of little consequence to the author of the note who described the subject of the portrait as "unknown young man."

The keepers of this curious canvas must have had a hard time believing that in the eighteenth-century ladies and gentlemen were incredibly adept at changing their sex by means of costumes, wigs, and make-up, and that cross-dressing was commonplace—at least among the capital's fops and members of high society. It is difficult to comprehend why scholars refuse to notice the pleasantly voluminous front of the young man's kaftan, precisely where a woman's breasts are usually found. And it is even harder to explain why they do not take into consideration the existence of male masquerade costumes for women, that is, Amazon suits (similar to those worn by Catherine II) patterned after men's fashions, or why they ignore the telling evidence of the small and smart tricorn of a type usually worn by ladies during that period. Were all this taken into account, it would become crystal clear why Rokotov left the "unknown young man" with a female face. There was never any young man to begin with. It is still the portrait of the same lady, except clad in a man's costume, possibly for a masquerade. And if we accept the Balbekova hypothesis as valid, then Rokotov's is a portrait of Olimpiada Sergeevna, the wife of the poet Nikolai Struiskii.

There were in fact innumerable instances of mischievous women arriving at masked balls dressed as young men. In February of 1782, Monsieur Picard, the keen-eyed tutor of Count Alexander Kurakin, attended a masquerade at court, which he related to his pupil in a letter: "There were a great many people there, many honorable individuals wearing costumes, incidentally, Count Chernyshev and his daughter [among them]; Countess Galitzin, née Olsufyeva, and the Vice-Chancellor's wife were dressed as men" (Pikar 1878, 46).

If writers of memoirs are to be trusted, then a number of women cross-dressed not only for masquerades but also in daily life. Tatyana Passek remembered a lady who spent her mornings in a men's house robe smoking a long pipe. Ivan Vtorov wrote about his fearless sister, who donned a man's costume and accompanied him to the theater in 1792. Enthralled by the Russian Amazons of the eighteenth century, Vladmir Mikhnevich insisted that "these plucky balls of fire, the new generation, were seen everywhere" (Mikhnevich 1895, 133), while Mikhail Pyliaev, an expert on Petersburg affairs and anecdotes, stated that "officers standing guard would wear house robes; on occasion an officer's wife would put on the husband's dress coat and serve in his place; during the Swedish war, the female colonel [Countess von] Mellin stood in for her husband, appearing in front of the troops in uniform" (Pyliaev 1990, 386).

Girls attending the Smolny Institute for Noble Young Ladies would put on men's coats, kaftans, and culottes. For graduation, they would give theatrical performances in which they skillfully portrayed male characters in corresponding attire. Catherine II was delighted with such entertainments. As she told Voltaire: "Our girls perform tragedies and comedies. Those playing male roles in comedies put on a long coat of the kind fashionable here [. . .]. For this carnival we had a fine fop, an original Blaise and a wonderful Madame de Croupillac, two charming *soubrettes*, a delightful Avocat Patelin and, finally, a very intelligent Jasmin."[5] Artist Dmitry Levitsky painted one of these performances in which Ekaterina Khrusheva in the part of a passionate shepherd named Colas gently touches the plain face of Ninette, a character played by Ekaterina Khovanskaia. Catherine's love of theater was wellknown, as were her dramatic works, so it is quite possible that the tsarina herself advised the girls as to what scenes to select for the performance.

Men in Drag

Troves of evidence from surviving memoirs inform us that Russian men would sometimes cross-dress, often at an empress's command. For example, in the winter and fall of 1744, Elizabeth I ordered a series of masked balls to be held at court. The empress herself compiled the guest list and strictly forbade anyone to appear in "their own" clothes. The ladies were to be dressed as gentlemen, and the gentlemen as ladies, without exception. The public—high-ranking aristocrats, many of them of advanced age—had to show up for these imperial entertainments as loyal buffoons. The men, as the script dictated, presented themselves in French-style dresses with décolletages and crinolines, and in wigs and powder. Women squeezed their bodies into men's narrow kaftans. Among those invited to the entertainments was the future empress, Catherine II. She left behind a description of a valet de chambre named Sievers wearing a woman's dress: "He was tall and wearing a crinoline, which the empress had lent to him. He was dancing the polonaise with me while Countess Gendrikova was dancing behind us. Sievers's crinoline knocked her over as he spun around to offer me his hand. As she fell, she pushed me so that I fell right under Sievers's crinoline, which had just risen toward me. He became entangled in his long dress, which was rocking violently, and we all wound up on the floor, with me directly under his skirt; I was choking with laughter" (Catherine II 1907, 56–7).

Elizabeth I's other favorite entertainment was attending theatrical performances given by cadets, who cross-dressed to portray the female characters. And, we are told, the empress herself designed the costumes. Thus, in 1750, she "herself dressed Cadet Svistunov, who was playing the part of Osnelda in a tragedy by Sumarokov" (Valishevskii 1911, 81). Later, she would do the same for Cadet Beketov.

Catherine II kept up the tradition of carnival entertainments inaugurated by Empress Elizabeth. On December 10, 1765, as reported in the official court record, known as the Kammerfurier journal, the tsarina first "partook in an evening repast," and then, in the Portrait Hall of the Catherine Palace, "amused herself by playing cards; all the while, the court musicians were playing the strings, ladies and gentlemen were dancing a contredanse, and some of the gentlemen in attendance were dressed up as ladies for entertainment" (*Kamer-fur'erskii zhurnal* 1765, 242).

Shortly thereafter, on December 25, Christmas Day, the tsarina held another costume ball. Drawing on Semyon Poroshin's papers, we are able to ascertain the names of those cross-dressers as well as descriptions of the outfits they had on that evening:

> While all these festivities were taking place, from Her Majesty's inner chambers appeared seven ladies, astonishing everyone. Dressed as women were Count Grigory Grigorievich Orlov, Chamberlain Count Alexander Sergeevich Stroganov, Chamberlain Count Nikolai Alexandrovich Golovin, Chamberlain Pyotr Bogdanovich Passek, Equerry Lev Aleksandrovich Naryshkin, Valet de chambre Mikhailo Egorovich Baskakov, Valet de chambre Prince Andrei Mikhailovich Beloselsky. They all had on blouses, skirts, and bonnets. Beloselsky was wearing a headscarf and was dressed worse than the rest, similar to the way the boyar women dress; he was playing Mother, and the rest of the young ladies were under her supervision. Upon arriving, they were seated at the round table and were served appetizers and punch. Much ensued, after which they rose to dance (Poroshin 1844, 548).

Another cross-dressing ball took place on November 10, 1790, at the Winter Palace. After the formal dinner, the guests, following the empress, approached the doors of the hall and read a royal order that had been posted there. It read: "Free masquerade here and costumes distributed on credit; ladies to the right, gentlemen to the left." Entering, the guests saw stalls marked "Clothes for Men" and "Clothes for Women." The ladies were expected to dress as men, and the gentlemen as women. Presented with no choice, they proceeded to purchase costumes "on credit" and then change into them. Male and female French comedians had been hired to act as tradesfolk.

Catherine was not without mercy—with the help of her state secretary, Alexander Khrapovitsky, she had designed the costumes in an Eastern style, effectively concealing bodily imperfections, which meant they looked good on both men and women. The appearance of the garments was recorded in the Kammerfurier journal: they were comprised of a white dress underneath, with something like a long pink belted cape layered over the dress; a turban of white gauze served as a head piece, with some modifications for women (*Kamer-fur'erskii zhurnal* 1790, 588). The masks purchased by the guests completed the outfits. The revelers remained dressed in these theatrical renditions of Asian attire until half past one in the morning and headed home without changing. It must have been a splendid sight.

Sadly, we have yet to discover a portrait of a Russian man in drag from the eighteenth century, despite the popularity of cross-dressing both in court life and theater during the period. One canvas, however, is worth considering: Anton Losenko's 1770 painting titled *Vladimir and Rogneda,* which is currently held by St. Petersburg's Russian Museum. To the best of our knowledge, this is the first painting by a Russian artist to be based on the history of ancient Russia. It is this painting that earned Losenko the title of scholar and professor at the Academy of Fine Arts. The artist's contemporaries, as well as nineteenth-century historians, commented on the artifice of this painting, the overall effect of which, from the fairytale-like costumes to the affected gestures of the subjects, bespeaks a theatrical influence. Both of the central characters in the work also have connections to the theater. Images of Prince Vladimir and Princess Rogneda of Polotsk were drawn from the same model: the renowned Russian actor Ivan Dmitrievsky, one of the first professional female impersonators on the Russian stage. Legend has it that he was so adept at transforming himself into a woman, moving so gracefully and dressing with such skill, that it was absolutely impossible to tell he was a man. Empress Elizabeth I took a liking to him, becoming his patroness. As far as we know, she gave him his stage name, Dmitrievsky (his real name was Narykov), allegedly because of his striking resemblance to a Polish Count of the same name. This gesture signaled Elizabeth's conviction that this actor would "become the tsar of the Russian stage." The tsarina herself dressed Dmitrievsky in women's costumes, lent him dresses from her personal wardrobe, and even presented him with her own diadem, which he would wear on stage when appearing in female roles. In the Russian theater of the 1760s, gifted actresses were still in short supply. It is therefore not at all surprising that Losenko should have chosen Dmitrievsky as his model, an actor who was accomplished at playing both male and female parts. Moreover, there might have been no exaggeration in the artist's representation of Rogneda's histrionic wailing as this was the grotesquely affected manner in which the actor portrayed distressed women on the verge of fainting. Nowadays, this style of acting comes off as a caricature, yet during the eighteenth century, such affected performances raised no objections and could in fact move credulous audiences to tears.

Conclusion

It might seem that the Russian culture of cross-dressing ended in the eighteenth century, at the end of a century of female rulers and of the rococo style that lent great freedom to behavior and dress. In the nineteenth century, there were no woman rulers, and historians have been unable to find any portraits of Russian men who dared to pose in woman's clothing. One might conclude from this that the phenomenon of cross-dressing did not exist in nineteenth- and twentieth-century Russia or was not reflected in visual culture. But such a conclusion is erroneous. Born in the eighteenth century, the culture of cross-dressing in Russia continued to develop into the nineteenth century. The habit of Empresses Elizabeth I and Catherine II of mixing in their dress masculine (military) elements and female (civilian) elements led in the nineteenth century to the curious phenomenon of special military uniforms for the female members of the House of Romanov who served as honorary heads of military regiments. (For more on this, see Khoroshilova 2018).

Moreover, it was in the nineteenth century that there appeared Russian military Amazons—women officers who took part in wars. Historians are very familiar with the portraits of the most famous of these: Nadezhda Durova-Aleksandrov. In these portraits, she is depicted in either men's military dress or men's civilian dress.

Until recently, we had no evidence of portraits of Russian men in women's clothing. And so, the opinion arose that such portraits did not exist. But I quite recently managed to uncover evidence of a portrait made of a cross-dressing Russian courtier in women's clothing, Count Mikhail Petrovich Rumiantsev (1751–1811); he wore such clothing in his daily life and received guests in it (for more on the portrait, see Khoroshilova 2021, 278–81). In addition, I found a very rare photograph of Russia's first professional female impersonator, Konstantin Puzinkovskii (1836–1915), entirely forgotten until now, who not only performed in women's dress but wore it in his everyday life (see Khoroshilova

2021, 152–7). These discoveries are discussed in my latest book, *Russian Cross-Dressing: In History, Culture and Everyday Life* (2021).

While working on that book, I was able to amass a number of very valuable and rare photographs of Russian cross-dressing, both among performers and ordinary people, who felt the need to dress in the clothing of the opposite sex. And while we know nothing yet of any paintings, we now have quite a few photographic portraits, which speaks to the fact that photography, as a less expensive, faster, and smaller scale, and, consequently, more intimate form of portraiture, became the most viable and in some cases the only possible means for members of Russia's queer community and cross-dressers to express themselves and to show their feelings to the world. I have discussed some of these photographs in my scholarly work, but their number is so great that the next step must be an exhibition of photographs of Russian cross-dressing in the nineteenth and twentieth centuries. I am confident that this would change the opinion of many, including Russian art historians, on this phenomenon and would compel them to reexamine the history of Russian visual culture.

Translated by Aleksei Grinenko

Notes

1 For more, see Khoroshilova 2017.

2 As for cameos and medallions— many copies for European collectors were made by James Tassie and still can be found in European collections, for example: https://www.worthpoint.com/worthopedia/original-glass-cameo-catherine-great-1761007865,

https://www.hillwoodmuseum.org/exhibitions/past-exhibitions/passion-empress-catherine-greats-art-patronage, https://www.rct.uk/collection/39437 as well as works by unknown masters, see: http://www.sothebys.com/fr/auctions/ecatalogue/2013/russian-works-of-art-faberge-and-icons-l13113/lot.594.lotnum.html

3 In the original Russian: "Soputnitsei byla, / Kogda s nebes na tron / Vozsest' Astreia shla; / A nyne—Apollon" (Derzhavin 1866, 350). The complete title of the work is: "K portretu knyagini Ekateriny Romanovny Dashkovoi, vo vremya ee presidenstva v Akademii nauk."

4 In the original Russian: "Se lik: / I baba, i muzhik" (Derzhavin 1866, 350. The title of this version was: "K portretu germafrodita" [On a portrait of a hermaphrodite]. It should be noted that the words Derzhavin uses to refer to the two sexes are not neutral but are in both cases colloquial and somewhat derogatory.

5 *Bumagi imperatritsy Ekateriny II, khraniaschiesia v Gosudarstvennom arkhive Ministerstva inostrannykh del*, vol. 1 (St Petersburg, 1871–1874), 227. The characters referenced here by Catherine II (Blaise, Baronne de Croupillac, Avocat Patelin, and Jasmin) are from the following French comedies, respectively: *L'Héritier du village* (1725), by Marivaux, *L'Enfant prodigue* (1738), by Voltaire, *L'Avocat Patelin* (1706), by David-Augustin De Brueys, and *L'Étété des couquettes* (1690), by Florent D'Ancourt.

References

Andreev, Vasilii. 1869. "Ekaterina Pervaia." In *Osmnadtsatyi vek: Istoricheskii sbornik, izdavaemyi Petrom Bartenevym*, Vol. 3. Moscow: Rys.

Bradford, W. (Mrs.) (ed.). 1840. *Memoirs of the Princess Daschkaw, Lady of Honour to Catherine II*, vol. 1. London: Henry Colburn.

Catherine II. 1871–74. *Bumagi imperatritsy Ekateriny II, khraniashchiesia v Gosudarstvennom arkhive Ministerstva inostrannykh del*, vol. 1. St. Petersburg.

———. 1907. *Zapiski imperatritsy Ekateriny II*. St. Petersburg: Izdanie Suvorina.

Derzhavin, Gavrila Romanovich. 1866. *Sochineniia Derzhavina s obyasnitel'nymi primechaniiami Ia. Grota*. St. Petersburg: Izdanie Imperatorskoi Akademii Nauk.

Gertsen [Herzen], A. I. 1957. "Kniaginia Ekaterina Romanovna Dashkova." In A. I. Gertsen, Sobranie sochinenii v tridtsati tomakh, vol. 12, 361–422. Moscow: Akademiia Nauk.

Kamer-furjerskij zhurnal 1765 goda. 1765. St. Petersburg.

Kamer-furjerskij zhurnal 1790 goda. 1790. St. Petersburg.

Khoroshilova, Ol'ga. 2017. "Smotr u derevni Khadykovki: chto nam izvestno o potemkinskoi rote amazonok." *Rodina* 3: 75–76.

———. 2018. *Voina i moda: ot Petra I do Putina*. Moscow: Eterna.

———. 2021. "Russkie travesti: v istorii, kul'ture i povsednevnosti." Moscow: MIF.

Lopukhin, Ivan. 1992. *Rossiia XVIII stoletiia v izdaniiakh Vol'noi russkoi tipografii A. I. Gertsena i N. P. Ogareva. Spravochnyi tom k zapiskam E. R. Dashkovoi, Ekateriny II*. Moscow.

Masson, Charles François. 1895. *Secret Memoirs of the Court of St. Petersburg*. London: Nichols.

Mikhnevich, Vladimir. 1895. *Russkaia zhenshina XVIII stoletiia*. Kiev.

Ogarkov, Vasilii Vasil'evich. 1893. "Ekaterina Dashkova, ee zhizn' i obshchestvenaia deiatel'nost'." Available at: http://az.lib.ru/o/garków_w_w/text_0050.shtml. Last accessed: May 21, 2021.

Pikar. 1878. "Pis'ma Pikara k kniaziu A. B. Kurakinu,." *Russkaia Starina* 22(5): 39–66.

Poroshin, Semen. 1844. *Semyona Poroshina zapiski: sluzhashie k istorii ego imperatorskogo vysochestva blagovernogo gosudarya tsesarevicha i velikogo knyazya Pavla Petrovicha*. St. Petersburg: Tipografiia K. Kraiia.

Pyliaev, Mikhail. 1990. *Staryi Peterburg*. Leningrad: Titul

Valishevskii, Kazimir. 1911. *Elizaveta I, Doch' Petra Velikogo*. St. Petersburg.

Wortman, Richard. 1995. *Scenarios of Power: Myth and Ceremony in Russian monarchy, Volume One: From Peter the Great to the Death of Nicholas I*. Princeton, NJ: Princeton University Press.

Chapter 3

The Queer Opacity of Alexander Ivanov's Nudes: Between Biblical Themes and Greek Love

Nikolai Ivanov

Alexander Ivanov is one of the most written about Russian artists of the nineteenth century; his famous work *The Appearance of Christ before the People* was created in Italy over the course of several decades. The painting evolved out of hundreds of studies, intermediary versions, and drawings, constituting, along with his "Biblical Sketches," the final stage of the artist's reflections on Christianity's actual and potential role in the development of the individual human and of all humanity.

Despite much art historical literature on Ivanov's engagement with such themes offering interpretations of his theological quest and its formal expression in his paintings, no scholar has yet offered a single more or less explicit hermeneutic paradigm with which to embrace the artist's Christianity-oriented works. Ivanov's diaries reveal his deep reflection on the ideas and moral principles of Christianity. His relationship to Christianity, however, changed over the course of his life, and a certain aloofness emerged in the artist's attitude toward theology during his final years. This has consequences for scholars whose writings on this topic are characterized by oblique definitions, a lack of clarity, and understatement.

The purpose of this chapter is to focus on what has yet to be adequately studied.[1] Namely, in examining the trajectory of Ivanov's life and work, the chapter will trace the representation of motifs that originate in sexual impulses that were prohibited from public expression in mid-nineteenth-century Russia.

The discussion will be divided into two parts. The first part will deal with the corpus of Ivanov's works depicting nude boys and analyze the range of opinions in the scholarly literature on the emergence of this rather extensive series of paintings, sketches, and drawings, and their place in the artist's legacy. The second half of the chapter will examine the artist's letters and notes as well as his contemporaries' reminiscences about him. It is there that we find the evidence to support conclusions about the contradictory nature of Ivanov's sexual identification. The published personal correspondence between the artist and his friends and relatives, as well as his diaries, serve as the basis for this line of argument. The scope of analysis involves abstractions from the transcendental, including sexuality, the possibility of homosexuality, and its manifestations in art/culture in the middle of the nineteenth century. The context in which Ivanov created his work and thought about the nature of human beings and their relationship to divinity does not presuppose self-identification as a homosexual: the subject of sexuality was not verbalized in public discourse.

Ivanov's Nudes

The ways in which the rhythm and tempo of Ivanov's life relate to the specificity of his creative process are evident in his protracted contemplation of ongoing events and their relation to notions of the sacred. The artist believed that any stretch of time he was living through called for concentration, seriousness, and deliberation. One might suggest that in his creative introspection and his dismissal of whatever appeared to be inconsequential, fleeting, or unimportant, Ivanov was following his father Andrei Ivanov's dictate to avoid "subjects that lead to moral depravity" (Botkin 1880, 24), as the artist frequently expressed his attitude toward his place in the world, and the stages of his artistic development and aesthetic positions: "I [. . .] will not miss the first opportunity to curl back into the snail in which my thoughts matured so peacefully over the course of eight years, thoughts that need at least four more years of Roman life before they come to full fruition. My snail is sacred like a mother's womb. To pry it open is to inflict death upon her and him" (Vinogradov 2001, 621). He is usually at his most explicit when it comes to expressing his overarching position on Christian morality and ethics. For example, in his letters and notes, Ivanov condemns other people's "unseemly" behavior, from the revelries of retired Russian artists in Italy to genre painting, which he considered base. True art, Ivanov maintained, does not favor "leaps into comic genres or watercolor, nor rainbow tones, nor hasty sketching" (Botkin 1880, 358).

Ivanov's series of works depicting nude boys might seem to clash with his dismissal of "fleeting" themes. His pictorial concentration on adolescent nudity in sketches and drawings, constitutes a striking cultural event, unprecedented in the history of Russian art in the mid-nineteenth century. Of all these paintings, his *Apollo, Hyacinth, and Cyparissus* has received the most attention from his contemporaries as well as later scholars. With his left arm, Apollo, the god of the sun, art, music, and poetry, embraces Cyparissus, who is leaning against him, while with his right hand he touches the knee of Hyacinth, who is playing the flute (fig. 1). Surviving material related to this work includes several sketches of the whole group and black chalk drawings of Hyacinth and Cyparissus.

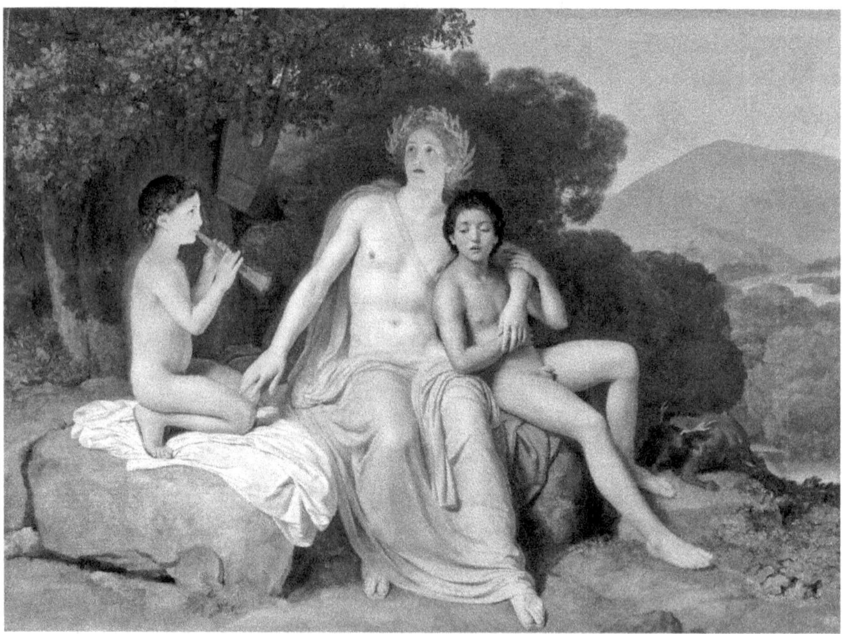

FIGURE 1. Alexander Ivanov, *Apollo, Hyacinth, and Cyparissus Making Music and Singing* (*Apollon, Giatsint i Kiparis, zanimaiushchiesia muzykoi i peniem*) (1831–1834). The State Tretyakov Gallery, Moscow

In contrast to other scholars' cautiously worded reflections about Ivanov's treatment of nude boys, Nikolai Romanov ends his enthusiastic discussion of this painting with a bold reference to Eros. Writing in 1916, he argues:

> The figure of Cyparissus in Ivanov's picture [...] is the artist's first step [...] toward style, his first insight that style is the only true substance; his "Eros" transformed the baseness of nature into an elevated representation of the free idea of art. [...] Refined and graceful, these images reach for the poetry of Plato's Eros, beguiling yet capable of fueling aspirations toward the lofty and the ideal. The artist drew his inspiration to seek the lofty, ideal Eros from the ancient myth about those favored by the gods, expressing this characteristically antique idea in his picture. [...] Ivanov grasped the delicate spiritual essence of the antique Eros. (Romanov 1916, 49)

Considering this painting to be one of his most important works, Ivanov would often bring it with him on his travels. The final version of the painting is considered to be unfinished. It traveled across Russia and Italy with the artist who felt compelled to finish it. However, he was unable to bring the painting to a satisfactory completion; he kept waiting to be in the right state to apply the finishing touch. In his letters to the Russian artist Mikhail Botkin, Ivanov called this picture "Apollo singing with his favorites Hyacinth and Cyparissus" (45). Museums and art historians would remove the word "favorites" from any subsequent discussion of the painting. This was the work of Soviet art historians who changed the name the artist had given the painting. There has never been any explicit reference to a homosexual subtext in the Russian scholarly literature on Ivanov's representation of the friendship between Apollo and the boys. When the work was still in progress, however, the Italian artist Vincenzo Camuccini, who was a friend of Ivanov's, saw the painting and, "tracing the figure of Hyacinth with an upward motion of his hand, said with a chuckle, 'C'è la natura, ma bruta natura.'" (Novitskii 1895, 34). Was the word "bruta" Camuccini's way of hinting at or reacting to the subject of pedophilia? And why then was the image of Hyacinth subsequently described, in the words of Mikhail Allenov (1980), as having an "element of vivid naturalness?" (Allenov 1980, 106). This prerevolutionary opinion on Hyacinth was even more daring: "The soft and gentle shape of his body gives him a semi-feminine character foreign to the ancient original" (Romanov 1916, 43). Yet the image of Cyparissus being embraced by the god is, according to Nikolai Romanov, "the most interesting image in the picture" (43). Writing about this boy, Allenov draws the following conclusion: "However, he [Apollo] draws Cyparissus into his embrace. [...]. Like an adult teaching or advising a child or an older friend kindly encouraging a younger one" (Allenov 1980, 105). We also have a record of sculptor Bertel Thorvaldsen's memories, pointing out a surprising playfulness in the pictorial representation of Apollo: "The smile on Apollo's face should not have been rendered so apparently, it prevents him from looking like a god" (Novitskii 1895, 35).

Russian art histories found in *Apollo, Hyacinth, and Cyparissus* "three stages of man's ascendance to perfection" (Alpatov 1959, 70), "the fine shade of an authentically antique spirit" (Romanov 1916, 37), and "a most spontaneous expression of a soulful intimacy" (Allenov 1980, 102). In this picture, "gods [. . .] partake of incomplete earthly joys" (18), "the spirit triumphs over the limitations of the inner life of the soul and breaks out from within toward nature and the sounds of the surrounding world" (104). The picture has a "striking authenticity of a nearly intimate order" (17).

Romanov discusses the academic techniques for treating the nude body in relation to this picture as follows: "Ivanov started working on this picture 'in order to draw nudity in lieu of a model drawing class'" (1916, 49). The author then goes on to state, "elements of truth and nature kept Ivanov's work away from an impersonal academicism, lending a touch of genuine grace to his picture" (47).

From the late 1830s to the early 1850s Ivanov made a series of album drawings depicting nude boys. Art historians such as Nikolai Mashkovtsev systematically commented on this tendency as "possibly the oddest part" of the artist's legacy (1916, 35). The first in this series is *Young Male Model Holding a Stick in His Left Hand,* dated 1824, followed by: *On the Shore of the Bay of Naples, Two Recumbent Male Figures on Red and White Drapes Against a Landscape Background and a Roughly Sketched Third Figure, Seven Boys, Nude Boy on a White Drape, Nude Boy, Half-figure of a Nude Boy, Four Nude Boys, Three Nude Boys, Three Nude Boys Standing Against a Blue Background, Recumbent and Sitting Nude Boys Against a Green Background, Four Recumbent Nude Boys, Three Recumbent Nude Boys,* and so on.

The artist painted these nude boys while in Italy. They are Italian boys. In going abroad, Ivanov was one of many Russian artists, writers, and architects for whom Italy was a particularly desirable artistic destination and one of the best places to study art and to perfect one's own art. The cult of Italy formed over the course of centuries. Artists tried to get to Italy and to stay there, competing for stipends from the tsar to support themselves. Artists who spent time in that country, familiarizing themselves with the methods of teaching art in the Italian academies, studying and copying the art of antiquity and masterpieces of Italian painting, and enriching themselves with the diversity of Italian art, acquired a special status back in their homeland, where they became conduits for new ideas from abroad. Any subject of Italian art assumed "authoritative" status, acquiring immediate legitimacy just because it had arisen in a country that was the repository of an enormous number of masterpieces, a country influenced by antiquity and by Christianity.

Before Ivanov, there were no representations of naked boys in Russian art. In Italian art, however, one can find this motif, which was often described as orientalism by foreign artists who found themselves in Italy; that is, researchers have pointed out that such artists cast an exoticizing gaze on the mores and freedoms of another country, and this is reflected in their art.

Ivanov's treatment of the motif of naked Italian boys corresponds to the work of Western artists, among which are the famous queer photographic series of Wilhelm von Gloeden. They are alike in the complete nudity of the boys, their poses, the introduction of attributes of the Golden Age (such as ancient musical instruments and garlands), and in their manner of artistic storytelling.

Art Historians on Ivanov's Nudes

Writing in 1997, art historian Mariia Nekliudova argues that nude boys for Ivanov constitute:

> a certain aesthetic and human ideal that speaks to the densely emotional and sensual part of the artist's ego, to the impulse he would often debate in moments in which he found himself contemplating, theorizing, and rationalizing while seeking aesthetic solutions. Both parts [of his ego] existed in a state of complex inner balance, within the total of his individuality as a human and an artist, but from time to time they would take turns asserting themselves (1997, 21).

Art historians have consistently attempted to assign some function to the images of nude children in Ivanov's work. As a rule, their interpretive trajectories were circumscribed by an academic tradition in which painting nude models was an essential phase in an artist's training, mandatory engagement with nature being integral to creative practices, including those of antiquity. These art historians also take care to balance discussion of the sensual and emotional in Ivanov's work with his constant worries about *The Appearance of Christ before the People*:

> Ivanov was censured for the large number of nude people who looked like bathers. [...] This eternal aesthetic endeavor, which should be traced

> to antiquity, did not and could not lose its appeal for the former student of the Academy; and its contents only grew in complexity, acquiring a new semantics thorough which to perceive refractions of nude people—young or old. [...] In their nude state these beings belong only to the sphere of nature, and not of morality (Nekliudova 1997, 18–9).

According to such interpretations, his study of three nude boys represents bodies in "spectral attitudes" (Mashkovtsev 1916, 35), that is, following the academic need for variety, while "the flexible expressiveness of each pose, undiluted, is the artist's tuning-fork, helping him discover values of plasticity in the amorphous conditions of reality" (35).

Art historical explanations of Ivanov's aestheticization of nude boys most commonly involve reflections about the world views of the ancients, how the ideas of Plato and Greek ideals of beauty were realized in these nude bodies: "Ivanov's boys, gawky and unprepossessing as they may be, nevertheless resemble ancient heroes" (Zagianskaia 1967, 14). "His figure, perfect in terms of proportion and shape, was associated with the aesthetic ideal of antiquity. By adopting the 'eloquence' of a body most beautiful, a posture, a movement, a gesture, the artist endeavored to capture the beauty, grace, and magnificent appeal of pagan antiquity, which he could not and would not forget" (Nekliudova 1997, 21).

Art historians, however, point out with some regularity that such an interpretation is incomplete and inconsistent with the Christian orientation of the artist's ideas and his other works. Making use of the glossary of generally accepted academic terms, Mariia Nekliudova, the most eminent authority on Ivanov, is unable to construct a stable interpretation of this tendency in his work: "memories of antiquity," "human nature with its postures and gestures," "through the prism of poetic perception," "a pantheistic world view." For an artist creating works reflecting the "essence of Christianity," such works are "nothing short of paradoxical" (40).

Nowhere in the existing Russian scholarship does one find so much as a hint at Ivanov's sexuality. The number of works depicting nude boys and their common representational techniques, however, compel art historians to address Ivanov's preoccupation with this theme, at times chiding Ivanov for paying excessive attention to it. Guarded allusions and hints as to the possibility of a different, inexpressible aspect of the artist's identity and pointing to the ambiguities underlying his commitment to representing nude children are often found in texts by art historians who comment on his "odd" choice of subject matter, his controversial, idiosyncratic treatment of the sensual realm dominated by the emotional, and the complications of his inner life. Dismissing these numerous works, which comprise such a sizable corpus, is even more difficult as art historians acknowledge a distinct point of view with regard to nude children.

These works stand out among his other creations: "They are the realization of the wholesome, harmonious contemplation of life the artist so longed for" (Nekliudova 1997, 39). In 1916, Mashkovtsev, admiring these pictures, stated that Ivanov's nude boys were "meditation through painting" (1916, 36). The corpus of these works, however, is not an exercise or some developmental phase on his way to his Christian canvases. They comprise a cohesive, fully formed, thematically linked series in which the author remains steadily invested during his mature creative period over the course of thirty years.

The abstract, covert nature of the boys' affective behavior, the restraint in the children's poses, and the recycled plotline in *Seven Boys*, compelled Mashkovtsev to point out that there is no "psychologism" in the work: "His treatment of the motifs of the standing, sitting and recumbent figures in their pure plasticity, is devoid of any hint of psychology" (1916, 35). Is this refusal to represent behavior that is more characteristic of children an indication of a different subtext, which Allenov later articulates as a "Schillerian image of 'lost childhood?'" (1980, 172). It is noteworthy that the nude boy series continues to be of interest to Russian art historians, and its aesthetic content is never questioned: "The nude boys are one of Ivanov's highest achievements in the field of open air painting" (Rakova 1960, 27); and these studies show "a great freedom in painting and a spectacular manifestation of creative individuality" (Nekliudova 1963, 14).

It has been suggested that some of the drawing exercises featuring images of nude boys were part of the artist's vision for a larger unmade picture. Given Ivanov's methods, Galina Zagianskaia argues, "These exercises in nude boys were created in conjunction with an idea for a completely independent painting, which comes closest to being realized in his small canvas *On the Shore of the Bay of Naples*" (Zagianskaia 1967, 15) (fig. 2). From the arrangement of the boys' poses to compositional concentration and projected colors—all the elements appear to function as meticulous, signifying points of emphasis, which, it can be argued, recur with regularity and, in this particular picture, stand out prominently.

Given the detailed development of the plot lines in Ivanov's other paintings and his multiple statements about their content, manner, and purpose, art historians are not used to dealing with the deliberate "simplicity" of narrative in his treatment of nude boys. "The artist's desire to speak of the human body

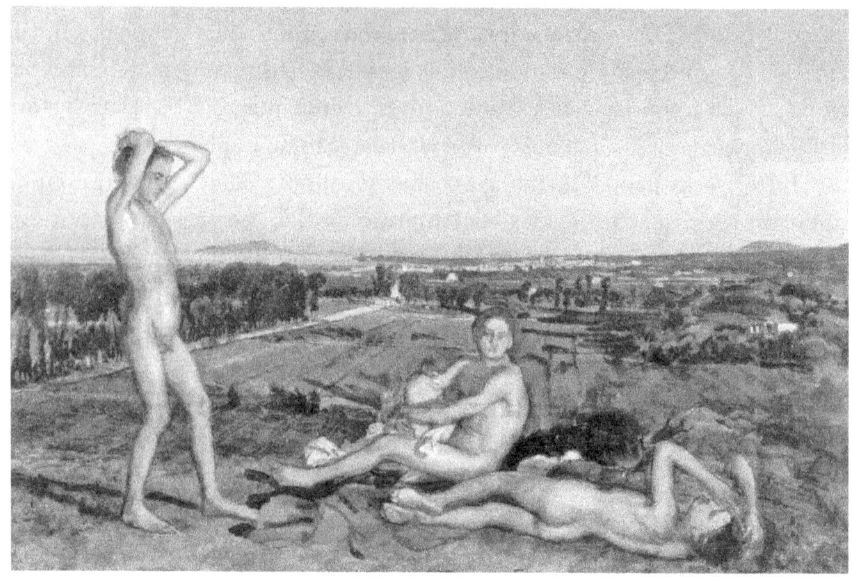

FIGURE 2. Alexander Ivanov, *On the Shore of the Bay of Naples* (*Na beregu Neapolitanskogo zaliva*) (late 1830s–1840s). The State Tretyakov Gallery, Moscow

in the idiom of pure painting" (Mashkovtsev 1916, 35)—such an interpretation is far removed from the artist's habitual "spiritual" quest. It does not square with his tendency to invest pictorial organization with sophisticated meaning, especially when it comes to illustrating plots bearing great significance for Christianity.

Ivanov on Ivanov

Surveying the artist's correspondence, the reminisces of his contemporaries, and notes made by Ivanov himself yields more or less definitive conclusions with regard to the sustainability of theorizing about the artist's sexuality. One of the letters contains a fleeting expression that can be understood as pointing to an unspeakable sexual desire banned from public discourse in the first half of the nineteenth century: Alexander Ivanov is "given to prohibited passions and pleasures" (Vinogradov 2001, 78). The depth of youthful torment and sincerity in his letter to his friend Pyotr Izmailov, which he wrote at the beginning of his Italian travels in 1831, is truly disarming:

> Pyotr! Our friendship can be lasting only if it is based on the rules of prudence; without it all is doomed! Without it, in my present circumstances, I should assure you that I would give up the whole of Italy for you alone, that you are everything to me; that without you I die. That I put myself completely at your disposal and that I should be happy even if you and I should find ourselves together in abject poverty, in vice. Thus, Pyotr, all these feelings are true ["true in my leisurely state" is crossed out] when a brief sensibility, separate from reason, takes hold of me in my leisurely state—then I weep—weep and demand your presence. I ask myself ["want to say" is crossed out] why I am removed from you . . . [One] must be educated then to be of use to one's country and home, to one's friend if ["he" is crossed out] should willfully prefer me to all else. —Stern, he does not know tenderness (Ivanov 1831).

The artist's correspondence and other people's memories of him, however, contain information about Ivanov's failed marriages and heterosexual relationships. Making use of the artist's own writings, one finds that, "having been innocent until the age of 30" (Vinogradov 2001, 660), Ivanov would later experience feelings and get into situations for which he would feel remorse: "meetings with young women drive my entire insides uncontrollably toward them, conversations with them intoxicate me like wine" (648); "the wench at the studio door," the scandal produced by "the woman who over the course of six years gratified my nature" (Zummer 1929, 392); "I do not know where and how my sense of attachment to the fair sex, a certain obligatory need to be with them, was first conceived in me.—First the captain's daughters, one after another, entertained me, then three or four girls in Albano, in different nooks of the city and so on. Either the time to marry had come, or it was the final stage of bidding farewell to the purpose of human life, it's just that love seemed to me not only a crime but also a certain necessity" (Vinogradov 2001, 359–60). Sexual license, according to the artist, conflicts with the "spiritual quest": "I must forsake Adultery—and remember the chaos of youth as material for communicating with people in a human language through the representation of passions in my art" (Zummer 1929, 393).

The artist is especially worried about venereal diseases: "The woman with whom I lived for eight years having no suspicions as to her health infected me with the clap" (Vinogradov 2001, 302). And elsewhere: "My last carnal union with a woman left me disarmed in the spiritual world. I now find myself in a state of fear that I might have contracted a disease that, once announced, will rob me of time to produce my work" (659).

The artist's reflections about marriage are also contradictory: "Woman was created to be man's helper: She is full of compassion for him, providing him with a marvelous respite from his mental strain, thus endowing him with strength for his further enterprises, and, by initiating him into her mysteries, endows his physical prowess with freshness and joy. Truly happy is he who is destined to be united with such a creature" (Vinogradov 2001, 436). At other times Ivanov finds marriage to be in the way of his "spiritual growth." The artist notes that "the sons of the resurrection" do not enter into marriage; the necessity for marriage, according to Ivanov, must be stated in the Scriptures, and the artist does not find it there:

> I almost found solitude in *picol' astagni,* but these tiresome boys once again drove me to my monk's cell. [. . .] Luke in ecstasy described of the last stage of marital perfection: they will neither marry nor be given in marriage like ordinary people, and their every action in life will earn them the name of God's Children.[2]—After reflecting and writing these words, I suddenly felt a quivering as if from a sort of fainting spell. I went out to the servants, and they trembled when they caught sight of my face (Zummer 1929, 408).

Several of the artist's correspondents noted his vacillation, detachment, and ambivalence regarding the role of family and marriage, but they drew different conclusions, at times characterizing Ivanov as an ascetic and a monk: "Ivanov truly leads a monk's life. And he would surely not refuse having a nun for his wife—a woman occupied with prosecuting her own vices!" (Vinogradov 2001, 12). "If you have been thinking about some sort of hearth, some family life and a woman, then know full well this is hardly your lot!" (12). Such was the advice Gogol gave the artist when considering his prospects for married life.

The most important thing, in the words of Allenov when considering the paintings with images of boys, is "signs of a free life" (1980, 18). The artist's engagement with this thematic realm, his indiscriminate heterosexual liaisons, his reflection on the role of marriage and celibacy make it possible to conclude that this artist's creative output to a large extent originates from his views on the interrelations between sexuality and morality and that sexual practices had complex and ambiguous consequences for the development of his artistic potential.

Conclusion

The range of interpretations explaining why the artist introduces naked figures into his paintings stretch between two contradictory points of view on nudity. The first expresses an opinion that is the most traditional in Russian art history; it holds that nudity in paintings has nothing at all to do with sexuality. This is opposed to the less frequently expressed opinion that a nude figure depicted by an artist is the incarnation of his sexual desire, that is, in the case of Ivanov, naked boys would point to his pedophilia. The context in which Ivanov's paintings were made, his letters, reminiscences about the artist and his works, and critical articles demonstrate that the sexuality of the artist and any discussion of it, let alone public discussion, was covert and sparse, but it was discussed. Naked boys in paintings are a motif in the Western history of art, which in the middle of the nineteenth century could be attributed to a variety of causes. First, the representation of naked children is a neoclassical expression of admiration for Antiquity. In the art of Ancient Greece and Rome, a naked youth was often the hero. The second reason associated with these manifestations of classicism is that naked children index the Golden Age, a time of innocence, when man and nature were one and when this oneness with nature was enough to bring happiness. This was a time before the fall, understood as the realization of one's sexuality. At that age, boys are allowed to engage in any activity and to do things that would be considered taboo for an adult. Third, the appearance of naked boys may be a religious motif. Their innocence alludes to Christ's statement: "Suffer little children, and forbid them not, to come unto me: for of such is the kingdom of heaven" (Matthew 19:14). The naked Christ child in Russian icons is often interpreted as indicating the high degree of closeness between the viewer of the icon and Christ.

At the same time, the realism of these paintings by Ivanov when accompanied by simple interpretations assumes qualities that could be called queer. And we might use queer to describe Ivanov's own sexuality. Questions of sexuality in the work of Ivanov are mediated by several different discourses—religion, neoclassicism, euphemisms of the time, and so on—which makes it impossible to attribute one definitive meaning to Ivanov's nude boys. These images arise with stubborn regularity in the work of the artist while in Italy; they are not concealed and appear to be important to the artist. But they are concealed, because their appearance in Ivanov's art and life is strange and indeterminate; psychological interpretations of the presence of naked Italian boys are strained. The nudity of

Ivanov's boys turns out to be discouragingly simple and yet illusory and strange. Is something lurking behind this queerness?

Translated by Aleksei Grinenko

Notes

1 Western Slavists have addressed the homoeroticism of Ivanov's work, beginning with Simon Karlinsky's psychobiography of Nikolai Gogol, *The Sexual Labyrinth of Nikolai Gogol* (1976, 190–191; 1997–201). More recent works include Rosalind Polly Gray's "The Homo-Erotic Paintings of Aleksandr Ivanov" (2001), and Allison Leigh's chapter "Aleksandr Ivanov: Desire and the Male Nude" in her monograph *Picturing Russia's Men* (2020, 103–145). It has also been addressed in Russia's gay subculture as well. For example, the first Russian anthology of gay literature *Love without borders* [*Liubov' bez granits*, 1997], edited by V. N. Dumenkov, features Ivanov's drawing *Two Nude Models* (1822) on the cover, and K. K. Rotikov's gay guide to St. Petersburg, *The Other Petersburg* [*Drugoi Peterburg*, 1998], devotes several pages to Ivanov. Those critical works, however, tend to interpret these figures as symptomatic of a homosexual orientation, which places them at odds with Ivanov's religious painting or as subverting them.

2 This is a reference to Luke 20:34–36: "Jesus replied, "The people of this age marry and are given in marriage. But those who are considered worthy of taking part in the age to come and in the resurrection from the dead will neither marry nor be given in marriage, and they can no longer die; for they are like the angels. They are God's children, since they are children of the resurrection."

References

Allenov, Mikhail. 1980. *Aleksandr Andreevich Ivanov*. Moscow: Izobrazitel'noe iskusstvo.

Alpatov, Mikhail. 1959. *Aleksandr Ivanov*. Moscow: Molodaia gvardiia.

Botkin, Mikhail. 1880. *Aleksandr Andreevich Ivanov. Ego zhizn' i perepiska. 1806–1858*. St. Petersburg: M.M. Stasiulevich.

Dumenkov, V. N. (ed.). 1997. *Liubov' bez granits. Antologiia shedevrov mirovoi literatury*. St. Petersburg: KET.

Gray, Rosalind Polly. 2001. "The Homo-Erotic Paintings of Aleksandr Ivanov." In *Gender and Sexuality in Russian Civilization*, edited by Peter I. Barta, 163–180. London and New York: Routledge.

Ivanov, Aleksandr. 1831. Correspondence from A. A. Ivanov to P. I. Izmailov. 1831, Rome. NIOR RGB. F. 111. K. 1. Ed. khr. 2. L. 9–9 ob.

Karlinsky, Simon. 1976. *The Sexual Labyrinth of Nikolai Gogol*. Chicago and London: The University of Chicago Press.

Leigh, Allison. 2020. *Picturing Russia's Men*: Masculinity and Modernity in Nineteenth-Century Painting. London and New York: Bloomsbury Visual Arts.

Mashkovtsev, Nikolai. 1916. "Tvorcheskii put' Aleksandra Ivanova." *Apollon* 6–7: 1–39.

Nekliudova, Mariia. 1997. *A. A. Ivanov. Zrelyi period tvorchestva*. Unpublished dissertation, Rossiiskaia akademiia khudozhestv, Moscow.

Nekliudova. Militsa. 1963. *Rannii period tvorchestva Aleksandra Ivanova*. Unpublished dissertation, Akademiia khudozhestv SSSR. Nauchno-issledovatel'skii institut teorii i istorii izobrazitel'nykh iskusstv. Sektor russkogo iskusstva, Moscow.

Novitskii, Aleksei. 1895. *Opyt polnoi biografii A. A. Ivanova*. Moscow: K. A. Fisher.

Rakova, Magdalina. 1960. *A. Ivanov*. Moscow: Iskusstvo.

Romanov, Nikolai. 1916. "Kartina A. Ivanova *Apollon, Kiparis i Giatsint*." *Starye gody* 1–2 (January–February): 36–49.

Rotikov, K.K. 1998. *Drugoi Peterburg*, St. Petersburg: Ligus Plius.

Vinogradov, Igor'. 2001. *Aleksandr Ivanov v pis'makh, dokumentakh, vospominaniiakh*. Moscow: XXI vek-soglasie.

Zagianskaia, Galina. 1967. *Rabota Aleksandra Ivanova nad naturoi*. Unpublished dissertation, Akademiia khudozhestv SSSR. Nauchno-issledovatel'skii institut teorii i istorii izobrazitel'nykh iskusstv. Sektor russkogo iskusstva, Moscow.

Zummer, Vsevolod. 1929. "Eskhatologiia A. Ivanova." *Uch. Zap. Nauchno-issl. kafedry istorii evrop. kultury. Kharkovskii un-t*. Issue 3, 387–409. Kharkhov: n.p.

Chapter 4

Prostitutes, Pierrots, and Priapus: The Queer Modernism of Konstantin Somov

Brian James Baer

In a review of the exhibition *Derain, Balthus, Giacometti: Une amitié artistique,* held at the Museum of Modern Art in Paris, June 2–October 29, 2017, Jed Perl argues for a more expansive understanding of modernism, beyond "the standard model of modern art as a drive toward ever-greater purity, simplicity, and abstraction" (Perl 2017, 12), to include artists, like those featured in this exhibit, for whom "the search for the past isn't a retreat [from modernism] but an advance—a new kind of avant-garde intervention" (12). The exclusion of such artists from the canon of modernism is, Perl argues, based on a fundamental—and erroneous—assumption:

> That specific artistic styles and sensibilities have some symbiotic or at least some close relationship with specific social and political tendencies. By this logic, many art historians are inclined to believe that classicism tends to be reactionary and that newer artistic styles, forms, or media (Dadaism, collage, video, and so forth) tend to be politically or ideologically progressive. That such assumptions aren't supported by the facts doesn't seem to matter."

Perl then goes on to cite the praise by Giacometti, "a hero among Left Bank intellectuals," of Derain, "by some arguments a collaborator and a reactionary," as evidence that "there are artistic affinities that cut across—or quite simply have nothing to do with—ideological lines" (12).

Perl then reinscribes Derain, Balthus, and Giacometti at the very center of modernist experimentation, describing them as "the metaphysicians of modernism, [who] burrow into the enigmas of style; they investigate the relationship between style and truth" (10). And while they "may reinstate certain traditional ideas about how an imaginary world is constructed on the canvas, [. . .] they reinstate those ideas with so much thoughtfulness and passion that they result in a painting with an entirely new, entirely modern power" (10). Perl ends the review by calling for increased interest in this "alternative modernism," which he describes as "nothing less than another side of the great modern adventure" (Perl 2017, 13,14).[1]

Of course, art historians in the West are not alone in arguing for an expanded definition of modernism and in seeing it as a contested concept. See, for example, *Modernism in Dispute. Art since the Forties*, edited by P. Wood et al. (1993), which contrasts the abstraction of American postwar art with the realist art of France. Russian art historians, too, are engaged in a rethinking of modernism, as evident in a recent exhibition at the Moscow Museum of Modern Art: *Modernism without a Manifesto*, 1920–1950, translated into English as "Implicit Modernism." In the exhibition catalogue, Nadezhda Plungian argues that the concept of modernism was very narrowly defined in official Soviet culture due to its association with "formalism." Understood as the "anti-art" of the Western world, modernism could not be applied to Soviet artists. This very restrictive understanding of modernism created a distorted view of Soviet art, blinding Soviet art historians to the modernist elements in Soviet art (Plungian 2017, 12).

Among Russian artists, perhaps none has been so clearly a victim of this narrow view of modernism than Konstantin Somov (1869–1839), a founding member of the World of Art group. His bourgeois background and emigration from the Soviet Union in 1923 (he spent a short time in the US, where he found the culture to be totally alien, then moved to Paris), his fascination with eighteenth-century libertine culture, his many commissioned portraits of the wealthy, and the homoeroticism of his émigré works, not to mention his refusal to engage directly in his art with the cataclysmic political and social events of his time, made him persona non grata in the Soviet Union until the late 1970s.[2] Not surprisingly, Soviet art historians were at pains to find anything new or modern in Somov's work, instead applying a host of "ideological clichés" to the artist's work (Golubev 2017, 21).[3] The art critic and historian Abram Efros ([1930]2007, 218; 41) described Somov as a "cynic" who "mocked the past (*starina*)," declaring that by the 1910s "he was already nothing more than a skilled craftsman and an unappealing practitioner of pastiche." This view is only slighted amended in the introduction to one of the few Soviet monographs dedicated to Somov's life and work, published in 1980:

> Somov was not only a creator of a particular retrospective genre, not only a "passéist," depicting life in "times gone by," he was also a thoughtful landscape painter who could lend a quiet charm to Russian nature, and a serious portraitist, who left behind a unique series of graphic portraits of representatives of the Russian intelligentsia of his time, which have now acquired the status of historical documents. (Zhuravleva 1980, 5)[4]

Here the critic attributes historical rather than aesthetic significance to Somov's portraits.

The Western view, however, was not much different, as evident in the assessment of Somov's work in John Bowlt's volume *The Silver Age: Russian Art of the Early Twentieth Century and the "World of Art" Group*:

> Unlike Bakst, Benois and Diaghilev, Somov has long been forgotten in the West, and only recently has he begun to receive attention in the Soviet Union. [. . .] Somov was an excellent technician, a man of elegant taste and wide culture. Like the World of Art as a whole, Somov was the summation of the finest traditions of the old Russian intelligentsia. And more than any of his World of Art colleagues, Somov embodied the disbeliefs, the frustrations and the presentiments of his age. His art was the decorative tail-piece to a society that was itself at the concluding stage of its development. (Bowlt 1979, 199)

Art historians in both the Soviet Union and the West tended to see Somov's representational style as traditional and dismissed his fascination with the eighteenth century as nostalgia, passéism, or even necrology, the last gasp of a dying culture.

Somov's friend and collaborator, the queer writer Mikhail Kuzmin (1872–1936), however, had a very different assessment of Somov's work, finding it deeply innovatory and thoroughly modern:

> The name of K. Somov is well-known to every educated person not only in Russia but also throughout the world. This is an international figure. And his fame is far from that of a master who has definitively expressed himself, who is complete (many like to replace that word with "finished"); his fame is that of a *creator*, who does not rest on his current accomplishments, who is changing, searching, with every step broadening his

> horizon and his freedom, after, it would seem, the unsurpassable charm of paints, once again occupying himself with new combinations of tones, with new enchantment. (Kuzmin [1916] 1979, 470; italics added)[5]

Kuzmin's appreciation of Somov's work as innovatory is no surprise as both men were not only "part of the intertwined society of poets and philosophers who perpetrated the revolt against the dominant canons of socially conscious realism" (Engelstein 1992, 388) but also "stood in Russia at the origin of a larger cultural movement seeking to emancipate and legitimize homosexuality" (Bershtein 2011, 75). Both Somov and Kuzmin explored ways of representing homosexual desire that were neither moralizing nor decadent—that were, in a word, modern. Somov's distinct engagement with queer beauty should, therefore, be considered not simply modernist but as a distinctly queer form of modernism, something that has been unappreciated by art historians who have traditionally "made no mention of the artist's homosexuality or focused on aspects of his oeuvre having nothing to do with this forbidden theme" (Golubev 2019, 14) or who have accepted a restrictive notion of modernism as "rough and masculine work," characterized by "a heightened and aggressively heterosexual masculinity" (Tickner 1994, 42, 55).

Homosexuality as an Aesthetic Problem, or Queer Beauty in the Russian Silver Age

The reforms that followed the First Russian Revolution of 1905 included the lifting of censorship restrictions and the lessening of the criminal punishment for homosexual activity, both signs of the modernization and liberalization of Russian society—for better or worse in the interpretation of contemporary critics. This led to unprecedented public debates—waged in newspapers and academic journals, as well as in literature and in the visual and performing arts—regarding the meaning of sex and sexuality (see Engelstein 1992). In those debates homosexuality often assumed the role of metonym if not symbol of nonreproductive sex, which was just as easily associated with modernity and progress as it was with decadence and decline. On the one hand, the liberal jurist Dmitrii Nabokov, father of the novelist, argued very eloquently for the complete decriminalization of homosexuality as part of the broader project of separating the public and private realms and protecting the latter from intrusion by the state. On the other hand, Grigorii Novopolin, in his treatise *The Pornographic Element in Russian*

Literature of 1909, decried the open discussion of sex and sexuality, including homosexuality, arguing that any discussion of love risks "slipping into erotomania and nymphomania" (quoted in Naiman 1997, 55).

In the realm of visual aesthetics this debate had been brewing for decades. Kantian aesthetics and other Neo-Platonist approaches to art that sought to contain the threat of queer beauty by advocating idealist abstraction regarding both works of art themselves and the position of the viewer were increasingly challenged by Realism and Naturalism in art and literature and by materialist philosophies, such as Marxism and Darwinism. From different perspectives, these philosophies alleged that "the doctrine of the beau idéal as a morally elevated norm had wrongly abstracted the cultural form, the work of art, from the real social relations of admiration, love, contest, status, and sexual desire" (Davis 2010, 45). Such critiques would lead to the validation of more bodily, sensual approaches to the making and the viewing of art. And so, while Dostoevsky's Prince Myshkin was horrified by Holbein's *The Body of the Dead Christ in the Tomb*, a work of Naturalism avant la lettre, declaring: "Why, a man's faith might be ruined by looking at that picture!" just a few decades later the Russian religious philosopher Nikolai Berdiaev would declare: "Eroticism is inextricably connected with creativity. [...] Likewise, eroticism is connected with beauty. An erotic shock is the path by which beauty appears in the world" (Berdiaev 1985, 260).

In this way, post-Kantian aesthetics offered a discursive opportunity for proto-gay liberations, such as Walter Pater, John Addington Symonds, and Elisar von Kupffer—and, as I will discuss below, Mikhail Kuzmin and Konstantin Somov—to force "acknowledgement of the diversity and depth—the empirical range and causal primacy—of human erotic instincts and motivations, including nonstandard and nonnormative ones" (Davis 2010, 6–7). In taking advantage of this opportunity, however, they faced a dual challenge, having to address not only the ontological question of whether homosexuality exists—whether the ancients really liked *that*—but also the epistemological question of *what* homosexuality is, which they saw as closely tied to the aesthetic question of *how* to represent homosexuality, namely, how to navigate between the Scylla of idealization and abstraction and the Charybdis of pathology and obscenity. Many queer writers and artists addressed the ontological question—do homosexuals exist?—by invoking historical periods in which queer sexuality was accepted, if not celebrated, such as Ancient Greece and Renaissance Italy, and by making lists of queer historical figures. As Thomas Cannon muses in the introduction to his eighteenth-century collection *Ancient and Modern Pederasty:* "What Charm then held so many Sages and Emperors, clear Heads and hale Hearts" (qtd. in Gladfelder 2007, 29). There was greater divergence in addressing the epistemological question—what is homosexuality? For example, in England, the work of sexologists played an enormous role in the work of early gay liberationists such as Symonds and Edward Carpenter. In fact, Symonds, a writer and poet, coauthored a textbook titled *Sexual Inversion* (1897) with the sexologist Henry Havelock Ellis, and the first edition of Radclyffe Hall's novel *Well of Loneliness* (1928) was accompanied by an introduction by Ellis. While certainly aware of what was going on in much of Western Europe at the time, Russians of the Silver Age chose or were destined to follow a path that was largely aesthetic. As Evgenii Bershtein (2018, 162) notes of Kuzmin, "[he] demonstrated remarkably little interest in scientific approaches to this topic. Kuzmin's project for normalization of homosexuality relied on models that were moral and aesthetic and ignored those that were pathologizing and scientific." And so, it is no great surprise that the hero of Kuzmin's novel *Wings*, Vania Smurov, succeeds in resolving the opposition of physical and spiritual love in Florence, Italy, the center of Renaissance art.

Somov attended a reading of Kuzmin's novel on October 13, 1905, and was captivated by it. As Kuzmin (2000, 57) records in his diary: "Somov was in such ecstasy from my novel that he tells everyone he passes, saying that he has never read anything like it, and now an entire group of people (L. Andreev, among them) want a second reading." Somov and Kuzmin belonged to a group of cultural figures in St. Petersburg at this time, referred to as the Silver Age of Russian art and letters, which included several individuals who were self-identified homosexuals. In addition to Kuzmin and Somov, there was the impresario Sergei Diaghilev, the author and critic Dmitrii Filosofov, the art lover and writer Walter Nouvel, and the music critic Al'fred Nurok. Among them, Kuzmin and Somov could be considered "out" in the modern sense.[6] As we now know from their detailed diaries, these men led active sex lives, participated in an established homosexual subculture, and felt little shame over their sexual orientation or any need to hide it, unlike the composer Pyotr Tchaikovsky, a generation before them, who felt compelled to marry in order to protect his public reputation, or their contemporary Filosofov, who was ultimately unable to accept his homosexuality.[7] Moreover, they produced an important body of queer art and literature.

Although Kuzmin was primarily a poet and prose writer and Somov, a painter, they had a lot in common: both were trained musicians, travelled in the same artistic circles, and read many of the same works (in several Western European languages). They were also related in their fundamentally aesthetic approach to addressing the problem of same-sex desire. In addition, both men dabbled in erotic art and literature. Somov produced mildly erotic drawings to accompany Kuzmin's story *"The Adventures of Aimée Leboeuf"* (1907). A year later, Somov produced illustrations for *Das Lesebuch der Marquise* (1908), commissioned by Franz Blei, and ten years later, for two expanded French versions under the title *Le Livre de la Marquise: Receuil de poésie et de prose* (1918), one of which, referred to as the "Small" Marquise, was censored, while the other, referred to as the "Large" Marquise, was not. The 1908 *Lesebuch*, which was published in Munich, contained German translations of excerpts from French eighteenth-century prose; the small *Marquise*, while "substantially larger than the German edition—including poetry as well as prose—lacks a whole series of plates and vignettes found in the 'Large' Marquise'" (Kasinec and Davis, 1999, 347). The 'Large' Marquise' was published clandestinely in St. Petersburg, by R. Golike and A. Vilborg, although the frontispiece lists the place of publication as Venice and the publisher as Cazzo e Coglioni, Italian for 'dick and balls.' Edward Kasinec and Robert H. Davis, Jr. (1999, 340) describe the "Large" Marquise as "one of [Somov's] principle achievements in this genre, and a classic nonpareil in the history of Russian erotic book design."[8] Kuzmin also contributed to a book of erotic art, *Zanaveshannye kartinki* (Covered Pictures, 1920), providing original poems and translations of poems by Henri de Régnier, which were accompanied by drawings by Vladimir Milashevskii. Unlike their work intended for a general audience, which approached the subject of same-sex desire with a certain seriousness, the erotic drawings of Somov and the erotic poems of Kuzmin were deeply imbued with a camp sensibility, which could be considered a distinct contribution of queer artists and writers to modernist aesthetics. The fact that the effete Kuzmin went by the moniker Antinous, the lover of the emperor Hadrian known for his incredible beauty, is a good example of their campy engagement with the queer beauty of the ancients.

Kuzmin's and Somov's sustained interest in erotic art reflected an aesthetic concern shared broadly among modernists in all fields of the arts, namely, how to represent sexuality in a "non-abstract way"—a phrase used by Kuzmin in his 1923 manifesto "On Emotionalism"—and how to liberate it from traditional associations with biological reproduction and, by extension, domesticity and bourgeois respectability. As Klaus Harer (1989, 50) puts it, "An apology for the naked body and for an erotics freed from the burden of procreation is an obvious commonplace not only in *Wings*, but also in the modernist world in which Kuzmin and his circle found themselves." Indeed, one of the running themes of Kuzmin's

1906 novel is that no physical act of love is in itself right or wrong; it is the intention behind the act that determines its morality. Hence, even same-sex physicality can be "good" if pursued out of true love and respect, as one imagines it will be with Vania Smurov and Larion Shtrup when, at the novel's end, Vania steps onto a sunlit balcony in Italy. This is the culmination of a sexual *Bildungsroman* during which the hero is exposed to horrifying examples of lustful sexual relations (both homo- and hetero-sexual) as well as abstract speeches on the beauty of same-sex love.

For all their commonalities, however, Kuzmin and Somov approached the problem of queer beauty differently. For example, while Kuzmin and his contemporary Vasilii Rozanov continued to frame homosexuality in religious terms (see Watton 199), except for a drawing of two libertine monks, religion has absolutely no place in Somov's world. Moreover, Kuzmin, like many of his contemporaries in both Russia and Europe as a whole, would look to the Italian Renaissance for a way to integrate queer beauty into life and art; Somov, on the other hand, would engage with a different cultural repertoire that had its roots in a historically later engagement with queer beauty, eighteenth-century *libertinage*. And while the progressivist narrative of Kuzmin's gay *Bildungsroman* has his hero leave behind vulgar lust for artistically mediated passion in the final scene where he emerges into the Italian sunlight, Somov's work is distinctly nonlinear, infused with a sexual energy that resists any attempt to render it developmental, let alone respectably bourgeois. Their approaches to queer beauty were also shaped by the different discursive opportunities for representing same-sex desire available at that time in the realm of literature and in the realm of the visual arts.

Queer Beauty in the Russian Visual Arts of the Early Twentieth Century

For writers across Europe in the late nineteenth and early twentieth century, the visual arts played a central role in the formulation of a modernist aesthetic. As Mieke Bal (2004, 61) notes, "Modernism's interest in questions of knowledgeability and epistemology lends itself to an exploration of vision." The visual arts appeared distinctly suited to questioning if not transcending the limits of "rational" verbal language, while offering an aesthetic alternative, where the traditional antinomies of western culture—that of mind and body, spirit and flesh, Christian and pagan—were resolved or rejected. Laying the groundwork for the emergence of a modernist aesthetics was an intense engagement with

Italian Renaissance art that took place across Europe, as reflected in an enormous body of literary and critical works devoted to the topic, many of them dealing quite overtly with sexuality, and several with homosexuality.[9] These include John Ruskin's *The Stones of Venice* (1851), Walter Pater's *The Renaissance: Studies in Art and Poetry* (1873), John Addington Symonds' seven-volume *Renaissance in Italy* (1875–1886), *Sketches and Studies in Italy* (1879), as well as his translation of *The Autobiography of Benvenuto Cellini* (1887) and his *Life of Michelangelo Buonarotti* (1893), Huysmans's *À Rebours* (1884), Pater's *Marius the Epicurean* (1885), Emile Zola's *L'Oeuvre* (1886) and *Rome* (1896), Oscar Wilde's "The Portrait of Mr. W.H." (1889) and *The Picture of Dorian Gray* (1890), Anatole France's *Le Lys rouge* (1894), Gabriele D'Annunzio's *Il fuoco* (1900), Akim Volynskii's *Leonardo da Vinci* (1900), Romain Rolland's *Vie de Michel-Ange* (1906), Edmondo Solmi's *Leonardo, 1452–1519* (1900), Wilhelm Jensen's *Gradiva* (1902), Freud's commentary on the latter (1907), Gide's *L'Immoraliste* (1902), Maurice Barrès' *La Mort de Venise* (1903), Henry James's *The Golden Bowl* (1904), Marie Herzfeld's *Leonardo da Vinci der Denker, Forscher und Poet* (1904), Elisar von Kupffer's *Heiland Kunst: Ein Gespräch in Florenz* [Redemptive Art: A Discourse in Florence] (1907), E. M. Forster's *A Room with a View* (1908), Sigmund Freud's *Leonardo da Vinci: A Memory of His Childhood* (1910), Woldemar von Seidlitz's *Leonardo da Vinci, der Wendepunkt der Renaissance* (1909), and Thomas Mann's *Death in Venice* (1912), among others.

While Winckelmann and Kant invoked the ancients to propose an aesthetics rooted in sublime perfection and in universal judgements of taste, free from subjective desire, by the end of the nineteenth century, the ancients were being invoked to validate the opposite: eroticism in art. Consider the following comment by the artist and art historian Igor' Grabar, writing in an 1899 issue of the journal *World of Art*:

> Erotic art is almost as ancient as any other form of art. Its history goes back to Egypt; it was found in Greece, it was cultivated by the Romans with particular enthusiasm, it was extremely widespread in the Italian Renaissance and in Holland; it sank its roots still deeper during the reigns of Louis XIV and Louis XV in France; and when in the middle of our century Europe had occasion to acquaint itself with a new art—that of the Japanese—it found there an eroticism in a very well-developed state." (qtd. in Granoien 1975, 398)

Conspicuously absent in Grabar's defense of eroticism, however, is any allusion to queer beauty, which is indicative of this historical period, when "new kinds of harsh, procreative, and virile masculinities were appropriated [by artists] in response to what was perceived as the depleted and effeminate influence of women, [...] and what Gaudier-Brzeska called the disgusting softness of modern life" (Tickner 1994, 47). While the two decades preceding World War I are often lumped together in histories of European homosexuality with the last two to three decades of the nineteenth century and/or the two decades following the Great War, for example, "The Homosexual Age, 1870–1940," by Florence Tamagne (2006) or "Secrets and Subcultures, 1900–1940" (Reed 2011), the early twentieth century was not especially welcoming to queer beauty in the visual arts, with the exception perhaps of marginal artistic forms, such as photography (for example, the photographs of Wilhelm von Gloeden), illustrations (for example, the drawings of Aubrey Beardsley), and political satire (see Bershtein 2018, 151–154)—or they were kept private, such as the erotic watercolors of Charles Demuth. Cecile Beurdeley (1994, 206) is one of the few art historians to make a clear distinction: "It was really only after the war of 1914–1918 that a small number of intellectuals found the courage to speak out and proclaim their homosexuality."

The marginalization of queer beauty in the visual arts of the early twentieth century in general, and in the subgenre of erotic art in particular, may have been a reaction to Oscar Wilde's widely publicized prosecution on charges of gross indecency in the 1890s and, later, the Eulenburg affair in Germany, in 1906–7. It may also be linked to the broader crisis of masculinity taking place among the upper classes, "one of a series of crises rising in response to the questions modernity was posing about proper sexual roles and behaviors" (McReynolds 2008, 133), a crisis that was felt acutely in artistic circles (see Tickner 1994). Symptomatic of this crisis was the increasingly visible culture of male physical fitness and body building, which led to the wide circulation of images of nude and seminude males, often wrestling, as in the Russian journals *Gerkules* [Hercules] and *Legkaia atletika*. As Richard Dyer argues, "the naturalness of muscles legitimates male power and domination" by presenting them as a biological fact. At the same time, "within a heterosexist and patriarchal society, it is usually forbidden for the male body to be marked explicitly as the erotic object of another male's gaze" (Smalls 1999, 471).[10] And so, the threat posed by homosexuality to masculinity in crisis results in what Eve Kosofsky Sedgwick theorizes as "homosexual panic," expressed in the often-hysterical renunciation or denial of queer beauty.

Consider Vasilii Rozanov's unequivocal rejection of ancient pederasty: "Hadrian and Antinous would have probably vomited at the disgusting bathhouse attendant Boris and his bathhouse adventures: did the ancients really like *that*?!! (qtd. in Bershtein 2011, 80). This circular logic—that the ancients, who are revered, could not have possibly engaged in activities that are today reviled—was quite common at that time. Vikentii Veresaev, for example, makes a similar appeal to common sense in his introduction to his translations of Sappho: "If the Hellenes had understood Sappho's songs in that way [as hymns to female love], then the profound respect that surrounded her in Iliad would have been completely impossible" ([1915] 2000, 11).

The denial of queer beauty was even more pronounced in art history of the time as evident in a series of books on art and visual culture published by the St. Petersburg-based publisher Sovremennye Problemy, or Contemporary Problems, founded by Nikolai Stolliar in 1907. Sovremennye Problemy published a variety of progressive works related to issues of sex and sexuality, including Russian translations of the following: queer Danish author Herman Bang's scandalous novel *Haabløse Slægter* (Families without Hope, 1880) about a young man who has an affair with a much older woman (*Driakhleiushchii vek*, 1913); Sigmund Freud's *Psychopathology of Everyday Life* (*Psikhopatologiia obydennoi zhizni*, 1910) and his psychological biography of Leonardo da Vinci (*Leonardo da Vinchi*, 1912); and Marc de Villiers's 1910 *Histoire des clubs de femmes et des légions d'amazones, 1793–1848–1871* (*Zhenskie kluby i legiony amazonok*, 1912). Sovremennye Problemy also published original works, such as Vladimir Friche's *The Triumph of Sex and the Fall of Civilization* (*Torzhestvo pola i gibel' tsivilizatsii*, 1908).

A significant number of works published by Sovremennye Problemy were on art and art history, and were issued in high quality, illustrated editions. These include: *Illiustrirovannaia istoriia nravov ot srednikh vekov do nastoiashchego dnia* (Illustrated History of Mores from the Middles Ages to the Present Day, 1912), in three volumes, by Eduard Fuchs; *Illiustrirovannaia istoriia eroticheskogo iskusstva* (Illustrated History of Erotic Art, 1914), also by Fuchs; *Nravstvennost' i beznravstvennost' v iskusstve* (Morality and Immorality in Art,1914) by Dr. Ernst Wilhelm Bredt; *Nagota v iskusstve* (Nudity in Art, 1914) and *Iskusstvo rokoko: Frantsuzskie i nemetskie illiustratory vosemnadtsatogo stoletiia* (Rococo Art: French and German Illustrators of the Eighteenth Century, 1914), by Dr. Wilhelm Hausenstein; and *Filosofiia iskusstva* (The Philosophy of Art, 1911) by Hippolyte Taine.

One of the obvious aims of these publications was to make eroticism respectable. This is evident in the title of doctor used for the German art historians Bredt and Hausenstein, as well as in the high quality of the editions. As described in the blurb for Fuchs's *Illustrated History of Erotic Art*: "A large, luxurious volume published in leather binding with gold lettering" and containing a great number of illustrations, ranging from 70 to 150. The price of ten rubles, which was quite high for the time, along with the luxury binding, might have been intended to shield these works from the charge of pornography.[11] The fact that the Russian publisher is named Contemporary Problems is also interesting, underscoring the distinct relevance of eroticism to early twentieth-century Russian culture. As stated in the blurb for the volume *Nudity in Art*: "Today, when we are again returning to the natural development of the body and when, after a long, one-sided understanding, the visual arts have begun to enter into the very essence of it, this book has profound significance."

Another way to make eroticism respectable at this time was to make it unambiguously heterosexual. We see this is in Taine's *Philosophy of Art*, where he avoids the issue of same sex desire altogether when discussing the ancient Greek culture of sport and its cult of the athletic body, making the point that women, too, exercised in the nude. The heterosexualization of erotic art is also evident in the distinctly different treatment of male and female nudes.[12] A cursory look at the artworks featured in the Silver Age journal *Zolotoe Runo*, for example, reveals an abundance of female nudes and almost no male nudes, a cultural shift in the visual arts foreshadowed perhaps by Édouard Manet's *Déjeuner sur l'herbe* (1862–1863), portraying a totally nude woman sitting in a park between two fully dressed men. When nude or semi-nude men are portrayed in Russian art of the Silver Age, there is a general avoidance of sensuality. Consider, for example, the artist Ivan Mashkov's *Portrait and Self-portrait* (1910). The painting features Mashkov himself sitting beside fellow artist Petr Konchalovskii, both wearing the tiny sports shorts that were popular at the time, indexing the contemporary craze for body building (see Bowlt 1996; McReynolds 2008; Katsuba 2006, 12–31); but they do not look at each other; they both look outward at the viewer. At the same time, their almost naked bodies are surrounded by cultural artifacts of high and low culture, exposing the highly performative nature of masculinity at this time, or what Norman Bryson (1994, 231) refers to as "the masquerade of the masculine." In fact, a program for a bullfight featuring two of the most famous bullfighters of the day, Bambita II (more commonly known as Bambita chico) and Fuentes, leans against the music desk of the piano, where the printed music would normally be. Another contemporary painting, Natalia Goncharova's *Wrestlers* (1908–9), which features two wrestling males, hovers on the edge of abstraction, with the two men crudely shaped, one painted a bright orange and yellow and the other green, a depiction that would appear to mitigate any sensual apprehension of the men.

The fact that the mainstreaming of eroticism in the visual arts at this time was predicated on its heterosexualization is also reflected in the marginalization of male-male couples in works of art history. For example, in Fuchs's magisterial *History of Erotic Art*, the only image that suggests male same-sex desire is one of the half-human Pan and Neptune. The situation in Fuchs's three-volume edition is somewhat more complex in that it devotes a considerable amount of space to phallic cult objects and sculptures of the god Priapus. That being said, except for one image of same-sex lovemaking on a Grecian vase, labelled simply "*Liebespaar*," there are no images of same-sex male couples. This means that queer motifs from Greek mythology and history, such as Zeus and Ganymede, Hercules and Ioläus, Hadrian and Antinous, Apollo and Hyacinth, Apollo and Cyparissus, and Achilles and Patroclus, not to mention "Orpheus (who turned his passionate attentions to young men after spurning women following the death of Eurydice), Narcissus, who rejected Echo in favour of his own, superior beauty, and Salmacis and Hermaphroditus" (Haughton 2015, 73), are not represented. Instead, we see a variety of heterosexual pairings from ancient mythologies: Jupiter and Galatea, Jupiter and Antiope, Zeus and Olympia, Venus and Satyr, Leda and the Swan, Neptune and Nymphe, Caesar and Cleopatra, as well as Adam and Eve. There is, however, a section in volume three that deals explicitly with lesbianism in art. That section is followed by one titled "*Die weibliche Sodomie*," in which sodomy is interpreted as bestiality, presenting images of women engaged in sexual acts with animals. While one image features an orgy among animals of various species, no image in that section presents a male figure, let alone two male figures. In fact, of the many images labelled "*Liebespaar*" across the three volumes, all but one are heterosexual. The idea that nudity is for women is also underscored on the cover of the Russian edition of *Nudity in Art*, which features a heterosexual couple lying on a couch; the fully dressed man is lying behind the woman, undressing her while a cupid off to the side aims an arrow at the woman's heart (see fig. 1). The same image is used for the covers of *Rococo Art* and *Morality and Immorality*.

The marginalization if not complete expulsion of queer beauty from erotic art is also evident in the drawings of Mihály Zichy, a Hungarian artist who occupied the position of court painter under Tsar Alexander II, Tsar Alexander III,

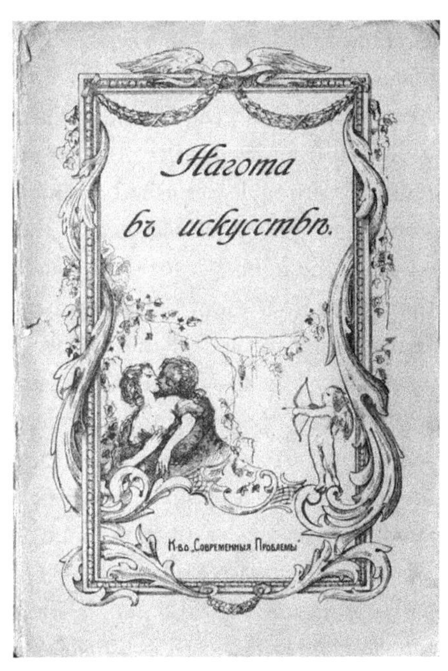

Figure 1. Artist unknown, Cover of the Russian edition of *Nudity in Art* (1914). Private Collection

and Tsar Nicholas II. The majority of Zichy's erotic drawings featured in the posthumously published edition of 1911 were of adult heterosexual couples—three of the drawings in fact feature a male artist fornicating with his female subject, a parodic commentary on post-Kantian aesthetics and the return of desire to aesthetic appreciation. The only allusions to male queer sexuality appear in two drawings of boys engaged in masturbation—one is of two schoolboys on a couch while the other is of three boys apparently in an insane asylum. In both cases, the dumb looks on the boys' faces appear to index the deleterious effects of onanism rather than the allure of queer beauty. And so, to fully appreciate Somov's queer modernism, it is necessary to situate it within the general heterosexualization of art, in general, and of erotic art, in particular, that was taking place in both art and art history at the time he began his artistic career.

Somov's Modernist Take on Queer Beauty

Somov's engagement with queer beauty was informed by two artistic repertoires—eighteenth-century French pornography and sixteenth-century Italian Commedia dell 'Arte. What we know from Somov's diary is that he was deeply interested in eighteenth-century libertinage, in particular, pornographic and scatological works, such as: *Le parnasse libertin, ou recueil de poésies libres* (The Libertine Parnassus, or a collection of free poetry, 1772), Anonymous; *La Prusse galante ou voyage d'un jeune français à Berlin* (The Gallant Prussian or the Voyage of a Young Frenchman in Berlin, 1801), Anonymous; the two-volume anthology *Le Parnasse satyrique* (The Satirical Parnassus, 1864–1881), by le Sieur Théophile; *Mémoires du chevalier de Grammont* (Memoirs of the Chevalier de

Grammont, edition unknown), by Anthony Hamilton (c. 1646–1720); *Thérèse philosophe* (Thérèse the Philosopher, 1748), attributed to Jean-Baptiste de Boyer; *L'enfant du bordel* (The Childe of the Bordello, 1800), attributed to Charles Pigault-Lebrun; *L'art de péter* (The Art of Farting, 1751) by Pierre-Thomas-Nicolas Hurtaut, although published anonymously; *Le nouveau Merdiana, ou manuel scatalogique* (The New Merdiana, or a Scatalogical Manual, 1870), Anonymous, although the publisher listed is: Une Sociéte de Gens sans gêne, or An Association of People without Embarrassment; and *Anti-Justine, ou les délices de l'amour* (Anti-Justine, or the Delights of Love, 1798), by Réstif de la Bretonne.[13]

Somov was also interested in historical works related to prostitution and sexual mores, underscoring his modernist preoccupation with non-reproductive sex. Exemplary in this respect are Pierre Dufour's illustrated *Histoire de la prostitution chez tous les peoples du monde depuis l'antiquité la plus reculée jusqu'á nos jours* (History of Prostitution among All Peoples of the World from the Most Distant Antiquity to Today, 1851-3) and the anonymous *Les dessous de la pudibonderie anglaise expliqués dans les divorces anglaise ou procès en adultère jugés par le banc du roi et al cour ecclésiastique d'Angleterre* (The Underside of English Prudery Explained in English Divorces of Adultery Trials Heard by the King's Bench and by the Ecclesiastical Court of Britain, 1898). Somov also read contemporary works of homosexual pornography, such as *Pédérastie passive, ou mémoires d'un enculé* (Passive Pederasty, or Memoirs of Someone Fucked, 1894–95), comically attributed to P. D. Rast; *Les cousines de la colonelle* (The Cousins of the Colonel, 1880–1882), by H. de Mannoury d'Ectot, although attributed to Madame la Vicomtesse de Coeur-Brûlant; and *La vengeance d'un fouteur* (A Fucker's Revenge, 1895), by A. Richequeue; as well as contemporary gay-themed literature, such as André Gide's *L'Immoraliste* (1902), and works of nineteenth-century literature dealing with themes of homosexuality and androgyny, such as Honoré de Balzac's *Sarrasine* (1830), a work that would be subjected to its most comprehensive analysis by the queer literary critic Roland Barthes in *S/Z* (1970).

I document the depth and breadth of Somov's reading on libertinage and nonreproductive sexuality and sexual pleasure to make the point that his erotic drawings should not be seen as some frivolous pastime, no matter how humorous or camp they may appear. Moreover, few of these works would have been available at the local bookstore and may have required considerable effort to obtain. All this suggests that Somov was pursuing an intellectual-aesthetic project, that of introducing the values of libertinage into Russian culture, and with it, the possibility of queer beauty, at a time when eroticism in the visual arts was being subjected to intense heteronormative regulation. As Pavel Golubev notes regarding Somov's *Livre de la Marquise*, "[it] is not a boudoir booklet meant to excite the emotions but an original manifesto of freedom" (2019, 41). That Somov saw himself as a philosopher of the sexual is suggested in an exchange with Kuzmin from 1906 recorded in Kuzmin's diary: "I asked K[onstantin] A[ndreevich]: 'Will our lives leave anything to posterity?' 'If our horrible diaries are preserved, then, of course we'll leave something; in the next epoch we'll be looked upon as Marquises de Sade'" (Kuzmin 2000, 223). It is, therefore, fitting that a painting by Somov adorns the cover of Alexei Lalo's *Libertinage in Russian Culture and Literature* (2011). At the same time, Somov critically engaged with libertine art by introducing queer content, which in the eighteenth century had been relegated to marginal art forms, such as book illustrations and pornography, into the prestigious form of painting.[14]

Deeply informed by materialist philosophy and inspired by ancient works of eroticism such as Ovid's *Ars Amatoria*, libertine pornography celebrated all forms of nonnormative and nonreproductive sexuality, rejecting sexual difference and placing pleasure above all else. For example, one of the short stories in an eighteenth-century English collection of erotic prose compiled by Thomas Cannon under the title *Ancient and Modern Pederasty* recounts the sexual encounter between a man and a woman; after an intoxicating bout of love making, the young woman reveals herself to be a male, but the lover is nonplussed. As Hal Gladfelder (2007, 33) comments "Amorio is happy to transfer the desire he thinks he feels for 'a Lady' to another object." In many eighteenth-century pornographic works of visual art, such as the illustrations to the works of Marquis de Sade, male and female figures gather in fornicating groups, making it difficult to determine the gender of those participating and suggesting by extension that their specific gender is irrelevant in the pursuit of sexual pleasure. As Kathryn Norberg (1996, 250) explains, "Sade's orgies always involve the switching of roles, with men sodomizing men, women performing cunnilingus on women, one sex on top some of the time, on the bottom the rest of the time, and all positions to be changed after a massive, communal 'discharge.'" Somov appears to capture the moments before such an orgy gets underway in the drawing from *Le Livre de la Marquise*, below (see fig. 2).

The Sadian orgy also implies a certain democratization of sex to the extent that, "in a materialist world, the only reward is bodily pleasure, and women are as entitled to this reward as any other human" (Norberg 1996, 249). Hence the political significance of claiming the right to sexual pleasure for women at a time

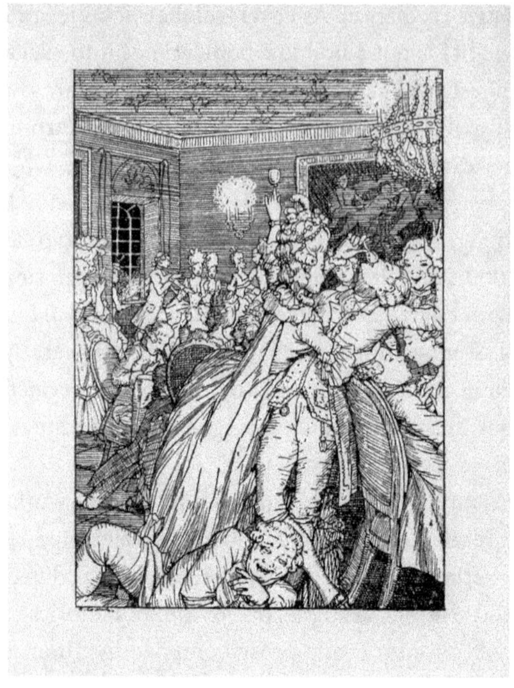

Figure 2. Konstantin Somov, A drawing from *Le Livre de la Marquise* (1918). Private Collection

when they were being literally and symbolically domesticated. Somov would invoke works of libertine art and literature to make a similar claim for queers.

That being said, the rejection of sexual difference—the idea that one can find pleasure with anyone and in any manner—makes the libertine world queer rather than identitarian, or gay. Indeed, there are very few same-sex couples featured in Somov's works. Perhaps the only overt rendering of same-sex desire features a rather poignant drawing of two lesbians, one quite a bit older than the other, both naked but wearing bonnets, with the older one's head lying on the younger woman's breasts (fig. 3).

While acknowledging Somov's erotic drawings to be "extraordinary both for the pre- and post-revolutionary periods," Kasinec and Davis (1999, 3888) note that there remains "much more to be said of Somov and his erotic illustrations." I will attempt to address that enduring gap by analyzing three central figures in Somov's drawings—some of which migrate into his paintings. They are the

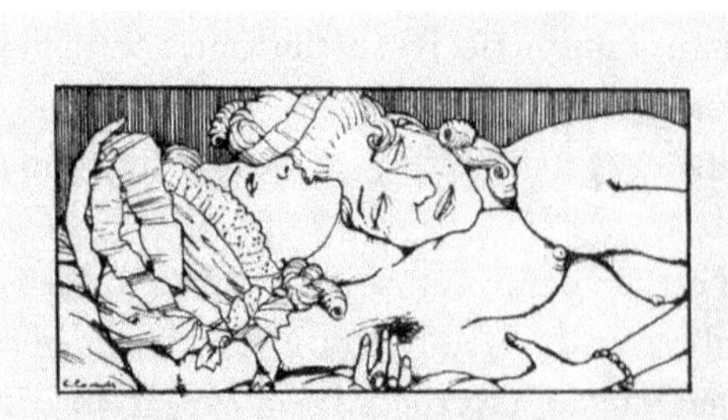

Figure 3. Konstantin Somov, A drawing from *Das Lesebuch der Marquise* (1918). Private Collection

libertine prostitute, Pierrot, and Priapus. Together they outline a libertine world that Somov hoped to conjure, not to copy.

The Libertine Prostitute

Somov's interest in libertine culture inspired one of the central figures in his erotic oeuvre: the libertine prostitute, or what Natalia Maslianinova (2021) refers to more coyly as the "rococo lady." The prostitute, it should be noted, is not merely a central figure in modern pornography; she stands at its very origin. As Lynn Hunt (303) notes, "The word *pornographe* had been used in 1769 by Restif de la Bretonne to refer to writing about prostitution," and the prostitute as first-person narrator was a common organizing principle in early pornographic writing, as reflected in Daniel Defoe's novel *Moll Flanders* (1720s). But during the European Enlightenment, a specific type of prostitute appeared, what Norberg refers to as the "libertine whore." As Norberg (1996, 240) explains:

> The libertine prostitute doesn't adhere to the new notion of womanhood. She is not modest, dependent, loving or maternal; she does not believe in romantic love and refuses to remain within the private, family sphere. Rather she is a public woman who, like Margot, is independent both financially and morally, intelligent, rational and responsible. Her reward is to end her days in comfortable retirement, on a country estate where she can lead a peaceful and measured existence. To the "virtuous courtesan" of Restif, Rousseau and Nougaret, she leaves modesty, dependency and victimization.

Somov's coding of his eighteenth-century heroines as libertine prostitutes in *Das Lesebuch der Marquise* and *Le livre de la Marquise* is accomplished in several ways. First, titling his erotic masterpiece *Le livre de la Marquise* (The Book of the Marquise) associates the marquise with pornography both as an author/compiler and as a reader. The title page underscores this connection by displaying a female figure in full eighteenth-century formal attire with the title written across the front of her dress, basically over her crotch. The drawing mentioned above of an older woman with her head on a younger woman's breasts may also code the women as libertine prostitutes, insofar as they were often associated with *tribadism*, or lesbianism (see Norberg 1996, 239). Somov's female figures are more generally coded as libertine prostitutes through their utter lack of modesty and shame; they are often pictured with a bare breast or breasts, typically sporting a beauty mark, and engaged in amorous relations without any sense of reserve or embarrassment. That being said, his female figures are almost never fully nude for, as Diderot wrote, "it is not a woman in the nude that is indecent, but a woman whose skirts are tucked up" (quoted in Frappier-Mazur 1996, 203)—directly referenced in Somov's drawing below (fig. 4).

In fact, it is quite typical for Somov's female figures to be dressed in formal eighteenth-century attire but with a breast exposed. One drawing features a woman sprawled out on a divan pleasuring herself while fully clothed. The male counterpart to this would be the silhouette of a shapely youth, naked except for a wig, the tip of his penis outlined between his legs. There is no nakedness in the libertine world, no innocent world before sexuality; the body and sexual desire are always already culturally mediated.

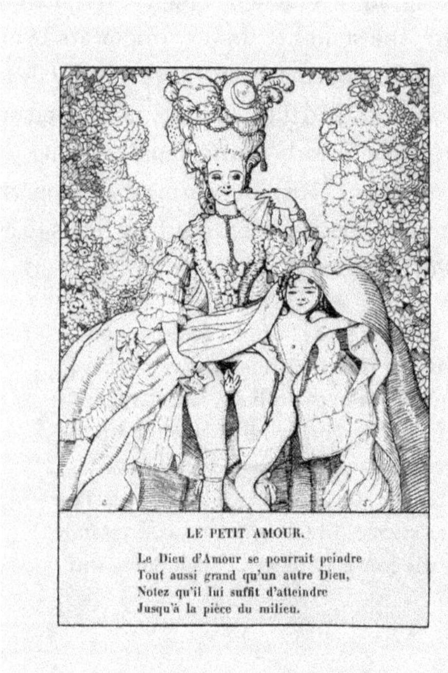

FIGURE 4. Konstantin Somov, A drawing from *Le Livre de la Marquise* (1918). Private Collection

Pierrot

The other great source of Somov's inspiration in creating his queer libertine world was the Commedia dell 'Arte.[15] We know from his diary that Somov read almost all the works of Carlo Gozzi, including Gozzi's autobiography, as well as works about Gozzi. Somov's interest in Commedia dell 'Arte appears to have inspired the other central figure in his queer world of art: Pierrot. While in traditional Commedia dell 'Arte, Pierrot is heterosexual insofar as he is hopelessly in love with Columbine, he is unable to capture and hold her affection, invariably losing out to Harlequin, who is associated with heterosexual promiscuity. As Olga Partan (2017, 226) comments:

> Harlequin is the most enigmatic and extravagant character of the commedia. His mask evolved over several centuries from being that of a servant and simpleton to that of an elegant lover and an emblem of artistic imagination and eroticism for modernist art. In older documents, Harlequin is sometime shown wearing a phallus, but in later incarnations his sword is used to symbolize his sexuality.

In opposition to the hyper-masculine, oversexed Harlequin, Pierrot is often portrayed as fey and sad.

Over the course of the nineteenth century, the gentle, loveless Pierrot was increasingly queered, portrayed not simply as fey but as effeminate and often homosexual. For example, in his poem of 1868, "Pierrot gamin," the French poet Paul Verlaine, lover of Arthur Rimbaud, portrays Pierrot "as a youthful androgyne whose appetites and tendencies are untempered. He is delicate, effeminate and acts beyond conventional morality" (Norman 2021, 63). Indeed, he is described not only as an éphèbe, but also as a prostitute: "Créature toujours prête // À soûler chaque appétit" (A creature (fem.) ready to whet every appetite). In 1896, Aubrey Beardsley portrayed an effeminate Pierrot serenading a man, while in 1900 a series of postcards was issued in France titled *Pierrot et Columbine,* in which Pierrot is portrayed by a woman and Columbine by a man in drag (see Norman 2021). In 1912, Arnold Schoenberg, in his "Pierrot Lunaire," associated Pierrot with the moon not long after the Russian writer and philosopher Vasilii Rozanov had described homosexuals as "people of the moonlight" (1907), coopting the traditional association of the moon with women.[16]

Somov codes his Pierrot as queer mainly through his effeminate gestures and poses, so it is interesting that Somov typically pairs Pierrot, not Harlequin, with a woman. That woman, however, is typically the libertine prostitute. It is clear in their "amorous" encounters and in many other amorous pairings in Somov's erotic drawings and paintings that these sexual relations have little in common with bourgeois heteronormative romance. For one thing, Somov's amorous pairs almost never look at one another, suggesting that they are not so much in love with their partner, but rather getting off sexually at the same time and place and, perhaps, anticipating a voyeur. This is most clearly represented in the 1910 painting *The Lady and Pierrot* and in subsequent erotic drawings on the theme, in which Pierrot is looking upward, flinging his arms in the air while the lady kisses him; in the erotic drawing, she appears to be preparing to masturbate his erect penis (see fig. 5).

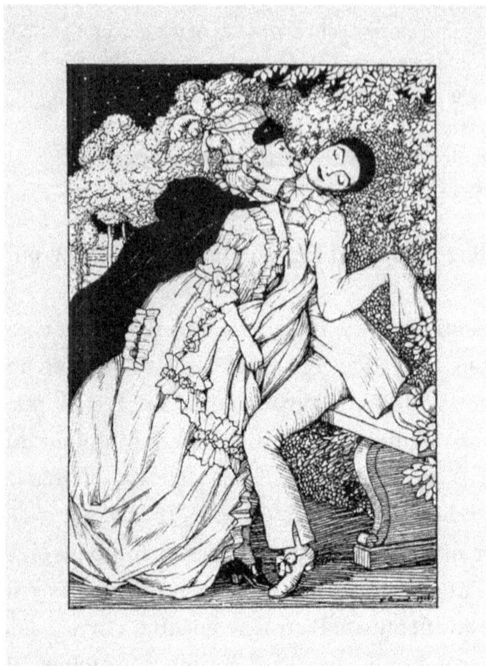

FIGURE 5. Konstantin Somov, A drawing from *Le Livre de la Marquise* (1918). Private Collection

Another queer pairing is featured on the frontispiece of *Le livre,* which portrays a male and female figure standing on either side of the drawing; the bare-breasted woman is coded as a libertine prostitute while the male figure is potentially queer insofar as the two figures do not look at each other but at the viewer, and the male figure has one hand over his robe and the other under his robe, resting in the area of his crotch. The libertine prostitute could be said to code the work as pornographic, given her central role in the genre, but so too does the male figure who, with his left hand under his robe and with a sly smile on his face, may be referencing Jean-

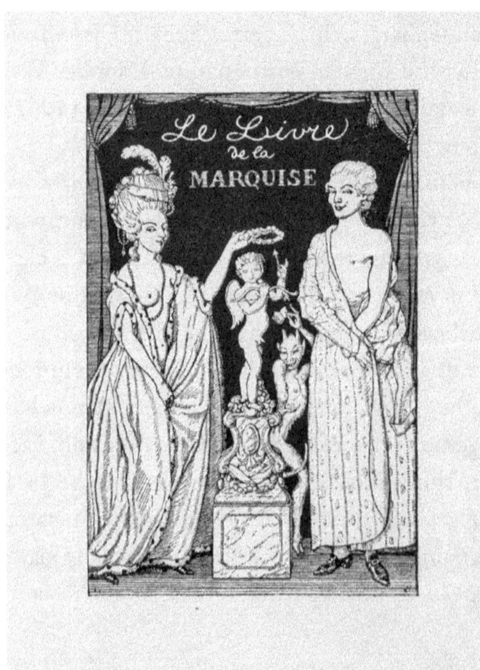

FIGURE 6. Konstantin Somov, Frontispiece to Somov's *Le Livre de la Marquise* (1918). Private Collection

Jacques Rousseau's euphemism for pornographic literature as "literature read with one hand." In addition, by dressing the male figure in a wig and a robe, Somov minimizes the gender differences between the two (see fig. 6).

That such literature may also be *written* with one hand is brought home in the frontispiece to one of the classic works of eighteenth-century pornography, *Histoire de Dom B---, portier des Chartreux* (Frankfurt edition, 1748), which features the author at his desk, fully clothed and wearing a wig. He holds a pen in his right hand and his erect penis in his left; the queer content of the book is suggested by the figure of Pan, also with a fully erect penis, who is leaning over the gentleman's shoulder, reading.

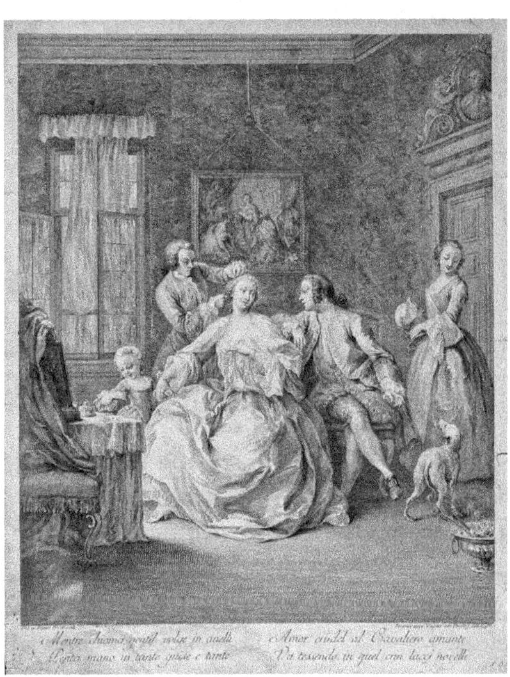

FIGURE 7. Charles Joseph Flipart, *A rilevar in poche note accolto...* (1748-1750). Wellcome Library, London

One of the campier depictions of such queer parings appears in Somov's drawing *La Toilette* (1910). Set in the eighteenth century, it features two men helping a young woman get dressed. While she gazes at herself in the mirror and her mother (or older lover?) looks on, one young man stands behind her, styling her hair, while the other sits and reaches his arm under hers to pet the dog lying on her lap. Her bare breasts code her as a libertine prostitute. The drawing underscores the queer allure of the eighteenth century where upper-class men and women both favored elaborate costumes and always wore wigs—in contradistinction to the bourgeois nineteenth century, when men's and women's clothing became sharply differentiated, with elite masculine dress losing much of its brilliance. When compared with a similar drawing by Charles Joseph Flipart from the eighteenth century, *A rilevar in poche note accolto . . .* (1748–1750), Somov's

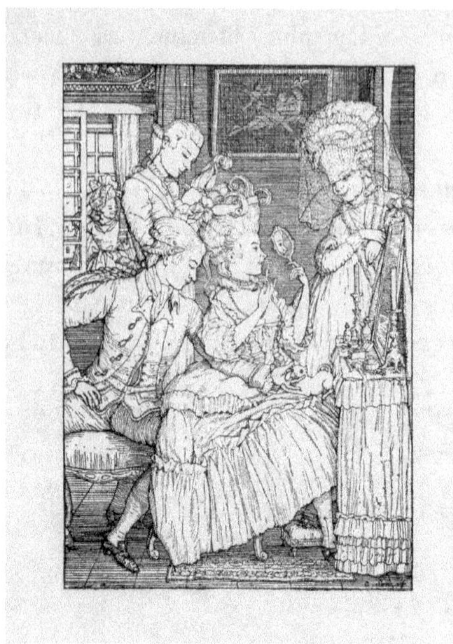

FIGURE 8. Konstantin Somov, A drawing from *Le Livre de la Marquise* (1918). Private Collection

distinctly camp sensibility becomes more evident (see figs. 7 and 8).

The queer union of the libertine prostitute and Pierrot was not restricted to Somov's overtly erotic drawings; it can be traced in other works as well, testifying to the centrality of this motif in his queer modernism. Consider, for example, an ex libris created by Somov for his friend and fellow artist Alexandre Benois (see fig. 9).

It features several material objects ostensibly indexing leisure class wealth and comfort, and specifically feminine refinement: pearls, an ornate jewelry box, a fan, tea roses, and a porcelain figurine of a woman in eighteenth-century dress. On the left-hand side of the ex libris, there appears to be a small imitation of Michelangelo's *David*, although the "real" David raises his left arm, not the right. In addition, Somov's *David* faces away from the viewer, showing his beautifully shaped backside. The small figurine of the woman holding a fan, situated on the far right of the ex libris, appears to be gazing in his direction, imbuing the drawing with a libidinal energy that juxtaposes nakedness

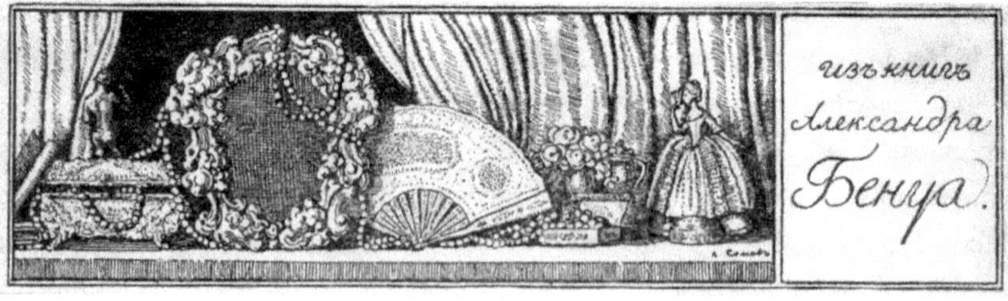

FIGURE 9. Konstantin Somov, Ex libris for Alexandre Benois (1902). University of Helsinki

with elaborate dress, high culture with the lower bodily strata, and so on. Moreover, the direction of her gaze invites the (queer) viewer to check out David's ass.[17] This citation of David, situated in a woman's boudoir, might also index the distinct appropriation of queer beauty that was taking place within the emerging gay subculture of the time, as evident in an entry from Mikhail Kuzmin's diary of 1906, in which he recounts the décor in the apartment of a gay acquaintance: "A small room; on the sill of the window opening onto the garden, there were flowers: tea roses, begonias, geraniums; over the commode there were photos: [my host] as a child, friends, Michelangelo's *David* . . ." (Kuzmin, *Diary*, September 6, 1906). The placement of the reproduction above the owner's commode achieves a similar juxtaposition of high and low, a characteristic feature of camp.

Priapus

Perhaps nothing symbolizes the libertine world's rejection of sexual difference in favor of polymorphous sexual pleasure than the sexual prosthesis, or dildo, whose queer origins lie in the myth of Priapus. As Whitney Davis (2020, 68) explains: "The specifically homosexual origin of the myth of Priapus was well known. Dionysius made the fig wood phallus (the prototype of the phallic herm commonly displayed at doors, in gardens, and other situations) as a substitute for the penis of his deceased boyfriend." Although a Greek god, Priapus became very popular in Roman art, where he was typically pictured with an enormous, permanent erection. As Charles Hupperts (2006, 49) notes, "Images of the Roman god Priapus were set up in entrances to homes and gardens to ensure fertility and prosperity and to protect property (the erect phallus was endowed with apotropaic qualities). Some images were accompanied by messages that threatened penetration of trespassers, male or female." There is also evidence that the image of an erect phallus was used in ancient Rome as a sign for a brothel, and "some of these signs bore the inscription *Hic habitate Felicitas* [Here dwells felicity]" (Beurdeley 1971). As a work of art meant to bring fertility to the home, Priapus precedes the act of coupling; he is neither the product nor the representation of that act, which, as the sign for the bordello suggests, need not result in procreation at all. Indeed, rendered alone, the phallus is a sexual prosthesis, capable of providing only pleasure, not offspring. Priapus was also associated with gardens, one of Somov's most frequently depicted locations. Somov's gardens, however, are heavily manicured French gardens, which associates them with artifice and pleasure, rather than reproductive fecundity.

In the early twentieth century, phallic worship represented a point of common interest between an emerging gay subculture and the self-conscious masculinity of heterosexual modernists, as hilariously represented in Aleksei Remizov's *Chto est' tabac: Gonosieva povest'* (1908), illustrated by Somov, featuring an ink drawing of the penis of Grigorii Potemkin, the legendary lover of Catherine the Great, on a silver tray. The penis sports a beauty mark.[18] The purported author of the work is a fictional St. Gonosii, whose name is formed from the root *gonos*, meaning 'seed,' from which the word gonorrhea and gonococcus derive. Remizov recounts the origin of the drawing of Potemkin's penis in his later work *O proizkhozhdenii moei knigi o tabake*.

There he describes a gathering at Somov's home of St. Petersburg writers and artists, including many members of the World of Art group and their friends, straight and gay (Benois, Dobuzhinski, Somov, Lanceray, Rozanov, Diaghilev, Nurok, Nouvel, and Kuzmin), to view a drawing of Count Grigorii Potemkin's phallus, which Somov supposedly borrowed from a private collection at the Hermitage Museum, where his father was the director. A beauty mark, which had been affixed to the drawing of the phallus, breaks off during the viewing, sending the guests crawling around on the floor to find it. It is supposedly at this point that Rozanov proposes the idea for the book to Remizov: "And what if you were to write this disavowed tale, and Somov were to illustrate it, in a visual way? That would be something, Vasilii said. Vasilii: Write it" (qtd. in Nivat 1989, 37). Remizov then reveals that Potemkin had a descendent who was a university student and that Somov brought him to his home, where "they played for three hours with his potemkinian talent" (ibid.). What had begun as a representation has by the end of the story turned into a real phallus, although referenced with a playful euphemism, thus replacing a patrilineal genealogy of biological inheritance with a queer genealogy of erotic pleasure.[19]

Dildos, in fact, abound in Somov's erotic drawings. One

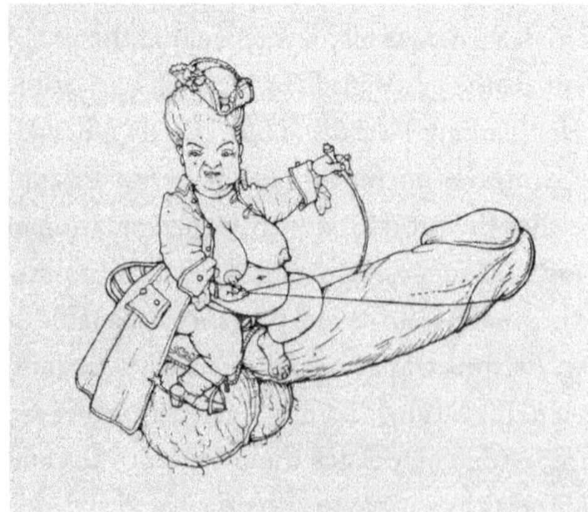

Figure 10. Konstantin Somov, A drawing from *Le Livre de la Marquise* (1918). Private Collection

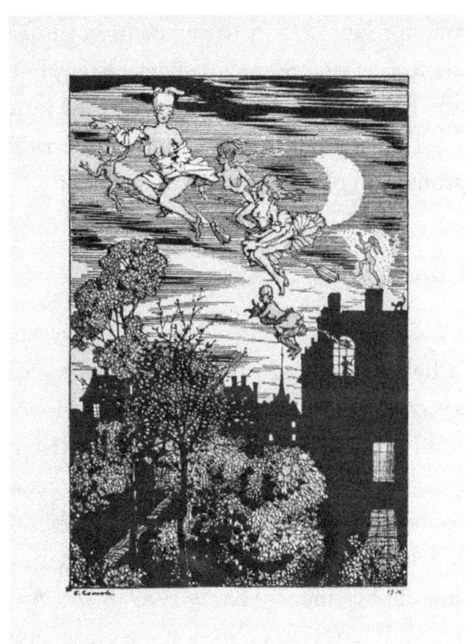

FIGURE 11. Konstantin Somov, A drawing from *Le Livre de la Marquise* (1918). Private Collection

features an old woman skillfully riding a phallus, while another presents a group of half-naked witches flying on brooms (see figs. 10 and 11).

A related image features a young woman, half-naked and recumbent in her bed, masturbating the penis of a man hidden behind the bed curtain.

In the world of libertine sexuality, anal penetration is analogous to the dildo for, as Norberg (1996, 250) explains, "Sade's *roués* all adore anal intercourse regardless of their gender, it being the form of copulation that comes closest to obliterating sexual difference by allowing either male or female to play the passive of the active role, since Sade's women are always armed with dildos." So, it is not surprising to find Somov's Marquise being entered from behind by a lustful monkey-like creature (see fig. 13), who resembles the devil as depicted in art and

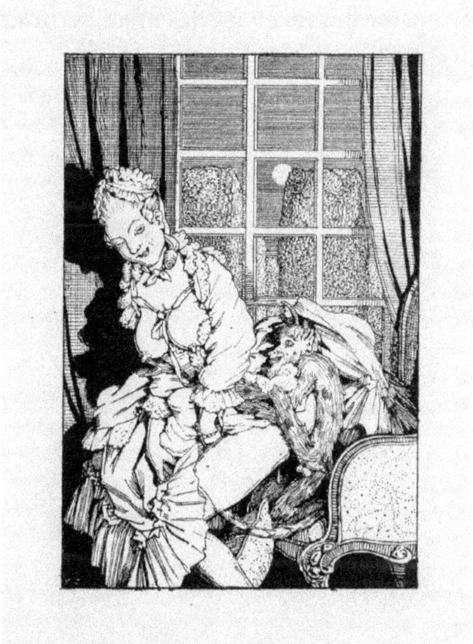

FIGURE 12. Konstantin Somov, A drawing from *Le Livre de la Marquise* (1918). Private Collection

folklore. Notice, too, the manicured garden framed by the window. And so, it is interesting that Somov depicts a hairy, horned devil figure grinning in anticipation behind an especially fey-looking Pierrot in his 1913 *Sketch for the Curtain.*

Dildos, anal sex, and old women riding penises are all connected in their promotion of nonreproductive sexuality.[20]

Conclusion

As a reaction to the reassertion of sexual difference and the promotion of "a heightened and aggressively heterosexual masculinity" (Tickner 1994, 55), which characterized modernism throughout much of the Global North and beyond in the late nineteenth and early twentieth century, Somov's queer indifference cannot be considered merely an act of nostalgia. Moreover, in the specific context of Russian art, Somov's contribution was especially significant and innovative given that "Russian culture lacked a link [to connect high and low art], the link of libertinage" (Nivat 1989, 30).[21] And so, his contemporary Erikh Gollerbach's description of Somov's work as "arch-bourgeois" seems off the mark, unless we interpret it to mean *archly* bourgeois, as Somov's queer world, anchored by the campy pairing of the libertine whore with the fey Pierrot, heralds an alternative modernity to the heterosexual, masculinist culture that would come to define the dominant modes of modernism in art and art history for most of the twentieth century.

Notes

1 Of course, Perl is not alone in arguing for an expanded definition of modernism and to see it as a contested concept. See, for example, *Modernism in Dispute. Art since the Forties*, edited by P. Wood et al. (1993). Russian art historians, too, are engaged in a rethinking of modernism, as evident in a recent exhibition at the Moscow Museum of Modern Art: "Modernism without a Manifesto, 1920-1950," translated as "Implicit Modernism." In the exhibition catalogue, Nadezhda Plungian argues that the concept of modernism was very narrowly defined in official Soviet culture due to its association with "formalism." Understood as the "anti-art" of the Western world, modernism could not be applied to Soviet artists, creating a very distorted view of Soviet art and a very restrictive understanding of modernism (Plungian 2017, 12).

2 Part of the rehabilitation of Somov in the Soviet Union involved the manipulation of excerpts from his diaries to make him appear "pro-Soviet" (Golubev 2017, 42).

3 This new edition of Somov's letters is remarkable in the Russian context, given that it was produced, in Golubev's words, "without a single excision" (2017, 21).

4 "Somov byl ne tol'ko sozdatelem svoeobraznogo retrospektivnogo zhanra, ne tol'ko "passeistom," rasskazyvaiushchim o zhizni "ushedshikh epokh," on byl i vdumchivym peizazhistom, umevshim peredat' tikhoe ocharovanie russkoi prirody, i ser'eznym portretistom, ostavivshim unikal'nuiu seriiu graficheskikh portretov predstavitelei russkoi intelligentsii svoego vremeni, priobretshuiu nyne kharakter istoricheskogo dokumenta" (Zhuravleva 1980, 5).

5 Somov's queer contemporary, the art critic Sergei Ernst, offered a similarly laudatory review of Somov's work in his 1918 monograph *K. A. Somov*: "In the fast-changing and uncertain world of contemporary Russian art, the work of Konstantin Somov lays down a unique and firm line—the burning soul of the artist, the charm and strength of his mastery bear true witness to the fact that our time too knows art that is ruled not only by a fleeting charm but also by the firmness of a tradition, the 'maturity' of its technique, the magic of its visions, which can withstand the test of time. This valuable and highly necessary assurance is contained in the magic garden of Somov's genius, which plays so lightly and gently with the rarest and most precious colors" (1918, 3).

6 As Malmstad (2000, 88) writes in regard to Kuzmin's diary: "The Diary provides no evidence whatsoever of moral or ethical qualms on Kuzmin's part about his sexual orientation. Quite the contrary, it sounds as 'utopian' in this regard as *Wings*."

7 As Malmstad (2000, 89) remarked about Filosofov: "The cousin and onetime lover of Diaghilev, he had helped found the 'World of Art,' but, unable to accept his own homosexuality and preoccupied by religious questions, he moved away from the whole movement and the people associated with it."

8 For a detailed comparison of the three editions, see Kasinec and Davis 1999.

9 As Tickner (1994, 46-47) points out, "The *kunstlerroman* or artist-novel reached the zenith of its popularity between about 1885 and the First World War, and large numbers of fictional and semi-documentary accounts of the artist and artistic life were avidly consumed by an expanding public. In the same period, a concern with sexuality and sexual identity emerged as the mark of the modern in art, literature, and social behavior."

10 It is interesting in this regard that D'Albert, the hero of Balzac's story "Sarrasine" (1830), is a sculptor who "falls in love with someone he believes to be a woman, but who turns out to be a highly feminized costrato" (1996, 108). Later nineteenth-century studies of sexual perversion include testimony from "pederasts" acknowledging their physical attraction not only to living males but to male nudes in works of art. As the French psychiatrist Henri Legrand du Saulle recounts: "He felt himself, on the contrary, invincibly attracted to men, to images, paintings, and statues representing male nudes" (quoted in Rosario 1996, 153).

11 By this time, the tradition of publishing pornography in expensive editions to keep them out of the reach of the "impressionable" working classes was firmly established and may explain why pornographic works were often referred to as "fancy books" (Berkowitz 2021, 136, 150).

12 Abigail Solomon-Godeau (1997, 7-8) associates the shift from male to female nudes with a crisis in masculinity that was occurring in France in the first part of the nineteenth century, "during which the beautiful male body ceded its dominant position in elite visual culture to the degree that the category 'nude' became routinely associated with femininity. It also refers to the transition from earlier courtly models of masculinity to recognizably modern, bourgeois ones, a transition fostered by the expulsion of femininity (and women) from increasingly masculinized cultural and political domains." This transition was more or less complete by the early twentieth century, and this was true across Europe. As Tickner (1996, 60) notes in regard to the "Post-Impressionist" exhibition held in London in 1910, "in a show containing a large number of landscapes and still lifes, between a quarter and a third of the paintings were paintings of women and almost all the sculptures were of women."

13 Libertinage describes not simply the lifestyle but the worldview of the libertine, as described by Marilyn Yalom (2013, 6): "Originally, in the seventeenth century, a libertine was something other than a ladies' man given to serial affairs. He was a person who refused the precepts and morality of the Church and claimed, instead, the right to free inquiry, as well as to sexual practices outside the norms of society. Eighteenth-century libertines were less interested in religious debate and more concerned with sexual freedom. In France as in England, libertine writers combined subversive ideas with erotic content to satisfy the demands of a large reading public increasingly addicted to titillating novels."

14 As Whitney Davis (1994, 188) notes, "Considering, however, that a flourishing subculture built around male-male sexual relations imagined and identified itself in many ways, one is not surprised to find that inter-male sodomitical relations could be depicted in quasi-pornographic images produced for specialized circulation or covert viewing. For example, in one of the two separate editions of Sade's *Justine* published by Girouard in Paris in 1791, certain copies—evidently they were made to interest a well-defined readership—contain illustrations of baroque sodomitical orgies populated by a large, almost entirely male cast of characters."

15 For a comprehensive overview of the Commedia dell'Arte in Russian culture, see Partan (2017).

16 That being said, there was precedence for such representations already in the eighteenth century, as evident in a series of engravings by the Dutch artist Gerard Joseph Xavery. Titled *The Marvelous Malady of Arlequin* (1748), the prints portray Harlequin and Pierrot as a married couple: "One scene captures Pierrot doing the laundry while Arlequin tends to the baby, while another depicts Arlequin dressing the child while Pierrot looks on with a sense of parental pride" (Norman 2021, 64).

17 The suggestion that Somov is inviting a queer gaze by portraying David from the back is supported by Patricia Lee Rubin's historical analysis of the shifting semiotics of the ass in western art. Rubin (2018, 8–9) traces the "transformation of the base bottom to high art, which constituted the beginning of a double life for masculine figures shown from behind. While continuing to have pejorative possibilities, rear views of well-formed men could also be objects of admiration and were used to characterize the heroic, the stalwart, and the brave. They also became surfaces for projecting desire."

18 Here I would disagree with Pavel Golubev's analysis of the figure: "It is especially interesting to look at a drawing by Somov for the first edition of [Kuzmin's] 'Adventures of Aimé Leboeuf' (1906). It is a black ink silhouette of a naked man in a wig in the style of the 18th century. The man is devoid of clothes not due to the erotic nature of the story: his figure can be interpreted as a symbol exposing the general nature of borrowing in Kuzmin and Somov—the representation of private, intimate life in the objective world of a stylized epoch" (Golubev 2017, 55). The wig, I would argue, represents Somov's libertine rejection of the romantic distinctions between public/private or nature/culture, although I would not disavow the erotic power of Somov's drawings, as Golubev appears to do.

19 The influence of Aubrey Beardsley is evident in Somov's erotic drawings. See, for example, Beardsley's illustrations for an edition of Aristophanes' comedy *Lysistrata*. Somov edited a collection of Beardsley's drawings that was published in 1906 by the St. Petersburg publisher Shipovnik. The relevance of Beardsley to Russian culture of that time is further evidenced by Nikolai Evreinov's study of Beardsley's work, which was published in St. Petersburg in 1910.

20 Given the fact that the slang used to refer to homosexuals by homosexuals at that time was *tetka* or *tante*, meaning 'auntie,' these images of older lustful women may have also served, among the initiated, as stand-ins for homosexual men.

21 That being said, the visual realm at that time was less receptive to open depictions of same-sex desire than the literary, which perhaps explains why Somov launched his series of male nudes only in the 1930s while living in Paris.

References

Bal, Mieke. 2004. "Dispersing the Gaze: Focalization." In *Looking in: The Art of Viewing*, 41–63. London: Routledge.

Berdiaev, Nikolai. 1985. Sobranie sochinenii, edited by Nikolai Struve. Vol. 2. Paris: YMCA Press.

Berkowitz, Erik. 2021. *Dangerous Ideas. A Brief History of Censorship in the West, from the Ancients to Fake News.* Boston: Beacon Press.

Bershtein, Evgenii. 2011. "An Englishman in the Russian Bathhouse: Mikhail Kuzmin's Wings and the Russian Tradition of Homoerotic Writing." In *The Many Facets of Mikhail Kuzmin: A Miscellany*, edited by Lada Panova and Sarah Pratt, 75–87. Bloomington, IN: Slavica.

———. 2018. "The Discourse of Sexual Pathology in Russian Modernism." In *Reframing Russian Modernism*, edited by Irina Shevelenko, 143–171. Madison: University of Wisconsin Press.

Beurdeley, Cecile. 1997. *L'Amour blue.* Translated by Michael Taylor. Fribourg: Evergreen.

Bowlt, John E. 1979. *The Silver Age: Russian Art of the Early Twentieth Century and the "World of Art" Group.* Newtonville, MA: Oriental Research Partners.

———. 1996. "Body Beautiful: The Artistic Search for the Perfect Physique." In *Laboratory of Dreams: The Russian Avant-garde and Cultural Experiment*, edited by John E. Bowlt and Olga Matich, 37–58. Stanford: Stanford University Press.

———. 2020. *Moscow and St. Petersburg, 1900–1920: Art, Life and Culture.* New York: Vendome.

Bryson, Norman. 1994. "Géricault and 'Masculinity.'" In *Visual Culture: Images and Interpretations*, edited by Norman Bryson, Michael Ann Holly, and Keith Moxey, 228–259. Hanover: Wesleyan University Press.

Davis, Whitney. 1994. "The Renunciation of Reaction in Girodet's *Sleep of Endymion*." In *Visual Culture: Images and Interpretations*, edited by Norman Bryson, Michael Ann Holly, and Keith Moxey, 168–201. Hanover and London: Wesleyan University Press.

———. 2010. *Queer Beauty: Sexuality and Aesthetics from Winckelmann to Freud and Beyond.* New York: Columbia University Press.

Dyer, Richard. 1992. "Don't Look Now: The Male Pin-up." In *The Sexual Subject: A Screen Reader in Sexuality*, edited by Mandy Merck, 265–276. London: Routledge.

Efros, Abram. [1930]. *Profili: Ocherki o russkikh khudozhnikakh.* St. Petersburg: Azbuka-klassika.

Ernst, Sergei. 1918. *K. A. Somov.* St. Peterburg: Obshchina Sv. Evgeniia.

Frappier-Mazur, Lucienne. 1996. "Truth and the Obscene Word in Eighteenth-Century French Pornography." In *The Invention of Pornography: Obscenity and the Origins of Modernity, 1500–1800*, edited by Lynn Hunt, 203–221. New York: Zone Books.

Gladfelder, Hal. 2007a. "In Search of Lost Texts: Thomas Cannon's *Ancient and Modern Pederasty Investigated and Exemplify'd*." *Eighteenth-Century Life* 31(1): 22–38.

Golubev, Pavel. 2017. "Predislovie." In *Konstantin Somov. Dnevnik. 1917–1923.* Moscow: Dmitrii Sechin.

———. 2019. *Konstantin Somov: Dama, snimaiushchaia masku*. Moscow: Novoe Literaturnoe Obozrenie.

Granoien, Neil. 1975. "*Wings* and the World of Art." *Russian Literature Tri-Quarterly* 11: 393–405.

Harer, Klaus. 1989. "Kryl'ja M.A. Kuzmina kak primer 'prekrasnoj legosti.'" In *Amour et érotisme dans la littérature russe du XXe siècle: Actes du colloque de juin 1989, organisé par l'Université de Lausanne, avec le concours de la Fondations du 450ème anniversaire,* edited by Leonid Heller, 45–56. Bern: Peter Lang.

Haughton, Ann. 2015. "Myths of Male Same-Sex Love in the Art of the Italian Renaissance." *Exchanges: The Warwick Research Journal* 3(1): 65–95. http://exchanges.warwick.ac.uk/index.php/exchanges/article/view/80

Hausenstein, Wilhelm. 1914. Nagota v iskusstve. Translated by Avgusta Gretman. Moscow: Sovremennye Problemy.

Hupperts, Charles. 2006. "Homosexuality in Greece and Rome." In *Gay Life and Culture: A World History,* edited by Robert Aldrich, 29–55. New York: Universe Publishing.

Kasinec, Edward and Robert H. Davis, Jr. 1999. "A Note on Konstantin Somov's Erotic Book Illustration." In *Eros i pornographiia v russkoi literature/Eros and Pornography in Russian Culture,* edited by Marcus Levitt and A. L. Toporkov, 338–395. Moscow: Ladomir.

Katsuba, Valery. 2006. *Phiscultura*. Madrid: Circulo de Bellas Artes.

Kuzmin, Mikhail. [1916] 1979. "K. A. Somov." In *Konstantin Andreevich Somov. Pis'ma. Dnevniki. Suzhdeniia sovremennikov,* edited by Iu. N. Podkopaeva and A. N. Sveshnikova, 470–473. Moscow: Iskusstvo.

———. [1920]1972. *Zanaveshannye kartinki.* Facsimile edition. Ann Arbor: Ardis.

———. 1999. *Kryl'ia*. In Mikhail Kuzmin. Plavaiushchie puteshestvuiushchie: Romany, povesti, rasskaz, edited by Nikolay Bogomolov, 45–106. Moscow: Sovpadenie.

———. 2000. *M. Kuzmin. Dnevnik 1905–1907,* edited and annotated by Nikolai Bogomolov and Sergei Shumikhin. St. Petersburg: Izd. Ivana Limbakha.

———. "Declaration of Emotionalism." In *Mikhail Kuzmin: Selected Writings,* edited by Michael A. Green, and Stanislav A Shvabrin, 162–163. Cranbury: Associated University Presses.

Malmstad, John. 2000. "Bathhouses, Hustlers, and a Sex Club: The Reception of Mikhail Kuzmin's Wings." *Journal of the History of Sexuality* 9(1–2): 85–104.

Maslianinova, Natalia. 2021. "'Something corrupt': The Queer Sensibility of Aubrey Beardsley and Konstantin Somov." AB 2020: The Aubrey Beardsley Society. https://ab2020.org/something-corrupt/.

McReynolds, Louise. 2008. "Visualizing Masculinity: The Male Sex That Was Not One in Fin-de-Siècle Russia." In *Picturing Russia: Explorations in Visual Culture,* edited by Valerie A. Kivelson, and Joan Neuberger, 133–138. New Haven: Yale University Press.

Merezhkovskii, Dmitrii. 1906. *Voskresshie bogi: Leonardo da Vinchi.* 3rd edition. St. Petersburg: M. V. Pirozhkov.
Naiman, Eric. 1997. *Sex in Public: The Incarnation of Early Soviet Ideology.* Princeton: Princeton University Press.
Nivat, Georges. 1989. "Le puritisme russe, pouquoi?" In *Amour et érotisme dans la littérature russe du XXe siècle: Actes du colloque de juin 1989, organisé par l'Université de Lausanne, avec le concours de la Fondations du 450ème anniversaire,* edited by Leonid Heller, 91–100. Bern: Peter Lang.
Norberg, Kathryn. 1996. "The Libertine Whore: Prostitution in French Pornography from Margot to Juliette." In *The Invention of Pornography: Obsenity and the Origins of Modernity, 1500–1800,* edited by Lynn Hunt, 225–252. New York: Zone Books.
Norman, Ana. 2021. *Miming Modernity: Representations of Pierrot in Fin-de-Siècle France.* Unpublished Master's Thesis, Southern Methodist University.
Panova, Lada. 2011. "A Literary Lion Hidden in Plain View: Clues to Mikhail Kuzmin's 'Aunt Sonya's Sofa' and 'Lecture by Dostoevsky.'" In *The Many Facets of Mikhail Kuzmin: A Miscellany,* edited by Lada Panova and Sarah Pratt, 89–139. Bloomington, IN: Slavica.
Partan, Olga. 2017. *Vagabonding Masks: The Italian Commedia dell 'Arte in the Russian Artistic Imagination.* Boston: Academic Studies Press.
Perl, Jed. 2017. "A Modernist Return to Reality." *New York Review of Books* LXIV 13 (August 17): 10–14.
Plungian, Nadezhda. 2017. "Sovetskii modernizm: Dovoennyi period." In *Modernism without a Manifesto, 1920–1950,* Vol. II, edited by Ivan Babichev, 9–22. Moscow: Moscow Museum of Modern Art.
Reed, Christopher. 2011. *Art and Homosexuality: A History of Ideas.* Oxford: Oxford University Press.
Rosario, Vernon A. 1996. "Pointy Penises, Fashion Crimes, and Hysterical Mollies." In *Homosexuality in Modern France,* edited by Jeffrey Merrick and Bryant T. Ragan, Jr., 146–176. Oxford: Oxford University Press.
Rubin, Patricia Lee. 2018. *Seen from behind: Perspectives on the Male Body and Renaissance Art.* New Haven: Yale University Press.
Smalls, James. 1999. "Homoeroticism and the Quest for Originality in Girodet's *Revolt at Cairo* (1810)." *Nineteenth Century Contexts* 20(4): 455–488.
Solomon-Godeau, Abigail. 1997. *Male Trouble: A Crisis in Representation.* London: Thames and Hudson.
Tamagne, Florence. 2006. "The Homosexual Age, 1870–1940." In *Gay Life and Culture: A World History,* edited by Robert Aldrich, 166–195. New York: Universe Publishing.
Thompson, Victoria. 1996. "Creating Boundaries: Homosexuality and the Changing Social Order in France, 1830–1870." In *Homosexuality in Modern France,* edited by Jeffrey Merrick and Bryant T. Ragan, Jr., 102–127. Oxford: Oxford University Press.

Tickner, Lisa. 1994. "Men's Work? Masculinity and Modernism." In *Visual Culture: Images and Interpretations*, edited by Norman Bryson, Michael Ann Holly, and Keith Moxey, 42–82. Hanover: Wesleyan University Press.

Veresaev, Vikenty. 2000. "Safo." In *Safo: Lira, lira sviashchennaia*, 5–16. Moscow: Letopis'.

Yalom, Marilyn. 2013. "Foreword: Libertine Love." In *The Libertine: The Art of Love in Eighteenth-Century France*, edited by Michel Delon, 6–7. New York: Abbeville Press.

Zhuravleva, E. V. 1980. *Konstantin Andreevich Somov*. Moscow: Iskusstvo.

Zichy, Mihály. 1969. *The Erotic Drawings of Mihály Zichy*. New York: Grove Press.

Chapter 5

Modernism as the Uncanny of Stalinism: On Alexander Deineka's Wartime Drawings[1]

Gleb Napreenko

When contemplating the mural, *The Noble People of the Soviet Country* (1937), Soviet viewers were prompted to feel as if they were looking in a mirror: Within the advancing solemn mass of Soviet citizens, one was supposed to find one's ideal self-image, in accordance with one's gender, age, and nationality. At the same time, what unifies all these marching "noble people" is the statue of Lenin, which, marking the highest point of the Palace of the Soviets, towers above them, pointing the way. Lenin here is reduced to a few cliché strokes facilitating recognition, such as, for instance, the sharp upward thrust of his arm. Two distinct degrees of idealization of the body are evident on the two levels of the mural: an individual ideal citizen of the USSR and a generalized ideal all citizens, representing the common denominator of their views of themselves; in other words, the two different functions that Jacques Lacan identified in Sigmund Freud's writing—the function of the ideal ego and the function of the ego ideal. In his *Group Psychology and the Analysis of the Ego* (1921), Freud argues that individuals within a group can be bound together by the same object, the leader, which takes the place of the ego ideal.

In one of his earlier paintings, *The Heroes of the First Five-Year Plan* (1936), which, from a compositional standpoint, parallels *The Noble People of the Soviet Country*, the figure raised over the marching heroes is that of the Winged Victory of Samothrace. In both paintings, the second—higher—ideal binding the group is identified with death: It is a statue—moreover, an ancient statue, a statue of a fallen civilization or of a dead leader. In this instance, however, death does not reveal its relation to the psychoanalytical notion of the drives, which would include the death drive; it appears to be simply an effect of elevating the body to the status of a symbol.

Similarly, sexual difference is reduced in Deineka's *The Noble People of the Soviet Country* to gender identity, that is, to the same attributes as national identity. There is no place here for sexuality as something that cannot be inscribed into the system of social relations or demonstrable characteristics, as something that might introduce a disturbance into the body. During the Stalinist period, the Soviet Union's official gender order was normalized: the criminalization of homosexuality and abortion was aimed at subordinating sexuality to procreation as a socially useful activity. The erotic imagination of Deineka's works of the 1930s is fixated on healthy athletic bodies—an imagination controlled by the perfection of visual form.

In a letter to Albert Einstein ("Why War?" 1932), Freud points out that in times of war one of the human drives—the death drive—directs its action toward external objects, taking the form of an impulse to destruction. The entire Stalinist period, with its enforced industrialization and repressions, can be regarded as a period of mobilization and militarization, the USSR's preparation for war, as the idea of defending the homeland of the Socialist Revolution is gradually replaced with the agenda of the Great Patriotic War. It is worth noting, however, that official Stalinist culture, engaged in the production of wholesome body imagery—the production of ideals—left little space for the representation of drives, which was a central preoccupation of modernism in the 1920s:[1] Dadaism and Surrealism in the West, or such Soviet movements as Constructivism or Productivism (recall, for instance, the play with oral fixation in Alexander Rodchenko's advertisements). Lacan describes the Freudian drive as montage, something akin to "a dynamo connected up to a gas-tap, [from which] a peacock's feather emerges, and tickles the belly of a pretty woman who is just lying there looking beautiful" (Lacan 1981, 169). But in the Stalinist art of the 1930s, montage gradually alters the function it had in the 1920s; the whole takes precedence over the parts, and the seams between the parts lose their autonomous value. Yet some artistic phenomena associated with the Great Patriotic War, including Deineka's field drawings, allow us to expose in retrospect the underlying cause behind the construction of the language of the visual arts of the Stalinist era—the system of official representation that took shape in the 1930s.

In several sketches dating from World War II, Deineka utilizes plasticity motifs characteristic of his earlier work, yet he reverses the affective resonance of his 1930s drawings, transforming the Stalinist cheer that had defined them into its bleak opposite. Thus, instead of a ball (as in the mosaic in the Mayakovskaya metro station, 1937), a 1942 drawing of a soccer scene features a human skull, while a skydiver's leap into the air (in his 1934 painting) becomes a motorcyclist's fatal fall (Deineka will reengage this motif later, in *A Downed Ace* [*Sbityi as*, 1943]) (figs 1 and 2). Such reversals are not limited to his drawings: The prototype of the 1942 painting *Burnt Village* (*Sgorevshaia derevnia*) is *Village* (*Derevnia*), made in 1934. During this period, the art historian Andrei Kovalev (2009, 80) suggests, Deineka's graphics suffer a kind of collapse, as the artist appears to lose his virtuosic power over form. The loss of authority over the kind of holistic gestalt that frequently coincided in Deineka's work with the image of a wholesome, robust body can be linked to the period's dissolution of the body itself, which lay at the core of the artist's production of form. Examples of this can be found in drawings of one-legged soldiers as well as macabre erotic fantasies: female nurses pictured as skeletons that nevertheless retain their gender attributes, shocks of hair on grinning skulls and ample bosoms sitting on top of what appears to be empty chest cavities (1942) (fig. 3). Explicitly manifest in these images of monstrous nurses are the Freudian drives: Death is no longer just a corollary of symbolic idealization as in Deineka's 1930s work, and gender is no longer a sum of attributes. Instead, death and gender here produce a visible breakdown of the montage of the drives within the body itself. These seemingly marginal drawings, as it were, these queer bodies can serve as a starting point for an examination of Stalinist culture and its relationship to modernism.

Deineka's wartime pictures express ambivalence toward his earlier "pathos formulas." Aby Warburg used this term in reference to bodily gestures and poses of extreme affect, hearkening back to the art of classical antiquity. As Carlo Ginzburg has shown, Warburg's concept of "pathos formulas" is linked to the question of inversions, or reversals in the expression of borderline affects, which Charles Darwin discusses in *The Expression of the Emotions in Man and Animals* (1897), a work that influenced Warburg's thinking.[2] The analogy between Deineka's images and the pathos formulas inherited from antiquity is not limited to the problem of ambivalence. We can recall here the artist's overall orientation toward antiquity in works like *The Heroes of the First Five-Year Plan* (1936), which features the Winged Victory of Samothrace. Yet the underside of the antique Apollonian ideal is the Dionysian orgy of passions. To express this in the terms of

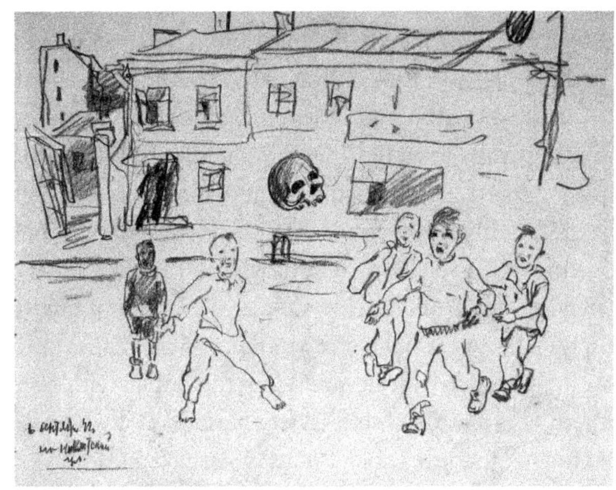

FIGURE 1. Alexander Deineka, *October 6th, 1942. Along Nikitskaya Street* (1942). © Дейнека Александр/РАО (Москва)/ 2017. Private Collection

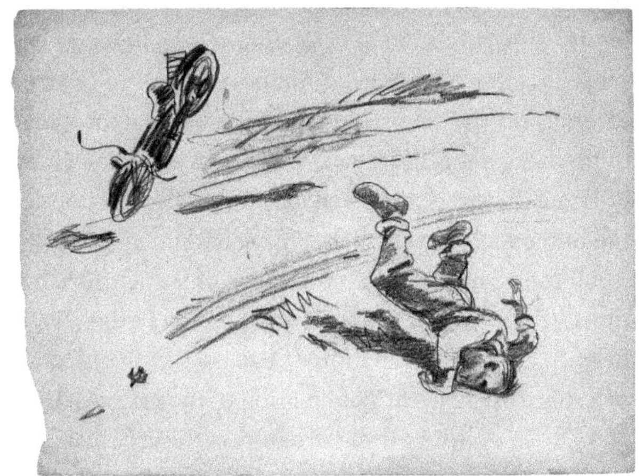

FIGURE 2. Alexander Deineka, *From the Frontline Drawings. (Motorcyclist)* (1942). © Дейнека Александр/РАО (Москва)/ 2017. Private Collection

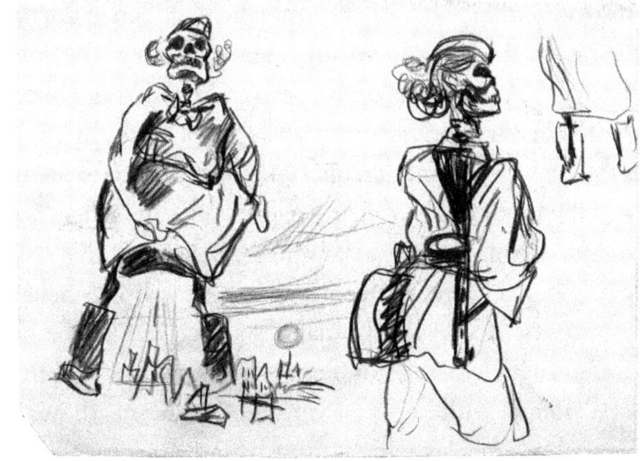

FIGURE 3. Alexander Deineka, *Wartime Fantasies. From the Frontline Drawings*. 1942–43. © Дейнека Александр/РАО (Москва)/ 2017. Private Collection

Freud's "Drives and Their Vicissitudes" (1915), the drive to control one's own body (as in sports, for instance) can transform itself into sadism or masochism.

In addition to ambivalence, Deineka's wartime drawings evince a crisis of these "pathos formulas" and bodily form as such. This crisis has to do with exposing the truths of death and mutilation and dissolving the image of a wholesome, readily legible body. The distinction between Good and Evil as essential features reflected in the bodily aspect of an individual or a class supplied the Soviet consumer of culture with a clear system of identifications and antipathies. In the 1920s, Deineka had been one of the main contributors to the cultivation of the imaginary ideal,[3] providing the public with visions of the ideal bodies of the "noble people of the Soviet country" or, by contrast, of the repulsive bodies of the bourgeoisie (as in, for instance, his caricatures for the *Projector* magazine). In his prewar period, Deineka exhibited a brilliant command of a whole range of bodily distortions, from caricature to idealization. Yet he never abandoned the sense of a flexible connection between the inner structures of the body and its exterior, on the one hand, and their separability analogous to the separability of the body's machinery from the sum of its social attributes, on the other. His wartime drawings, however, destabilize the relations between the backbone and the outer shell, between the image and its underside. Deineka's skeleton nurses recall the scrubbed-down buildings of the Khrushchev era—Stalinist constructions stripped of their "skin" (moldings and other ornamentations) following the decree "On the Elimination of Excesses in Design and Construction" (an effect of a sharp break in the sublimation of the imaginary ideal).

Observable here is the structure of the Freudian "uncanny" (*unheimlich*), with its shocking exposure of the ambivalent in the habitual, the invasion of quotidian reality by what had until then remained hidden in the background, in phantasy—that is, by the breakdown and fragmentation of the body (Freud 1955, 217–52). Under the conditions of the Second World War, Deineka brought together two motifs that had hitherto run on separate tracks in his oeuvre—the motif of war, as we see, for instance, in his 1934 illustrations for Henri Barbusse's novel *Le Feu*, and the motif of peaceful Soviet existence. It is this combination—the incursion of war into his country's daily life—that generates a sense of the uncanny, a sense of the horrible and alien coming to light in things held intimately close and dear.

Death as a drive also manifests itself in Deineka's postwar drawings. As his student Igor Dolgopolov recalls, the artist showed him an unfinished painting of a woman with her skeleton visible underneath her fur coat. Deineka accompanied this display with a quote from Romain Rolland: "To create is to destroy death" (Dolgopolov 1988, 222). Here, as in his wartime sketches of nurses, we encounter the ambivalence of Eros and Thanatos.

A similar reversal is evident in two paintings by Deineka's comrade in arms, Iurii Pimenov—*New Moscow* (*Novaia Moskva,* 1937) and *Front-line Road* (*Frontovaia doroga,* 1944). The shiny new buildings of Stalin's Moscow turn into bleak ruins in what is, from a compositional standpoint, an identical picture. The experience of war, however, did not engender the kind of paradoxical shifts and reversals in Pimenov's oeuvre as it did in Deineka's, which is likely due to the comparatively insignificant role played by the body in Pimenov's works.

Pimenov addresses the motif of death in his anti-modernist statement "The Art of Life and 'the Art of Nothing'" (1960), which was inspired by the artist's trip to the Venice Biennale. In making his case, Pimenov invokes war experiences, suggesting that the kind of art exhibited at the biennale comes from a lack of appreciation for life; Pimenov contrasts the avant-gardist "posturing" with an art born of wartime suffering (Pimenov 1966, 83–84). In fact, he draws equivalencies between the baring of the device in modernism and wartime destruction, between modernism and death.

There are multiple examples of Soviet artists circling back to modernist aesthetics to capture the essence of the experience of war. Among them are some of the almost Dadaist photographs of Evgenii Khaldei, the grotesque scenes of violence in Mark Donskoi's film *Rainbow* (*Raduga,* 1944), which was shot on the home front, or the "Blockade" poems (1942–1944) of Gennadii Gor. In each of these instances, the modernist devices employed (for instance, Gor's use of bodily fragmentation echoing the OBERIU group's poetry) shift the work's description of the horrors of war from the register of the subjective or the metaphorical into the register of the objective or the literal, as if buttressing Pimenov's notion of equivalency between war and modernism as destroyers of life. Gor did not expect to see his "Blockade" poems in print (moreover, he would not show them even to those close to him); just as Deineka did not anticipate the publication of his curious drawings. Yet it is noteworthy that Gor's cycle of war poems marks the peak of his clandestine engagement with modernism throughout his career. Here is one of Gor's poems from that cycle:

With an air wave in my ears,
With a cold moon in my soul
I shot myself to madness. I am my own
Check and mate. I am mute.

I am already nothing and run toward nothing.
I am already no one and rush toward no one.
With an air wave in my mouth,
With a cold moon in the dark,
With a foot in the corner and a hand in the trench
With eyes fallen from their sockets
And a forgotten finger in a hospital,
With a useless moon in the dark. (Gor 2011, 244)[4]

Thus, the axis around which Stalinist anti-modernism revolves (or the hidden core from which it springs) is in fact nothing but modernism, with its tendency toward baring the device. But what brought this hidden core to light was the crisis of the well-oiled machine of Stalinist representation, a breakdown precipitated by the artists' need to deal with the reality of the war. Within the regime of Stalinist representation, the asceticism of modernism so crucial to the radical avant-gardes of the 1920s is perceived as a pernicious or inhumane assertion of death, which should be kept at a distance. A similar position is discernible in Deineka, who, as Dolgopolov suggests, delays indefinitely the completion of his pictures featuring the figure of Death. This kind of strenuous repudiation of modernist origins is traceable to the cultural purges of the 1930s, which began with the anti-formalist campaign. In this light, ambivalence is seen as immanent in Stalinism's mimetic language, which is based on the repression or concealment of its modernist origins, even as they survive in the form of the uncanny, in the ambiguity of the image and in its inherent defect— like the amputated leg of a female subway construction worker in Andrei Platonov's *Happy Moscow* (*Shchastlivaia Moskva*, 1932–1936), a loss that turns the heroine into a figure of eroticized attraction. This admixture of ambivalence and repression intrinsic to Socialist Realism became an aesthetic basis for Sots Art both in literature (for example, Vladimir Sorokin) and art (for example, Vitaly Komar and Alexander Melamid).

The eradication of modernism in Stalinist culture ran parallel to the repressions, the Great Terror, the Gulag. And the proximity of Stalinist repressions to the "normal" daily reality of Soviet society also found its cultural expression in the uncanny: that is, the uncanny that resides alongside you without being seen. Alexander Solzhenitsyn describes the Soviet individual's entire life as lived next to a fence, which hides the unknown from view and which can be ignored. But when the individual is out of luck, they may find themselves behind the fence, in the parallel world of Stalin's camps (Solzhenitsyn 1973).

The war becomes an alibi for baring, first, the concealed or repressed ambivalence of the image, and second, the rejected language of modernism itself, calling attention to the stylization and montage-based construction of the image. Moreover, these two kinds of baring occur both in works created "for the drawer" and in pieces designed for public consumption.

A characteristic example of such deliberate ambivalence of the image can be found in the first part of Dmitri Shostakovich's *"Leningrad" symphony* (1941), in which a spirited march-like melody, by degrees, becomes ambiguous and eventually menacingly aggressive. Written before the war, it had not been performed for the general public until the designation of the symphony as a work about the war and the Leningrad blockade enabled public performances of this ambivalence.[5] According to a later interpretation (supported by the composer himself), in this piece Shostakovich expressed not only the experience of war but also the Soviet people's common experience of suffering, that is, the experience of Stalinism.[6]

Thus, the theme of war opened possibilities for employing repressed modernist devices and for laying bare the disavowed function of these devices in Stalinist culture. At the same time, this theme became an indirect way of speaking publicly about the hardships of Soviet life, Stalinism, and the repressions. An early example of this way of speaking is evident in texts by Olga Bergholz, who, having survived the repressions, struggled with the impossibility of giving voice to this taboo experience in a novel she had conceived in the 1930s. The war gave her an opportunity for transforming the experience of internal violence into a representation of invasion from the outside. Bergholz defined this connection thus: "The prison is the root of our victory over fascism, because we knew: the prison is fascism, and we are fighting against it, and we knew that tomorrow the war would come and we were ready for it" (Bergholz 2010, 112). It should be noted that during the siege of Leningrad, Bergholz, while suffering alongside the other inhabitants of the city, was privileged to work as a radio announcer. Therefore, when she writes to Georgy Makogonenko during her short-term stay in Moscow as an evacuee that mundanities or surfaces rule here, while in Leningrad it is bare existence, freed from surfaces, and that she wants to return there (126), her words should be read not as the voice of an ordinary person from Leningrad but as that of an author who gets to speak about something that lies beyond mundanity.

Bergholz's emphasis on bare existence as a counterweight to the mundane brings us back to the origins of the Soviet project and the poetics of asceticism as an aesthetic regime offering an alternative to high Stalinism. This contradiction is clearly manifest in the question of the bodily image. The rejection of Stalinist flesh—the robust body comprising the primary gestalt of Stalinist culture—is articulated in Bergholz's short story "Blockade Bathhouse" ("Blokadnaia bania," 1962). The female bodies during the blockade are terrifying because they have been stripped of their outward shell of beauty, but what proves really terrifying is the arrival in the bathhouse of a woman who has a healthy, Deineka-style body. She is called a "slut" and kicked out.

The blockade body, which functions as an alternative to the Stalinist body while at the same time exposing its hidden core, also makes an appearance in Lidiya Ginzburg's *Blockade Diary* (*Zapiski blokadnogo cheloveka*, 1942–1983). Her account of the exercise of will power, which de-automatized the most habitual movements (Ginzburg 2011, 313–14), as well as the precisely calculated daily schedule of blockade living (321), sound like a blood-chilling parody of Vsevolod Meyerhold's biomechanics, Viktor Shklovsky's de-automatization, and Aleksei Gastev's vision for the organization of labor. Describing the rubble of buildings destroyed in the bombings, Ginzburg compares them to stage sets in theatrical productions by Meyerhold, who had by that time been executed (324).

In her book *Blokada v slove*, Irina Sandomirskaia traces the continuities between Ginzburg's texts from the late 1920s–1930s and her *Blockade Diary*, suggesting that the state of the blockade individual in Ginzburg reveals the truth about what it meant to be a writer in the 1930s (Sandomirskaia 2013, 192–203). But to be a writer in the 1930s also means to inherit, in a distorted form, elements of the leftist modernist priorities from the previous decade, the priorities of groups like LEF or OPOIAZ (Ginzburg was affiliated with the latter). In the 1930s, such modernist priorities as the conscious mastery of writing techniques and the notion of the author as a manufacturer (an idea to which Ginzburg never subscribed) became foundational to a mechanized approach to perfecting the craft of writing. According to Ginzburg, the writers were now only engaging in the manufacture of an ersatz product—the glorified image of a writer divorced from authentic realities, from existence. As for "the device," Ginzburg writes, "one had better hide it away" (Sandomirskaia 2013, 186).

In conclusion, I will try to trace links between engagement with the uncanny, the destructive, and the deadly, on the one hand, and modernism, on the other, in artistic works of two kinds: those operating in the field of public representation and those contained within the private realm. This distinction is evident, for instance, in the configurations of the blockade body. In Ginzburg, the dystrophic body functions as a kind of existential truth, or, as Sandomirskaia puts it, the truth of Stalinism as such. This resonates with Bergholz's stated preference for the bare existence of Leningrad over the mundanities of Moscow. Yet "Blockade Bathhouse" constructs and authenticates the blockade body, first of all, by directing everyone's righteous anger at the woman who does not share in the plight of her people, and second, by reducing the scope of the narrative's subject matter to its wartime setting: Bergholz ends her short story by presenting a monstrously emaciated old woman as an allegory of war.

We see more of the same in other examples. Within the framework of "private perception" (for instance, in Ginzburg or Gor), the horrors of war are interpreted as realities that are immanent and subject to analysis without foregone conclusions. By contrast, in the context of public representation (as in Pimenov, for instance) these horrors are subject to condemnation and rejection as something alien to the common view of reality. The first position can be seen as modernist, the second as anti-modernist. And this anti-modernist position is best characterized by the words of its proponents. Take Deineka's comment about creativity as the destroyer of death, which is echoed almost verbatim by Bergholz (2012, 301–02) in "Your Way" ("Tvoi put'," 1945):

> . . . And the one,
> Whom I joyously and tirelessly
> Grieve, mourn and miss,
> Whom I praise with a nameless glory –
> A mute glory, the highest on earth –
> You are merged with everything that was greater than life
> dreaming,
> the soul,
> the fatherland,
> existence –
> and your grave is everywhere for me
> and everywhere is your resurrection.
> Moscow's last trumpet
> repeats this over and over,
> when it,
> shaking the nocturnal sky,
> praises the fallen and the living alike
> and predicts a death sentence for Death . . .[7]

Both speakers, especially Bergholz, reference the Christian belief in "death conquered by death" through Christ's resurrection. Stalinist culture is frequently discussed in terms of its quasi-religious or eschatological elements. The context of the modernism/anti-modernism question pertaining to the representation of the war experience endows Stalinist religiosity with another meaning. This meaning crystallizes in a tension with modernism, whose interest in immanence was based on a materialist theology and skepticism regarding the divine nature of Christ and his resurrection. It is therefore not surprising that, alongside the macabre motifs, Deineka's wartime fantasies should incorporate an image of the winged goddess of victory soaring over a dead Soviet soldier (1942).

This split into two levels brings us back where we began: Deineka's large scale pieces, *The Noble People of the Soviet Country* and *The Heroes of the First Five-Year Plan,* which also evince a vertical split between the individual Soviet citizen and the ideal that governs them. And once again, his wartime drawings expose the underside of his art works from the 1930s—what was once aloof idealization has turned into the reality of a dead body, the reality of a human life lost.

Translated by Aleksei Grinenko with Brian James Baer

Notes

A version of this chapter was first published in Russian in the volume *Epizody modernisma: ot istokov do krizisa*, by Gleb Napreenko and Aleksandra Novozhenova (Moscow: Novoe literaturnoe obozrenie, 2018). The text was expanded and revised for translation in the — current volume. The revised Russian text is available at: https://syg.ma/@sygma/glieb-naprieienko-modiernizm-kak-unheimlich-stalinizma

1 Modernism is posited here as antithetical to Stalinism, although this article is in many ways concerned with the ways in which modernism was in fact the underside of Stalinist culture.

2 Carlo Ginzburg spoke about it in a lecture in Moscow on June 2, 2015, and, more briefly, in the article "Ot Varburga do Gombrikha. Zametki ob odnoi metodologicheskoi probleme." See Ginzburg (2004).

3 The image of the "ideal ego" as understood by Freud and Lacan.

4 This poem was translated by Brian James Baer.

5 See, for instance, Dmitrii Shostakovich, Simfoniia #7 "Leningradskaia." Available at: http://music-fantasy.ru/materials/dmitriy-shostakovich-simfoniya-no7-leningradskaya/. Last accessed: March 4, 2016.

6 As Shostakovich himself explained: "Even before the war, in Leningrad there probably wasn't a single family who hadn't lost someone, a father, a brother, or if not a relative, then a close friend. Everyone had someone to cry over, but you had to cry silently, under your blanket, so that no one would see. Everyone feared everyone else, and the sorrow oppressed and suffocated us. It suffocated me too. I had to write about it, I felt it was my responsibility, my duty. I had to write a requiem for all those who died, who had suffered. I had to describe the horrible extermination machine and express protest against it. But how could I do it? I was constantly under suspicion then, and critics counted what percentage of my symphonies was in a major key and what percentage in a minor key. That oppressed me, it deprived me of the will to compose. And then the war came and the sorrow became a common one. We could talk about it, we could cry openly, cry for our lost ones. People stopped fearing tears" (Volkov 1979, 135–136).

7 This poem was translated by Brian James Baer.

References

Berggol'ts, Ol'ga. 2010. *Zapretnyj dnevnik*. St. Petersburg: Azbuka.

Darwin, Charles. 1897. *The Expression of the Emotions in Man and Animals*. New York: D. Appleton and Co.

Dolgopolov, Igor'. 1988. *Mastera i shedevry*. vol 3. Moscow: Izobrazitel'noe iskusstvo.

Freud, Sigmund. 1955. "The Uncanny," in *The Standard Edition of the Complete Psychological Works of Sigmund Freud*, vol. XVII, trans. and ed. James Strachey. London: Hogarth Press.

Ginzburg. Karlo. 2004. *Mify-emblemy-primety: morfologiia i istoriia*. Moscow: Novoe izdatel'stvo.

Ginzburg, Lidiia. 2011. *Prohodyaschie kharaktery: Proza voennykh let. Zapiski blokadnogo cheloveka*. Moscow: Novoe izdatel'stvo.

Gor, Gennadii. 2011. "Blokada: Stikhi 1942–1944 gg." *Toronto Slavic Quarterly* 38 (Fall): 239–247.

Koval'iov, Andrei. 2009. "Zashchita Deineki: sil'nyj mittel'shpil'," *Deineka, Grafika*. Moscow.

Lacan, Jacques. 1981. *The Four Fundamental Concepts of Psychoanalysis*, translated by Alain Sheridan, *The Seminar of Jacques Lacan, Book XI*, edited by Jacques-Alain Miller. New York: Norton and Company.

Pimenov, Iurii. 1964. *Iskusstvo zhizni ili "Iskusstvo nichego."* Moscow: Iskusstvo.

Sandomirskaia, Irina. 2013. *Blokada v slove: Ocherki kriticheskoi teorii i biopolitiki*. Moscow: Novoe izdanie.

Solzhenitsyn, Aleksandr. 1975. *Arkhipelag Gulag*. Paris: YMCA Press. Available at: http://www.lib.ru/PROZA/SOLZHENICYN/gulag.txt. Last accessed March 4, 2016.

Volkov, Solomon. 1979. *Testimony: The Memoirs of Dmitri Shostakovich, as Related and Edited by Solomon Volkov*. Translated by Antonina W. Bouis. New York: Harper and Row.

Chapter 6

Carnivalesque Carnality: The Queer Potential of Sergei Eisenstein's Homoerotic Drawings

Ada Ackerman

> "Had it not been for Leonardo da Vinci, Marx, Lenin, Freud and the movies, I would in all probability have been another Oscar Wilde."[1]

> "Eroticism is far too strong a force not to be used."[2]

> "I started from 'erotic' croquis, and then I came to be interested not in the eroticism *of the croquis, but in the eroticism of* the croquis."[3]

Peter Greenaway's 2015 film *Eisenstein in Guanajuato,* dedicated to the Soviet filmmaker's 1931 stay in Mexico while shooting his unfinished movie *¡Que Viva Mexico!,* focused in a very explicit way on Eisenstein's presumed sexual experiences in Mexico, and specifically on his homosexual affair with Palomino Cañedo, a scholar of comparative religion with whom, at the age of 33, the Russian director supposedly lost his same-sex virginity (Salazkina 2009, 130–136). This episode is alluded to in a letter Eisenstein sent from Mexico to his secretary and very close friend Pera Atasheva, whom he would marry in 1934 (Eizenshtein 1997/1998, 234–236). In this letter, Eisenstein explains with excitement and bewilderment that, for the first time in his life, he was "experiencing and not evaluating," that he had "crushed the complex that has been weighing down on [him] for ten years (or more)," that he has managed to go "all the way" with a love object; in short, that he was able to complete the sexual act while being in love, and to thus experience a full orgasmic sexual experience, which brought him a feeling of extraordinary happiness.

The film surprised viewers around the world and caused a scandal in Russia (Gray 2015; Greenaway 2015), where the government's antigay policy had been intensifying over the past few years, culminating in the 2013 law banning "homosexual propaganda" (Elder 2013). Greenaway's film, however, only added to an already long list of studies dedicated to Eisenstein's appetite for men, something that did not escape even his earliest biographers (Seton 1960: 203), nor did it escape his contemporaries. For instance, the actor Mikhail Nazvanov, who played Andrei Kurbsky in *Ivan the Terrible* (1944–1946), reported to his wife how, during the shooting of the movie, the filmmaker would flirt with young men on the set (Nazvanov 1998: 129). Film scholars have discussed at length the homoeroticism in Eisenstein's movies: his glorification of the masculine body in *Battleship Potemkin* (1925) and *October* (1927), which aligns with the agenda of building a New Socialist Man, endowed with a healthy and vigorous constitution; his fascination with scenes of transvestism (especially in *October* and *Ivan the Terrible*) and of gender inversion; and his clear phallic imagery, such as the erect cannons in *Potemkin* (1925) or the milk separator in *The General Line* (1929).[4] Eisenstein scholars have also written about his privileged relationship with his assistant, Grigori Aleksandrov, as well as his deep fascination with his "spiritual father" Vsevolod Meyerhold.[5] Prominent gay filmmakers such as Kenneth Anger have made explicit references to Eisenstein's suggestive scenes in their own movies,[6] and several encyclopedias on homosexuality, gender studies, and queer culture include entries on Eisenstein.[7]

It is not surprising that as gay studies gained greater legitimacy, scholars would begin to treat such a major Soviet avant-garde figure within this theoretical frame. Nevertheless, it would be reductive to label Eisenstein as "exclusively" homosexual since he was attracted to both men and women throughout his life and had intimate experiences with members of both genders. He described himself as a bisexual, understanding bisexuality as a manifestation of the core dialectics within the human body, "wired deeply in everyone's memory" (Tsivian 2002, 65). That said, Eisenstein's interest in men cannot be underestimated. In that respect, and despite the numerous studies dedicated to his homoeroticism quoted above, one body of material remains understudied: his "sex drawings," as Joan

Neuberger labels them (Neuberger 2012). Departing from purely biographical considerations and psychoanalytical interpretative models, Neuberger's pioneering article analyzes the creative functions of Eisenstein's "sex drawings" within his work, and especially his theoretical writings. But Neuberger tackles the issue without taking into consideration the peculiarities of Eisenstein's representations of homoerotic relations, the significance of which cannot be overestimated.

Eisenstein made thousands of drawings from childhood until his death.[8] Often displaying a great sense of humor, sometimes provocative to the point of blasphemy, these visual works are remarkable for their thematic and stylistic variety, which reveals Eisenstein's multifaceted imagination. Eisenstein experienced drawing as a subversive, carnivalesque practice, in which he could enjoy a freedom he could find neither in the collective practice of film, which had to be submitted to the State for approval, nor in the context of Soviet society. As such, drawing provided a marginal space that allowed Eisenstein to maintain his psychological balance and to cope with external pressure, thus enabling him to carry on with his other creative activities. In his drawings, Eisenstein blurred all lines and categories, turning the world upside down and creating unexpected junctures between various cultures and myths. He used these drawings to explore his fantasies and to illustrate his theories of art and the human psyche (Christie and Kleiman 2017, 20 23; 131 135). Far from being a peripheral practice, drawing represented for Eisenstein an essential tool and a theoretical laboratory in which he could test his ideas, especially those regarding artistic processes and methods (Christie and Kleiman 2017, 162 164). Drawing also provided Eisenstein with a space for "post-analysis," in which he could reflect upon his work and highlight its specific features.

Eisenstein dedicated a significant part of his impressive graphic output to "sex drawings." Staging innumerable situations in which sex is associated with violence but also with laughter, these drawings are hard to categorize. According to Neuberger, they are "sexy and repellent, funny and sadistic, charming and creepy" (Neuberger 2012, 7). They are neither pornographic nor erotic, since they do not generally aim so much to arouse the viewer's sensuality as to awaken his laughter; "to the extent they address the viewer, they distance the viewer at the same time" (Neuberger 2012, 7 9).

Together with his diaries and personal writings, these drawings reveal much about Eisenstein's ambivalent views on sex and its place within his creative activity.[9]

In these drawings, Eisenstein questions and exorcizes his fears about sex while addressing and exploring all kinds of sexualities: heterosexual, gay, lesbian, zoophilic, and pedophilic, thereby subverting all categories and genres. According to his friend, the anthropologist Anita Brenner, whom he quotes in an article dedicated to the analysis of his drawings, "Eisenstein appears as an erotomaniac monk and a mystic from the Middle Ages. [. . .] A singer of orgasms of all known and unknown varieties" (Eizenshtein 2002a, 494–496). This pansexualism, close to the kind advocated by D. H. Lawrence, whom Eisenstein greatly admired, makes him part of the "culture of gender and sexual dissent" described by Dan Healey (2001) in his pioneering study of homosexuality in Soviet Russia. To the extent that it does not fit the ideological and social agenda of the Soviet state, which was based on an *etacratic* gender order (Zdravomyslova and Temkina 2003, 463), this sexuality represents potentially transgressive values (Healey 2001, 12).

A Complicated Relationship with Sex and Homosexuality

The erotic fantasies displayed in Eisenstein's drawings must be understood through his problematic relationship to the body and to sex. In his *Memories,* he describes at length how the troubled relationship between his father and his mother deeply affected him. Their divorce was caused in part by Yulia Ivanovna's seductive behavior: "Mom was, as Americans say, 'oversexed.' Papa in his turn was 'undersexed'" (Eisenstein 1995a, 425).[10] Some of his drawings suggest that Eisenstein believed that his mother had intercourse with several lovers when pregnant with him, therefore forcing him, as a mere embryo, to have sex with men (fig. 1). This belief nurtured his perception of sex as an insecure and threatening sphere. Moreover, young Sergei held resentment toward his father, the architect Mikhail Eisenstein, because of his authoritarian view of education and his refusal to explain the laws of reproduction: "Mikhail Osipovich was endlessly evasive when questioned about the 'secrets' of biology" (Eizenshtein 1995a, 444 46). The "obedient, polite, [. . .] typical boy from Riga" (Eizenshtein 1995b, 16) found some shocking answers in his mother's flat when he stumbled upon some hidden books, not suitable for a child, some of which contained illustrations: Octave Mirbeau's *The Garden of Torments* (1899), Leopold Sacher-Masoch's *Venus in Furs* (1870), Marquis de Sade's *The Story of Juliette or Vice Amply Rewarded* (1800), mistakenly remembered by Eisenstein as *The Stages of Vice,* and later, Richard von Krafft-Ebing's *Psychopathia sexualis* (1886) (Eizenshtein 1995c, 488–92). These books deeply impressed the young Sergei and vividly

FIGURE 1. Sergei Eisenstein, *Premiers souvenirs d'enfance* (First childhood memories) (1932). Published in *Eisenstein. Dessins secrets*, Paris, Seuil, 1992, no. 40. Courtesy of Rada Alloy

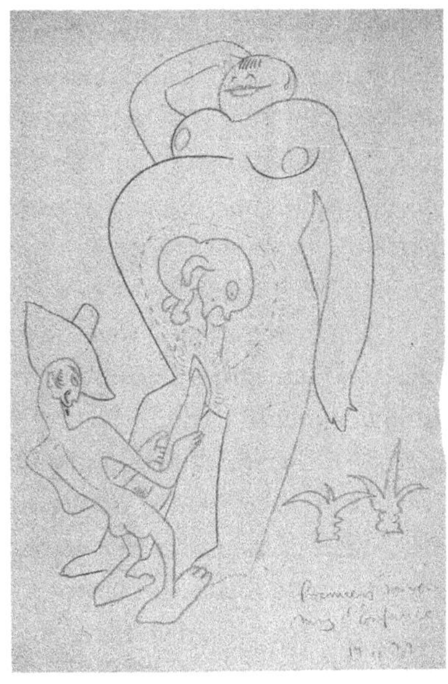

stimulated his imagination. As he would admit, these "unhealthy" images were the first images of "sensuality" (Eizenshtein 1995c, 492) he came across, and without a doubt, they informed his own erotic and pornographic drawings. As a youngster and later as a young adult, Eisenstein suffered from a poor body image and had trouble entering relationships with women, even though many women were attracted to him. His mother was greatly disturbed by this and even enlisted a psychoanalyst, Aaron Zalkind, to help with the matter (Bulgakowa 2001, 41–43).

Eisenstein's reading of Freud's *Leonardo da Vinci and a Memory of his Childhood* (1910) in 1918 also had a significant impact on him, providing him with the notion that sex could be sublimated into creativity, as well as the hypothesis that da Vinci was homosexual and that his masculinity had been crushed by an excessively powerful mother (Bulgakowa 2001, 11).[11] Identifying himself with the Italian genius and taking him as a model, Eisenstein would play with this interpretation in his drawings, presenting the Renaissance master in the company of attractive young men. Of similar importance was Otto Weininger's *Sex and Character* (1903), which he read one year later. Weininger's concept of universal bisexuality received much attention in fin de siècle Russia—his work was first translated into Russian in 1909—and the disjunction between sex and gender he proposed caught Eisenstein's attention.[12] Later, Weininger would play a key role in Eisenstein's theoretical work, in particular, his reflections on the phenomenon of "ex-stasis" in art. Eisenstein elaborated his own conception of bisexuality, which he viewed as a powerful dialectical unity of opposites, and which he construed as a reenactment of a primordial stage in one's evolution, before sexual differentiation. As such, images of bisexuality answered a deeply rooted desire in every human being to erase inner divisions and to go beyond fixed identities.[13]

The explanatory models of homosexuality provided by these readings proved insufficient to fully satisfy Eisenstein about the evolution of his sensual drives and attractions. Moreover, despite increasing sexual liberalization following the legalization of divorce and abortion, Soviet society of the 1920s remained ambivalent about homosexuality; no longer punished as a crime, it was nevertheless perceived as a temporary aberration, as a "sexopathology" (*seksopatologiia*) and a sexual perversion (*polovoe izvrashchenie*) to be treated by science and medicine. Understood as products and remnants of a decadent bourgeois mentality, all sexual minorities (*seksual'nye menshintsva*), it was believed, would dissolve in time under the new social conditions established by socialism (Healey 2001, 122–26). Therefore, the dominant medical discourse presented homosexuals as sick people who needed to be cured. For instance, Vladimir Bekhterev, one of the fathers of modern reflexology, actively sought out ways to use hypnosis and reflexology to reestablish "correct" sexual drives among his patients. Eisenstein must have been aware of these conceptions and of the extensive literature available on the subject; Bekhterev's work was one of the major sources of inspiration for his concept of the "montage of attractions" (Eizenshtein 1988, 39–58). Eisenstein was convinced that his troubles with women were an illness to be treated by specialists, as his diaries suggest, and he sought help from several of them (Bulgakowa 2001, 79–80).

Nevertheless, his doubts about himself took a new direction when he discovered a gay, lesbian, and queer scene on public display during his time in Europe and the United States between 1929 and 1931. These encounters and experiences prepared him for the new relationship he would establish with his body and his sexuality in Mexico. According to various testimonies, Eisenstein expressed fascination with these alternative milieux. For example, the dancer Valeska Gert, who spent some time with Eisenstein in Paris, wrote, "We went to Magic-City Bal, the place where all Parisian homosexuals and transvestites meet. This is where the entire beautiful world of haute couture, much more elegant and eccentric in their evening costumes than the most elegant women, gathered" (Gert 2002, 121). During his stay in France, Eisenstein also went to Toulon and Marseille, discovering their brothels and, in particular, the practice of male prostitution (Barna 1973, 48). In Berlin, Eisenstein visited many "gay" places, including the famous Eldorado Café on Lutherstrasse, known for its transvestite shows (Tamagne 2007, 38), and bought several erotic books (Marcadé and Ackerman 1999, 14). In New York, the writer Lincoln Kirstein and the associate director of MoMA Jere Abbott took Eisenstein on a tour of "New York City's queer lowlife," as the filmmaker had mentioned to Kirstein that he'd "been amused by a 'small drag' show he'd seen in Harlem" and asked him "why it was that all 'sex books' in New York drugstores were priced at sixty-nine cents (Duberman 2007, 137–138).

In Berlin, Eisenstein visited the Magnus Hirschfeld Institute for Sex Research. Hirschfeld was actively working to decriminalize homosexuality in Germany (one of the reasons he would later incur the hatred of the Nazis), and his works on sexual and gender dissent were wellknown and promoted in Russia, especially within social hygienist circles—Hirschfeld himself was invited to Russia in 1926 as a sex specialist (Healey 2001, 132–38). At the Hirschfeld Institute, Eisenstein discussed topics such as homosexuality and his own sexual proclivities, and even considered beginning psychoanalysis there (Kleiman 2002, 480).[14] Eisenstein wondered whether homosexuality was a regressive trend and was concerned about its potential effects on his creativity and art (Marcadé and Ackerman 1999, 14; Bulgakowa 2001, 104). As Eisenstein himself reported, during his visit to the Institute he met a Bulgarian engineer wearing feminine clothes and a wig, who explained that he needed to do this to feel like a complete and normal human being, which Eisenstein attributed to a desire to return to the primordial state of "androgeny" (Eizenshtein 2002, 285–86). After his visit, Eisenstein wrote to Hirschfeld several times, looking for further information, as in a letter dated May 23, 1931: "A second request concerned the sexual type of Hegel, the father of modern dialectics, and of possible traces of bisexuality in him (and to what extent they were expressed)" (Bulgakowa 1998, 96).[15]

A Delayed Graphic Diary and a Means of Escape

Eisenstein's sex drawings testify to the vividness of the impressions made on him by his encounters with an open gay life in Europe and United States. A significant number of drawings incorporate dates and places where Eisenstein witnessed memorable sights. However, one cannot fail to notice that in almost all cases, these drawings were made quite a while afterward. Many drawings are dated 1931 and 1932, when Eisenstein was in Mexico, but they refer to events that happened in 1929 and 1930. For instance, many drawings from the "Marseille series," which depict scenes of (male and female) prostitution that he had witnessed in Marseille in 1929, were sketched on letterhead from Mexican hotels in 1931. One drawing from the series depicts a male couple sitting at a café—one was probably a prostitute, dressed in a sailor suit, and the other his client—and is titled "Marseille, Café, 1931" (fig. 2). This caption is striking in that it fuses two distinct moments: the scene recorded in the drawing (1929) and the drawing's realization (1931). Such a temporal bridge suggests that the context of Mexico, and the freedom he experienced there, reactivated Eisenstein's memory of his European experience and scenes of a new way of life that he had to digest and assimilate before he was able to transform them into graphic material. These drawings thus appear as a delayed record of powerful visual data.

Once the Mexican experience triggered the memory of European gay life, Eisenstein seems to have been in a hurry to visually register all the details he had so carefully observed. This confirms Joan Neuberger's statement, following Ian Christie's, that Eisenstein's sex drawings should not only be construed as the "expression of an otherwise repressed libido" (Neuberger 2012, 7) through the Freudian lens of sublimation, no matter how relevant this model may seem to Eisenstein's case. As Neuberger remarks, it is precisely when Eisenstein enjoys pleasurable sensual and sexual experiences that his drawings proliferate (Neuberger 2012, 11)—this convergence being particularly noticeable during his stay in Mexico. In these cases and elsewhere, Eisenstein does not censor or suppress his desires to sublimate them into art but, on the contrary, enhances them in drawing, boosting his creativity and his imagination, to further explore the sexual sphere in all its possible relations with his anthropological and aesthetic concerns, which these drawings in turn fuel (Neuberger 2012).

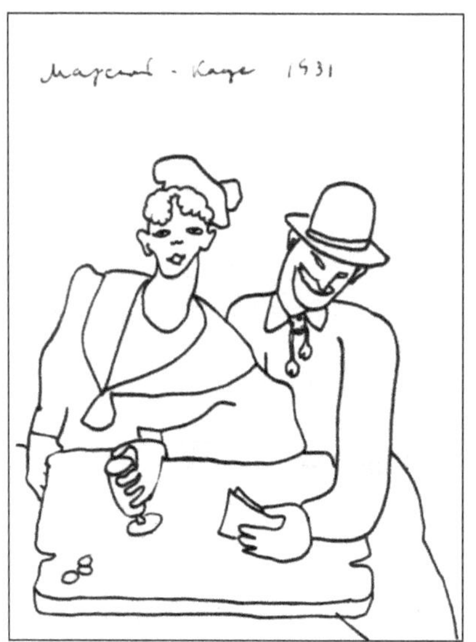

FIGURE 2. Sergei Eisenstein, *Café à Marseille, 1931* (1931). Published in *Risunki Eizenshteina*, Moscow, Iskusstvo, 1961, p. 110

A number of sex drawings express Eisenstein's curiosity toward gay couples, mainly male prostitutes with their customers, whom he depicts in different situations in the fashion of an ethnographer: walking together, resting, chatting, sleeping, and so on (fig. 3). He also pays attention to queer life, observing this world with the fascinated gaze of an outsider, making use of his favorite tools of physiognomy and "type." Some drawings reveal his interest in male transvestites, whom he depicts

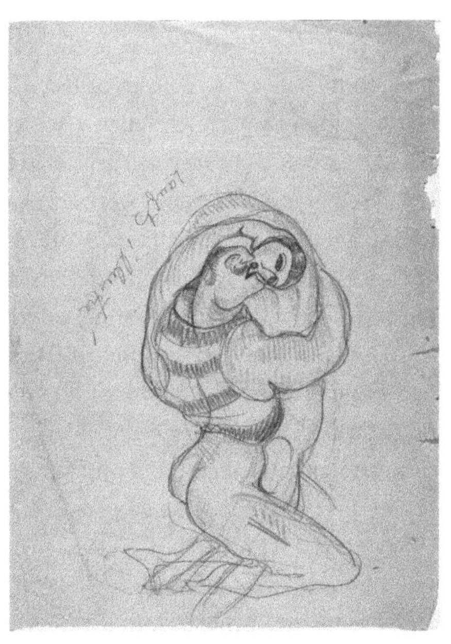

FIGURE 3. Sergei Eisenstein, *Untitled* (n.d.). Private Collection, Courtesy of Alexander Gray Associates, New York and Matthew Stephenson, London

as exotic and desirable, as embodiments of an attractive otherness. Taken together, these drawings form the equivalent of a documentary catalogue of European gay life, especially in France. Stylistically, they can be compared with Jean Cocteau's homoerotic illustrations in *The White Book* (1928), which Eisenstein might have seen during his stay in Paris since, according to his diaries and *Memories*, he was friends with Cocteau and met with him several times in Paris (Eizenshtein 1995d, 240–254; Bergan 1999: 174–176). Their friendship is well-evidenced in a letter dated February 13, 1930, in which Cocteau invites Eisenstein to attend the general rehearsal of *La Voie humaine*. It concludes with these words, "I love you and admire you. Please try to come and see this attempt of an artist to come out of himself and become anonymous" (Cocteau 1930, 11–12). Moreover, Eisenstein's knowledge of Cocteau's drawings is revealed by Eisenstein's later comments on Cocteau's "ecstatic" graphic style, which was a result of his use of opium (Eizenshtein 2009, 106).

In some cases, Eisenstein relies on his encounters with homosexual life in Europe and America to nurture his imagination, developing imaginary scenes and exploring fantasies

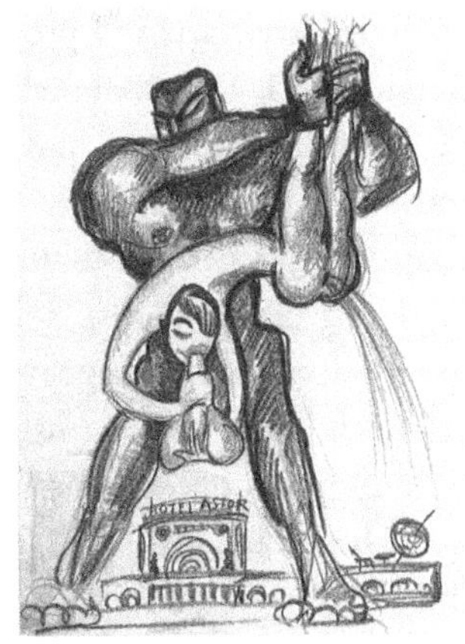

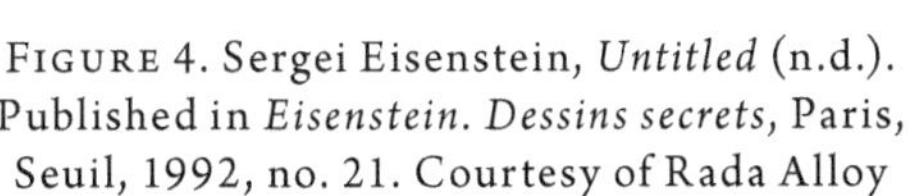

FIGURE 4. Sergei Eisenstein, *Untitled* (n.d.). Published in *Eisenstein. Dessins secrets*, Paris, Seuil, 1992, no. 21. Courtesy of Rada Alloy

of his own. He transforms past situations and places visited in Europe into his own crude scenarios. In one of them, an extremely vigorous Black man forces a young man to perform fellatio, with the Hôtel Astor, where Eisenstein spent his December 1929 stay in Paris, visible in the background (Hansen 2012, 23) (fig. 4). It is as if Eisenstein were acknowledging how much these places aroused his imagination. As such, these erotic drawings appear to function as an intimate and secret diary of Eisenstein's dreams and desires, as well as a site for concentrating and storing the creative energy derived from sex.

Drawing acquired another function when Eisenstein returned to the USSR in 1932 following the failure of his Mexican project. He faced trouble with the Soviet authorities, partly because of his alleged "unconventional" sexual orientation, an accusation fueled, for instance, by the writer Upton Sinclair who, during his conflict with the filmmaker over *¡Que Viva Mexico!*, sent letters of complaint to several Soviet officials about Eisenstein's sexual behavior and his "very elaborate obscene drawings" (Bergan 1999, 232–33). The American poet Kenneth Rexroth reported that before Eisenstein left the US for the USSR, the filmmaker expressed his concern over the fact that "they" had some compromising information about his homosexuality that "they" were threatening to reveal (Brakhage 1997, 98–99). If the anecdote is true, Eisenstein's worries were not exaggerated as the status of homosexuality was changing in the USSR as state policy took a conservative turn. As Laurie Essig explains, "by the end of the 1920s, daily life under the Soviets was increasingly politicized. Conversations, letters, diaries, dress and, of course, desire were becoming matters of state. In the panopticon of Stalinist Russia, sexual practices were no longer affairs of the individual, but indicative of political systems" (Essig 1999, 5).

The Party started to promote the family as the social nucleus of the regime (Healey 2001, 196–203; Stella 2014, 28–30), and homosexuality was considered a crime against the state, and the workers' society and was increasingly associated with fascism as expressed in Maxim Gorky's famous call to the proletariat to "crush homosexuality in order to make fascism disappear" (Gorky 1953, 238). From the beginning of the 1930s, "socially harmful elements" (*sotsvredniki*) became the targets of police campaigns against public disorder (Hagenloh 2009, 117–118). In March 1934, *muzhelozhstvo* (lying with a man) became a crime, punishable with five years of imprisonment in the labor camps, and homosexuals were arrested beginning in 1933 (Gessen 1994, 8). In this context, many famous homosexuals were encouraged to enter straight unions (Essig 1999, 5). Probably for this reason Eisenstein married Pera Atasheva in 1934 (Karlinsky 1989, 360–61).

Eisenstein's relatives and friends regularly destroyed his explicit drawings, especially the homoerotic ones, as it was too *risky* to keep such compromising material (Ivanov/ Goriaeva 2006, 22).[16] Ironically, it so happens that Muscovite gays frequently met right near Eisenstein's flat on Chistye Prudy (Neuberger 2012, 23).

Under these conditions, with Eisenstein under suspicion and deprived of the possibility of travelling abroad again, drawing offered him the opportunity to revive scenes of sexual freedom. Drawing became a medium for nostalgia, an act of mourning for an unrepeatable joyful past. His drawings function as markers of a lost sensual paradise and as a form of escapism and fantasy. In some cases, Eisenstein returns to scenes witnessed more than a decade earlier: "Pacific Coast, Mexico, 1931" was drawn in 1942 and features a gorgeous young man lying sensually on the beach. Made on September 26, 1942, "*On se coudoie au 'Magic'*" [One mingles with each other at the Magic] restores a scene experienced in Toulon, France. In "Drag New York," executed the same day, Eisenstein reconstitutes the queer life he witnessed in the US (fig. 5). In "*Berlin raté*" [Failed Berlin], made in 1933, Eisenstein depicts homosexual intercourse, which appears to inspire bliss in the one character whose face is visible (fig. 6). It is as if Eisenstein were regretting not having indulged in such pleasures when he was in Berlin, knowing it would be difficult, if not impossible, to find them again in the USSR.

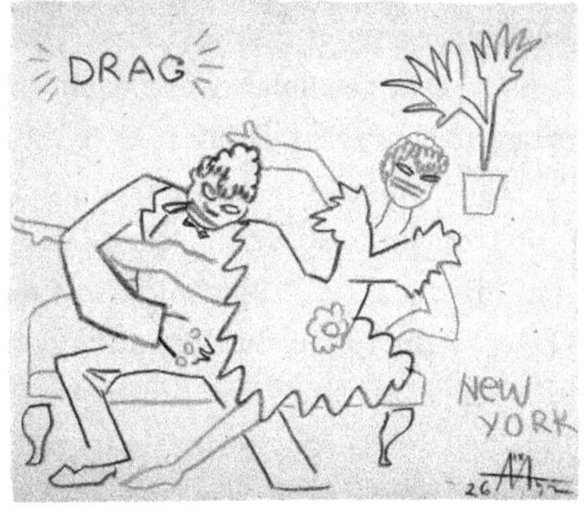

FIGURE 5. Sergei Eisenstein, *Drag New York* (September 26, 1942). Private Collection, Courtesy of Alexander Gray Associates, New York and Matthew Stephenson, London

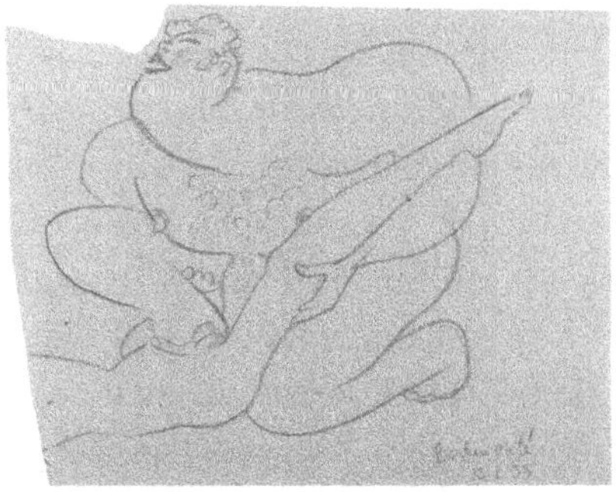

FIGURE 6. Sergei Eisenstein, *Berlin raté* (Spoiled Berlin) (January 13, 1933). Published in *Eisenstein. Dessins secrets*, Paris, Seuil, 1992, no. 60. Courtesy of Rada Alloy

A World of Cruelty and Shame

Looking at Eisenstein's homoerotic drawings, one is struck by the violence depicted between the partners. As Viacheslav Ivanov notes, Eisenstein's erotic drawings convey mixed feelings; their comic quality is, in most cases, deeply interwoven with tragedy and a gloomy quality (Ivanov 2006, 17). One of Eisenstein's favorite motifs consists of a huge partner forcing a smaller one to have sex, dominating him and humiliating him (fig. 4). This is not surprising as Eisenstein's imagery—in his movies as well as in his drawings—is filled with cruel and sadistic scenes of violence exerted by one group over another as a highly efficient means of conveying pathos.

The recurring theme of violent homosexuality is related not only to Eisenstein's conception of sex as struggle and as a terrifying sphere but also to his shame over his sexual drives; his initial fear that they were "of an unhealthy sensuality" (Eizenshtein 1995c, 492) could only be enhanced by the homophobic context of Stalinist Russia. Some drawings reveal how Eisenstein interiorized and assimilated the straight norm, as reflected in self-hatred and in shame over his own potential gayness.[17] For instance, in some captions Eisenstein uses homophobic expressions borrowed from French and English slang: "harlots," "*tapettes* [fags]," "the love that dare not speak its name," and so on. Often, the characters depicted make gestures of shame or attempt to hide themselves.

It is no wonder that Eisenstein's imagery so often features masks and costumes. The motif of the mask, especially in self-portraits, embodies the alienation felt by the subject from himself as a result of aspects of the self that he does not wish to acknowledge and accept. Of course, the mask also alludes to the necessity for the *homo Sovieticus* to hide anything compromising. Therefore, in Eisenstein's iconography transvestism and disguise acquire a broader meaning; not only do they reveal his fascination with the queer world, but they also function as a metaphor for the strategy of protecting oneself in a totalitarian society.

Eisenstein's ambivalent attitude toward his gay tendencies might explain why he returned repeatedly to the motif of Saint Sebastian in his drawings and in his films. Visual images of the martyrdom of Saint Sebastian present a desirable, young male, pierced and penetrated by arrows, whose torments can be construed as sensual ecstasy (Kaye 1996, 86–105; Kaye 1999, 269–303). In numerous drawings dedicated to Saint Sebastian, Eisenstein indulges in the pleasure of representing an athletic male body, which he tortures at the same time, as if to get rid of the shameful object while taking revenge on it through the guilty

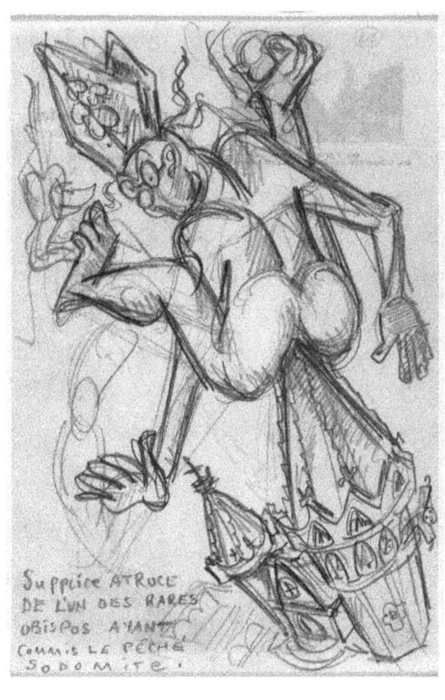

Figure 7. Sergei Eisenstein, *Supplice atroce de l'un des rares obispos ayant commis le péché sodomite* (Excruciating torture of one of the few obispos having indulged in the sodomite sin) (c. 1931). Private Collection, Courtesy of Alexander Gray Associates, New York and Matthew Stephenson, London

excitement it provides. This same binary—of repression and excitation—structures scenes in which Eisenstein represents gay couples having sex while one of the partners is being crucified. This wish to expurgate himself of shameful desires through art appears very clearly in some of his most violent compositions, in which Eisenstein imagines corporal punishment and torture for people indulging in anal intercourse, such as priests sodomized by church towers, Mexican peasants raped by huge cactuses, and so on (fig. 7). Here Eisenstein fuels his compositions with memories of satirical Soviet antireligious propaganda, which often emphasized the clergy's alleged depravity by highlighting its homosexual lust, which was meant to disgust the "straight" and honorable Soviet citizen (Healey 2001, 153–156).

The introduction of homosexuality as a shameful element is also evident in Eisenstein's provocative

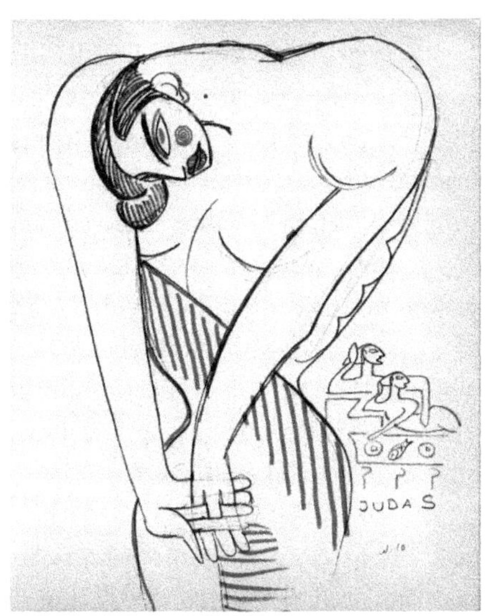

Figure 8. Sergei Eisenstein, *Judas* (n.d.). Published in *Meksikanskie risunki Eizenshteina*, Moscow, 1969, p. 45

and blasphemous depictions of Biblical scenes. Drawing inspiration from Baroque Mexican art and relying upon a rich iconographic tradition emphasizing Christ's effeminacy—or at least his gendered indeterminacy and ambivalence (Ward 1998, 170–92; Stevens 1993, 118–149)— Eisenstein transforms Jesus into a languorous transvestite, exhibiting his semi–nude legs adorned with a garter. In a similar fashion, Judas, the traitor, as rendered by Eisenstein, becomes an effeminate man with a slim waist and heavy makeup, while the other apostles appear in the background, tenderly holding one other (fig. 8). Here effeminacy becomes a symbol of treason—like the effeminate Kurbsky in *Ivan the Terrible*—and functions as evidence of the shame experienced by the artist and of his desire to keep the gay world at a distance.

Gay Models

During that same time, Eisenstein was looking for homosexual models to legitimize his own attractions and support his theories about bisexuality, art, and the human psyche. In his writings, for instance, he frequently quotes Oscar Wilde, with whom he felt a strong affinity.[18] An important cycle of Eisenstein's drawings feature the seductress Salomé, whose extravagant sexual and sadistic qualities recall Wilde's scandalous play *Salomé* conceived with his young lover Lord Alfred Douglas and illustrated by Aubrey Beardsley. (Wilde wrote the play in French and Douglas translated it into English.) Eisenstein might have feared finding himself in a situation similar to that of Wilde, who was famously tried for "acts of gross indecency" and condemned to two years in prison (Foldy 1997, 31).

In his drawings, Eisenstein appears obsessed with the lives of famous gay couples. Many drawings are dedicated to Socrates and his young male lovers, to "Greek philosophy" as a historical period when homosexual relations were normal and considered a means of acquiring wisdom. In one drawing, a smiling Socrates is harmoniously coupling with his young lover, as in the famous image from *The Symposium*. The couple is perfectly framed by the building behind them (supported by exaggerated phallic columns) as if to suggest that their union is organically inscribed in the social order of that time. In this respect, both the cycle devoted to Socrates and the one where Eisenstein imagines an ideal love and sexual life between male angels celebrate a golden and mythical age of same-sex love.

In some of the more explicit drawings, Eisenstein depicts the passion between Nijinsky and Diaghilev, or between Rimbaud and Verlaine ("Arthur et

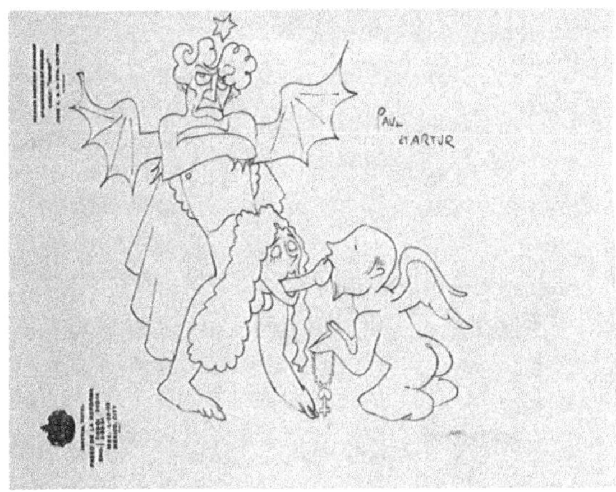

FIGURE 9. Sergei Eisenstein, *Paul et Arthur* (Paul and Arthur) (n.d.). Published in *Eisenstein. Dessins secrets*, Paris, Seuil, 1992, no. 46. Courtesy of Rada Alloy

Paul"), whose sexual life he renders with vivid and humorous details, making fun of Verlaine's attachment to Christianity (fig. 9). In this regard it is worth noting that Eisenstein might have discovered specific information about Verlaine at the Hirschfeld Institute, which possessed important archival material about famous homosexuals (Eizenshtein 2002b: 286).

Conclusion

It would be a mistake to reduce Eisenstein's homoerotic drawings to mere autobiographical data. What is also at stake in Eisenstein's representations of homo—or any nonnormative sexuality—is related to his exploration of art as transgression and as a creative force enabling the transformation of the world and the refashioning of categories and norms. This is a quality that Eisenstein labeled "plasmaticity" and which, according to him, found one of its most refined expressions in Walt Disney's protean art (Eizenshtein 2012, 15). In that respect, it is worth considering Eisenstein's erotic drawings in relation to the circus. Fascinated with the circus from an early age, Eisenstein valued its transgressive, subversive, as well as timeless qualities, which allow it to remain free from ideology (Eizenshtein 2002c, 431–39). In a Bakhtinian way, the circus imagery enables Eisenstein to carnivalize the world and turn it upside down, to invert existing categories, and to redefine and transgress borders and boundaries. It is no wonder then that Eisenstein invests many of his homoerotic drawings with a circus theme.

Mediated through the circus, homosexuality appears in Eisenstein's drawings as a stage upon which identities can be playfully renegotiated and transformed.

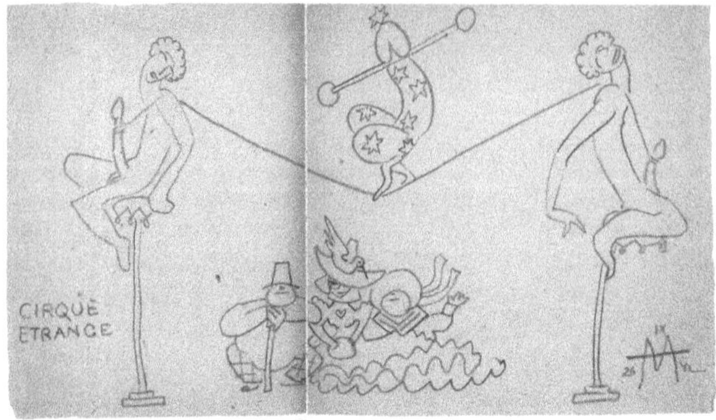

FIGURE 10. Sergei Eisenstein, *Cirque étrange* (Strange circus) (September 26, 1942). Published in *Eisenstein. Dessins secrets*, Paris, Seuil, 1992, no. 90. Courtesy of Rada Alloy

In one drawing, labeled "*Cirque étrange*" [Strange Circus], Eisenstein expresses his fascination with the male anatomy. By employing a favorite device that he called "*pars pro toto*," or part for whole, he transforms an acrobat into a giant phallus trying to keep its balance on a rope and mimicking a bird (fig. 10). This fantastic and comic scene, informed by Eisenstein's anthropological research on phallic cults as well as by his passion for Walt Disney and for Nikolai Gogol, finds a parallel in Eisenstein's staging of *Enough Stupidity in Every Wise Man* in 1923, where his close collaborator, the handsome Grigori Aleksandrov, had to cross a tightrope, which was not without danger, and so represented an "attraction" (as understood in Eisenstein's concept of "montage of attractions"). This drawing functions as a kind of manifesto in which Eisenstein posits the "strange circus" of homosexuality as a place where social norms and identities can be radically transformed and subverted: The autonomous phallus joyfully and provocatively dominates the typical bourgeois family watching him. The phallus is not only emancipated from the classic model of the family but also from the very body to which it belongs, accessing therefore a new status and identity—an obscene parody of Gogol's "Nose." The circus thus embodies a space of absolute freedom in which one can define and redefine oneself in a protean fashion ad infinitum. As such, the circus for Eisenstein maximally echoes a lifelong fascination with shape-shifting processes and a rejection of fixed forms (Jach 2018).

Eisenstein's drawings, intimate as they are, allow us to get closer to the hidden Eisenstein. However, rather than confining Eisenstein to a hermetic sexual category and label, his homoerotic drawings are evidence of his curiosity and fascination with the gay world as one possible identity among many. Above all, they assert the power of fantasy, imagination, and art in times of censorship and control.

Notes

1 Eisenstein's interview for the American newspaper *New Masses,* quoted in Bulgakowa (2001, 80).

2 S. M. Eizenshtein, "Imitation as Mastery" (Eisenstein 2006, 16).

3 Eisenstein's diary, 1931, quoted by Kleiman (2017, 274).

4 See for instance Britton (2009, 282–301); LaValley (2001); Tyler (1972, 320–323); Waugh (1996, 124–125; 132–137); and Waugh (2004, 59–68).

5 On Eisenstein and Aleksandrov, see Bergan (1999, 71–72; 121); on Eisenstein and Meyerhold, see Kozlov (1971) and Zabrodin (2005).

6 *Fireworks* (1947) alludes to the ecstatic milk separator in Eisenstein's *The General Line*'s (1929); in *Inauguration of the Pleasure Dome* (1954), Kenneth Anger references Eisenstein's use of masks in *¡Que Viva Mexico!* (1932), for which Anger provided the editing while he was working with Henri Langlois at the French Cinémathèque.

7 Taylor and Haggerty (2013, 271–272); Howes (2001, 170–171); Pendleton and Gerstner (2006, 201–202); Stern (2009, 162); and Chin and Summers (2012, 105–106).

8 The latest and most complete study on Eisenstein's graphic practice can be found in Christie and Kleiman (2017).

9 On Eisenstein's erotic drawings and their agendas, see Neuberger (2012, 5–52); Ivanov (2006, 15–32) and Marcadé and Ackerman (1999). Eisenstein's erotic drawings have been exhibited several times, for instance, during the Cannes Film Festival in 2006 in the exhibition *A Mischievous Eisenstein* and in New York in 2017 at the Gray Gallery in the exhibition *Sergei Eisenstein: Drawings, 1931 1948.*

10 The words "oversexed" and "undersexed" are written in English in the original text.

11 Eisenstein's choice to "sublimate" his homosexuality into creativity can be compared to Jean Epstein's conception, according to which the sublimation of sexuality leads the homosexual artist to reach his personal imaginative potential (Epstein 2014, 99).

12 On Weininger in Russia, see Essig (1999, 26) and Engelstein (1992, 301–302; 328 329), on Eisenstein and Weininger, see Bershtein (2004, 64–89).

13 On Eisenstein and bisexuality, see Tsivian (2002, 60–73).

14 As evidenced in the collections from the Moscow State Central Film Museum, Eisenstein possessed in his library at least three books by Hirschfeld: *Das Erotische Weltbild* (1929), *Die Weltreise eines Sexualforschers* (1933), which he had in its 1935 English translation, *Men and Women. The World Journey of a Sexologist,* and *Sittengeschichte des Weltkrieges* (1930). I am grateful to Vera Rumyantseva from Moscow State Central Film Museum for providing me with this information.

15 This translation is by the author.

16 As Ivanov points out, in the USA too, people got rid of Eisenstein's prurient works, as did Upton Sinclair, fearing they might be perceived as a supporter of pornography.

17 On shame experienced by gay and lesbian communities, see Halperin and Traub 2009.

18 Eisenstein calls him the "great aesthete" in his *Memoirs* (Eizenshtein 1997a: 290). He mentions *Salomé* with Beardsley's illustrations (Eizenshtein 1997b: 83).

References

Barna, Yon. 1973. *Eisenstein*. London: Secker and Warburg.

Bergan, Ronald. 1999. *Sergei Eisenstein. A Life in Conflict*. London: Overlook Press.

Bershtein, Evgenii. 2004."Tragediia pola: dve zametki o russkom veiningerianstve," in *Erotizm bez beregov: sbornik stat'ei*, edited by Margarita Mikhailovna Pavlova, 64–89. Moscow: NLO.

Brakhage, Stan. 1997. *Film Biographies*. Berkeley: Turtle Island.

Britton, Andrew. 2009. *Britton on Film*. Detroit: Wayne State University Press.

Bulgakowa, Oksana. 2001. *Sergei Eisenstein. A Biography*. Berlin: Potemkin Press.

———. 1998. *Eisenstein und Deutschland*. Berlin: Akademie der Künste.

Chin, Daryl. 2012. "Sergei Eisenstein." In *The Queer Encyclopedia of Film and Television*, edited by Claude Summers, 105–106. New York: Simon and Schuster.

Christie, Ian and Kleiman, Naum. 2017. *Eisenstein on Paper. Graphic Works by the Master of Film*. London: Thames and Hudson.

Cocteau, Jean. 1930. "Letter to Sergei Eisenstein." Eisenstein Archive, RGALI, Moscow, 1923-1-1867.

Duberman, Martin. 2007. *The Worlds of Lincoln Kirstein*. New York: Knopf.

Engelstein, Laura. 1992. *The Keys to Happiness. Sex and the Search for Modernity in Fin-de-Siècle Russia*. Ithaca: Cornell University Press.

Eisenstein, Sergei. 1930. "Diary." RGALI, Moscow, 1923-2-1109.

———. 1988. "The Montage of Film Attractions." In *Selected Works. Vol. 1. Writings 1922–1934*, edited and translated by Richard Taylor, 39–58. London: British Film Institute.

———. 1995a. "Wie sag' ich's meinem Kinde?!" In *Beyond the Stars: The Memoirs of Sergei Eisenstein*, edited by Richard Taylor and translated by William Powell, 424–456. London: BFI/Seagull Books.

——— 1995b. "The Boy from Riga (An Obedient Child)." In *Beyond the Stars: The Memoirs of Sergei Eisenstein*, edited by Richard Taylor and translated by William Powell, 16–22. London: BFI/Seagull Books.

———. 1995c. "*Monsieur, Madame et Bébé*." In *Beyond the Stars: The Memoirs of Sergei Eisenstein*, edited by Richard Taylor and translated by William Powell, 487–506. London: BFI/Seagull Books.

———. 1995d. "*Épopée*." In *Beyond the Stars: The Memoirs of Sergei Eisenstein*, edited by Richard Taylor and translated by William Powell, 184–257. London: BFI/Seagull Books.

———. 1997a. "Knizhnye lavki." In *Memuary*, vol. 1, edited by Naum Kleiman, 284–306. Moscow, Muzei Kino.

———. 1997b. "Svetloi pamiati markiza." In *Memuary*, vol. 2, edited by Naum Kleiman, 67–114. Moscow, Muzei Kino.

———. 1998. "Letter to Pera Atasheva, 1931." *Kinovedcheskie zapiski* 36/37: 220–224.

———. 2002a. "Konspekt dlia stat'i Annity Brenner o moikh risunkakh dlia *Creative Art*." In *Metod*, vol. 1, edited by Naum Kleiman, 494–496. Moscow: Muzei Kino.

———. 2002b. "Zdvig na biologicheskii uroven'." In *Metod*, vol. 1, edited by Naum Kleiman, 285–286. Moscow: Muzei Kino.

———. 2002c. "Misteriia tsirka. Struktura kak siuzhet." In *Metod*, vol. 1, edited by Naum Kleiman, 431–439. Moscow: Muzei Kino.

———. 2006. "Imitation as Mastery." In *The Eisenstein Collection*, edited by Richard Taylor, 11–19. London: Seagull Books.

———. 2009. "El Greco y el cine." In *Cinématisme, peinture et cinéma*, edited by François Albera and translated by Valérie Pozner, 65–128. Paris: Les Presses du réel/Kargo.

———. 2012. *Disney*, edited by Oksana Bulgakowa and Dietmar Hochmuth. Berlin: Potemkin Press.

Elder, Miriam. 2013. "Russia Passes Law Banning Gay Propaganda." *The Guardian* (June 11). Available at: https://www.theguardian.com/world/2013/jun/11/russia-law-banning-gay-propaganda. Last accessed May 21, 2021.

Epstein, Jean. 2014. *Ganymède, essai sur l'éthique homosexuelle masculine. Photogénie de l'impondérable et autres écrits*, edited by Nicole Brenez, Joël Daire, Cyril Neyrat. Dijon: Independencia Editions.

Essig, Laurie. 1999. *Queer in Russia. A Story of Sex, Self and the Other*. Durham: Duke University Press.

Foldy, Michael S. 1997. *The Trials of Oscar Wilde. Deviance, Morality, and Late-Victorian Society.* New Haven: Yale University Press.

Gert, Valeska. 2002. "I Witch." *Kinovedcheskie Zapiski* 58: 121.

Gessen, Masha, 1994. *The Rights of Lesbians and Gay Men in the Russian Federation*. San Francisco: IGLHRC.

Gorky, Maksim. 1953, "Proletarskii gumanizm." In *Sobranie sochinenii*. Vol. 27, 233–241. Moscow: Goslitizdat.

Gray, Carmen. 2015. "Greenaway Offends Russia with Film about Soviet Director Gay's Love Affair. *The Calvert Journal* (March 30). Available at: http://calvertjournal.com/articles/show/3767/peter-greenaway-Eisenstein-in-guanajuato-berlinale-interview. Last accessed: May 21, 2021.

Greenaway, Peter. 2015. "Vozmozhno, v Rossii na menia obidiatsia." Interview with Tatiana Rosenshtain. *Ogoniok* (February 23). Available at: http://www.kommersant.ru/doc/2669010. Last accessed May 21, 2021.

Hagenloh, Paul. 2009. *Stalin's Police: Public Order and Mass Repression in USSR, 1926 1941*. Baltimore: John Hopkins University Press.

Halperin, David M. and Traub, Valerie (eds.). 2009. *Gay Shame*. Chicago: University of Chicago Press.

Hansen, Arlen J. 2012. *Expatriate Paris: A Cultural and Literary Guide to Paris of the 1920s.* New York: Arcade.

Healey, Dan. 2001. *Homosexual Desire in Revolutionary Russia.* Chicago: University of Chicago Press.

Howes, Keith. 2001. "Sergei Eisenstein." In *Who's Who in Contemporary Gay and Lesbian History: From World War II to the Present Day,* edited by Robert Aldrich and Garry Wotherspoon, 170–171. London: Routledge.

Ivanov, Viacheslav. 2006. "Eisenstein's Risqué Drawings and the 'Cardinal Problem' of His Art." In *A Mischievous Eisenstein,* edited by Tatiana Goriaeva, 15–32. St. Petersburg: Slavia.

Jach, Aleksandra. 2018. *Shapeshifting: Eisenstein as a Method,* Exhibition catalogue. Łodz, Muzeum Sztuki, June 22–September 23, 2018.

Karlinsky, Simon. 1989. "Russia's Gay Literature and Culture: The Impact of the October Revolution." In *Hidden from History: Reclaiming the Gay and Lesbian Past,* George Chauncey, edited by George Chauncey, Martin Duberman and Marta Vicinus, 360–361. New York: NAL Books.

Kaye, Richard A. 1996. *"Losing His Religion: Saint Sebastian as Contemporary Gay Martyr."* In *Outlook and Gay Sexualities in Visual Cultures,* edited by Peter Horne and Reina Lewis, 86–105. New York: Routledge.

———. 1999. "Determined Raptures: St. Sebastian and the Victorian Discourse of Decadence." *Victorian Literature and Culture* 27(1): 269–303.

Kleiman, Naum. 2002. "Kommentarii." In *Metod,* vol.1, edited by Naum Kleiman, 444–492. Moscow: Muzei Kino.

Kozlov, Leonid. 1971. "L'hypothèse d'une dédicace secrète." *Cahiers du Cinéma* 226/227: 57–66.

LaValley, Al. 2001. "Maintaining, Blurring and Transcending Genre Lines in Eisenstein." In *Eisenstein at 100: A Reconsideration,* edited by Al LaValley and Barry P. Scherr, 52–64. New Brunswick, New Jersey: Rutgers University Press.

Marcadé, Jean-Claude and Ackerman, Galia. 1999. *Dessins secrets.* Paris: Le Seuil.

McLaughlin, Eleanor. 1993. "Feminist Christologies: Re-Dressing the Tradition." In *Reconstructing the Christ Symbol: Essays in Feminist Christology,* edited by Maryanne Stevens, 118–149. Mahwah, N.J: Paulist Press.

Nazvanov, Mikhail. 1998. "Prokliataia kartina": Pis'ma k Ol'ge Viklandt so s'emok fil'ma "Ivan Groznyi" (1944). *Iskusstvo kino* 2. Available at: https://old.kinoart.ru/archive/1998/02/n2-article20. Last accessed May 1, 2020.

Neuberger, Joan. 2012. "Strange Circus. Eisenstein's Sex Drawings." *Studies in Russian and Soviet Cinema* 6(1): 5–52.

Pendleton, David. 2006. "Sergei Eisenstein." In *Routledge International Encyclopedia of Queer Culture,* edited by David A. Gerstner, 201–202. London: Routledge.

Salazkina, Masha. 2009. *In Excess. Sergei Eisenstein's Mexico.* Chicago: University of Chicago Press.

Seton, Mary. 1960. *Sergei Eisenstein.* New York: Grove Press.

Stella, Francesca. 2014. *Lesbian Lives in Soviet and Post-Soviet Russia.* Basingstoke: Palgrave Macmillan.

Stern, Keith. 2009. "Sergei Eisenstein." In *Queers in History: The Comprehensive Encyclopedia of Historical Gays, Lesbians and Bisexuals, and Transgenders,* edited by Keith Stern, 162. Dallas: BenBella Books.

Tamagne, Florence. 2007. *A History of Homosexuality in Europe. Berlin, London, Paris, 1919–1939,* vol. 1. New York: Algora Publishing.

Taylor, Richard. 2013. "Sergei Eisenstein." In *Encyclopedia of Gay Histories and Cultures,* edited by George Haggerty, 271–272. New York: Routledge.

Tsivian, Yuri. 2002. *Ivan the Terrible.* London: BFI Classics.

Tyler, Parker. 1972. *Screening the Sexes: Homosexuality in the Movies.* New York: Rienhard and Winston.

Ward, Graham. 1998. "The Gendered Body of the Jewish Jesus." In *Religion & Sexuality,* edited by Michel Hayes, Wendy Porter and David Tombs, 170–92. Sheffield: Sheffield Academic Press.

Waugh, Thomas. 1996. *Hard to Imagine: Gay Male Eroticism in Photography and Film from Their Beginnings to Stonewall.* New York: Columbia Press.

———. 2004. "A Fag-Spotter's Guide to Eisenstein." In *The Fruit Machine: Twenty Years of Writing on Queer Cinema,* 59–68. Durham: Duke University Press.

Zabrodin, Vladimir. 2005. *Eizenshtein o Meierkholde.* Moscow: Novoe Izdatel'stvo.

Zdravomyslova, Anna and Temkina, Elena. 2003. "Sovetskii etakraticheskii genderny poriadok." In *Sotsialnaia istoria. Ezhegodnik 2003. Zhenskaia i gendernaia istoriia,* edited by N. L. Pushkareva, 436–463. Moscow: ROSSPEN.

Chapter 7

Moscow Conceptualism's Erotic Objects

Yelena Kalinsky

The title of this paper is meant as a provocation. There's something off about the idea of the erotic in Moscow Conceptualism: The categories don't match. The "black-and-white" conceptualism of the 1970s was "immaterial, intangible, and elusive," in the words of Sven Gundlakh, who accused it of "bec[oming] overburdened with such a quantity of documentation that it was not clear what, in essence, was the work of art" (1983, 3).[1] With sources either juvenile (children's book illustrations and fairy tales) or sacred (Orthodox icons, Zen Buddhism, asceticism), it is hard to imagine Moscow Conceptualism engaging with the bodily, the perversely gendered, or the profane. And yet, once we go looking, examples proliferate, from Andrei Monastyrski's early visual poetry ("Excessive Tension," 1973), to actions by Gnezdo (*Fertilization of the Earth*, 1976), to Kabakov's obscene *brani*, or invective (for example, *Go to . . .*, late 1980s, silkscreen), to recent work by Vadim Zakharov. There is a profane thread running through Moscow Conceptualism that has rarely been discussed. In this chapter, I will address several works by Zakharov and his various collaborators from the 1970s to the present that seem in one way or another to touch on themes of the erotic and the profane. Reading these works through a queer lens, I will argue that erotic imagery—in particular, phallic and vaginal imagery—is queered in various ways in order to grapple with the problem of individual and collective artistic identity.

I begin with a recent work by Vadim Zakharov, *The Archive Is My Vagina* (2019), which he posted on his Facebook feed on September 9, 2019, with the comment "self-portrait is now a complete identity" (2019a) (fig. 1). The work consists of two readymades: a seated figurine with an oversized phallus cast out of an unspecified hard material and a black two-ring file binder, the latter alluding to Zakharov's self-designation as the *arkhivarius* of the Moscow Conceptualist circle. Since the early 1980s, Zakharov has served as one of the circle's chroniclers. He was the editor of the second MANI *papka* (published in June of 1981, with Viktor Skersis) and produced the first edition of *Around the Workshops* (*Po masterskim*, 1982–83, with George Kiesewalter), a collection of photographs of artists in their studios and interviews with said artists. Over the following three decades, Zakharov compiled a personal archive consisting of texts and documents, purchased and gifted artworks, and documentary videos of individual and group exhibitions that he recorded in Russia and abroad between 1989 and 2014. In addition, between 1992 and 2001, he published nine issues of *Pastor*, an annual journal that gathered in thematic collections texts and dialogues from all three generations of Moscow Conceptualists on such topics as Moscow Conceptualism's publications, artistic identity, and interest in the East.

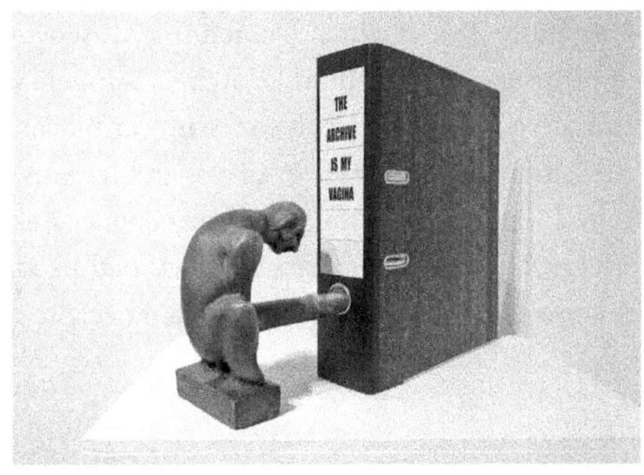

FIGURE 1. Vadim Zakharov, *The Archive Is My Vagina* (2019), found object and archive box. Courtesy of the artist

Zakharov's activities as a collector, publisher, and archivist have long intersected with his activities as an artist. In his *History of Russian Art from the Avant-Garde to the Moscow Conceptual School*, a large-scale installation produced by Zakharov in 2003 and exhibited at the Guggenheim Museum's 2005 exhibition *Russia!*, the archive takes the form of gigantic black binders that serve as a stage set that viewers can performatively "enter." "The magic of the Archive," writes Zakharov, "is in being able to hold in one's hands another historical moment, even if just for a second. This creates a sense of the miraculous, an incredible realization of time and understanding of the people around you" (2015, 124). The ability to enter Zakharov's stage-set installations, like *The History of Russian Art*, stands in for the possibility of holding in one's hands an actual fragment of the past. It is an imperfect equivalence, whereby the materiality of fragile archival documents is replaced with the frisson of physically engaging with a work in a museum. Nevertheless, both the archive and its artistic representation as stage set produce a kind of temporal enchantment that Zakharov might call "magical."

This sense of temporary euphoria, however, has a dark side, which Zakharov has characterized as the "Killer Archive," which threatens to annihilate the artist's identity, usurping the place of authorship, "completely obscuring the artist, forever burying him in its catacombs" (2009). Recently, Zakharov renounced his role as *arkhivarius*, depositing his archive with the Garage Museum of Contemporary Art, which marked the occasion with an exhibition featuring a selection of the 228 videos now in the Garage collection, entitled *Vadim Zakharov. Postscript after RIP: A Video Archive of Moscow Artists' Exhibitions (1989–2014)* (on view August 24–October 25, 2015) (fig. 2). Here, too, the characteristic archive binder is adapted as a metaphor of temporal passage and possible transformation: The videos documenting Moscow artists' exhibitions were installed in furniture-sized, coffin-like archival binders arranged in a minimalist grid and containing video monitors in the upward-facing holes in the binders' spines. The exhibition and the transfer of the archive was, according to Zakharov, a liberation. In his essay in the show's catalogue, Zakharov wrote, "the burden of the Archive's constantly increasing mass had become unbearable. [. . . C]lothed in the suit I was born in, . . . I once again became an artist" (2015, 124–5)

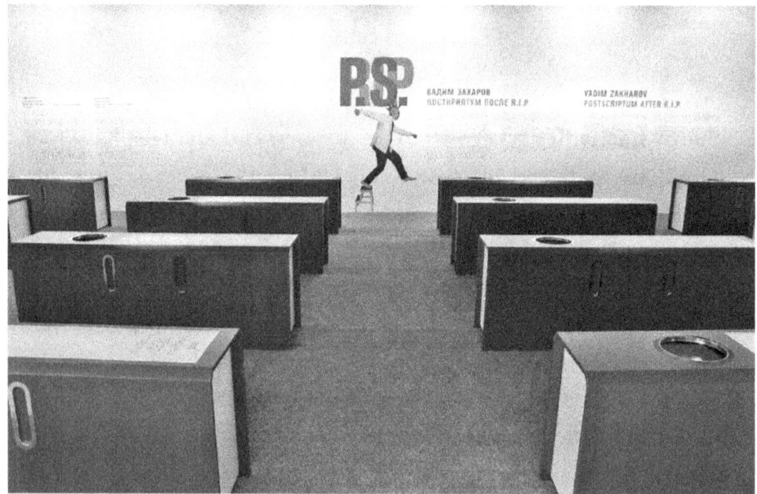

FIGURE 2. *Vadim Zakharov: Postscriptum after R.I.P. A Video Archive of Moscow Artists' Exhibitions (1989–2014)*, August 24, 2015–October 25, 2015, Garage Museum of Contemporary Art, Moscow, Installation view. Courtesy of the artist

Considering the central role the archive plays in Zakharov's oeuvre and its inseparability from the figure of the artist himself, we might look at the second part of his profane double readymade—the phallic statuette—as a figure of artistic identity, the fertile male artist depositing his works directly into the archive-as-vagina. Here we might recall the action *Fertilization of the Earth,* from the series *Helping the Soviet State in its Struggle for the Harvest* of 1976 by the group Gnezdo. In that work, Gennadii Donskoi, Mikhail Roshal', and Viktor Skersis stripped naked, prostrated themselves on the earth, performing exertions to help the flagging Soviet harvest. (1975 had seen shortfalls in Soviet grain production due to a sustained drought, leading to increased imports at high prices [U.S. Department of Agriculture Economic Research Service 1975, 7]). Lara Weibgen has read this work in the context of the *Helping the Soviet State* series of actions by Gnezdo beginning in the mid-1970s, as well as Zakharov's early collaborations with Igor' Lutts, such as *Visit to Red Square, Gestures of Appeal,* and other civic participation performances of the late 1970s and the early 1980s. In Weibgen's reading, these second-generation Moscow Conceptualist artists perform a deconstruction of the official youth paradigm by enthusiastically posing as productive Soviet citizens to subvert the already bankrupt category of Soviet youth with which they themselves could no longer identify. Instead, Weibgen argued, their over-identification "allegorizes the plight of alternative artists, whose efforts yielded few if any concrete returns, and for whose projects Soviet society seemed to have little use" (2011).

For Weibgen, however, the single documentary photograph of Gnezdo's dubious contribution to the Soviet harvest presents an ambiguity in its simultaneous registration of the "sexual potency and . . . boundless productive energy associated with the figure of the young communist constructor" and a "queering of the official youth paradigm [that] can only be understood as a gesture of desublimation" (2011). In the "proximity of the artists' naked bodies to one another and the blunt presentation of their buttocks to the viewer," she sees a nonprocreative homoeroticism that could serve as "an avatar or perhaps even a role model for the alternative artist" who does not need to construct or bring things into the world to claim an artistic identity in a system that explicitly excludes and dismisses them.

Returning to the twin themes of the Artist and the Archive, Zakharov's work takes on a similarly ambiguous cast. The readymade "self-portrait" as a prolific artist penetrating the archive with his substantial phallus reveals itself as a fantasy of the "idiot" ex-archivist who needs to assert himself to maintain a stable identity as an Artist, a word whose "stench," Zakharov claims, "causes him to vomit"

(2015, 125). Like his and Lutts's zealous Soviet youths overperforming their civic duties, Zakharov seems to be overexerting himself in performing the role of the Artist after his final execution of the Archivist. This ambivalence is evident in the phrasing of the title. While Zakharov claims ownership over the archive-as-vagina ("the archive is [mine]"), the title also suggests a transsexual artistic identity ("my vagina"), in which his attempt to kill the archive is incomplete and the archive-as-vagina continues to inhere in his artistic practice. To be sure, I am not arguing that Zakharov is claiming a transgender identity, but rather that, like he and the other second-generation Moscow Conceptualists had in the 1970s and 1980s, he is desublimating the masculine ideal of the Artist—whether the Soviet constructor, in the earlier case, or the contemporary name brand artist in the latter—in favor of something more ambiguous and fluid.

There is, however, a difference between the two moments that troubles this analogy and casts Zakharov's later work in a more pathetic light. The late-1970s second generation, according to Weibgen, successfully pilloried the ideal of the artist-modernist (whether Soviet or Western) in favor of a performative, non-productive, collective practice. This subversive collective practice then blossomed into a second wave of colorful, exuberant performances, exhibitions, and outdoor happenings that we today associate with APTART, Mukhomor, and the "new wave" of the 1980s (Tupitsyn 2009, 87). By analogy, Zakharov's recent position seems to take the reverse view. The constantly expanding Archive that oppresses him also contains within it the collectivity that had sustained Moscow Conceptualism from its beginning by serving as audience, curator, collector, and critic at a time when artistic institutions were hostile or nonexistent. It is no wonder that Zakharov finds it difficult to kill this collectivity off and claim his own proper name outside the circle. The figure of the pathetic, hunched over onanist fucking the undead corpse of the archive-as-vagina (while also unconsciously identifying with it) is a maudlin allegory of the Moscow Conceptualist circle's double bind in the present system of contemporary art.

Zakharov says as much with a pair of works he made in 2008 for Kapiton, an artist collective consisting of Zakharov, Yuri Leiderman, and Andrei Monastyrski, who met throughout 2008 to share and discuss works that each member made specifically for these encounters (2008). For the ninth and final meeting, Zakharov offered a pair of excessively referential assemblages: *Nightmare: The Cock of Contemporary Art Discovered in the Inkwell of Moscow Conceptualism*, consisting of a latex phallus inserted into a glass inkwell and capped by the inkwell's brass lid; and *Three Darknesses for the Cunt*, or *Moksha, Covered by Kapiton*, or *The Struggle for Style,* a silicone vulva set on top of the 1936 Marxist tract *The Struggle for Style* by Ivan Arkhipovich Vinogradov, hidden beneath three bowler hats that, when removed in the course of the work's demonstration, reveal the vulva (figs. 3, 4, and 5). Zakharov decodes the works during the group discussion, which was recorded and later published in a volume documenting the collective Kapiton experiment:

> It was important to me to make a work, every detail of which would in itself connect the sum total of the signs and associations belonging to the artistic tradition that continues to be important to us. What's more, this tradition of Collective Actions, Leiderman, "Inspection Medical Hermeneutics" passes in an instant into Duchamp, Magritte, Broodthaers, etc. [. . .] [T]he cock of contemporary art [in *Nightmare: The Cock of Contemporary Art Discovered in the Inkwell of Moscow Conceptualism*] is the horror of a living dullness (*tupost'*) that has grown in the center of our conceptual (*umozritel'nogo*) creative work. Our center is in the inkwell, in the ocean of words. And it is precisely there [. . .] that this living member, like a mushroom of a foreign contemporary art tradition, has sprung up. We have no access to the ink. Nowness (*aktual'nost'*) in the form of the cock blocks all paths to the creative well. And this is why we are discussing in one way or another precisely this problem: how to remove this fuckery (*khuinia*) from our brains, from our present situation. For me, it is important that in our context, any nowness and aliveness carry a *negative sense.* We keep running into this cock-spectacle (*chlen-attraktsion*) and cannot get to the ink. It seems to me that this work describes very precisely today's situation. This member won't let us do anything; it blocks everything in sight with its erection (2008, 186).[2]

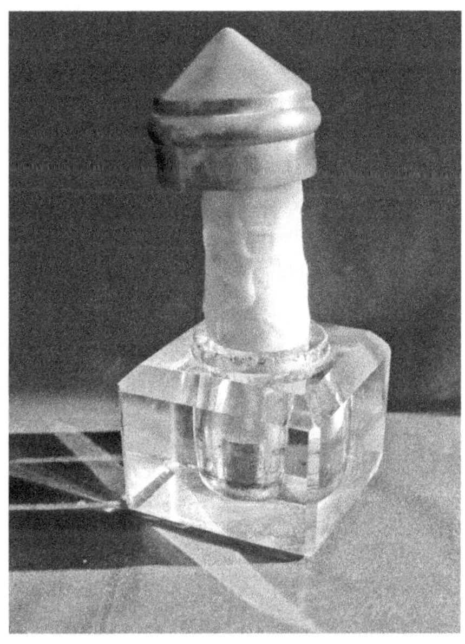

FIGURE 3. Vadim Zakharov, *Nightmare: The Cock of Contemporary Art Discovered in the Inkwell of Moscow Conceptualism* (2008), latex phallus, glass inkwell with brass lid. Courtesy of the artist

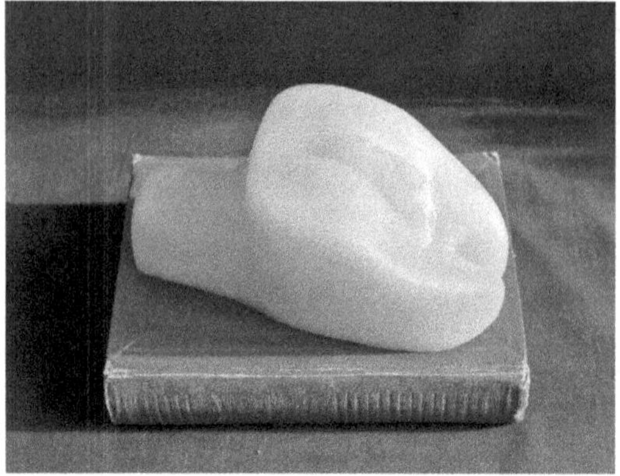

FIGURE 4. Vadim Zakharov, *Three Darknesses for the Cunt*, or *Moksha, Covered by Kapiton*, or *the Struggle for Style* (2008), silicone vulva, three bowler hats, and the book *The Struggle for Style* by I. A. Vinogradov (1936). Courtesy of the artist

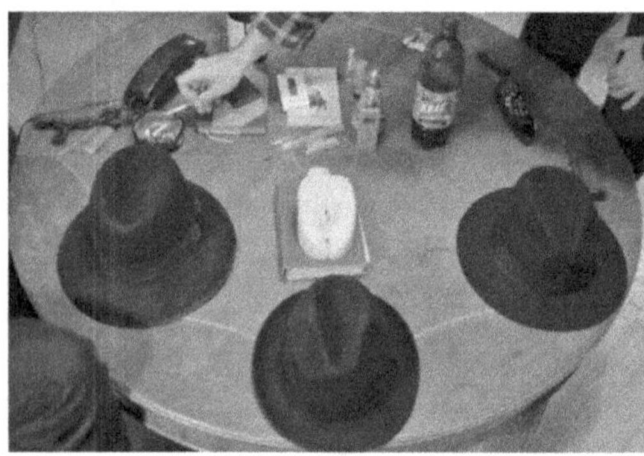

FIGURE 5. Vadim Zakharov, *Three Darknesses for the Cunt* performed at the Ninth meeting of Kapiton, December 29, 2008, photodocumentation. Courtesy of the artist

In response to Monastyrski's question of whether the phallus could be inserted into the vagina and turned on, Zakharov responds negatively:

> No, that's the whole point. There should be no intercourse. [. . .] The vagina possesses a certain positive quality, a sacrality, a mystery. The aggressive male mushroom that's grown up in the wrong place covers up and chokes all sacral feelings. If we cut it off, the mushroom's base will still remain, and from it another mushroom will grow. How to get it out of there is the whole question (2008, 187).

Zakharov laments the narrowing of artistic discourse in favor of novelty under extreme market conditions. In compensation for this creative loss, he crams his works full of obvious references to works such as Marcel Duchamp's *Female Fig Leaf* (1950); Man Ray's photograph of Duchamp as *Rrose Sélavy* (1923); René Magritte's use of the bowler hat, as in *Le fils de l'homme* (1964); and the

Collective Actions' performance *For Panitkov* (*Three Darknesses*) of February 17, 1980 (in which Nikolai Panitkov was encased in three paper enclosures from which he had to break out), among others. Almost nostalgically, Zakharov includes the Marxist tract *The Struggle for Style*, ready once more to battle Soviet aesthetics with his conceptualist maneuvers. Zakharov's wish to rid contemporary art of the phallic assault of novelty in favor of the plenitude of collective discourse is an echo of the second generation's embrace of the nonproductive, which Weibgen read through a queer lens.

The combination of direct references to works that were canonical in the Moscow Conceptualist tradition, like Duchamp's *Fountain* (1917), and an identification with the archive-as-vagina of discursive plenitude is not a new theme for Zakharov. In the case of Duchamp's *Fountain*, he plays on the feminized image of the Madonna of the toilet to construct an allegory of flowing discourse. Named "Common Place" (*Obshchee mesto*) on the label, *Fountain* was made to mark the publication of the first issue of *Pastor*, the journal of artists' texts that Zakharov (in the guise of his alter ego Pastor Zond) produced for the Moscow Conceptualist circle throughout the 1990s. In 2019, however, Zakharov's position between Artist and Archivist, the self and the collective, the phallic and the vaginal, is less secure, more contradictory. Rather than flowing into each other, these roles seem incompatible. Not exactly subversive, the self-deprecating bravado of the 2019 work betrays an uncertainty about the artist's function.

In 1983, the creative duo SZ (Zakharov in collaboration with Viktor Skersis, one of the members of Gnezdo) staged a solo exhibition at APTART, a makeshift gallery space organized in fellow artist Nikita Alekseev's Moscow apartment. As was the practice at APTART, the exhibition space was crammed full of objects, photographs, and texts that visitors had to navigate. The pair adopted a trickster aesthetic, spray painting graffiti on the yellow walls and posing nude in baroque poses for the photo series *Caresses and Kisses Make People Ugly*. This queer posturing extended to a series of silhouettes of a mannered Centaur and Minotaur wrestling, and another photo series of pairs of matches in what appear to be conjugal poses, entitled *The Anatomy of Matches* (1982). SZ's exhibition was raided by KGB agents, and the pair were accused of sodomy and faced five years' imprisonment, which, according to Zakharov, they barely managed to escape (2019b). The ordeal was enough to scare the group away from such explicit provocations, and APTART decamped for the outdoors, staging "APTART in Nature" (May 23, 1983) and "APTART behind the Fence" (September 25, 1983) before finally ceasing to exist.[3]

It is notable that the three works under discussion here were each exhibited outside the major circuits of the contemporary art market. APTART was a self-organized collective that exhibited in a private apartment, among other places, between 1982 and 1984. Kapiton was also a collective enterprise staged in a private apartment; its production consisted of a series of published discussions. (The Kapiton collective was also small, consisting of the three artists themselves with no outside public other than occasional invited guests.) And finally, Zakharov's *The Archive Is My Vagina* was posted to his Facebook wall, a space that members of Zakharov's circle, as well as many other Russian artists and poets, often use to share works, carry on discussions, and open their personal archives to commentary from fellow participants and viewers. Each of these alternative exhibition spaces privileges presence, engagement, and discourse, and produces documentation, images, and texts. In their own ways, their users attempt to preserve the discursive plenitude that Zakharov values and fears losing.

Throughout his career, Zakharov has risked scandalizing his audiences to elicit a response that would ensure the further development of artistic discourse. In his early photo series *Hand Inscriptions* (*I Made Enemies*) (1982), for example, he applied the Futurist "slap in the face of public taste" to his own narrow circle of unofficial Moscow art. By confrontationally criticizing four "classic" nonconformist artists at the risk of damaging his personal relationships with them, he tried to shake the older generation of artists out of what he saw as their complacency. Zakharov's erotic objects from 2008 and 2019 seem to me to originate in this tradition. Responding to a specific set of artistic conditions, they lodge a provocation, seeking to get a rise out of their viewers. They also put under pressure on received artistic positions—who is a "classic" and who an upstart, who is an Artist and who a mere Archivist. The answer is not always clear, but that may not actually be the point.

Notes

1 The original translation has been clarified.

2 "The Third Meeting," *Kapiton* (Vologda: BMK, 2008), 186. Emphasis added.

3 On the history of APTART, see Margarita Tupitsyn, Victor Tupitsyn, and David Morris, eds., *Anti-Shows: APTART, 1982-1984* (London: Afterall Books, 2017).

References

Gundlakh, Sven. 1983. "APTART: Pictures from an Exhibition." *A-Ya* 5 (1983): 3.

Leiderman, Yuri, Andrei Monastyrski, and Vadim Zakharov, eds. 2008. *Kapiton*. Vologda: Biblioteka Moskovskogo Kontseptualizma.

Tupitsyn, Margarita, Victor Tupitsyn, and David Morris, eds. 2017. *Anti-Shows: APTART, 1982–1984*. London: Afterall Books.

Tupitsyn, Victor. 2009. *The Museological Unconscious: Communal (Post)Modernism in Russia*. Cambridge: MIT Press.

U.S. Department of Agriculture Economic Research Service. 1975. "USSR's Coarse Grain Output Down 12%, Spurs Imports." *Feed Situation*. September.

Weibgen, Lara. 2011. "Juvenilia as Style: Moscow Conceptualist Performances of Youth." Paper delivered at the ASEEES 43rd Annual Convention, Washington, DC, November 17.

Zakharov, Vadim. 2009. "The Shiva Method: Archive, Collection, Publisher, Artist." *Annual International Festival of Collections of Contemporary Art. Collection and Archive by Vadim Zakharov*, n.p. Moscow: Pastor Zond Edition.

———. 2015. "P.S." *Vadim Zakharov: Postskriptum posle R.I.P. Videodokumentatsiia vystavok sovremennykh moskovskikh khudozhnikov, 1989–2014*, edited by Sasha Obukhova. Moscow: Garage Museum of Art.

———. 2019. "Vadim Zakharov © 'The Archive is my Vagina,' 2019 Self-portrait is now a complete identity." Facebook, September 9, 2019. Available at: https://www.facebook.com/pastorzond/posts/10215395485260063. Last accessed March 30, 2023.

———. 2019. Email to the author, November 6.

Chapter 8

Queering Socialist Realism: The Case of Georgy Guryanov[1]

Maria Engström

In her article on Soviet material culture in Moscow Conceptualism, the noted Russian art philosopher and critic Keti Chukhrov noted: "If we return to the Soviet socialist realist space, what we will notice is the extent to which it is [. . .] desexualized, its libidinal economy transformed into the Eros of collectivism and various forms of enthusiasm" (Chukhrov 2009). One of the strategies of aesthetic resistance to the capitalist post-Soviet space is the *resexualization* of the socialist body. The first of these "recyclings" or "remixes" of socialist realism in visual art was done in the late-eighties to early nineties by Petersburg artist Georgy Guryanov (1961–2013), widely known in Russia and in the post-Soviet states as the drummer in the band Kino.

Although the Moscow and Petersburg art scenes of the late eighties and early nineties were characterized by melancholia and work with Soviet "ruins," interpretations of Soviet heritage were often quite the opposite. In place of conceptualist and socialist realist irony, Guryanov uses another device—*queerification*—or reworking the visual canon through the lens of queer optics. Guryanov offers an alternative to the Moscow intellectual art of the text: the sensual art of the body. As an alternative to "trash" aesthetics, he offers imperial rigor and military dandyism. To the representational performance of the conceptualists, he offers the incessant and unfixed performance of life, the living experience of art. Guryanov was the first to violate the normative late-Soviet binary and create examples of a "third" art: un-Soviet, but also not anti-Soviet. He integrated a new homoerotic sensuality into the aesthetics of the "old regime" and reanimated socialist realism through an avant-garde queer utopia.

"My Greatest Artwork Is Myself."

The creative center of queer visuality in the nineties was Petersburg, where the first and leading queer art community in post-Soviet Russia—the New Academy of Fine Arts—was founded by artist and art theorist Timur Novikov (1958–2002) in 1989. Novikov was a key figure in the cultural revolution that took place during the Perestroika period of the 1980s and of the Russian queer revolution of the nineties.

The mock institution, the New Academy of Fine Arts, of which Georgy Guryanov was a professor, was one of many counterculture communities founded by Timur Novikov. In 1982, Novikov founded the New Artists movement, of which practically all the major players of the Leningrad art and music underground were members: Georgy Guryanov, Viktor Tsoi, Sergei Kurekhin, Evgeny Kozlov, and Oleg Kotelnikov, among others.[2] A defining characteristic of the New Artists was their orientation toward contemporary Western music and art. A particular stylistic feature of the artists and musicians in Timur Novikov's circle was working with Soviet found objects (readymades), a style popular in the West at that time. Guryanov worked on remakes of Soviet posters.[3] The second common denominator was life creation. The main goal of the New Artists was not to produce an art product; rather, they worked to produce themselves, to create an alternative lifeworld. A distinguishing characteristic of this community was their ambition to make works of art from themselves, from their own bodies, from their daily lives. Not only was the artefact, exhibition, or museum important, but life itself was, as was the flow and fabric of aestheticized life. Appearance became very important: the face, figure, and clothing of the artist or musician, their style, speech, and everyday behavior.

In 1986, Novikov and Guryanov organized the Friends of Mayakovsky Club, which was chaired by the artist Sergei Bugaev (born 1966), also known as "Afrika." One of its members was Andy Warhol.[4] This nonconformist community of artists and musicians unexpectedly chose "official" Soviet poet Vladimir Mayakovsky as their aesthetic ideal. This move ties in with the strategy of the artists and musicians in Novikov's circle to appropriate and "recompose" Soviet culture, which, as will be described below, would be fully realized only after the fall of the USSR. Georgy Guryanov admired Mayakovsky for his synthesis of heroic romanticism and narcissism, seeing in the poet a model for an approach to the self as a stylistic object:[5] "Of course I loved Mayakovsky's elegant clothes. Fascination with Mayakovsky's appearance explains everything. The most important thing is self-admiration. [. . .] I tried out several of my favorite characters. But Mayakovsky was the most handsome of them all" (Andreeva 2007, 141). Guryanov's personal style was always characterized by perfectionism, rigor, and minimalism in clothing, "stylishness," with an orientation not so much toward protest rock as toward intellectual glamor and the queer aesthetics of the British New Wave. Later he would say, "My greatest artwork is myself."

In the 1980s, queer visuality was not conceptualized by Novikov and Guryanov as an artistic strategy. It entered the late-Soviet cultural context subtly, as the style of the New Wave and the New Romantics, which provided aesthetic form to the Perestroika period and the social changes of the late eighties. This style in clothing, music, and art is known to a wider audience thanks to the 1988 film *Assa*, which captured the life world of the Leningrad underground and the band Kino. Guryanov, who was not only the drummer of Kino but also the band's stylist and one of the major New Romantics of the USSR, played a key role in the formation of this style: "We put on makeup, we wore earrings. I adopted this style right after it appeared around 1980–81. I took this very seriously" (Andreeva 2007, 139).

Guryanov's dandyism in the 1980s was not only a form of aesthetic resistance to the squalor of late-Soviet life but also a heroic act of rejecting the collective identity prescribed by Soviet society. This was pointed out by Dmitry Volchek (2013, online):

> Georgy Guryanov was one of the most beautiful people in Leningrad. In the 80s there were almost no beautiful people; they were all downtrodden, identical, and dressed stupidly. One of my classmates was attacked by some werewolves on Nevsky Prospect only because he was wearing an earring, which they took great pleasure in ripping out, along with his earlobe. Looking today at archive photos of Gustav (as he was called at that time—later he grew to dislike this pseudonym), young people don't understand the bravery it took to dress and wear makeup like that in 1984, imitating the British New Romantics.

No less important for Guryanov was distancing himself from non-conformist normativity, from the image of the dissident or the hippy. In the first half of the eighties, Guryanov belonged to the Teddy Boys society. He took the name Gustav and was one of Leningrad's most prominent hipsters. The strict style of Leningrad's Teddies—black trousers, white shirts, black ties, pointed-toe shoes, bangs, and the back of their heads shaved—was radically different from that of the hippies or the Leningrad rock clubs. Guryanov was always criticizing Leningrad's rock underground not only for its music but also for its bad style: "I would see them performing in some rock club as my polar opposite: they were drunks, degenerates, slobs. What else can I say? Nothing good. I didn't identify myself with that group, no way!" (qtd. in Andreeva 2007, 140).

Already in the late eighties, the Petersburg Neoacademicians realized the power of media images and new technologies and substituted "unfashionable violence with fashionable seduction." As the art historian Andrei Khlobystin writes,

> Leningrad art worked not with the old, non-conformist, modernist understanding of power that was inscribed in the triad "sex-power-violence," but with the real power that was being defined at that moment: media power, which was transformed from a form of repressive power into a seductive one, and the mass media began to carry it out. (Matveeva 2014)

The artists of the New Academy began early on working with glossy journals. They worked in advertising and fashion and were directly responsible for the massive success of "Soviet retro." Georgy Guryanov, in particular, used his Neo-socialist realist works to create flyers and posters for rave parties in the first Russian rave club DanceFloor, which he and Timur Novikov founded at the first Russian squat-club, 145 Fontanka.[6]

Petersburg Neoacademism and the Queer Revolution of the 1990s

Following Warhol's principles for organizing the artistic process, Novikov simultaneously created different groups and invited his friends to join them, creating the illusion of a large and powerful movement. In 1986 he organized not only the Friends of Mayakovsky Club, but also his "Factory," or the New Academy of Any Arts (Novaia Akademiia Vsiacheskikh Iskusstv), in which most of the New Artists participated, including Guryanov. In 1989 Novikov changed the name and goal of this mock institution. "Any arts," a term that refers to Russian avant-garde artist, illustrator, set and costume designer Mikhail Larionov and his "*vsyochestvo*"—a neologism formed from the word *vse,* meaning 'all' or 'everything,' which defined art that could be made out of anything—was replaced with "fine arts," while the New Wave aesthetics à la Jean-Michel Basquiat and Keith Haring[7] gave way to academism and neoclassicism. Thus, the New Academy of

Fine Arts was born, becoming the center of avant-garde queer visuality in post-Soviet Russia.

What was radically different and maximally provocative for the early nineties was not so much the search for the limits of sexual identity, but their "suspicious," classicizing figurative art, which came too close to Soviet totalitarian aesthetics. In several manifests, articles, and speeches in the early nineties, Novikov interpreted classical and socialist realist art as the most modern form of art, while contrasting social criticism to aesthetic populism, such as camp and kitsch. The Neo-academician reading of socialist realism was developed in their polemics with the art establishment of that period: Moscow Conceptualism and actionism. The neo-socialist realism of the New Academy should be interpreted as a radical break with the anti-Soviet sensuality of the late-Soviet underground, which became mainstream in the nineties and displayed features of aesthetic repression. In Guryanov's works, which continue the tradition of Alexander Samokhvalov (1884–1971), Alexander Deineka (1899–1969), and Ivan Shagin (1904–1982), the theme of "Soviet (homo)eroticism" is put forward, and Soviet art of the high Stalinist/post-constructivist period serves as an inexhaustible aesthetic and conceptual resource. In a 1991 interview for the exhibition *Contemporary Art from Leningrad* in Helsinki, Guryanov indicated the relevance (!) of socialist realism and socialist realist corporeality:

> To me, the widespread idea that socialist realism has lost its timeliness seems premature. Socialist realism replaces avant-garde art, which had developed extremely fast. In the West, these processes are considerably more delayed. But I think these strait-laced people will soon understand that it is much more sensible to see before oneself a strong, tanned young body basking in the rays of the sun and the sea winds than to stare with a wise expression at a black square . . . [C]ritics should immediately put an end to the mess of contemporary art. Otherwise, we must seek inspiration in museums of classical art or on the beach.
>
> [. . .] to see before yourself a strong, tanned, young body, illuminated by the sun's rays and winded by the sea breeze, is a lot more reasonable than staring at a black square with a smart look on your face. (Guryanov, quoted by Lahtela, Eskelinen 1991, 19)

Neoacademism is only one of the artistic movements that has exploited the aesthetic of socialist realism. However, if Sots Art, while admiring the rich figurativeness of socialist realism, deconstructs it according to all the rules of postmodernism, then Neoacademism, which at first glance appears to resemble Sots Art,

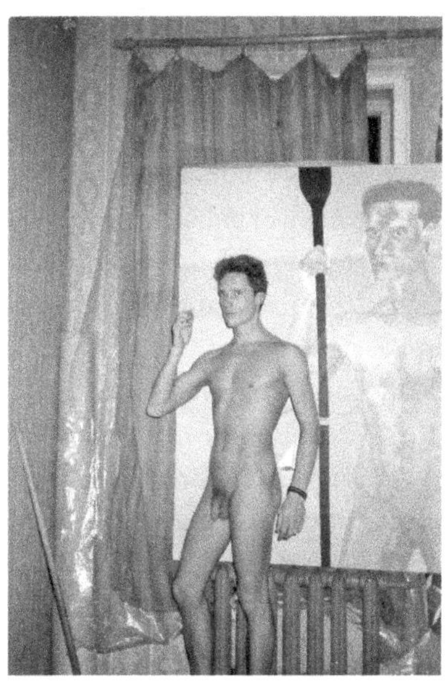

Georgy Guryanov in front of his portrait *A Stern Young Man* (1987) by Timur Novikov. Archive of Timur Novikov

makes a different ideological and artistic move. The language that allows artists to admire heroic socialist realist images while simultaneously distancing itself from them, but without critically deconstructing them, is the language of queer.

In turning to the Soviet visual tradition the moment the USSR collapsed and when everything associated with it was completely rejected, the Neoacademicians, first and foremost Novikov and Guryanov, were following a revolutionary queer model. In a 1998 interview with Slava Mogutin, the prominent Canadian director Bruce LaBruce (born 1964), one of the major representatives of New Queer Cinema, mentions the non-conformist nature of queer, its readiness to radically challenge anything mainstream:

> The most exciting thing is the possibility to be different from others, to be a rebel, to go against the establishment, to act within the limits of normal culture, while at the same time going beyond those limits and observing what's going on from the sidelines. It's no coincidence that in primitive cultures, homosexuals were often shamans and witch doctors . . . I like Jean Genet's revolutionary model of homosexuality. Wherever there was some revolutionary situation, he was always there. He was for those ideas until they were institutionalized and became dominant. Then he would betray them and start fighting for something else. I think that's a good metaphor for how homosexuals should behave. They're privileged when compared to the majority of normal people: their identities are not solidified in culture or ideology. Homosexuals can flow from one identity to another, change their roles and betray them. If we don't like the direction the gay movement is moving in, we are free to completely destroy it and start over. (Mogutin 1998, online)

It is worth noting that Novikov radically changed his aesthetics and came out with a Neoacademic project after a trip he and Guryanov took to France and the

U.S. in 1989, during which he became acquainted with the Paris and New York gay culture of the clubs and galleries.[8] Transnational queer culture, oriented toward the legacy of classicism and contrasted with modernism as a global (hetero-) mainstream, was interpreted by Novikov as an avant-garde aesthetic ideal reflecting the hope of independent artists of the 1990s that Russian art would be on an equal footing with the international art community. Neoacademism opposes the patriarchal national-gendered approach to art. It called for erasing temporal and spatial borders and interpreted art as a united field of freedom. In this way, Neoacademism was initially conceived as a global and transcultural project, rather than a local Russian one. Queer figurative art and neoclassical aesthetics, with its cult of (male) corporeality, was the universal language that was supposed to give Russian artists access to the international art market. Having lived in Europe and the US for a while in the nineties, Guryanov reconceived and reinterpreted the Soviet legacy through a queer lens, overcoming its localness and inscribing Russian art of the twentieth century into the global context. This desperate attempt to break free from the imposed colonial framework of the "Russian artist" and to show the universality of Russian culture should be interpreted as an important political and emancipatory aspect of this artistic movement.

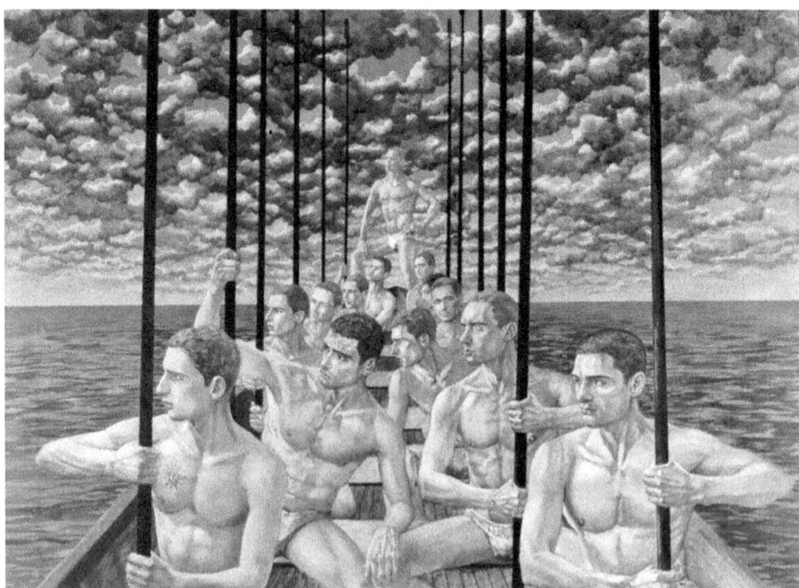

Georgy Guryanov, *Argo/Rowers* (1998-2000).
Collection of Shalva Breus

The New Academy was a place of absolute modernity, the avant-garde of the sexual revolution of the 1990s, and the first and most visible artistic community in post-Soviet Russia to create recognized masterpieces of gay art. However, what interested Timur Novikov, Georgy Guryanov, Vladislav Mamyshev-Monroe, Bella Matveeva, and other artists of this movement was not in the identity of sexual minorities or the progressive fight against their oppression, but life creation and perfect corporeality. Neoacademic Apollonism consciously distanced itself from the LBGT political agenda and turned toward the conservative European tradition of dandyism and aristocratic heroism (the Pre-Raphaelites, Oscar Wilde, Ludwig of Bavaria, and Ernst Jünger, among others). The orientation toward the atemporal canon was a device that allowed them to steer the conversation away from relevant political topics to the mystical. Exceptions are the posters Guryanov created for the Gay Games in Amsterdam in 1998, but even those contain no contemporary references and so read as timeless.

Timur Novikov found examples of dandyist protest the spirit of the times in Petersburg Hellenism of the early twentieth century (Andreeva 2011), as well as in contemporary Western art. As the main model for his Neoacademic project, Novikov chose the work of the avant-garde queer photographer of the eighties Robert Mapplethorpe (1946–1989) and his concept of binding antiquity with modernity, and counterculture (punk and gay underground) with neoclassical visuality. Mapplethorpe talked of photography as a new type of sculpture[9] and became a model for all Neoacademicians as a master of "sculptural photography," or the photographing of the living as the dead and the dead as the living.[10] Following in Mapplethorpe's footsteps, Novikov accentuated the neoclassical tendencies in photography and wrote of the importance of preserving through photography the heritage of European plastic arts, such as architecture, sculpture, and fashion. Following Mapplethorpe (for an example, see his work *Apollo*, 1988), Novikov proclaimed a new cult of Apollo and created visual manifestos of Neoacademism: *Apollo Trampling a Black Square* (1990) and *Apollo Trampling a Red Square* (1991).

In the very early nineties, the aesthetics of the American gay underground was reconceived and presented by Novikov and several other curators close to Neoacademism (Ekaterina Andreeva, Olesya Turkina, and Andrei Khlobystin) to a broad Russian public in numerous exhibitions in the best museum spaces in Moscow and St. Petersburg. Thanks to Novikov, Mapplethorpe's photographs were exhibited in Russia for the first time. So, in 1994, Novikov and Ekaterina Andreeva organized the photography exhibition *Renaissance and Resistance* at the

State Russian Museum, which was dedicated to "the heroes of aesthetic resistance": Oscar Wilde, von Gloeden, and Mapplethorpe. Ten years later, in 2004–2005, the prominent Petersburg curator Arkady Ippolitov organized several exhibitions of Neoacademic art, as well as the international exhibition *Robert Mapplethorpe and Classical Tradition. The Art of Photography and the Engraving of Mannerism,* which followed the Neoacademic practice of mixing contemporary and classical art.[11]

"Soviet Antiquity" and Post-Irony

In reconstructing classical images, Novikov followed Warhol's theory of the economy/recycling of images and Shklovsky's theory of the deautomatization of perception. The principle of recomposition, which Novikov formulated before 1982 and made the basis of the work of the New Artists and the New Composers, was applied in the 1990s to update the historical legacy, including that of the Soviets.[12] A distinct feature of Neoacademism is an interest in Soviet visual culture of the 1930s–1950s, not only for its neoclassical aesthetic, but also as a source of homoerotic themes and visual dominants. A paradoxical result of the reception of queer visuality in the form of Mapplethorpe's classicism was the strengthening of Russia's identity as European. The neoclassicism of American queer art and, more broadly, Western postmodernism, fits into a long-standing tradition of Russian Palladianism, which dates to the eighteenth century, and represents a new manifestation of the European project of the Enlightenment. While most works of modern art deal with pain and "Soviet" trauma, the Neoacademics, chiefly Novikov and Guryanov, in an avant-garde gesture turned their attention to "Soviet" beauty and "Soviet" enjoyment. The strategies of remembering practiced by the artists in this movement are clear. They selected only those features of the Soviet aesthetic project that most vividly embodied classical ideals: elevation, architecture, sports, corporeality, hierarchy, and the priority of space over time. The realm of the sublime in Neoacademism, just as in Stalinist post-constructivism,[13] is first and foremost that of the ideal human body, ideal architecture, the golden mean, and classical proportions.

One of the first artistically convincing experiments to inscribe the legacy of socialist realism in the context of queer visuality was an exhibition of Guryanov's works entitled *Willpower,* curated by Novikov. The exhibition was held in the summer of 1994 in St. Petersburg, in the New Academy's exhibition space. In November it was shown in the Moscow gallery *Rigina.* In this exhibition,

Guryanov's famous triptych *A Stern Young Man* was displayed. This work is a queer remix of images of "Soviet antiquity": shots from the 1936 Abram Room film of the same name. Although the exhibition *Willpower* featured Guryanov's paintings, at their foundation were stills from Room's film.

In Guryanov's remakes of socialist realist themes, homoerotic tension coexists with dandyist detachment and suprahistorical coldness. Therefore, Guryanov's style is often characterized as "romantic" or "raw," which also hearkens back to the "raw style" of the 1950s and 1960s in socialist realism. The heroic individuality of the neo-socialist realism of Guryanov must also be emphasized: When drawing the slender ranks of sailors or athletes, he gives them the faces of his friends—musicians from Kino or his colleagues from the New Academy—or he gives them his own face, introducing into the process the theme of narcissism in art. The hero and Eros in Guryanov's work are individual rather than collective. His is the Eros of the "last hero" of the age, the dying dandy.

As originals for his paintings, Guryanov takes models not just from Soviet art, but also from Western art of the 1930s, a gesture intended to emphasize the universality of the cult of the body and of queer masculinity in the era of interwar modernism. As an example, in several photo projects, he freezes the Discus Thrower in a pose, copying a shot from Leni Riefenstahl's film *Olympia.* In the 2002 painting *The Fitter,* he uses the work of American industrial and military photographer Margaret Bourke-White (1904–1971) *Man on a Turbine Shell, Dnieprostroi* (1930) as his foundation, while in his painting *Parallel Bars,* he cites Riefenstahl's *Olympia.*

In appropriating Western images, Guryanov creates models of the homoerotic "eternal Soviet." In a 2008 interview for the magazine *Rich Style,* he emphasizes the fundamental atemporality of the images he creates, which opens possibilities for endless interpretation:

> *Rich Style*: In your opinion, do your works refer back to images of the bygone Soviet era or to the "era of totalitarian art," or are these modern images viewed through the prism of that time?
>
> G. G.: I want to show atemporality. I don't want my work to be tied to a certain era. I want a work to be relevant in 1,000 years and in 100 years. (Vol'de 2017, 97)

In this respect, the works of Guryanov follow the same principles of universality and atemporality that are typical of the songs of the rock band Kino:

> We had no interest at all in politics. But Viktor's songs are such a universal thing that everyone can find something in them for themselves. For example, the song "Change!" is a purely philosophical treatise without a drop of anything political, and it was written even before Gorbachev's reforms, having no relationship to them whatsoever. It's another thing that we saved it for the film *Assa*: Viktor agreed to this with Sergei Solovyov, that's why the song's not on a single album. After the film it became basically a symbol of Perestroika. It's precisely in the freedom of interpretation where the beauty of a work of art lies. (Vol'de 2017, 100–101)

In conclusion, it is worth mentioning that the turn toward socialist realism and its interpretation as a "new antiquity" in the years before and after the fall of the Soviet Union was not only a successful commercial move that allowed Novikov and members of his Academy to occupy the neoclassical niche nobody else wanted at that time (nowadays Guryanov is one of the most highly valued contemporary artists). Novikov's Neoacademic project became one of the first experiments in post-ironic art in post-Soviet Russia of the mid-nineties. A defining characteristic of post-irony is the use of the possibilities of irony for realizing a serious idea. As the Russian philosopher and publicist Kirill Martynov notes:

> Post-irony is the condition when the limits of seriousness and irony become blurred. Post-ironists deliberately admit the ambiguity of their speech. Their game is to make you doubt: are they being serious or not? [...] post-irony can lead to a "new sincerity," that is, it can allow the ironist to speak about serious things. The final aspect is the most remarkable: post-irony is becoming a cultural mechanism for breaking with postmodernism. (Martynov 2015, online)

Art historian Ekaterina Andreeva emphasizes the importance of Georgy Guryanov's works as an art of "direct expression": "Guryanov's role is especially meaningful because he was the first to approach taboo totalitarian iconography and to work with it seriously, eye-to-eye, without hiding behind the protective mask of Sots Art conceptual irony" (Andreeva 2011, 53). At first glance, there appears in Guryanov's work a search for a hero and a desire for the sublime, which distances it from postmodernism, which is fundamentally unheroic, bringing it closer to a new cultural dominant that has fully appeared only recently—metamodernism.

Translated by Ryan Green

Notes

1 This article was written as a part of the research project "Visuality without Visibility: Queer Visual Culture in Post-Soviet Russia," Swedish Research Council, no. 2016-02341.

2 For more on the New Artists movement, see Andreeva and Podgorskaya 2012.

3 In creating avant-garde music, Soviet readymade was, for example, used by the New Composers.

4 Novikov and Guryanov knew Warhol indirectly through the musician Joanna Stingray. In 1986, Warhol sent autographed tomato soup cans, silkscreen prints of Marilyn Monroe's portrait, and a few copies of *The Philosophy of Andy Warhol: from A to B and Back Again* to Novikov, Guryanov, Kurekhin, Grebenshchikov, Tsoi, Krisanov, Bugaev-Afrika, and Kotelnikov. For more see Novikov 2003, 22.

5 Later, in 1998, Guryanov played Mayakovsky in the short film by New Academy artist Olga Tobreluts, *The Love Story of Marilyn Monroe and Vladimir Mayakovsky*. Monroe was played by Egor Ostrov.

6 For more, see Tsodikov, 2019.

7 Besides Andy Warhol, these queer artists had the largest influence on the New Artists' style. In particular, the square-headed figures of Viktor Tsoi and Andrei Krisanov's drawings and paintings refer to Haring's work.

8 Novikov visited New York gay clubs (Jackie 60 et al.) dressed in a red wig and women's clothing, see Khlobystin 2017, 153.

9 See, Mara Hoberman's article in the *New York Times*, "Mapplethorpe: A Sculptural Perspective," April 15, 2014. Available at: https://www.nytimes.com/2014/04/15/arts/artsspecial/mapplethorpe-a-sculptural-perspective.html

10 On the importance of Mapplethorpe for Neoacademism, see A. Ippolitov on the exhibition *In Memory of Mapplethorpe and the End of the 20th Century. Bella Matveeva* (2011). Available at: http://www.ilovepetersburg.ru/content/pamyati-meppltorpa-i-kontsu-xx-veka-bella-matveeva

11 The exhibition *Robert Mapplethorpe and Classical Tradition. The Art of Photography and the Engraving of Mannerism* was held in 2004–2005 in Berlin in the Deutsche Guggenheim, in the Hermitage, and in the Moscow House of Photography. The curators were A. Ippolitov and D. Chelant.

12 For more on the device of recomposition see Novikov 1996.

13 See Selivanova 2016.

References

Andreeva, Ekaterina and Nelli Podgorskaya. 2012. *Novye khudozhniki*. Exhibition catalogue. Moscow: Maier.

Andreeva, Ekaterina. 2007. *Timur. Vrat' tol'ko pravdu!* St. Petersburg: Amfora.

———. 2011. "Leningradskii neoakademism i peterburgskii ellinizm." In *Novaya Academiya. Saint Petersburg*, edited by A. Ippolitov and A. Kharitonova, 49–73. Exhibition catalogue. Moscow: Cultural fund "EKATERINA."

Chukhrov, Keti. 2009. "Sovetskaia material'naia kul'tura i sotsialisticheskaia etika v moskovskom kontseptualizme." *Prostory* 29. Available at: http://prostory.net.ua/ua/translate/227-2009-10-28-14-40-51. Last accessed: May 14, 2021.

Engström, Maria. 2018. "Metamodernizm i postsovetskii konservativnyi avangard: Novaia akademiia Timura Novikova." *Novoe Literaturnoe Obozrenie* 151(3). Available at: https://www.nlobooks.ru/magazines/novoe_literaturnoe_obozrenie/151/article/19762/.

Khlobystin, Andrei. 2017. *Shizorevoliutsiia: Ocherki peterburgskoi kul'tury vtoroi poloviny XX veka*. St. Petersburg: Borei Art.

Lahtela, Päivi, and Kirsi Eskelinen, eds.1991. *Nykytaidetta Leningradista: Neljä elementtiä =Nutidskonst från Leningrad = De fyra elementen = Contemporary Art from Leningrad: Four Elements*, 7–31. Exhibition catalogue. Vantaa: Vantaan kaupungin kulttuuritoimi, Helsingin juhlaviikot.

Martynov, Kirill. 2015. "Chto takoe postironiia?" *The Question*. July 7, 2015. Available at: https://thequestion.ru/questions/19960/chto-takoe-postironiya. Last accessed: May 14, 2021.

Matveeva, Anna. 2014. "Andrei Klobystin: 'Perestroit' nemodnoe nasilie v modnoe soblaznenie.'" *Artgid*. May 15, 2014. Available at: http://artguide.com/posts/592-andriei-khlobystin-pieriestroit-niemodnoie-nasiliie-v-modnoie-soblaznieniie. Last accessed May 14, 2021.

Mogutin, Iaroslav. 1998. "Pornograf ponevole. Interv'iu s rezhissorom Brius Liabriusom." *Inoekino*. http://www.inoekino.ru/newsOne.php?id=944. Last accessed May 17, 2021.

Novikov, Timur. 1996. "Teoria perekompozitsii." *Kabinet* 11: 85–101.

———. 1998. *Novyi russkii klassitsizm*. St. Petersburg: Palace Editions.

———. 2003. *Lektsii*. St. Petersburg: Novaia Akademiia Iziashchnykh Iskusstv, Gallereia D137.

Selivanova, Aleksandra. 2016. "Sovetskoe ar-deko, ili Chto takoe postkonstruktivizm." *Arzamas*. November 11, 2016. Available at: https://arzamas.academy/mag/368-ardeco. Last accessed May 14, 2021.

Tsodikov, Oleg. 2019. *Made in Dance 1991–1999. Khroniki elektronnoi klubnoi stseny v Rossii*. Moscow: Izd. Olega Tsodikova.

Volchek, Dmitry. 2013. "Statuia diskobola." *Radio Svoboda*. July 25, 2013. Available at: https://www.svoboda.org/a/25056320.html. Last accessed: May 14, 2021.

Vol'de, Metsur. 2017. Georgii Gur'ianov: "Ia i est' iskusstvo." Moscow: ACT.

Chapter 9

A Russian Schizorevolution? Observations on the New Academy of Fine Arts and Queer Issues in the Late 1980s and Early 1990s[1]

Andrei Khlobystin

At the end of the twentieth century, Russia saw another revolution, which was unlike the social, industrial, sexual, or other revolutions at the beginning of the century but was a fateful event for the entire world. The rebuilding or *perestroika* of the Soviet "body," which took place over the course of a decade, from 1986 to 1996, can be defined, in the spirit of Gilles Deleuze and Felix Guattari (*Capitalism and Schizophrenia,* 1972–1980), as a "schizorevolution." The French philosophers do not use the term "schizorevolution" in their writing, but their entire philosophy explores, in one way or another, an anticapitalist revolution, which their original method of "schizoanalysis" inaugurates.

In the USSR, a world that had previously appeared to be invincible and rigidly structured shattered into innumerable pieces. In addition to the global "external" changes, which can be characterized as geopolitical shifts, a stupendous semiotic catastrophe took place—things lost their names; ideology, text, and narrative vanished; a total crisis of identity occurred, like an eternal Zen void gaping wide. Life accelerated at the insane pace of Shiva's divine dance, the tandava, crushing old forms and immediately exploding everything that came into being.

Given these processes, it is interesting to consider the significance of the cultural upheaval that took place in Leningrad in the late 1980s to early 1990s, a subject that is just beginning to receive scholarly attention. This upheaval was engineered by the children of the generation of the Khrushchev Thaw, the first post-Stalinist "perestroika." In Leningrad independent culture became a youth culture. These young people failed to inherit the "genetic" fears of their fathers and grandfathers. At first this was a rather small circle of people, but their local subculture and lifestyle spread via the half–discernible sounds of tape recordings, films of dubious quality, such as *Assa* and *Rock*, and "blind" samizdat and word of mouth, winning the hearts of Soviet young people enchanted by the aura of authentic freedom, joy, and dignity. At the same time, Leningrad performed its archetypal function as a "window onto Europe": it is the point of origin for Russian rock, squatters, alternative cinema, the dance club movement, gay culture and so forth, practices that then spread throughout the country. The Leningrad of that period became a kind of textbook example of "schizorevolution." It is also significant that this new avant-garde "theater of life" inherited the creative strategies of dandies and holy fools specific to Saint Petersburg's distinct artistic culture and revived the aesthetics of "oddballs and mavericks" glorified by Mikhail Pyliaev. The man in the street may have found these radical changes nightmarish and chaotic, but the youth who were dropped into the sea of this "schizorevolution" felt completely in their element.

The peak of Neoacademism coincided with the breakdown of the paternal language, with no one left to protest such displays of rebellion. At the same time, the Soviet brand of Puritanism had bottled up the queer concerns of this generation: Emotional experiences typical of teenagers overtook those in their thirties, causing many to lose themselves in delayed libertinism and all manner of daring experiments, which sometimes cost them their lives and sanity. Tragic tales of passionate affairs abounded; one was hard–pressed to name one normal family. Given the period's fantastic changes, which, among other things, made travel to the hitherto fable–like West a reality, artists had a sense that there was no center or periphery, that "life is everywhere" and it is less exciting to sit around stuck in some "capital" or in some internal state than to move between them, to be in transit, in transformation, in a trance. New York City's and Berlin's most sinister back alleys were studied with no less zeal than the art market itself. According to eyewitnesses, the secret paths of Tiergarten Park buzzed with legends of extraordinarily powerful Russian neophytes.

Let us turn our attention to one salient feature of the artistic processes endemic to a "schizorevolution," namely, the dissolution of what was once experienced as an intact whole, including the artist and their body. In the late 1980s, the problem of gender turned the body into a fashionable and ubiquitous discourse. "The discursive ascendance of the 'human' and the 'body' [. . .] defines our current cultural situation, which I interpret unreservedly as a Renaissance," wrote Timur Novikov (1958–2002), a leader of the 1980s and 1990s youth avant-garde, in 1996. In Leningrad, the body was not just a topical issue but a lived experience and a practice hearkening back to ages past.

An ever-shifting kaleidoscopic refraction of perpetual metamorphoses, a new type of artist and human, irreducible to final definitions, emerges in the 1980s and becomes dominant in the 1990s. A kind of fluid identity—a meandering of masks—is a salient feature of this period of change. In Leningrad, a center of narcissism and faddism, people cultivated personal "avatars" as art works by which to both create and communicate. When conversing with the Azerbaijani chair of the Artists Union, Tair Salakhov, Novikov became Taymoor; in an Orthodox setting, he was Timofei Petrovich; Novikov the Westernizer preached the ideas of Mikhail Larionov, a proponent of the Native Soil movement and a patriot; the persona of a gay activist appeared next to that of a reactionary conservative; an old man with a gray beard could suddenly transmogrify into a young fop, and so forth. It should be noted that such external shifts were not a sign of omnivorousness, indecision, or some deficit in his constitution. Inner integrity in a state of constant becoming, coupled with a heroic world view, was recognized as one of the principal distinguishing values of this community.

These ideal or concealing self-images—what I call the Petersburgers' "avatars"—could change at a kaleidoscopic pace. The term "avatar" is suitable here both in the routine modern sense of a computer-generated icon, an image representing a user, and in the Hindu-philosophic sense of the coming of the Brahman, a human incarnation of a deity. The "avatar" of the Leningrad-Petersburg tradition was not just a mask, a persona, but primarily a manifestation of a practice that, as an archetype, hearkened back to Buddhist and Orthodox traditions. In his discussion of the Hesychasts' fight against Monothelitism, which insisted on God's dualistic nature, David Zilberman writes: "For them, neither the mind nor the body is a separate entity: the body is whole and the body has reason. [...] The main feature of the philosophy of Hesychasm was the postulation of the body as an immanently active, fundamental substance" (2014, 117–118).

The specificity of Leningrad's creative milieu could be described as body- and image-based art, as opposed to Moscow's "iconoclastic," conceptual art, which tended toward imagelessness and bodily abjection. In contrast to nonconformist Gnosticism, which saw the world as hostile and alienated, the young artists of Leningrad's "new wave" were wild, new romantics who bravely confronted life and, instead of attempting to break down the wall of the public's incomprehension, wound around it, like a vine, covering and suffusing it with their ornamentation. They did not fight for freedom so much as they actualized it through practice. This was the first generation of self-assured, cheerful people at ease—the "smiling" generation. For them, both officialdom and dissident nonconformism belonged to the same base, aggressive impulse (Yurchak 2005).

Within the nonconformist movement, this aggressiveness made itself felt along gender lines. Natalia Malakhovskaia, who edited the first Russian feminist samizdat journal *Maria* (1979–1982), speaks about "particular women and women's initiatives in general being explicitly and openly humiliated, which, paradoxically, was a trend among advocates of freedom."[2] As Malakhovskaia explains:

> Whereas within the European student movement of 1968 women were allowed to serve the male protesters ("making coffee"), the women involved with Leningrad samizdat were graciously given access to the technical aspects of the enterprise (typing and binding samizdat journals), while only those who had "a male mentality" and composed "male poems" (such characteristics then figured as the highest praise) were allowed to publish their own writing. Thus, only through self-abdication and self-negation could women reach the reader. Similar things were happening in the nonconformist artist milieu.[3]

Unlike the hermetic and patriarchal circles of the Moscow conceptualist intelligentsia, who conceived of "partisanship" along national, gender, political, social, and other lines, the "New Artists," a group founded by Novikov in 1982, did not much care for such stratifications or regarded them as an eccentric touch. In late 1980s Leningrad, the nonconformists' suppression of queerness was lifted, and women, who in Moscow had to remain in the shadow of the men, became influential gurus, "queens," and heads of clans, schools, and salons, with their share of faithful students and fans.

After the 1980s art scene, Leningrad became dominated by the "New Artists" movement, and the artistic schools of the two capitals grew substantially apart. The artists differed in terms of their philosophy of art, lifestyle, and external appearance. "Leningrad, I have come to understand, is always a relief after Moscow," wrote American writer Andrew Solomon, who visited Leningrad in 1988, when mass media and pop culture were gaining a lot of traction there (Solomon 1991, 59). He goes on to note:

> Whereas most of the Moscow artists look like vagabonds fresh from the streets—even by Soviet standards—the Leningrad artists are beautiful to behold. They have the right haircuts, the right clothes, and also the right faces and bodies. [. . .] In a country in which homosexuality is both illegal and ill-regarded, many of the Leningrad artists are gay; the other are comfortable with this. The drugs are endless. Stoned, beautiful, and totally cool, the Leningrad artists sit in attic rooms holding paintbrushes. [. . .] This work looks, as the artists themselves look, straight out of the East Village (60).

The early roots of neoacademist striving for a beautiful self-image, one that is reflected in the image of their city and of those around them, is discernible in the cult of fashion among "new wave" and "new romanticism" groups. With the 1950s *stiliagi* movement, fashion became primarily a street phenomenon, a series of initiations via risqué socio-sexual displays. Back in 1983–1984, the streets of Leningrad saw the messy hippies and punks eclipsed by the "teddy-boys" (or "twisters"), fierce young people dressed in the style of the 1960s. As Georgy Guryanov (1961–2013), Saint Petersburg's leading dandy-artist and the percussionist of the extremely popular Russian rock band Kino, reminisced to me, with a smile: "Ah, the twisters, they were my retinue." In the late 1980s, the neoclassical imagination of the neoacademists offered an even more radical image, that of the pop star's beautiful and, at the same time, media-structured body. Reformatting the massive stress of a borderline situation constituted by a total identity crisis, the rave and dance epidemic culture that sprang into being at the same time as neoacademism shaped new bodies and souls.

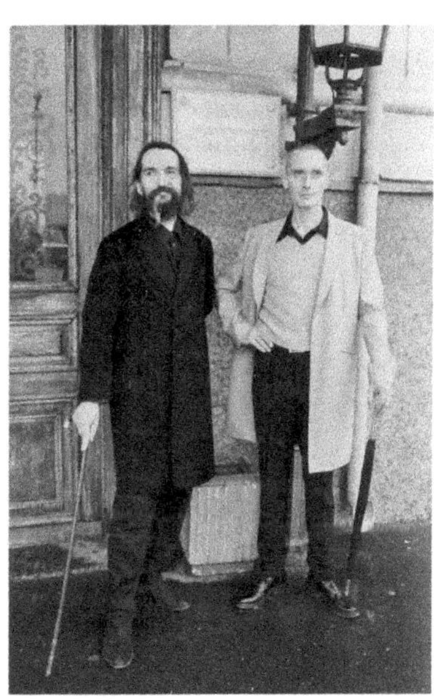

Timur Novikov and Georgy Guryanov by the Director's Entrance of the State Hermitage Museum (1998). Photo by Isabel Roman. Collection of Andrei Khlobystin

The First Manifestations of Neoacademism and the Gay Movement

In the late 1980s–early 1990s, Novikov reformatted the "new wave" movement, which he had created in the early 1980s and which had reached a point of bifurcation, into "neoacademism," which argued for a return to the classical ideals of "beautiful art." The cultured public found it puzzling when these notoriously freewheeling innovators performed a backflip that invited comparisons to a counterrevolution. They announced that they were disillusioned with contemporary art and were determined to rediscover traditional craftsmanship, praising Saint Petersburg with its neoclassical architecture, the Hermitage, and its ballet, as the last bastion of classical art amid a perilous ocean of modernism. "Down with modernist monstrosities and back to beautiful art!" was the straightforward and clear war cry of academicism, which appealed to a generation of young romantics who would be called "the new serious" crowd in the future. They sought in art the sublime and the authentic, recoiling from ugliness, negativity, and the politicized, vulgar gag of Sots Art. At first, the nonconformist art intelligentsia, accustomed to the quips and pranks of the "New Artists," who were now crowning themselves with laurels, calling each other "professors" and their center of operation the "New Academy of Fine Arts" (NAFA), did not take it seriously.

Yet soon enough, the obscurantist speeches and rallies of these self-appointed "academics" began to whip up indignation and horror. Neoacademism was accused of all the mortal sins attributed in the twentieth century to neoclassicism, from kitsch to the paradoxical coupling of fascism and homosexuality. "Such was probably the response to pop-art among the abstract expressionists, or to Sots Art among Moscow's underground artists," claimed the critics (Fomenko 2001). Novikov always enjoyed hearing negative, scandalized responses to the movements he started, criticism that he himself would initiate, a practice that predated the advent of such media strategies in Russian show business and politics by many years. Novikov was gratified by the polemics that accompanied neoacademism throughout its history; he embraced the art of public relations, as Pushkin had once embraced dandyism, at a time when its energy was new and unknown.[4] He never fetishized such manipulative energies; he used them not so much to ridicule or debase as to draw out the sublime essence of things. Neoacademism became Russia's most prominent movement at the end of the twentieth century and its biggest media project: It became clear that a new artistic leadership had come to power. Supplanting the repressive authority of the Soviet state, this new authority emanated from the seductive mass media, which the Leningrad milieu put to good use in inaugurating a new phase of artistic development in the 1990s, even as Moscow Conceptualism, which had mooched off the paternal mono-language of power, followed the exit of that language into the wings, becoming obsolete.

Dance ushered in the last decade of the twentieth century. With records spun by Janis Krauklis, a DJ from Riga, the first Leningrad discotheque party took place at the Communication Workers' Palace of Culture in January of 1990. Novikov and Guryanov were the creative engine behind the event. The dance hall was decorated with large-scale, neo-classicism-inspired paintings: Novikov's nude portrait of Guryanov, Guryanov's self-portrait, and a nude portrait of Denis Egelskii, all of which displayed a new type of male beauty and could easily be interpreted as homoerotic. Later, Novikov would call this event NAFA's "first art campaign" (Novikov 1998, 15). Russian rave and neoacademism thus emerged as fraternal twins.

Acid house music, a DJ, a cheerful, fashionably dressed crowd, a door policy, event-specific print fliers, and, above all, a staunch denial of mundane reality—these were the defining characteristics of the first bona fide Russian techno party. This was also the first gay party. "I am ashamed to remember being part of those disgraceful goings-on. [. . .] I can recall the exact developmental trajectory: new artists—faggots—neoacademists—rave," wrote NAFA professor Egelskii to me in a text message; he had been a party animal in those days and later, naturally, would lead the Holy Inquisition, a virulent orthodox fundamentalist wing of new-academicism. The event also constituted the social debut of Vladik Mamyshev *aka* Monroe, a future star of Russian collaborative art, as he stepped out for the first time wearing what would become his canonical look. No one had seen anything so gloriously outrageous before. This is how Novikov describes that night in a piece characteristically entitled "How I Invented Rave":

> It was the first dance party with house music and techno elements. To step up the fun, we developed a show called "The Alternative Singing Female Voice." Our alternative female singers were the now famous Vladislav Yurievich Mamyshev (Monroe), a less famous person named "Alla Pugacheva," and one "Sandra," still less famous and now residing in Germany. These three were the hostesses of the main program in between DJ sections. Since sexual minorities express themselves quite boldly when it comes to their appearance, dressing for maximum effect and using make-up, we invited a large number of people representing sexual minorities. They paid a lower cover charge than the rest. The prices were laughable,

> general admission was 10 rubles, it was 5 for sexual minorities. I worked the door and decided how much to charge. It wasn't of course only gays and lesbians who got a discounted rate. The cheaper tickets were offered based on one's appearance, and those with particularly exceptional looks could get in for free. Our friends—and there were a lot of them—got in for free too. The prices were symbolic, just to raise enough to pay the facility's landlord. The DJ as well as all the performers worked for free, just to support the idea. The first DJ-led discotheque party was thus simultaneously the first sexual minority party and the first drag queen show. There was also an exhibition as well as a chill-out area, which is called a VIP room nowadays. We basically incorporated all nightclub models (Novikov 1996).

A rave-olution swept over the USSR. The rave emerged as a new space for different kinds of freedom—social, semiotic, sexual, gender, economic, psychedelic, musical, bodily, and so on.

Those associated with the traditional nonconformist culture of the Soviet underground viewed both rave and neoacademism as disgraceful. They had a point. Dedicated taxonomists would be right to classify both movements under the umbrella of post-punk. Punk consists of crude challenges to convention, which in Leningrad were intensified through a philosophy of cynicism inherited from the New Artists. The prefix in "post-punk" referenced the "ascetic" quality of the movement (*post* in Russian means "fasting" or "abstinence"), a quality that would become apparent in the years to come as the lava of punk hardened into neoacademism.

Novikov's 1987 portrait of Guryanov, which was shown at a Communication Workers' Palace of Culture exhibition and took its title and much of its style from Abram Room's 1935 film *A Stern Young Man*, became a programmatic artwork of "proto-academicism," anticipating some essential features of the art scene of the following decade. The canvas projects an image of a nude Guryanov against a nautical landscape with a tiny yacht in the distance—a typical Novikov motif. While the picture, overall, tends toward an expressionistic style characteristic of Novikov's 1980s portraits, it is worth noting his recourse to the imagery of so-called totalitarian art, characterized by a penchant for the butch nude aesthetic as evident in its most representative expressions (Deineka, Breker, the Foro Italico/Mussolini sculptures). This work can be regarded as a sincere act of worship, or an ironic commentary on the grandeur of totalitarian neoclassicism ("a girl with an oar" was a staple of classical Soviet iconography and folklore), on gay discourse, and on Guryanov's heroic profile. This kind of image "fluidity" would come to define Novikov's mature work.

Guryanov's pieces that are based primarily on photographs from the totalitarian era are products of the same period. Presented in bright acrylic with a near "acid" fluorescent effect, the grandiose personae inhabiting these canvasses—aviators, athletes, workers, and female tractor drivers—have a clear pop art poster quality, which is further enhanced with captions like "Let's go!" and "Goal!" Displayed at multiple Leningrad parties, Guryanov's large-scale self-portrait (1990), which is reminiscent of Novikov's *A Stern Young Man*, is also representative of early neoacademism. Andrew Solomon describes Guryanov's image and art circa 1988 this way: "He is very cool, perhaps the best-looking Soviet I have met, and he cut not only Timur's hair, but also his own hair. His visual sense is keen: his work, which is ultra-slick and super-commercial-looking, shows the same sense of balances as his haircuts. At its best, its riveting smoothness can be deeply erotic" (Solomon 1991, 63).

In 1989–1990, Egelskii, who had just returned from "the torture-chambers of the Brezhnev-era,"[5] and Bella Matveeva began to work in a similarly exaggerated manner painting bodies, depicting the silhouettes of brown male torsos against ornate backgrounds, often with appliques made of cloth. Bella's plot-driven, witty pictures, such as *The Crude Son of the People*, which shows a semi-nude sailor punching Venus of Tauris in a palatial interior, dovetail with Denis's exquisitely sensual male nudes as well as his robust graphics, which far surpass the cloying piousness of his later period. These artists could not care less about being called mawkish or vulgar. On the contrary, nothing was "too much"; excess excited the public, while art historians, armed with the obscure language of "discourse," uttered magic spells: "postmodernism," "kitsch," etc.

The years 1989 and 1990 also saw the neoclassical watercolors of Oleg Maslov, the leader of the "New Savages," who, with a childlike naturalism, depicted garden sculptures coming alive as shameless bodies of flesh accessorized with modern shoes and purses, as envisioned by Konstantin Vaginov in 1922: "The statues gave up the pedestals to people. As the marble became animated, the human bodies grew paler and paler until, finally, they froze" (Vaginov 1922, 13–14).

While early neoacademism was utterly devoid of decadent sluggishness and intellectualized aestheticism, works belonging to this new direction developed the rudimentary, decorative side of "New Artists" painting, echoing the "primitivism, lubok, icon" of Mikhail Larionov (1881–1964), which Nikolai

Khardzhiev defined as the "national accent" (Vrubel-Golubkina 2014).[6] It should be noted that "proto-academicism" was fully aware of itself as primitive—which helps account for the presence of Larionov's *Venus* in the background of a Matveeva painting depicting a crude confrontation between a revolutionary sailor and a pince-nez-wearing officer. Early neoacademism was in fact far removed from the qualities of cold technicality, glossiness, and lifelessness, for which the academicism of the seventeenth through nineteenth centuries has traditionally been criticized. The form of late 1980s–early 1990s painting—the neoacademist "archaics"—is frozen in a stupid smile, with its awkwardly violated proportions, reckless coloring, tasteless ornamentation, and carnal sensibilities. Novikov explained his use of ornamentation on carpet textiles during that period as "bedside" art, located "as near as possible to a human being at his most intimately felt moments" (Novikov 2003, 122). At the same time, such works are unrestrained, relaxed, and tranquil, a hallmark of neoacademism, in stark contrast to the general pool of busy art productions at that time of semiotic catastrophe. These self-assured, provocative, and joyful artists introduced what seemed at that moment to be the most brutal and marginal kind of art, suffused with a residue of exuberant classical beauty: the glamourized, salon-style "lubok," totalitarian imagery, the aesthetics of homoeroticism and pop culture, all of which delighted the fashionable young crowd and the progressive critics, while befuddling and enraging the purveyors of a righteous modernism. Lacking classical academic skills or unwilling to exploit them, the early neoacademists defined a contemporary sense of beauty much more eloquently than the polished graduates of the Soviet Academy of Arts, who had no idea what they were doing or why.

Novikov writes that in 1991, the Marble Palace, then still the Lenin Museum, housed "the first exhibition called 'Neoacademism.' [. . .] The first wave of neoacademism can then be said to have formed by 1990."[7] This "first wave" had a pronounced sensual emphasis, which Ekaterina Andreeva describes as "erotic":

> There was a particular erotic quality to the first neoacademicist film *Voskresenie*, shot in a 16 mm format by Bella and Vladimir Zakharov, as well as Russian art video pioneer Yury Lesnik's *Contrast*, in which Georgy Guryanov performed a striptease. One might see them as precursors to today's selfies and home videos, yet this comparison would not be entirely accurate. In early neoacademism, self-worship emanated not just from youthful passions but, more importantly, from a kind of aesthetic love that permeated Timur's community, that is a love that proceeds from

> admiration rather than compassion. In this connection, the ethos of early neoacademism was best formulated by artist Ivan Movsesian: "Content was to be located aesthetically, in erotic provocations." (Andreeva 2015, 28).

The late 1980s marked the ascendance of sexual freedom, a new chapter in the country's sexual revolution, which now included the coming into visibility of Russian gay culture. This process had been underway before the emergence of the neoacademist movement—in the space of the New Artists' aesthetic forms and public expressiveness. I remember a massive crowd of diverse, curious people, including reporters, who came to the Trade School Students' House of Culture on Sophia Perovskaia Street to hear American gay movement veterans talk about how they had teamed up with the Communists, organizing collective farms in the USA and plowing the prairies on tractors, as well as about a medieval order of destitute monks, who, persecuted by the authorities yet supported by the people, would spin around dancing, their soutanes lifting in the manner of "the twirling dervishes," etc. Novikov did not like missing out on hot trends and would exploit them in promoting Russian art in the West, where, according to the word on the street, the gay mafia was omnipotent. As can be surmised from the statements by Egelskii, late neoacademism tended to disavow or deny this dimension of the movement in its early stages. With all due respect to the guardians of neoacademism's serious image, the effort to silence this part of its history is unreasonable[8] and, from a scholarly point of view, unprofessional.[9] It generates inept, reductive interpretations of the past.

In 1989, the conversation of Sergei Bugaev (Afrika) and Novikov with Margarita Tupitsyna, Viktor Tupitsyn, David Ross, and Elisabeth Sussman (the Whitney Museum) included the following exchange:

> Elisabeth Sussman: *How much do you know about gay freedom in America?*
>
> Timur Novikov: Not sure how much . . . To the extent that the situation allows . . .
>
> Sergei Bugaev: To the extent of 20 centimeters!
>
> T.N: Soviet law only prohibits anal intercourse. If a homosexual, let's say, doesn't do anal penetration but only, to be blunt, blowjobs, he cannot be legally prosecuted. There is no law for them. It was actually Stalin who introduced laws policing sexuality. Before 1933 we had different laws that allowed pretty much everything! Moreover, the Soviet registry offices recognized same-sex families, between men and between women. I read about it in the Soviet Encyclopedia published in 1932.

> It says that because gays and lesbians were victimized in bourgeois countries (and in pre-revolutionary Russia) our country now provided them with favorable living conditions.
>
> Viktor Tupitsyn: *Lately you have been open about your sexual orientation. You are both homosexual, right?*
>
> T.N. and S.B: Yes!"[10]

Following this candid interview, the Leningrad art scene became strongly associated with gay identity. This "homosexual fame" in turn affected the reception of neoacademism, which was now attacked not only by generally homophobic people, but also by Anatoly Osmolovsky and other members of Moscow's radical, "leftist" intelligentsia, who proved to be hard core philistines suffering from a bad case of male chauvinism.

In 1990, soon after this first and last schizorevolutionary coming out in Russian art, Novikov, Guryanov, Goncharov, Egelskii and other young men from Leningrad travelled to Budapest, where Agnesh Khorvat, who was a close friend of this group and especially Guryanov, organized an exhibition called "Novye iz Peterburga" ("The New from Petersburg"). Khorvat was surprised to observe the changed behavior of her guests, who had been "normal men" just a couple of years ago. As Leningrad artist and poet Oleg Kotelnikov would say: It is as if one "left on a reconnaissance operation as a boy (the Russian *boi,* which means 'battle' or 'combat,' is also the transliteration of the English word *boy*) and returned as a gay." It was not long before the glamorous gay image, which this small company of friends cultivated to a large extent as a playful provocation, ceased to reflect the makeup of the movement, as neoacademism expanded to include more and more people. Only Guryanov, who never cared what others thought of him, showed consistency in this respect. Back in the summer of 1990, he displayed his 2x3m painting of two multicolored penises at the base of a raised leaf of the Palace Bridge on the Hermitage embankment, in a sense, the first ever show of monumental kinetic street art in the city. Yet during that time, this gesture was hardly seen as anything scandalous. Among the young generation of Petersburg bohemians, who were typically accepting of, if not indifferent to, each other's private lives, gay imagery, as mobilized by the formerly punk, neoacademist artists, would often be riddled with mockery, which was similar to the way it was exploited by the mooning artists of the necro-realist persuasion in the 1980s. In this connection, it should be noted that anti-gay propaganda would often borrow images from art works and performance projects by two NAFA professors, Oleg

Maslov and Viktor Kuznetsov, a pair of butch collaborators and fathers to several families.

Yet no more than a year later, in January 1991, in his interview in *Kabinet* magazine, Novikov said the following:

> Olesya Turkina: *But your life was always prone to signal danger, that is to say, a double danger: first of all, as an avant-garde artist, and secondly, as a member of the sexual minorities.*
>
> Timur Novikov: It is a mistake to consider me a member of the sexual minorities. I do serve on the board of a sexual minority organization, because I have always cared for people that are victims of discrimination. As for me, though, I'd rather call myself a member of the sexual majority. I think all these horrible things happened because the Bolsheviks did not care for the Mensheviks. We have to care about our neighbors. (Turkina 1992, 42)[11]

It should be noted that as general views on homosexuality become more lenient, a process that includes the cessation of legal persecution (criminal code article 121, criminalizing sodomy, was abolished in 1993), Novikov loses interest in this topic and begins to distance himself from gay discourse. And so, we get an entirely different take from a blind Novikov in a 1998 interview:

> Reporter: *Some critics identify academicism with feminine origins.*
>
> T.N.: There is a Krylov fable about a pig that went to have a look at newly built rooms. Upon the pig's return, they ask "How do the rooms look?" The pig replies: "Nothing remarkable. I took a walk around the courtyard—there is dirt in every single corner." And as Krylov sums up, so do certain critics see only dirt in beautiful new rooms. Pigs will always find dirt. And some people see gay culture in the purest ideals of neo-academism. Everyone interprets things to the best of their depravity: the homosexuals see in it a gay culture, the perverts see deviations, the nymphomaniacs see narcissism, etc.; one can go on like this forever, of course, masochists see masochism.
>
> Reporter: *Gay culture—does it constitute a powerful generative resource in contemporary art?*
>
> T.N.: I often get these questions about gay culture. My answer is always the same: "Yes, there are perhaps some select individuals at our Academy who could be called homosexuals. Yet the percentage of homosexuals at our Academy is much lower than the average percentage across the country." (Golybin and Molok 1998, 71)

During a memorial art program dedicated to the five hundredth anniversary of Girolamo Savonarola's death at the stake, Novikov burned his 1989 work *Pink Evening*, a work he himself declared to be "pure propaganda of homosexuality."[12] This, however, did not prevent the leader of neoacademism from cutting off his grey locks and beard on a fine summer day in 2001, shaving his legs, putting on shorts and going out with his cheerful comrades-in-arms for a stroll through the neighborhoods of their former conquests, an event captured in photos by the Moscow-based neoacademist Natalia Zhernovskaia.

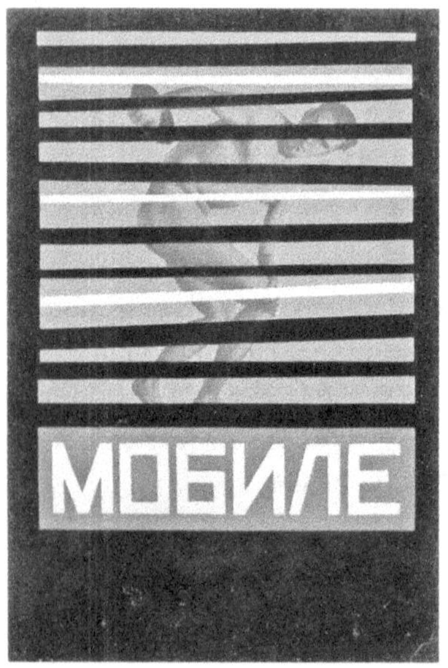

Georgy Guryanov, poster of the rave "Mobile-party" (1992). Collection of Andrei Khlobystin

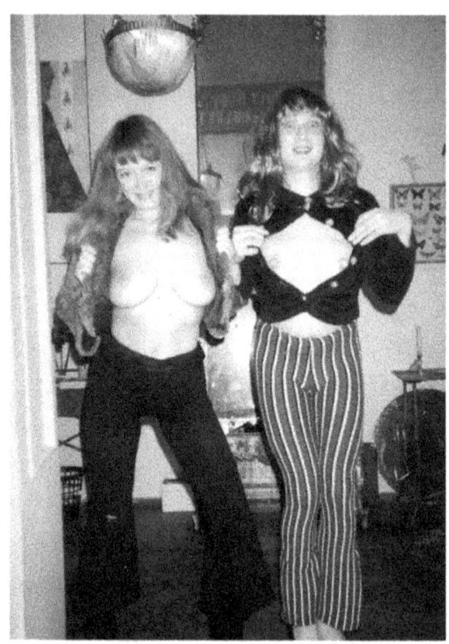

First Russian female DJ Lena Popova and Vladislav Mamyshev-Monroe in drag as Lena Popova (1993). Photo by Andrei Khlobystin. Archive of Garage Museum of Contemporary Art, Collection of Andrei Khlobystin

Cross-dressing

It should be noted that during the early years of neoacademism, Leningrad artists did not conceive of the body as something definitive, nor did they locate its essence in a straightforward gender binary or in the opposition between flesh and prosthetics, between the natural and the artificial, and so on (Kurekhin 1991). A Petersburg tradition dating back to the court balls of Russian empress Elizabeth I in the eighteenth century, this schizorevolutionary fluidity of selfhood, of psychosomatics, and of external image formation manifested itself not only in the mask and "avatar" practices but also in nudity and cross-dressing. The latter, far from being exclusive to "minorities," was characteristic of theatrical techniques, dandyism, shamanism, criminality, the genre of comedy, traditional religious and folk rituals, etc.[13]

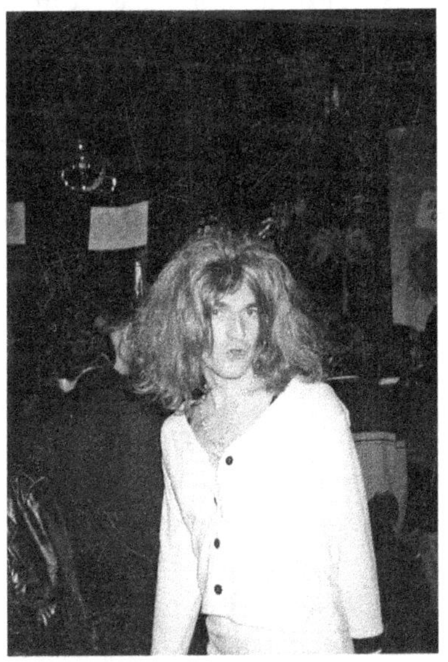

Timur Novikov wearing a wig and a dress by the club Jackie 60 (1990). Photo by Andrei Khlobystin. Archive of Garage Museum of Contemporary Art, Collection of Andrei Khlobystin

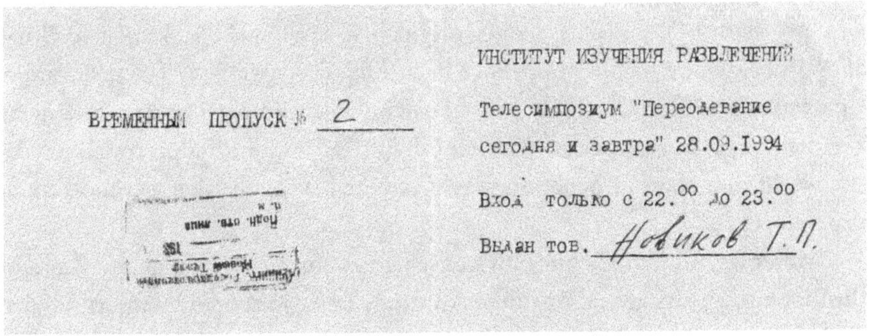

ВРЕМЕННЫЙ ПРОПУСК № 2

ИНСТИТУТ ИЗУЧЕНИЯ РАЗВЛЕЧЕНИЙ

Телесимпозиум "Переодевание сегодня и завтра" 28.09.1994

Вход только с $22.^{00}$ до $23.^{00}$

Выдан тов. Новиков Т.П.

An invitation card for the TV symposium "Dressing Up Today and Tomorrow" (party "Frickadelika") of the Institute of Entertainment Studies (1994). Archive of Garage Museum of Contemporary Art, Collection of Andrei Khlobystin

One of the more extreme manifestations of narcissism specific to Petersburg was the career of Vladislav (Vladik) Mamyshev-Monroe (1969–2013), whom Novikov calls "Russia's first official transvestite" (Novikov 2003, 47). Vladik became a front man for Soviet videoart, appearing in the wildly popular *Pirate Television* (1990–1993), whose programming was co-created by Novikov and Yuris Lesnik at 22 Naberzhnaia Moiki. While the network's aesthetic is hard to pinpoint definitively, it was an admixture of styles reminiscent of *Monty Python,* John Waters's films starring Divine, and other forms of art trash that exploded into prominence in the late 1960s—early 1970s. What set Monroe apart from Yasumasa Morimura and Cindy Sherman—and from the Moscow Actionists with their animalistic image—was that he would transform himself not only when positioned in front of a camera or an audience but also in the privacy of his own home—it was simply his way of life. Stanislavsky's "here and now" demanded that an actor expend a great deal of effort to transform himself into a character, which entailed an exacting regimen of preparation and an uncompromising commitment to role-playing/catharsis on stage, followed by a sense of being drained, a kind of acting hangover (akin to a shapeshifter's bodily suffering).

Monroe, however, pursued the more radical tradition of always being in the state of the "here and now"; he was a human wave, a Terminator-like body of liquid crystals, gliding and shimmering. His wit and recklessness were done with considerable foresight (we shall avoid discussing his sense of responsibility here). Like Kino's leader Victor Tsoi, Novikov, Guryanov and other heroes of that culture, Monroe stood out from the general crowd by virtue of his self-indulgence, radiating a seductive energy. Overall, this lent him the appearance of a magical personality rather than a cunning imitator. Indeed, one of his images was "professor of the department of originality" at the NAFA. Similar to Guryanov and Novikov, he did not believe in curbing his passion. When asked about "freedom," Tsoi would say; "I am a free man because I have always done what I wanted to do and refused to do what I didn't."[14] These willful personalities saw the world in a state of becoming, as if strained through their psychosomatic experiences.

Moreover, under the conditions of schizorevolutionary change, they felt the thrill of buccaneers at sea. At times, Monroe's behavior could be interpreted as an "echo": like the old man who, having miraculously materialized in a temple, responds to everyone's questions by repeating them, Monroe merely mirrored those around him. These acts could be seen as mockery if he had not conducted them as exchanges of energy generally gratifying to both sides. Thus, when

Jacques Derrida, the grey-haired philosopher star who was obviously aware of his good looks, visited the NAFA museum at 10 Pushkinskaia Street in 1994, he was greeted by a young-looking old man in a trek suit, a gold Olympic medal dangling off his neck. While Monroe, who was twenty-four years old at the time, knew little about the person he was there to mirror, he somehow managed to achieve a subtle resonance with the creator of deconstruction. Monroe was known for his risk-taking. According to eyewitnesses, he once marked National Aviation Day by dressing up as Marilyn Monroe and hitting on drunk military men; he showed up in Alla Pugacheva drag at his own court hearing for drug possession; and having risen to stardom in Moscow's art scene, he was spotted riding around the capital's Azerbaijani markets, after 9/11, in an Osama bin Laden disguise.[15]

Despite Monroe's fame, the first cross-dresser on the Russian art scene was in fact Bugaev-Afrika, who wore a dress during a *Kino* rehearsal, which was featured in the French TV movie *Rock around the Kremlin* (1985).[16] Vladimir Sorokin, Oleg Kotelnikov and others from the brutal punk scene likewise appeared in drag at a Pop-Mechanics concert at the Rock Club in 1985. In March of 1988, Afrika, appearing under the drag name of Irena Belaia, became a finalist in the first perestroika-era beauty contest, organized by Sergei Kurekhin and Lenfilm director Vitalii Aksenov at the October Concert Hall. As photographer Vladimir Peshkov remembers it: "It transpired during the last moments of the event that contestant #24, the beautiful and insanely sexy blonde Irena Belaia, who was regarded as one of the likeliest winners, was in fact . . . a man made up as a woman. And not just any man but the famous Afrika, who had passed through all preliminary parts of the contest and was a serious contender on par with the other finalists. It's a relief he didn't win."[17]

In the late 1980s, playful engagement with the provocative side of current gender discourses became in vogue not only in early neoacademism but also in the entire avant-garde scene in the Leningrad of the schizorevolutionary era. In 1989 Olesya Turkina and Viktor Mazin held an exhibition called "Women in Art" at the Exhibition Hall of the Museum Association of the Leningrad Region. The male artists, whose works were shown alongside those of the women, assumed female names: Gul'barshin Temirgalieva (Vadim Ovchinnikov), Natasha Rostova (Viktor Tuzov), Lida Sossura (Vlad Gutsevich), Rebecca Kreutzer (Timur Novikov), Nadezhda Nevynosimova (Vladimir Sorokin), Valentina Tereshkova (Georgy Guryanov), Pivitsa Ivanova (Ivan Movsesyan), etc. Gender antics became integral to the club and rave cultures. For example, in 1994, the Institute of Entertainment Studies (Institut Izucheniia Razvlechenii), created by Novikov, hosted two parties at the Tunnel Club, where large swaths of Petersburg bohemians had a chance to let loose in drag. I remember borrowing fishnets, a mini skirt, and tall laced boots from Lena Popova, who would one day become Russia's first female DJ. Accompanied by an acquaintance in a red striped dress, we emerged on Nevsky Prospect, hailed a taxi, got to the Tunnel, danced up a storm, and happily returned home. It was okay back then, even though on the streets a crime spree was underway, and people were extremely agitated. By the mid-1990s drag was regarded, at times rather naively, as a conduit to social prestige. Writer Almat Malatov thus describes a young man's experience in 1995: "If you never appeared in a public place wearing an evening gown, your career as a socialite was over. Done. Leave the group, crawl under a rock—if you have not impersonated a transsexual or a drag queen, you are a scumbag, a lowlife, and absolutely not on trend" (Malatov 2007, 188). Nevertheless, as Novikov's interviews quoted above demonstrate, in the early 1990s the leader of neoclassicism was already disengaging neoacademism from queer discourse.

Nudity

The "evolution" of the body in Leningrad art during the second half of the twentieth century inaugurates "human wave" somatics (Monroe is constantly changing his appearance, even his own weight) and the masquerade of bodies in neoacademism of the late 1980s–early 1990s. Within the enclaves of neoacademism, *Pirate Television*, Pop-Mechanics, and other such art phenomena during the period, the significance of the figures of "Genius" and "Hero" had to do with evolving ideas about avatar-bodies and increased attention to "surface," "texture," the "external," which was then being freed from censure, and the "outfit" or the "look." Given to dreaming and endless fantasy, these artists concentrated on external effects, which bespeaks the significance of the *ideal image* (one of Novikov's favorite expressions).

In neoacademism, nudity was one of the crucial refractions of this ideal image. The history of getting naked among these artists had an idiosyncratic trajectory. Nudity was barely present either in nonconformist art or in Soviet photography. There were of course proponents of nudism and some amateur photographers who were interested in the subject, but they kept a low profile. For example, poet Konstantin Kuzminskii strolled around naked under a parachute stretched across the ceiling of his apartment, which served as a space for many independent art exhibitions. Photographer Gennady Prikhodko captured nude bodies outdoors in the wild, but, as Valery Valran writes, in the 1970s these images "would certainly have been classified as 'pornographic'" (Valran 2002). Novikov told me that while working as a projectionist, he had pieced together a collage of scenes with nudity, which he had compiled from all the films he had access to.

Young people, particularly those brought up by progressive parents belonging to the 1960s generation in home environments free from prudery, would get naked without a second thought. I remember that in the 1980s my art historian college mates—Katya Andreeva and Alla Mitrofanova, the future founder of Russian cyber-feminism—would casually take off their clothes at a Crimean beach in Morskoe. Passing cars would honk at them from the road along the beach, while an admirer, too shy to approach them, decorated pebbles with graceful drawings of their figures. The cult of naturalness and nature had also been a part of the hippie movement, with which everyone had come into contact in one way or another in the 1970s.

In punk circles, Evgeny Yufit, the founder of Leningrad's necro-realism, and Svin (Andrei Panov), the leader of Russia's first punk band Avtomaticheskie Udovletvoriteli, would get naked for attention and provocation. The first nude act by the "New Artists" looks cheerfully scandalous: A naked Novikov, captured by Oleg Kotelnikov in 1984, lies on his stomach, his back side to the audience, wearing headphones and listening to a state-of-the-art portable player (now in the Russian Museum collection).

The nude male body, a popular Socialist Realist motif that had entered Soviet Art from the prerevolutionary era, was beginning to be seen as suspect in the 1980s, even as neoacademism pushed the boundaries of this tradition (Kon 2005, 194–222). Himself an image of a nude hero akin to an ancient Greek god, warrior, or athlete, Guryanov stood proud and tall on the stage of life, asserting that a man looks his best when he is nude, and only in the absence of remarkable qualities does he cover himself in elegant suits. Guryanov's toilette in front of his admirers recalled the hours-long ceremonials of the Sun-King's court. He would get naked at the first opportunity.[18] I remember Arkadii Dragomoshchenko telling me about a squabble that took place before a Pop-Mechanics concert: Guryanov wanted to go on completely in the buff, while Kurekhin insisted that he at least leave his speedo on. Guryanov was not only an eminent practitioner but also a theorist of nudity in the bohemian enclaves of Leningrad. A truism of his was: ". . . to look at a strong, tan young body, illuminated by rays of sunlight and blown by sea winds, is far wiser than to stare at a black square with an intelligent air."

In Petersburg, the boundaries between life and art were typically porous. Neoacademist genres—painting or staged photography beholden to the ideals of antiquity—abutted the realm of the mundane. Thus, Maslov and Kuznetsov based their first neoacademist series of paintings, *Golubaia Laguna* (Blue lagoon), on ordinary photographs of young men and women relaxing at the gay beach in Simeiz, Crimea. A tourist once told me that while strolling through the parks of Petergof he had been accosted by a group of naked young people with lyres and wreaths, asking him to take a picture of them. That sounds like one of Maslov and Kuznetsov's out-of-town photo sessions. The old genre of *tableau vivant* regained its currency. The neoacademists would use readily available objects as material for costumes, scenery, and props: A toilet seat, for instance, could be turned into a lyre. Soon, these neoacademist shows would include nudity not only by the "academics" themselves but also by people from all sorts of creative communities.

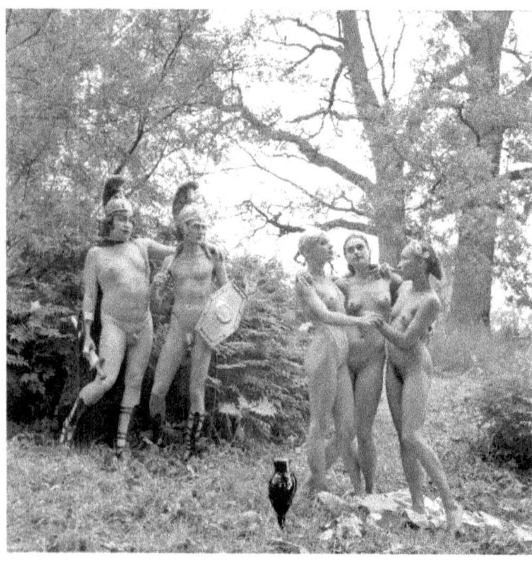

Oleg Maslov and Viktor Kuznetsov, from the series *Secrets of the Sacred Grove* (1995). Courtesy of the artists

In his essay "Nudity," Giorgio Agamben takes a trip through Christian theology to arrive at an analysis of nudity in relation to garments, both material and supernatural. Nudity represents man's original state, before falling into sin, when he had been clothed in grace, "in the glory of God." As the Italian scholar writes, "The nudity of the human body is its image—that is, the trembling that makes this body knowable" (Agamben 2011, 84). Neoacademist photo sessions in pastoral, natural settings extended traditions that can at the very least be traced from William Blake to the Die Brücke artists in Germany and, later, to the Soviet "Down with

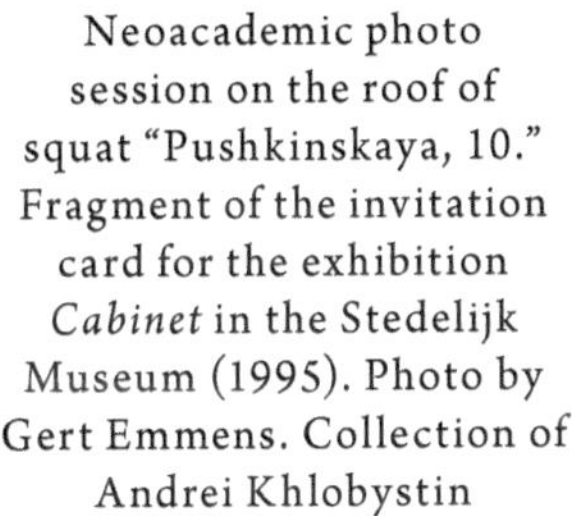

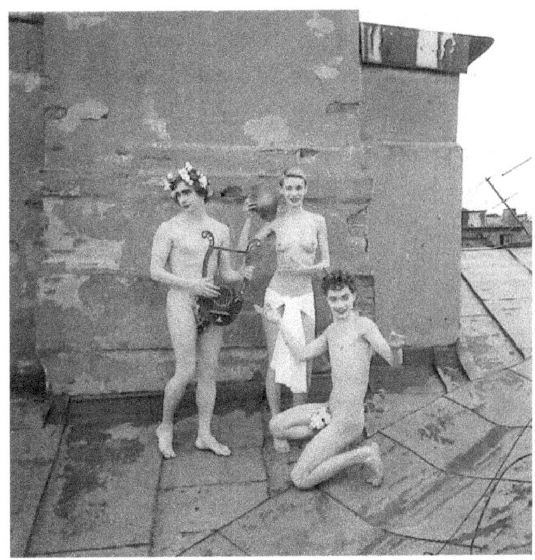

Neoacademic photo session on the roof of squat "Pushkinskaya, 10." Fragment of the invitation card for the exhibition *Cabinet* in the Stedelijk Museum (1995). Photo by Gert Emmens. Collection of Andrei Khlobystin

shame" movement and the rise of nudism in the 1960s. While depicting the nude body, often ironically, as deviant in their paintings and photographs, Neoacademicist artists in fact aspired to recreate "garments of light" and beauty. Committed to nudity as the appearance of beauty (Agamben 2011, 85),[19] they shrugged disdainfully at the antics of 1990s Moscow's Actionists. The experiments of these Leningrad artists preceded the pornographic affect-ridden bodies of the capital's art scene by more than a decade.

Conclusion

The splintering of our picture of the world—from atoms to living beings—over the course of the twentieth century has resulted in the emergence of the ubiquitous twenty-first-century human who has no real appearance or ultimate essence. The eccentric body and shimmering identity of the bohemia of the 1990s established new horizons and conditions for daily artistic life that are still around. Today, anyone can change their identity several times a day: A clerk who begins his day at work by logging on to social media under an alias may later find himself waiting in line at the housing authority, stopping by a political rally, joining a *Game of Thrones*-style quest, then a techno party, and ending his day somewhere in the vicinity—only to hop a plane to Turkey in the morning to get away from it all. During the schizorevolution, however, artists were people of the unrestricted lands of the Wild Fields, of the frontier, of the zone of expansion; they were adventurers, pioneers, gold diggers, and freebooters who had left the borders of the old world behind. The generations that succeeded them—agronomists, prospectors, and miners working hard to master the natural world and the discourses outlined by the schizorevolution—barely lifted their eyes to look at the horizon and didn't even consider making a ridiculous attempt to break open that illusory line.

Translated by Aleksei Grinenko

Notes

1 The essay is based on materials from the book *Shizorevoluziia. Ocherki peterburgskoi kul'tury vtoroi poloviny XX veka* [Schizorevolution. Notes on the St. Petersburg culture of the second half of the 20th century], St Petersburg: Borei-Art, 2017.

2 From the article "Leningradskii feminizm 1970-kh godov," by Natalia Malakhovskaia. The article was deleted from Wikipedia but was republished by permission of the author on May 7, 2013 at: http://ravnopravka.ru/2013/05/leningrad_feminism/.

3 From the article "Leningradskii feminizm 1970-kh godov," by Natalia Malakhovskaia (See footnote 2).

4 In addition to appearances on radio and television programs, public speeches, and internet activity, the NAFA bibliography includes hundreds of publications in Russian and abroad. See *Bibliographiia Novoi Akademii Izyashchnykh Iskusstv* (St. Petersburg: n.p., 2004), 56–87. http://www.newacademy.spb.ru/4itzal.html and http://www.newacademy.spb.ru/Timur/bibliography.html.

5 Quoted from Egelskii's biography, written by Novikov in 1991. Retrieved from: https://russianartarchive.net/ru/catalogue/document/D5509.

6 Retrieved from: http://ro-ko-ko.ru/blog/intervju-iriny-vrubel-golubkinoj-s-nikolaem-hardzhievym-dlja-zhurnala-zerkalo, https://daily.afisha.ru/archive/vozduh/books/nikolay-hardzhiev-serebryanyy-vek-eto-mif-vydumka-ochen-glupaya/.

7 Timur Novikov, *Autobiography*, 16; Exhibition, "Academicism and Neoacademicism," opened on April 6, 1991; Vladislav Mamyshev's interview with Timur Novikov is available at: http://www.youtube.com/watch?v=V5SyLwd2C6k.

8 The aforementioned article by Alexander Yastrebov is an example of a recent amateurish treatment of gay art and neocademicism in the press. "Gay-art or not gay-art." *ARTGID* (November 2, 2011). Available at: http://artguide.com/posts/841?page=20.

9 Thus, Gasan Guseinov, director of the Center for the Humanities at the Presidential Academy, states: "When considering Antiquity, all of Antiquity, we can clearly see that various aspects of same-sex love or same-sex relationships have a great significance there. We cannot comprehend or explain them without exploring this phenomenon not only on a linguistic level but also on all levels pertaining to human existence. Whoever says that this can be overlooked is a liar. This cannot be overlooked. [. . .] If I can clearly explain to a 20-year-old the problem of same-sex love in Homer or Plato or the problem of democracy and tyranny in, once again, Plato or the tyrant Dionysius, then I am indeed a scholar." This is an excerpt from an episode of the television program *Perspektivy*, hosted by Ivar Maksutov, titled "Iazyk klassikov i iazyk sovremennosti," during which the philologist Gasan Guseinov discusses classical philology, the need to study one's own language, and the mutual interaction between philosophy and philology (PostNauka, December 13, 2012); available at: http://postnauka.ru/tv/6575; see also Sergei Averintsev, "O tom chto takoe paideia," described as "a course of lectures delivered at the Moscow State University in 1989 about the ways in which attitudes toward same-sex love in ancient Greek and Judaic traditions relate to those people's relationship to history and about the ways in which philosophers, mathematicians, astronomers, poets, and artists developed a sense of community and difference from the rest."

10 This interview was first published in the Russian version of *Flash Art* 1 (1989).

11 This is the first major interview of the Leningraders, given to the well-known art critic Olesya Turkina, and has been published many times. Initially it was printed in the Russian publication of the "leading European art magazine," *Flash Art* 1 (1989) under the title "Razgovor s Timurom." After, it was printed in English in a slightly abridged version in *Flash Art* 151 (March/April 1990): 122–125). Later, it appeared—with permission of the magazine *Kabinet* of which Novikov and Bugaev were editors—in the almanac *RISK* 1 (1995): 79–82). Then, it was published in Viktor Tupitsyn, *Drugoe Iskusstvo: Besedy s khudozhnikami, kritikami, filosofami, 1980-1995* (Moscow: Ad Marginem, 1997): 303–304; available at: http://yanko.lib.ru/books/art/tupicin-drugoe-isskustva.htm. Finally, it appeared in the exhibition catalogue *Neoakademizm i elektronika. Vystavka sovremennogo iskusstva iz Sankt-Peterburga.* (Cheboksary: Chuvashiia, 1999: 5–10). Notably, in 1999, Novikov ordered the pages of this interview to be torn out from all the copies of this last publication.

12 Egelskii asserts that he created a major part of this painting.

13 For more, see Andrei Khlobystin. "Merlin Makhno." *Dantes* 2 (1999): 53–55. Available at: http://www.mitin.com/dj02/hlob.shtml.

14 Quotes taken from various interviews given by Tsoi circulate on the Internet; often the source of the interview in some provincial newspaper is virtually impossible to find, but these words and sayings have become associated with him like apocrypha or koans. They exist in the form of original quotation collections, such as this one: https://rockcult.ru/po/viktor-tsoi-quotes/

15 See *Pirate Television* coverage here: https://www.facebook.com/PiratskoeTelevidenie/videos/443053032871/?theater

16 See 19:00–21:39, available at: https://www.youtube.com/watch?v=7hcV3ozs0Ms https://www.youtube.com/watch?v=Nf0aXQSNQys.

17 Vladimir Peshkov, *Konkurs Krasoty*. Available at: http://bogemnyipeterburg.net/retrograund/materials/krasota1988.htm and http://ed-glezin.livejournal.com/799360.html.

18 See video of this famous moment during a Kino rehearsal in Guryanov's apartment, available at: https://www.youtube.com/watch?v=dAuiObJUpko.

19 As Agamben (2011, 89) writes: "Only because beauty remains to the end an 'envelopment,' only because it remains 'inexplicable' [etymologically, that which cannot be unfolded], can appearance—which reaches its supreme stage in nudity—be called beautiful."

References

Agamben, Giorgio. 2011. "Nudity." In *Nudities*. Translated by David Kishik and Stefan Pedatella, 55–90. Stanford: Stanford University Press.

Andreeva, Ekaterina. 2015. "Novaia akademiia iziashchnykh iskusstv: dvadtsat' let spustia." In *Neoakademizm v Sankt-Peterburge: Katalog vystavki v muzee Ludviga (Budapest)*, 28. Ekaterinburg-Budapest: UVC Art Gallery.

Deleuze, Gilles and Félix Guattari. [1972] 2004. *Anti-Œdipus*. Translated by Robert Hurley, Mark Seem and Helen R. Lane. London: Continuum, 2004.

———. [1980] 2004. *A Thousand Plateaus*. Translated by Brian Massum. London: Continuum, 2004.

Fomenko, Andrei. 2001. "Geneologia neoakademizma." *Khudozhesvennyi Zhurnal* 32. http://www.guelman.ru/xz/362/xx32/xx3204.htm. Last accessed: May 23, 2021.

Golybin, Vasilii and Nikolai Molok. 1998. "Akademik s toporom." *Itogi* 71. Available at: https://timurnovikov.ru/storage/docs/articles/1998_academik_s_toporom.pdf. Last accessed May 23, 2021.

Kon, Igor'. 2005. "Obnazhennoe muzhskoe telo v russkom izobrazitel'nom iskusstve." In *Telo v Russkoi kul'ture*, edited by Galina Kabakova and F. Kont, 194–222. Moscow: Novoe literaturnoe obozrenie. Available at: http://www.fedy-diary.ru/html/112010/11112010-03b.html. Last accessed May 23, 2021.

Kurekhin, Sergei. Aired May 17, 1991. *Lenin–grib. Pyatoe koleso* on Leningrad Television. Available at: https://www.youtube.com/watch?v=h2cs8QLnxlU, https://www.youtube.com/watch?v=ExXDxpBFFR0. Last accessed May 23, 2021.

Malatov, Almat. 2007. *Immoralist. Krizis poludnia.* Moscow: ACT.

Novikov, Timur. 1996. "Kak ya pridumal reiv." *OM* (March). Available at: http://www.timurnovikov.ru/index.php?option=com_content&view=article&id=48&Itemid=18&lang=ru. Last accessed May 23, 2021.

———. 1998. *Retrospektiva.* St. Petersburg: Novaia Akademiia.

——. 2003. "Moe raskaianie Malevicha." Lecture at Novaia Akademiia Iziashchnykh Iskusstv, St. Petersburg.

———. 2003. "Peterburgskoe iskusstvo 1990 godov." Lectures. St. Petersburg. Available at: https://timurnovikov.ru/storage/docs/lecture/90_peterburgskoe_iskusstvo.pdf. Last accessed May 23, 2021.

Solomon, Andrew. 1991. *The Irony Tower.* New York: Knopf.

Tupitsyn, Viktor. 1997. "Timur Novikov and Sergei Bugaev (Afrika) with the participation of Margarita Tupitsyna, David Ross, and Elizabeth Sassman." In *"Drugoe" iskusstva. Besedy s khudozhnikami, kritikami, filosofami: 1980-1995*, 303–304. Moscow: Ad Marginem. Available at: http://yanko.lib.ru/books/art/tupicin-drugoe-isskustva.htm#_Toc152007894. Last accessed May 23, 2021.

Turkina, Olesia. 1992. "Razgovor s Timurom." *Kabinet* 1: 41–42.

Vaginov, Konstantin. 1922. "Monastyr' gospoda nashego Apollona." *Abraksas* 1: 8–15.

Valran, Valerii. 2002. "Gennady Prikhodko. Obnazhennaia. Iazycheskii tsikl." Exhibition at the "Art-Kollegiia" Gallery, November 1–30. Available at: http://www.arteria.ru/photomarathon/left10.htm. Last accessed May 23, 2021.

Vrubel-Golubkina, Irina. 2014. *Razgovory v zerkale*. Moscow: Novoe Literaturnoe Obozrenie.

Yurchak, Alexei. 2005. *Everything Was Forever, Until It Was No More: The Last Soviet Generation*. Princeton: Princeton University Press.

Zilberman, David. 2014. *Pravoslavnaia etika i materiia kommunizma*. St. Petersburg: Ivan Limbakh.

Chapter 10

The Lure of Implied Transgression as Revolutionary Retrospective: The Illicit as *la Belleza* in Bella Matveeva's Art

Helena Goscilo

We always long for the forbidden things, and desire what is denied us.

—François Rabelais

Matveeva's *Modus Vivendi et Pingendi*

"Beauty is a short-lived tyranny."

—Socrates

Dostoevsky's over-quoted prophecy that "beauty will save the world" (*krasota spaset mir*), articulated by Myshkin in *The Idiot* (1869), clearly belongs to the domain of utopia. Yet it helped to salvage the Neoacademists' artistic reputation, and perhaps especially that of Bella Matveeva (b. 1961), whose very name in Italian denotes beauty. Indeed, beauty in various registers and variously understood constituted the group's artistic credo and calling card in their effort to revive the aesthetics of a classical, remote past as a means of self-legitimation.

Frequently omitted from general commentaries on the Neoacademists, Matveeva joined them in 1990 as the first woman in the group.[1] A native of Troitsk/Chelyabinsk, resident of St. Petersburg since 1977, graduate of the Restoration

Department at the Serov College of Art (1981), and fabled hostess of a risqué salon,[2] she subsequently became a painting instructor at the New Academy of Fine Arts (Novaia Akademiia Iziashchnykh Iskusstv), which opened in St. Petersburg in 1993, boasting a faculty of so-called 'professors,' several of them lacking the advanced academic degrees normally requisite for such a designation. An emerita today, in 2014 Matveeva moved her studio to the house on Tavricheskaia Street previously inhabited by Viacheslav Ivanov, where approximately a century ago convened such literary luminaries as Anna Akhmatova, Nikolai Gumilev, and Zinaida Gippius. To mark Matveeva's quarter-century of artistic production, in the same year, Tat'iana Nikitina's Art Holding, with considerable pomp and ceremony, orchestrated a sizable exhibition there, whimsically titled *Bella Vita: Retrospective*. With only a handful of survivors from the original Academy left and the group disbanded, Matveeva finally had arrived.[3]

One of few women in the male-dominated Neoacademist coterie—which included Ol'ga Tobreluts, Iuliia Strausova, and Irena Kuksenaite—Matveeva adopted the dominant device of queer or same-sex allusiveness that characterized the group's aesthetic and that briefly brought media attention to the pop-music duo of t.A.T.u shortly thereafter, before the regime under Putin clamped down on any manifestation of LGBTQ-related phenomena.[4] Inspired by nineteenth-century academic art and Art Nouveau, Matveeva began producing large paintings that are instantly identifiable by her exclusive preoccupation with young bodies and her signature 'decadent' stylization.[5] Relying on lush colors, seductive skin tones, copious decorative detail, lavish textures, and an extensive use of gold,[6] Matveeva conveys a wealth of sensations through her trademark opulent style and recourse to earlier painterly conventions connoting wealth and/or exoticism. In a revival of *fin de siècle* genres, thematics, and methods, she embodies in voluptuous form a cult of luxurious beauty, the eroticism of androgyny, and sundry modes of implied transgression,[7] leading one admirer somewhat fancifully to label her mode of painting "spicy academism" (*prianyi akademizm*) (Nikolaeva 2014, 8). Her works typify yet simultaneously depart from several fundamental Neoacademist precepts and have evolved over three decades while retaining a perceptible consistency. Unlike such fellow Neoacademists as Georgy Guryanov, who focused exclusively on males and particularly male bodies,[8] Matveeva, especially in the early phases of her career, tended to engage the female form and its expressive capacities.

The Body Beautiful

"And your very flesh shall be a great poem."

—Walt Whitman

The human body, its allure, and its signifying potential constituted the heartbeat of the Neocademists' art, particularly that of Matveeva, Guryanov, Vladislav Mamyshev (also known as Vladik Monroe),[9] Oleg Maslov, and Viktor Tsoi.[10] Ancient Greeks, whose influence on Western art would be impossible to overestimate, considered the body's beauty reflective evidence of its divine creator's perfection and the ideal to which all humans should strive. Analyzing Greek statues, Kenneth Clark, in his watershed monograph *The Nude: A Study in Ideal Form* (1956), maintains:

> The nude gains its enduring value from the fact that it reconciles several contrary states. It takes the most sensual and immediately interesting object, the human body, and puts it out of reach of time and desire; it takes the most purely rational concept of which mankind is capable, mathematical order, and makes it a delight to the senses; and it takes the vague fears of the unknown and sweetens them by showing that the gods are like men and may be worshiped for their life-giving beauty rather than their death-dealing powers. (Clark 1956, 25)

For the most part classical art depicted individual bodies of pagan divinities as incarnations of sublime beauty, whether of Apollo, Venus, or Hermes. These works invite/d contemplation. In contrast, Matveeva prefers to arrange her human bodies in couples or with an animal in evocative attendance. That preference implies a dynamic interplay between those near-naked bodies—a narrative plot intimated yet never made explicit by the relationship of the two or three forms, frequently recumbent and located on couches, beds, or in abstract, unidentifiable contexts. What such juxtapositions urge is not contemplation but explication, the impulse to deduce the precise nature of the connection between or among these figures and the artist's motivation for presenting such combinations.

The Power of Implication

Any visitor to Matveeva's salon could testify that she thrived on suggestion and suggestiveness, preferring intimation to intimacy and persistently courting the forbidden as a source of inspiration. Thus nakedness, sexuality outside traditionalist socially approved mores, and scenarios that imply purportedly perverse desires are the norm in her canvasses and in her publication titled *Aesthetics of the Classical Bordello* (*Estetika klassicheskogo bordelia*, 1994), containing photographs of self-consciously staged activities envisioned as transpiring in a *fin-de-siècle* brothel. The poses and arrangement of near-naked female bodies presuppose heterosexual male viewers (or possibly lesbians), abetted by the three fully clothed males in the strategically choreographed sepia photographs and accompanied by a rambling, confused text addressed to Matveeva by a certain Nikolen'ka Kuchukova, whose efforts at perceptual and poetic sophistication are lamentably naïve.

While Matveeva's predisposition to embrace the uncensored, on the one hand, may smack of standard juvenile rebellion, on the other, it reprises the tendencies of the late nineteenth and early twentieth century, when modernism's revolutionary impetus to explore prohibited terrain dovetailed with Sigmund Freud's pioneering efforts to jettison imposed propriety by delving into the darker recesses of the human psyche and unacknowledged aspects of sexuality—an enterprise reflected in the Austrian Otto Weininger's (1880–1903) condignly controversial *Sex and Character* (*Geschlecht und Charakter*, 1903).[11] Seeking to define identity through quantitative verification grounded in the body, Weininger rejected anatomy as the basis for distinguishing males from females, instead positing a chemically based, universal sexual indeterminacy, whereby individuals' "relative" sex depends on the degree to which they possess male or female plasmic dominance. Weininger proselytized a system of gradations, with every human being oscillating between the femaleness and the maleness of her/his constitution. With 'pure' maleness as the unattainable Ideal, homosexuality, according to him, was the condition of the intermediate sexual forms, while women were either prostitutes or mothers (Weininger 2005, *passim*).[12] Just as in the official anti-sodomy statute (article 121) added to the Soviet criminal code under Stalin in 1934, female queerness received no mention in this misogynistic tract.

Matveeva's work instantly if imprecisely evokes not only Weininger's unaccountably influential ideas, but also sundry literary texts by his contemporaries, the Symbolists, particularly Fedor Sologub, Zinaida Gippius, Valerii Briusov, Konstantin Bal'mont, and Vasilii Rozanov—the last an advocate of a 'healthy sexuality' sympathetic to homosexuality, thus doubtless violating homophobic readers' tastes. The pictorial precedents, however, sooner suggest Gustav Klimt (1862–1918), who owed his artistic passion for gold to his goldsmith father, and

Nikolai Kalmakov (1873–1955), one of the most melodramatic and understudied figures of Russian decadence, who until recently suffered complete neglect. Like most contemporary artists, Matveeva borrowed liberally from Russia's painterly past; and Neoacademism's artistic values, particularly the primacy of beauty, youth, and a focus on the body, explain her attachment to the decadent contingent of Symbolist painters and writers.

Play with Taboos

"Things forbidden have a secret charm."

—Tacitus

A quintessential early work showcasing Matveeva's characteristic manner, the diptych titled *End of the Second Part* (*Konets vtoroi chasti*, 1990) conjures up the Liudmila-Sasha relationship of Sologub's *Petty Demon* (*Melkii bes*, 1907), in which the pagan Liudmila cross-dresses the sexually undifferentiated, young male student Sasha as a geisha, who coquettishly 'plays' the feminine, thereby anticipating by nearly a century Judith Butler's notion of performing gender, and enjoys phenomenal popularity at the masquerade ball they attend[13] (fig.1). In a kindred vein, the left segment of *End of the Second Part* portrays a minimally clothed, bare-breasted, bejeweled beauty, kneeling, right arm raised toward a completely naked young man reclining in an indolent pose evoking classic representations of female odalisques.[14] Illicit sexual desire (and, possibly, activity) is suggested by the ambiguously gendered Dalmatian who visually links the two human figures in a number of ways: through his/her sleek body and long

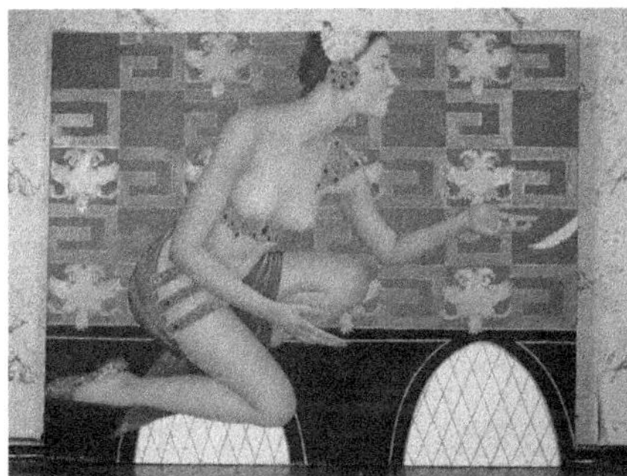
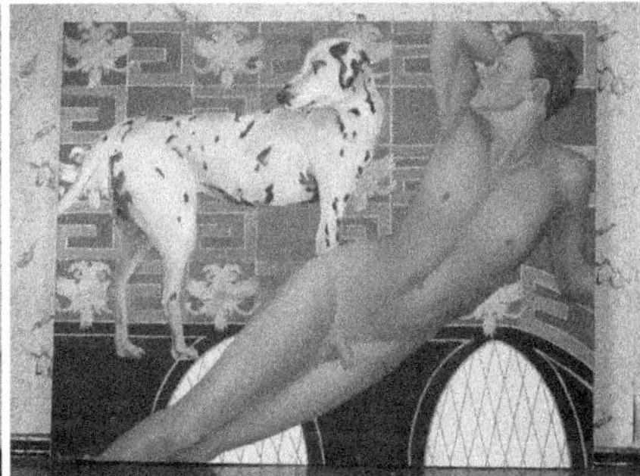

Figure 1. Bella Matveeva, *End of the Second Part* (1990), diptych, oil on canvas. Courtesy of Ekaterina and Vladimir Semenikhin

legs, which echo the male form; through the spots of her/his coat, which parallel the jewels at the woman's ears, shoulder, and torso; and above all through the gaze, which installs triangulation, for both humans watch the dog, who stares at the woman. Moreover, this oblivious preoccupation with one another creates a closed world as if suspended in the strange setting and relegates the viewer to the status of voyeur. Furthermore, the woman's left arm seems to summon the dog, while the tip of the dog's tail rest overly eloquently on her thumb, his/her front legs, partly hidden by the male body, perfectly aligned with the latter's exposed groin, as if the youth's penis were an extension of a paw.

In addition to the titillating play with gaze and constellation that unites the trio, the two human forms imply a gendered role reversal,[15] both in their postures (the sprawled, languorous odalisque as male, with the female as half-robed pursuer) and in the specifics of their depiction: elongated, boyish, completely devoid of hair, in shape, the male body, even apart from its downplayed genitalia, verges on that of an adolescent girl. In contrast, the straps and jewels of the woman's outfit peculiarly conjure up armor, though her right foot—a longstanding object of male fetishism, as evidenced in Réstif de la Bretonne's (1734–1806) prose[16] and Pushkin's verses—quite astoundingly, is missing.[17] The eroticization of the male body via the traditions of female odalisques, as well as the tingling aura of 'decadence' that imbues the scene (intensified through the overly ornamented yet mysterious setting), carried a shock value within the Soviet context no less powerful than that of the vagina motif in Judy Chicago's *Dinner Party* (1973) when unveiled before the American public in the 1970s. The painting teems with tabooed possibilities, such as the human couple enjoying 'female' or 'male' queer relations with each other, one or both indulging in sexual intimacies with the sleek dog, or a triangulation of all three bodies seeking whatever pleasure may be possible.

As part of recuperated Silver Age praxis (that is, Diaghilev, Gippius, Kuzmin, Nijinsky, Sapunov, Somov, Sudeikin),[18] a concern with sexual orientation and a performance of transgendered roles were staples of Neoacademists' self-presentation and artistic production from the start.[19] Sexuality and gender identity resided at the core of Neoacademism, whether its members favored public disclosure, secrecy, or coyness. Quite simply, male Neoacademists' choices of subject, treatments of male bodies, and close-knit self-presentations inarguably opted for queer aesthetics and identification. They cited and engaged with specifically gay writers and artists such as Oscar Wilde, Pierre et Gilles, Robert Mapplethorpe, Andy Warhol, and a host of others. As Iosif Bakshtein in his internet eulogy to the late Vladislav Mamyshev aka Vladik Monroe noted, Mamyshev's frankness about his gayness elevated him to the status of an icon among Russian gays, largely because Russia's adamant homophobia discourages homosexuals from acknowledging their sexual orientation, particularly under the 'macho' Putin (Backstein 2013). Mamyshev's openness also made explicit what his various cross-gendered impersonations, especially that of his signature Monroe transformation, implied. By contrast, Guryanov remained reticent about his sexual proclivities even while exclusively depicting paragons of male physicality and engaging with such explicitly gay sources as Rainer Werner Fassbinder's film *Querelle* (1982), based on Jean Genet's novel (1947), fueled by homosexual fantasies of male sodomy amid violence, murder, and drugs. The frisson of the forbidden vitalized the concept of beauty embraced by the group. As one of the few female members of Neoacademism (alongside the more widely exhibited and professionally venturesome Tobreluts[20]), Matveeva opted to follow same-sex subjects and flirt with queer identity, paralleling the musical duo t.A.T.u, whose assumption of lesbian personae cultivated media attention and anticipated lucrative marketability, particularly in the West. Like Guri'anov, though more subtly, Matveeva in her art scrupulously sidestepped explicitness, extracting the maximum possible erotic charge from calculated juxtapositions and dispositions of near-naked bodies portrayed in such a way as to hint at commonly interdicted physical interactions and intimacies—rarely heterosexual and sometimes bestial. In short, the calling card of Matveeva and the Neoacademists was queerness.

Myth and Kalmakov

> "It would be difficult for me not to conclude that the most perfect type of masculine beauty is Satan, as portrayed by Milton."[21]
>
> —Charles Baudelaire

As the neo- (*novyi*) in its very title indicates, Neoacademism by definition was a retro movement, and Matveeva's aesthetics manifestly revisited the *fin de siècle*. Of all Russian predecessors from this period, the artist to whom Matveeva owes the greatest debt is the half-Italian Nikolai Kalmakov, a second-generation Symbolist notable for his decadent demonism and passion for myth, influenced by the Pre-Raphaelites, Gustave Moreau (1826–1898), and Franz von Stuck (1863–1928). Until recently sunk in oblivion, he has been rediscovered by the *cognoscenti*, especially those specializing in the Silver Age, such as the prolific, astute John Bowlt.[22] It is no accident, of course, that Kalmakov designed bookplates for Sologub—author of *The Petty Demon* and *The Created Legend* (*Tvorimaia legenda*, 1914) as well as a devotee of nubile bodies, tabooed topics, myth, and folklore. Clearly, Matveeva appropriated some of Kalmakov's devices, such as a focus on enticing bared flesh, vividly patterned backgrounds for supine figures, an accent on decorativeness, frisson-inducing juxtapositions, and pairing of mythic figures. Following Léon Bakst (1866–1924) and Valentin Serov (1865–1911), Kalmakov nurtured a passion for Greek mythology, especially the myth of Narcissus, in which he sought the key to his own identity (Bowlt and Balybina 2008, 247–49). His undisguised predilections clearly provided artistic signposts for Matveeva, raised in a less intellectual era and patently eager to reprise *fin-de-siècle* models.

In its visionary and transcendental pursuits, Symbolism turned to myth as an instantiation of what Friedrich Nietzsche (1844–1900), another proponent of myth—though with a different valence—called the Eternal Return.[23] One of Kalmakov's major obsessions was the ancient myth of Leda and the Swan, which he tackled in a number of canvasses. Matveeva trod in his footsteps, as evident in her unorthodox *Youth with Peacock* (*Iunosha s pavlinom*, 1990), which recasts the classical Leda and Swan scenario.[24] According to the myth, Helen of Troy was conceived when her mother, Leda, wife of the Spartan King Tyndareos, was raped by Zeus in the form of a huge swan. Falling into her lap while pursued by an eagle, he had his way with her. Popular during the Renaissance and repeatedly pictorialized through the centuries,[25] the myth occupies a focal place in Matveeva's oeuvre. Like Kalmakov, she returned to it again and again. In her first foray in 1990, a resplendently gorgeous male peacock stands at the sexually strategic juncture of the thighs of a supine, dark-skinned, naked androgyne languidly stretched out on a brightly colored bedcover. The peacock's legs protrude suggestively from between the apex of the youth's thighs, and the atmosphere of decadent sensuality derives partially from the *absence* of eye contact: the peacock gazes off into the distance, while the androgyne's eyes are abashedly averted. An uneasy (or, for some viewers, perhaps titillating) aura of violated prohibitions, of uninhibited voluptuousness, permeates the unusual 'coupling' of unclothed, gleamingly muscled human and evocatively luscious bird. Peacock replaces swan and youth replaces Leda, but the roles enacted by human and bird are analogous, with the male peacock here implicitly invading the (possibly same-sex) human. The displacement onto the bird would seem to seek propriety, were it not for the fact that it actually intimates bestiality. This sort of questionable move typified Matveeva's art and that of many Neoacademists, whose works smuggled the prohibited in the guise of the "proper," aesthetically rendered.

Furthermore, serving a function here akin to that of the pedigree dog in Matveeva's diptych, the peacock evokes the environment that normally frames it, one of aesthetically saturated affluence, for only owners of large estates can accommodate them. At the time both canvasses pushed back the boundaries of eroticism in Russian art and ultimately did so in terms of female or queer viewers' pleasure. That is probably why Matthew Cullerne Bown and Brandon Taylor in their study *Art of the Soviets* (1993) implicitly endorsed Aleksandr Borovsky's reductive assertion, "Matveeva proposes a feminist interpretation of woman's sexuality that would be familiar to an audience in the West" (Borofski 1993, 202). Rather than allying herself with feminism Matveeva consistently courted the tabooed—or at least the tabooed in a Soviet Russian context, just as Kalmakov did in his tsarist-era stage design for Oscar Wilde's *Salomé*, with his lover, Vera Kommissarzhevskaia, in the title role. Predictably, the Holy Synod closed that performance after opening night.[26] As Bowlt and Balybina (2008, 374) remarked, "To Kalmakov, fascinated by transgression, the legend of Salomé, like those of Gorgona and Medusa, assumed a prominent place in his pictorial arsenal and he returned to it on many occasions and in diverse transfigurations." The same holds for Matveeva's preoccupations. Feminism plays no role whatever in her art, which some might even associate with soft porn, given its obsession with the display of bared female flesh in often provocative positions and hinting at queer or bestial intimacy. While one could argue that certain paintings, such as *End of the Second Part*, convey agency, the insistence on women as predominantly beautiful bodies to be viewed and delectated hardly conduces to a feminist interpretation of her oeuvre, *pace* her 'liberated' behavior in her salon.[27]

In more direct and straightforward engagement with the myth of Leda, Matveeva grouped eight of her paintings into the series *Leda and the Swan* (*Leda i lebed'*), the title of a 1995 ballet on which she collaborated with the young choreographer Sergei Vikharev (b. 1962) and which premiered at the Hermitage Theater.[28] Without having seen the ballet, on the basis of available visuals I can only hypothesize that Matveeva adhered to the myth's disposition of gender roles, with the wispily garbed young male as the swan. As is typical of Matveeva's 'perverse' manner in most of her works, here Leda's nudity consorts with an elaborate headdress. And as background for both personae, Matveeva provides her customary abstract, gold-heavy, ornate designs, but here in flowing lines much more elegant than the fussy patterning of her earlier canvasses. This overt invitation to scopophilia has been a constant of Matveeva's works, as of Neoacademists in general, which renders their works a borderline case of performance, for cynosural display is a primary principle of their narcissistic aesthetics. Most obvious in Mamyshev's wholesale metamorphoses into various personae, it also features prominently in the various members' canvasses and photographed enactments.

Disavowal of a stable identity and enactment of roles were commonplace during Russia's 1990s. Of the Neoacademists, Mamyshev may have been the most visible example, but Matveeva also posed as the silent-era actress Louise Brooks (1906–1985) and drew on film director Evgenii Bauer's (1865–1917) favorite female star, Vera Kholodnaia (1893–1919), just as the music group Lyube in its early recordings assumed various personae, as also did the rock ensemble Leningrad, fronted by Sergei Shnurov (b. 1973).[29] That trend, especially in a nostalgic vein, has continued across sundry genres into the twenty-first century. Illustrated by Verka Serduchka's (b. 1973) stage numbers and recordings, it is most vividly and comprehensively exampled in Ekaterina Rozhdestvenskaia's photo project called *Private Collection* (*Chastnaia kollektsiia,* 2000), featuring contemporary celebrities who adopted the clothing and poses of famous historical personalities (for example, Konstantin Khabenskii as Chopin) or brought a famous painting to life (for example, Ingeborga Dapkunaite as Vermeer's *Girl with a Pearl Earring* [c. 1665]) and 'copied' it. This theatrical tendency, underpinned by a loss of imposed identity, liberated *Kulturarbeiter* to explore previously prohibited possibilities; the result was an array of posited selves, often of an *outré* nature, such as the adopted personae of the patently faux-queer duo t.A.T.u or Leningrad helmsman Shnurov's creative self-identification as a boozing, drug-taking, misogynistic lout.[30] In St. Petersburg's streets it also assumed the form of cosplay, as groups of young men and women garbed in the elaborate costumes of a bygone era accosted passersby, issuing invitations to an exhibition, a concert, or a new restaurant, in a blend of nostalgia and marketing stratagems. Putin's presidency rather quickly terminated such ludic initiatives.

Matveeva's painterly method varied little during the 1990s. Her *Youth with Pheasant* (*Iunosha s fazanom,* 1990) played variations on the paintings already discussed above, with the 'bonding body' interplay between dog and youth thought-provokingly contrasted to, yet in hues and placement echoed in, the inert (exhausted?) pheasants lying at the level of the youth's crotch. The manifestly queer *Roulette* (*Ruletka* 1990), with the potentially female symbol of a cupola pulling the viewer into the vortex of the painting's center, shows two androgynous youths playing the pleasurably dangerous game of symbolic penetration with swords as surrogates.[31] (fig. 2) In structure and disposition *Roulette* reworks Kalmakov's painting of *Artemis and Sleeping Endymion* (1917), which illustrates the Greek myth of the chaste goddess of the hunt who falls in love with a sleeping shepherd. Matveeva, however, once again de-heterosexualizes the couple, transforming both figures in her painting into young males who, the citation of Kalmakov leads us to believe, are enamored of each other. And she transplants the dog in Kalmakov's painting who guards Endymion while he sleeps to her *End of the Second Part*, where his (her?) role vis-à-vis the two humans is appreciably more ambiguous.

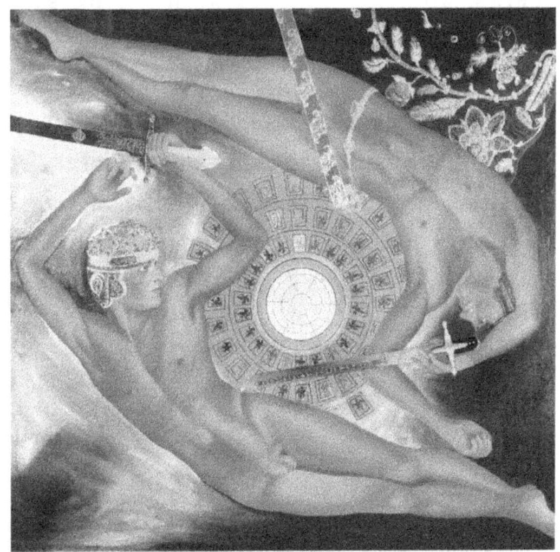

FIGURE 2. Bella Matveeva, *Roulette* (1990), oil and collage on canvas. Courtesy of Ekaterina and Vladimir Semenikhin

A similar queering strategy operates in such canvasses as *My Little Fox* (*Lison'ka,* 1990),[32] which pairs two naked young women and evidences the influence of Japanese art and the gold-infused background of Kalmakov's *Expectation (Farewell)* (*Ozhidanie* [*Proshchanie*], 1927). (fig.3) The bird on the right shoulder and the "little fox" on the other shoulder of the young woman with her face in profile signal exoticism, simultaneously evoking Frida Kahlo's *Self-Portrait with Thorn Necklace and Hummingbird* (1940) but appear utterly incongruous in light of the backdrop and the women's unclothed bodies. While the frontally displayed woman with the boyish haircut holds a mirror or fan and gazes vacantly into space, the other stares intently at her. Ambiguity resides in the very title of the painting, *My Little Fox*. On the one hand, it may refer to the miniature fox (redolent of wealth and luxury) that the attentive companion wears partly on her head. On the other, it also may serve as a term of endearment for the young woman with the mirror (fan?), whose hair color on both head and pubis duplicates that of the fox's fur. The longstanding sexual connotations of fur, founded on its similarity to body hair,[33] is perhaps most famously illustrated in art by the Swiss Surrealist Mèret Oppenheim's (1913–1985) startling *Object* (*Luncheon in Fur*) (1936), comprising a fur-covered cup, saucer, and spoon. As Robert Hughes observes, the work "has [. . .] retained a long, secret life as a sexual emblem. The action it implies, the artist bringing her lips to a hairy receptacle full of warm fluid, makes Oppenheim's cup the most intense and abrupt image of Lesbian sex in the history of art" (Hughes 1991, 243).[34] Such an object would not accord with Matveeva's concept of beauty, but its suggestiveness doubtless would appeal to her passion for allusiveness. Though the nakedness and proximity of her female duo implies intimacy, abetted by the parallelism and continuous line of their limbs, the explicit nature of their relationship is withheld. Are they geishas? Lovers? Both? Leaving the answers to those questions up to viewers, Matveeva surely anticipates that at least some would be likely to interpret the scenario along queer lines.

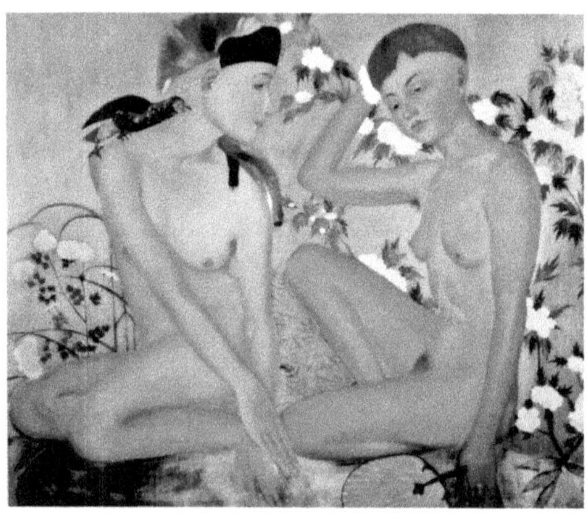

FIGURE 3. Bella Matveeva, *My Little Fox* (1990), oil and mixed media on canvas. The State Russian Museum, St Petersburg

Several years later, *Mirror and Shadow* (*Zerkalo i ten'*, 1995), to which Matveeva subsequently added the subtitle *These Are Dreams*,[35] likewise implies encounters of the unmistakable kind amid a rhythmically rendered, undefined setting dominated by decorative fabrics that bring the smooth, naked flesh of the two dreamy women into relief. (fig. 4) The angles of their heads as well as the curves of their bodies are perfectly aligned as they grasp each other's hands. One end of the diaphanous blue scarf that strategically hides the pubic hair of the frontally presented woman is wound around the foot of her companion (the heel

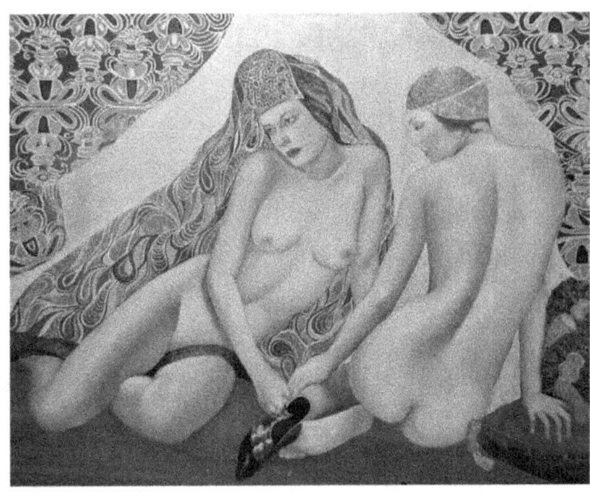

FIGURE 4. Bella Matveeva, *Mirror and Shadow* (1995), oil on canvas. Private Collection

of which in shape and position evokes an erection) and runs provocatively between the other's thighs. Consequently, their unity or union seems a carnal one. Whether such a union constitutes the dreams referenced by the subtitle one can only speculate, but like *My Little Fox* and several later paintings under the collective rubric of *Ibsen's Doll House* (2002) that depict naked women reclining or sitting side by side, *Mirror and Shadow* in its eroticism not only entertains but actually urges a queer reading.

Matveeva's absorption with titillating and sumptuous aesthetics explains her participation in the 1990s Petersburg fashion for collecting souvenirs—old albums, photographs, and random bric à brac—from bygone eras, particularly the late nineteenth century. This phase reflected aspects of the previous *fin-de-siècle* St. Petersburg captured in Aleksei Balabanov's film *Of Freaks and Men* (*Pro urodov i liudei*, 1998), which concocts a heady cocktail of polymorphous perversity, voyeurism, and sadomasochism, primarily through photographic representation—a rapidly proliferating 1990s mode. Matveeva's retro activities in 1989–1990 included a series of mixed-media works (collages, installations) dedicated to the silent film actresses Louise Brooks and Vera Kholodnaia, and the coproduction (with Vladimir Zakharov) of a film signally titled *Resurrection* (*Voskresenie*), which focuses on bodies and stylizes *fin de siècle* aesthetics. Her *Aesthetics of the Classical Bordello*—the album of photographs collected in a slim brochure, which she assembled in 1994—likewise belonged to this phase. It conflated her preoccupation with the body, voyeurism, fetishism, love of texture and mixed forms, and transgression across boundaries of genre, gender, time periods, and heteronormativity.

The album, with Matveeva's lovely painting titled *Old Album* (*Staryi al'bom*) on the cover, would fit quite comfortably into Balabanov's film. And in 2004, true to her habit of moving forward by looking back, Matveeva recuperated not only the theme of the bordello, but also the surface motifs of the East in her painting *The Seraglio.* Characteristically, the East as such held little interest for her, but the seraglio as a site of seduction, sexuality, and possible experimentation in bodily pleasures tapped into her abiding interests. Technically proficient and enamored of forebears who shared her fascination with the beautifully forbidden, Matveeva concentrated on large canvasses that tended to play variations on a circumscribed number of themes articulated in colors and arrangements that migrated from one painting to another without necessarily acquiring additional depth and resonance with the years, for enticing surface largely ruled her aesthetics. If she aspired to the status of 'the bad girl' in art, then she indisputably succeeded as the bad girl in love with the striking beauty that she consistently featured. No children, middle-aged, or old people appeared in her canvasses, which confined themselves to young specimens of physical pulchritude.

Evolution as Pseudo-Consolidation

Two new tendencies marked Matveeva's work in the new millennium. The first was the collation, if not meaningful integration, of earlier works subsumed into series: the already mentioned *Leda and the Swan* and *Ibsen's Doll's House* (*Kukol'nyi dom Ibsena*), both expanded with new paintings. From the latter grouping one could deduce that for Matveeva, Ibsen's play of 1879 functions as a loose umbrella concept, above all, for sexual liberation of all stripes. Subsequent series followed, such as *Silver Garters* (simply a renaming of *The Aesthetics of a Classical Bordello*, posted on her Facebook page) and *The Coronation of Poppea* (2013), as well as another painting of *Leda and the Swan* in an appreciably pared down, less decorative style.

The second, more interesting novelty was her sudden absorption with the *Nibelungenlied* (c. 1200) or, more probably, Richard Wagner's operatic cycle, *Der Ring des Nibelungen* (1876) (comprising *Das Rheingold, Die Walküre, Siegfried,* and *Götterdämmerung*). Wagner drew on Old Norse sources[36] more than on the medieval epic poem, and extracts from the various operas within the cycle have accompanied sequences in countless films, most notably Luchino Visconti's *The Damned* (*La caduta degli dei,* 1969) and Werner Herzog's *Nosferatu* (1979).[37] Given the primacy of myth, armed conflict, the union of love and death, sexual couplings, and incest, as well as otherworldly beings such as the superhumanly empowered female Valkyrie in the myth and the Ring cycle,[38] one can readily understand how Matveeva's perennial preferences guided her to this material.

The latter teems with semi-divine beings, sensualized battles, and Valhalla—the immense, gold-rich Hall of the Slain presided over by the god Odin in Norse mythology that in Wagner's *Rheingold* is likewise the castle housing the gods to which noble heroes ascend after their death, escorted by the armed Valkyrie. There the skillful warriors undergo preparation for "the final battle" through combat with one another.

Most striking about Matveeva's renditions here were her modifications of her previous manner: these figures, though central and naked as before, are neither projected against an aestheticized background nor supine and indolent. Instead, they are bellicose, dwell in an indefinable setting as if in air, and appear framed primarily in gold. Spatially, they lack expanse and ease, caught violently engaged in inimical pursuit or fatal conflict within a narrow, sometimes constrictive, frame. Moreover, Matveeva's depiction of Valhalla is devoted exclusively to violence, with no reference to the feasting that traditionally transpires there. In other words, for reasons that are far from clear Matveeva collapsed into Valhalla itself the lethal clash that usually precedes posthumous entry into that sphere or will follow at some future date. Presumably her combatants were training for the final confrontation. What *is* clear, however, is that sexualized/sensualized conflict, with swords unsheathed but not playfully as in *Roulette*, was critical to Matveeva's purposes. For instance, her *Valhalla: The Battle* (2004)[39] (fig. 5) shows two young warriors, one in the upper register presented frontally, clad in a light blue codpiece and crimson cloak draped over his upper arm, both hands grasping his sword above his head. His naked antagonist, seated with his back to the viewer, holds onto a javelin of which the upper part draws attention to the crotch of the upright warrior, who gazes intently at him. Once

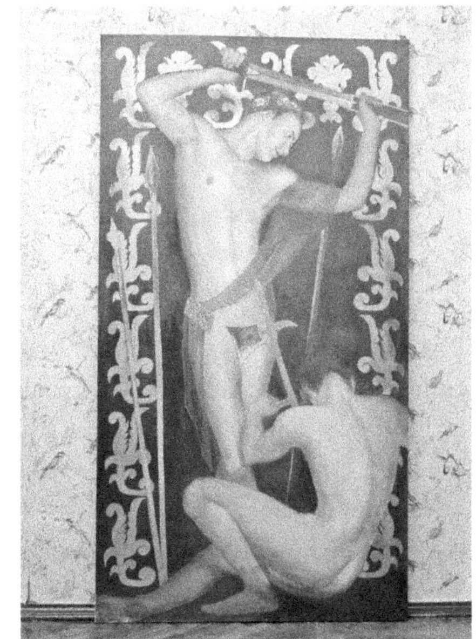

FIGURE 5. Bella Matveeva, *Valhalla* (2005), oil and mixed media on canvas. Collection of Greis Karvalecsene

again, the relationship between the two is evocatively enigmatic. Are they enemies, as the title of the work seems to indicate? Or do they sooner belong to the same side, enjoy the love made famous by Achilles's "friendship" with Patroclus, and are merely readying for the titular battle with an unspecified enemy? Given the bowed head of the warrior in the lower register, it is even possible that he is dead and simply being examined by his victorious foe. Whatever the situation, the proximity of the two bodies and the focal location of the crotch, emphasized by the placement of the javelin, would certainly justify a queer interpretation of the scene. It is also worth noting that Matveeva's probable familiarity with Kalmakov's *Le Courroux des Cieux* (*Heavenly Wrath*, 1915) may have inspired her interest in Valhalla, though during the 2000s she appeared to have liberated herself from Kalmakov's shadow as a source of citations.

While her paintings of this period depict strife and armed conflict—as usual, in idealized, beautiful form—Matveeva also turned her hand to the genre of the non-cinematic screen as a mode of seclusion and concealment. To it she brought her older style: the reclining, near-naked female bodies against a gilded, ornate, often Asian-motif background, and an aura of appreciative voyeurism. These are images meant exclusively for audiences' aesthetic pleasure, and the Art Nouveau style almost makes one forget that the subjects, carefully positioned and lovingly painted, with a proposed continuity between bodies and flowers or reticulating motifs, are nudes. And the screen, of course, is an item that automatically conjures up something that requires concealment, even if temporarily; that "something," of course, has normally been the unclothed body, whether in a doctor's office, a theater's changing room, or a brothel—all venues associated with examination, spectatorship, or consumption of the flesh. Like the veil, the screen stimulates the desire to see what is behind it.

A Coven of Queering Female Artists?

From the start, Matveeva violated Russian pictorial traditions by exploring the entire range of officially prohibited alternatives to heterosexual, reproductive, missionary-position sexual activity by portraying the naked body in a fashion avoiding explicitness yet simultaneously hospitable to queer interpretation. She could be placed alongside other women artists of the 1990s likewise making exposed female flesh the *dominanta* of their works, such as Aidan Salakhova (b. 1964) who during her early career celebrated the shapely, generous contours of feminine forms.[40] The St. Petersburg artist Anastasiia Neliubina (b. 1960), though embracing a more avant-garde aesthetic[41] than Matveeva, also hosted a salon, dwelled on bodies, nudity, sexual activity, and painted several works in various media,[42] inviting a queer reading. Particularly her revealingly titled album, *From Kiss to Orgy* (*Ot potseluia do orgii,* 1998), interspersed with literary quotations, features bare representatives of both sexes playing instruments, readying to eat (forbidden) fruit, and enjoying sexual intercourse, including incest and onanism. *Leda and the Swan, Susanna and the Elders,* as well as the eponymous *Minotaur* enchanted by the sight of a female nude constitute only a few of Neliubina's many mythological and painterly citations. While animals such as a bull and a monkey figure in implied perverse narratives that revolve around a red couch, the two queerest renditions show a duo of naked women, their genitalia exposed, sprawled beside each other on it. *Two Girls on a Red Couch* (*Dve devushki na krasnom divane*) has the foot of one directly pointing at the vagina of the other. Its companion piece, *Girls Trying a Pear* (*Devushki probuiushchie grushu*) shows one of the women holding a pear—shaped like buttocks—at the level of her breasts while the other crawls toward her, mouth open. Obviously, the orgy includes same-sex intercourse and Neliubina in her graphic depiction of orgiastic delights approached the explicitness that Matveeva invariably eschewed. Tobreluts, whose oeuvre is incomparably more varied in genre, subject, and medium than her colleagues', also revised mythological figures and focused on alluring bared flesh, as in her *Dance* (2003),[43] *Sirens* (2004), *Adam* (2005), *Eve* (2006), and *Battle of the Bare* (2011), but is perhaps best remembered for pioneering digital technology in art during the 1990s, which she subsequently abandoned.

Revolutionary Retrospective

As the above selective examples evidence, Matveeva was hardly the sole female artist in the post-Soviet era to explore the potential of allusive images that conjured up titillating scenarios open to, even courting, queer interpretations. Her canvases reprised the ancient Greek aesthetics of the human body as the pinnacle of beauty, but in suturing her exclusive fascination with the naked form to a pronounced sexuality/sensuality, same-sex pairing, luxurious backdrops, and an aura of voluptuous indolence she departed from the classical invitation to contemplate the beautiful. For it she substituted an invitation to a voyeuristic identification and/or the expectation of illicit relationships or activities. In that regard her paintings were revolutionary vis-à-vis Soviet caveats and conventions.

Whereas nineteenth-century Russian painting largely focused on genres other than nudes, during the prudish Soviet era artists such as Alexander Deineka (1899–1969) and Alexander Samokhvalov (1894–1971) in their widely exhibited works rationalized nudity by such contexts as sports, work, and the *bania.* Deineka's primary interest was the human body in motion, whether at war, in sports, or in dance, as his most frequently reproduced and analyzed paintings amply illustrate (Goscilo 2017, *passim*). Nudes at rest by such fellow artists as Boris Kustodiev (1878–1927), Vladimir Lebedev (1891–1967), and Iurii Pimenov (1903–1977) number among their lesser-known works, as corroborated by the extraordinary exhibition *Venus Sovietica: 90th Anniversary of the Great October Socialist Revolution* at the Russian Museum and the resultant book/catalogue (Petrova 2007). These bodies—many of them hefty and far from seductive—are associated with productive labor, healthy sport, and hygienic ablutions, not languid, sensual self-indulgence. Alexander Borovsky, in his introductory essay within the volume, views the eroticism of the World of Art group and especially Bakst as derived from classical mythology and therefore not innovative, commending instead the originality of Filipp Maliavin's (1869–1940) ample, energetic peasant woman in national costume (!) as a "homegrown Venus." He proceeds, unaccountably, to demonize Lebedev's *Kat'ka* (1918?)—a luridly rouged but fully dressed and rather awkwardly posed brunette—as a "provocative, feminine, openly sinful and wildly licentious" female image (Borovsky 2007, 9–13). Yet by comparison with Matveeva's nudes, Kat'ka may as well be a nun with heavy makeup. As Marina Stekolnikova in another essay in the publication rightly observes, early Soviet female images in their fleshliness sooner resemble Amazons than Venuses (Stekolnikova 2007, 43) and scarcely inspire viewers' desire or function as aesthetic ideals of harmony and proportion. Briefly tracing the fate of photographed nudes throughout Russia's history, Alexei Longinov illuminates the problem, citing a representative view of nudity in art from 1929: "'The eroticism of contemporary Western European art (both painting and photography) is nurtured by rich, satiated idleness and the intellectual/bohemian lifestyle. For Soviet art this is unseemly.' Here lies the reason for the struggle against all manifestations of the nude genre in Soviet art" (Longinov 2007, 58). Indeed, such a freighted ideological stance explains why post-Soviet art, in rejecting its predecessors' concept of politicized appropriateness, resuscitated the nude in diverse subgenres: graphics, painting, performance, and photography.

While sundry works by several Neoacademists (Guryanov, Maslov and Kuznetsov, Tobreluts) centered on the bare or scantily clad body, within that cohort Matveeva is unique in painting solely exposed eroticized bodies in various configurations, with her addiction to the decorative resplendence and gorgeous textures anathematized during the Soviet era resurrecting the decadence of the *fin de siècle*. Although her art is representational, it deviates from the conventions of realism. Its categorical dismissal of Soviet prohibitions is revolutionary, and the constellations of figures in her scenarios may be described as performative insofar as they hint at 'readiness to perform' illicit deeds. Ultimately, her distinctive creative signature does not fit comfortably into any readymade niche. For all the repetitiveness and eclecticism of her oeuvre, where arrestingly beautiful surfaces, erotic inventiveness, and the blurring of gender distinctions are concerned, she has few if any rivals among recent Russian artists. *Pace* Socrates, beauty in her art may constitute teleological tyranny, but is definitely not short-lived. Whatever else may have changed, it has been her dominant aesthetic principle for three decades, and precisely that constancy may be called, paradoxically, conservative in its revolutionary endeavor.

Notes

My gratitude to Bożenna Goscilo for her helpful response to this piece.

1 She joined the group shortly after it became constituted in late 1989. For information on Matveeva, see her website, http://www.bella-matveeva.narod.ru, ever a work in progress; the brochure accompanying the exhibition of paintings, graphics, and installations organized in St. Petersburg in 1995, *Zhenshchina i ee vremia: sorokovye-devianostye*; the interview in *Zhenskie otvety* 29–31; and the catalogue *Bella Matveyeva. Painting*. It is characteristic of male commentators to bypass Matveeva and other female members of the group in their publications. See, for instance, Ivor A. Stodolsky, "A 'non-aligned' intelligentsia: Timur Novikov's neo-avantgarde and the afterlife of Leningrad non-conformism," Studies in East European Thought 63.2 (May 2011): 135–45. See the list of members provided on p. 137, fn. 3. Here he lists members of the 1982 New Artists but adds no names for the New Academy. By 2013, relations among the Neoacademists had so degenerated, that several Neoacademists took Bugaev "Afrika" to court and won the case, forcing him to return their paintings, which he had appropriated and was offering to sell back to them. See Andrei Khlobystin, "New Artists Win Their Case against Sergey Bugaev-Afrika," *Baibakov Art Projects* (November 6, 2013), available at: http://baibakovartprojects.wordpress.com/2013/11/06/new-artists-win-their-case-against-sergey-bugaev-afrika/ (last accessed June 14, 2014). Another court subsequently reversed that decision.

2 For a bemused account of his attendance at the salon, see the brief article by journalist Nick Crowe (1997, 38–43).

3 The following ten members and associates died before reaching their mid-fifties—two, in fact, perished in their twenties and one in his thirties: Sergei Dobrotvorskii (1959–97), Aleksei Feoktistov (1959–2009), Konstantin Goncharov (1969–98), Georgy Guryanov (1961–2013), Vladislav Mamyshev (1969–2013), Andrei Medvedev (1957–2010), Timur Novikov (1958–2002), Vadim Ovchinnikov (1951–96), Kirill Sluchainyi (1962–2005), Viktor Tsoi (1962–90). For more on the Neoacademists, see the cluster of articles orchestrated by Helena Goscilo, *The Allure of Retro: Neoacademism after the Fall, Russian Review* 78.2 (April 2019): 183–271.

4 The then teenage duo comprised of Iuliia Volkova and Elena Katina, aged fourteen and fifteen, respectively, discovered in 1999 by thirty-three-year-old Ivan Shapovalov, a former child psychologist turned advertising executive, who in 2000 introduced them to the Russian public via radio with the single "Ia soshla s uma" (I've Lost My Mind). Their promoted lesbianism was utterly fraudulent, as, in the perception of many, was the homosexuality of some male Neoacademy members. On this issue, see Thomas Campbell's commentary on what he calls the "homo-device." The eager, automatic identification of beauty with homosexuality stems from Russians' rather simplistic traditions inherited from the fin-de-siècle and their rediscovered championship of Oscar Wilde.

5 Earlier, she also produced a few installations, at least one featuring herself as Louise Brooks, but subsequently abandoned that genre.

6 Both Russian icon painters and artists such as Gustav Klimt relied on the associative properties of gold, as did Matveeva.

7 Her eagerness to work with different forms and genres—painting, installations, photographs, films, stage sets—likewise revived the aesthetics of the fin de siècle, which witnessed a mingling of genres, styles, and cultural forms.

8 According to Maria Engström, Guryanov's sole known work depicting women was a poster of female tractor drivers and three girls, designed for lesbians in Berlin. Private correspondence, December 14, 2015.

9 On Mamyshev, see Julie Cassiday, "Vladislav Mamyshev-Monroe, Frog-Princess of Neoacademism," *Russian Review* 78. 2 (April 2019): 221–44.

10 See Helena Goscilo, "Maslov and Kuznetsov: Camping and Revamping Classical Scenarios," *Russian Review* 78. 1 (April 2019): 245–71.

11 Weininger's male-supremacist tract, which underwent a plethora of editions and elicited the admiration of August Strindberg, Ludwig Wittgenstein, and numerous European *Kulturarbei ter*, embraces overt anti-Semitism and misogyny, perhaps clarifying why such a horrendous worldview would lead the gay, Jewish 'thinker' to commit suicide at the age of twenty-three soon after the publication of the work.

12 Though superficially his notion of sexual indeterminacy seems to anticipate Adrienne Rich's idea of a lesbian continuum; in fact, he legislates sexuality along a rigid hierarchical axis, whereas Rich makes an argument for fluidity and inclusion along a vertical line. See Adrienne Rich, "Compulsory Heterosexuality and Lesbian Existence," in her collection of essays titled *Blood, Bread, and Poetry: Selected Prose 1979–1985* (New York: W.W. Norton & Co., 1986: 23–75).

13 For an incisive analysis of the androgyne during this era see Olga Matich, "Androgyny and the Russian Silver Age," *Pacific Coast Philology* 14 (1979): 42–50. She contrasts sexual ambiguity during the *fin-de-siècle* to the ancient concept of the androgyne as the exemplar of sexual wholeness. Of course, in his numerous metamorphoses Mamyshev-Monroe regularly resorted to gender performance, assuming the identities of both men and women.

14 See, for instance, those by Henri Tanoux (1625), Françis Boucher (c. 1749), Delacroix, several by Ingres, Guillaume Seignac, Boris Kustodiev (1919), and dozens of other painters.

15 In Western praxis, such reversals include Sylvia Sleigh's *Philip Golub Reclining* (1971) and *The Turkish Bath* (1973)—the title of Delacroix's famous painting also appearing as that of Tat'iana Antoshina's transgendered baths, where male bodies replace Delacroix's female counterparts. In many of her works Antoshina used her husband as a model the way male artists traditionally have relied on women (often their lovers) to pose for their art. On this phenomenon in non-Slavic art, see Chadwick 1990, 323–24.

16 See, for example, his revealingly titled novel *Le Pied de Fanchette* (1769).

17 Note especially the pertinent passage in *Evgenii Onegin* ("O nozhki, nozhki, gde vy nyne . . ."). On this topic, see Helena Goscilo, "Feet Pushkin Scanned, or Seeming Idée Fixe as Implied Aesthetic Credo" *SEEJ* 32.4 (1988): 562–73.

18 For a long list covering tsarist and Soviet Russia, see *The Russian Out* List, available at http://community.middlebury.edu/~moss/ROL.html.

19 Timur Novikov was the 'theorist' and early popularizer of the group before Andrei Khlobystin took over the role of its popularizer.

20 On Tobreluts, see Jonathan Brooks Platt, "Olga Tobreluts: *Stiob* Beauty," *Russian Review* 17. 2 (April 2019): 201–20.

21 [I]l me serait difficile de ne pas conclure que le plus parfait type de Beauté virile est Satan,—à la manière de Milton. Charles Baudelaire, *Fusées*, I (1887).

22 The first sizable, illustrated monograph on Kalmakov's oeuvre is the volume by John Bowlt and Iuliia V. Balybina, pointedly titled *Nikolai Kalmakov i labirint dekadentstva*. See bibliography.

23 Unlike Nietzsche, who found inevitable recurrence horrifying, the Symbolists revered myths as a source of confirmation of their inner visions and a repository of psychological/spiritual paradigms.

24 And one of Matveeva's later conceived series was, indeed, *Leda and the Swan*.

25 In addition to a Roman marble statue (possibly by Timotheos) and a mosaic in Cyprus (c. third century AD), these include paintings by Correggio, a copy of a lost or destroyed Michelangelo, Cesare da Sesto's copy of Leonardo's lost original (1515–20), and extant works by Gustave Moreau and Paul Cezanne. Probably the best-known literary work on the theme is W. B. Yeats's poem "Leda and the Swan" (1928).

26 Some claim that the reason was the first act, where Wilde set the scene in what he called the "temple of love." "Kalmakoff designed a temple of huge proportions, based on a woman's sex," as one commentator euphemistically put it. Reportedly, Kommissarzhevskaia, who had promoted Kalmakov, "lost all her money, and was forced to go on tour in the provinces to recuperate some of her losses. She died, one year later, far from St. Petersburg" (La Caruana 2004). This report is controversial, not the least because the play is not divided into several acts but is explicitly identified by the author as "a tragedy in one act." Such reports as the one cited, however, are telling, for they reflect Kalmakov's reputation as a sex-obsessed artist.

27 On that behavior, see the jejune comments by Crowe (1997, 42–43).

28 Five of the paintings reportedly almost filled the stage during the performance of the ballet.

29 In the hilarious rock opera *Babarobot*, Sergei Shnurov does a superlative imitation of Vladimir Vysotskii.

30 For Leningrad's self-presentation, see Helena Goscilo, "Lewd and Ludic, and Flaunting It: Leningrad's Highly Profitable 'Nenormativnaia Leksika,'" in *Translating Russia: From Theory to Practice*, edited by Brian James Baer, 37–62. *Ohio Slavic Papers*, Vol. 8. Columbus, OH: Ohio State University Press.

31 The sword and the knife, of course, are time-honored symbols for the phallus. See, for example, Guillaume Apollinaire, *Alcools* (1912). Ekaterina Andreeva (Andreyeva) sees the figure to the left as "a girl," which strikes me as inaccurate, for she lacks breasts, and her body is shaped analogously to that of "the youth" to the right. I read this painting as much less 'innocent' than Andreeva's notion of it as a heterosexual 'dream' implies. See the exhibition brochure *Bella Matveyeva: Painting,*, St. Petersburg: KRIN, nd., np.

32 This is the title of the painting listed on her personal site, and of a film by her collaborator Vladimir Zakharov, with whom she also made a nineteen-minute film, *Voskresenie* (1990).

33 That likeness elucidates the slang term "pussy" for a woman's vagina, which the James Bond film *Goldfinger* (1964) mined for the unsubtle innuendo regarding the character of Pussy Galore, who quickly abandons her lesbianism for the manly charms of the improbably irresistible spy.

34 Thanks to Bożenna Goscilo for drawing my attention to the Oppenheim's object.

35 Matveeva tends to alter titles of her works. For instance, in an attractive card advertising the exhibition of her works at the Chetwood Stapylton Gallery in Portland, Oregon from September–October 11, 1997, the title of this painting appeared in French as *La Voyeuse* (The [Female] Voyeur).

36 Matveeva's familiarity with the medieval Icelandic *Poetic Edda* or *Prose Edda* (thirteenth century) and other myths that inspired Wagner seems extremely unlikely.

37 Herzog creatively uses the lush music from *Das Rheingold* for the protagonist's transition from the bourgeois human world to that of the otherworldly domain of the vampire. For the extensive incorporation of Wagner's music into films, see Wagneropera.net at http://www.wagneropera.net/Themes/Wagner-In-Movies.htm.

38 By virtue of being able to decide who should perish and who should survive on the battlefield, the Valkyrie exercised enormous control over armed conflicts. Their power doubtless is what partly led to the concept of their superior size, though in some German myths they are identified not with physical force and might, but with the graceful swan.

39 The original date of 2004 now has transformed into 2003 on Matveeva's Facebook. See https://www.facebook.com/bella.matveeva. Such changes are part of her kaleidoscopic shifts regarding her oeuvre.

40 Salakhova's paintings, however, are appreciably more diverse and independent of predecessors.

41 For example, whereas Matveeva directly invokes Kalmakov, Neliubina in *Orgy* (*Orgiia*) borrows from Matisse's *Dance* (1910).

42 These include lithographs, graphics, and painted etchings. For commentary on these works, see the introductory essay by Ol'ga Kasianenko in Neliubina (1998, 11–48).

43 Like Neliubuna, she revises Matisse's Fauvist original.

References

Art Daily."'Absolute Beauty': Neoacademism in Saint Petersburg on view at the Ludwig Museum." 2015. Available at: https://artdaily.cc/news/80812/-Absolute-Beauty-Neoacademism-in-Saint-Petersburg-on-view-at-the-Ludwig-Museum#.YKP0aKh-Kg2w. Last accessed May 18, 2021.

Backstein, Joseph. 2013. "Life as Art." *The Calvert Journal* (March 20). Available at: http://calvertjournal.com/comment/show/624/life-as-art-joseph-backstein-remembers-iconic-performance-artist-vladislav. Last accessed July 6, 2014.

Borofski, Aleksandr. 1993. "Non-conformist Art in Leningrad." In *Art of the Soviets: Painting, Sculpture and Architecture in a One-party State, 1917–1992*, edited by Matthew Cullerne Bown and Brandon Taylor, 196–204. Manchester: Manchester University Press.

Borovsky, Alexander. 2007. "Venus Sovietica." In *Venus Sovietica: 90th Anniversary of the Great October Socialist Revolution*, edited by Yevgenia Petrova, 9–28. St. Petersburg: Palace Editions.

Bowlt, John E. and Iuliia V. Balybina. 2008. *Nikolai Kalmakov i labirint Dekadentstva 1873–1955*. Moscow: Iskusstvo—XXI vek.

Chadwick, Whitney. 1990. *Women, Art, and Society*. London: Thames & Hudson.

Clark, Kenneth. 1957. *The Nude; A Study in Ideal Form*. 2nd edition. New York: Pantheon Books.

Crowe, Nick. 1997. "Arty St Petersburg Seen through Its Bars." *The European Magazine* (February 20–26): 18–19.

———. 1997. "Queen of the Bordello." *Creator* 5 (Spring): 38–43.

Dijkstra, Bram. 1988. *Idols of Perversity: Fantasies of Feminine Evil in Fin-de-Siècle Culture*. Oxford: Oxford University Press.

Goscilo, Helena (ed.). 2019. *The Allure of Retro: Neoacademism after the Fall*. *Russian Review* 78(2): 183–271.

Goscilo, Helena. 2017. "Deineka's Heavenly Bodies: Space, Sports, and the Sacred." In *Russian Aviation, Space Flight, and Visual Culture*, edited by Vlad Strukov and Helena Goscilo, 53–88. London: Routledge.

Goscilo, Helena and Elena Kornetchuk. 2002. "Canvassing Gender: Recent Women's Art" [Zhivopisuia gender: Sovremennoe zhenskoe iskusstvo]. In *Femme Art* [Iskusstvo zhenskogo roda], 144–70. Moscow: Tretyakov State Gallery.

Holmgren, Beth and Helena Goscilo. 1999. "Introduction." In Anastasya Verbitskaya, *Keys to Happiness*, xi–xxix. Bloomington, IN: Indiana University Press.

Hughes, Robert. 1991. *The Shock of the New*. New York: Alfred A. Knopf.

Khlobystin, Andrei. 2002. "Neoakademizm: Neokonchennaia p'esa." *ARTCHRONIKA* 1: 96–103.

Kriel, Janet. 2005. "Radical Classical." *Passport* (Summer). Available at: http://www.passportmagazine.ru/article/252/. Last accessed May 18, 2021.

La Caruana. 2004. "Kalmakoff, The Forgotten Visionary," visionary revue, Paris (Spring 2004), http://visionaryrevue.com/webtext3/kal1. html.

Longinov, Alexei. 2007. "Forbidden Genre." In *Venus Sovietica: 90th Anniversary of the Great October Socialist Revolution*, edited by Yevgenia Petrova, 51–61. St. Petersburg: Palace Editions.

Neliubina, Anastasiia. 1998. *Ot potseluia do orgii/Du baiser à l'orgie*. St. Petersburg: Nani-T.

Nikolaeva, Elina. 2014. "Prianyi akademizm." In *Bella Matveeva: BellaVita retrospektiva*, 8–9. St. Petersburg: ART HOLDING.

Petrova, Yevgenia (ed.). 2007. *Venus Sovietica: 90th Anniversary of the Great October Socialist Revolution*. St. Petersburg: Palace Editions.

Stekolnikova, Marina. 2007. "A Word on Goddess." In *Venus Sovietica: 90th Anniversary of the Great October Socialist Revolution*, edited by Yevgenia Petrova, 43–49. St. Petersburg: Palace Editions.

Stodolsky, Ivor. 2011. "'A Multi-Lectic Anatomy of Stiob and Poshlost': Case Studies in the Oeuvre of Timur Novikov." *Laboratorium* 1. Available at: http://www.soclabo.org/index.php/laboratorium/article/view/235/548. Last accessed November 4, 2015.

———. 2011. "A 'non-aligned' intelligentsia: Timur Novikov's neo-avantgarde and the afterlife of Leningrad non-conformism." *Studies in East European Thought* 63: 135–45.

Strukov, Vlad and Helena Goscilo, eds. *Russian Aviation, Space Flight, and Visual Culture*. London: Routledge, 2017.

Weininger, Otto. 2005. *Sex and Character*. Translated by Ladislaus Löb. Bloomington: Indiana University Press.

Chapter 11

Sexual and Gender Dissent in a Bipolar World: Georgy Guryanov and Vladislav Mamyshev-Monroe

Andrey Shental

One Russian art critic has justly remarked that the posthumous fame of many Western artists is based on their association with gay discourse, while in Russia even mentioning the topic is strictly prohibited as it would lead to the artist's marginalization (Kovalev 2008). And this was the case long before the Russian Duma passed the infamous "anti-gay propaganda law" in 2013, the same year that Russia lost two major queer/gay artists: Vladislav Mamyshev, who died on March 16 at the age of forty-three, and Georgy Guryanov, who passed away on July 20 at the age of fifty-two. This double tragedy—which coincided with the first open attack on LGBTIQ+ rights since the fall of the Soviet Union—might have triggered a curatorial, critical, or theoretical "queering" of Russian art history, but this did not happen. Most of the posthumously published texts about these artists remain deceptively hagiographical and mythopoeic, while the sexual and gender aspects of their works, if mentioned at all, tend to be pushed to the margins (Turkina 2014).[1] The aim of this essay is therefore two-fold: to recontextualize their practices within a (post-)Soviet sexual and gender matrix and to reconceptualize that matrix through the lens of their work.

Guryanov and Mamyshev both started their careers as part of the Leningrad underground art scene under the influence of the homosexual artist Timur Novikov, who died of AIDS in 2002. Novikov, who was older, more experienced and mature, became their mentor and guide in the world of contemporary art, and his new friends followed almost all the stages of his dialectical evolution from the rebellious neo-Expressionism of the New Artists movement, through the short-lived quasi-institution *Pirate TV* project, to the conservative neoclassical New Academy. In the 1990s, however, their artistic paths went in different directions. If one could speak in such essentialist terms, Mamyshev-Monroe traded "iconophilic" Saint Petersburg, with its painterly tradition, for "iconoclastic" Moscow, which was associated at that time with the more avant-garde movements of Conceptualism and Actionism. As for Guryanov, he remained faithful to the sensual, decadent style and dandyism of Russia's Northern capital. While the former preferred the mediums of photography, video, performance, intervention and installation, the latter shifted his focus to quasi-traditional large-scale canvas painting. In terms of subject matter, Mamyshev mimicked and impersonated public figures, making humorous, self-critical and sometimes overtly political statements. Guryanov, on the other hand, celebrated transhistorical ideals of beauty with total earnestness, depicting perfectly shaped young men in paintings filled with historical allusions.

In Russian criticism, it is acknowledged that the Leningrad artistic practices of the 80s were aligned with global art history under the aegis of postmodernism.[2] According to critics associated with the journal *October*, the art of that period was not homogenous but must be critically divided into "rival postmodernisms." On the one hand, we have "neoconservative postmodernism," which reflects the reactionary politics of that time in its return to figuration and its promotion of artistic individuality and historical memory. On the other hand, there is "poststructuralist postmodernism," which corresponds to the intellectual tendency to put into question both the originality of artistic expression and the authority of artistic tradition (Foster et al. 2016, 596–7). The mature paintings by Guryanov, which are made in the Neoacademic style, are reminiscent of the kitschy Italian *Pittura colta* movement or the homoerotic academism of someone like Michael Leonard or Delmas Howe. Following *October*'s line of argument, one could say Guryanov followed the "reactionary" trend. Mamyshev's photographic and video works, on the other hand, would approximate appropriation art and particularly the Pictures Generation artists who applied pop-culture imagery to put into question the reigning conventions of representation (especially Cindy Sherman and Yasumasa Morimura). Nevertheless, to subsume their works under categories suggested by American critics would be limiting, reductive or even uncritical. Guryanov's canvases that are based on film stills and photography cannot be reduced to conservative "pastiche," while Mamyshev, who created a cult out of his own persona, should not be identified exclusively with the post-structuralist, anti-romantic ideal of citationality.

The reason for this is obvious: They were born, lived and worked in a completely different historical context—that of "actually existing socialism" and then the post-Soviet condition. While in the "West" the 1980s was a time of reaction, in the USSR it was a time of renewal when Perestroika and Glasnost led to a profound revision of the Soviet past. It was followed by the more radical and liberating, though economically devastating and humiliating, period of the 1990s. At that time people achieved certain civil rights and democratic institutions and experienced a kind of "sexual revolution," which was mainly driven by mass culture. Thus, these artists' reference to metahistorical "ancient systems of order," to use Benjamin Buchloh's expression, was already mediated by Socialist Realism and Soviet pop culture. What escapes certain Western and even local scholars is the fact that these visual systems were not an aberration from the universal modernist narrative, but rather a particular aesthetic regime, in which a younger generation of authors subjected the universal modernist narrative to revision.

Following this theoretical stance, I would claim that Guryanov did not wish to restore the eternal neoclassical patriarchal order, while Mamyshev did not pursue a relativist intertextual game using historical events and persons as ready-made material. What they were both engaged in was in fact a critical reappraisal of Soviet modernity in a way that was similar to Walter Benjamin's redemptive logic. In saving it from oblivion, they sought to rehabilitate and awaken the emancipatory potential lying dormant within that culture. To demonstrate this, I will focus on the darkest period of that history, namely Stalinism, referring to works by both artists that appropriated Stalinists aesthetics and to recent theoretical interpretations of that era.

From Homosociality to Homosexual Desire

Guryanov began his career with neo-Expressionist, wild, punk graphics based on mass culture artifacts, but in the late 1980s he gradually shifted to monumental easel paintings. He shared certain aesthetic principles with his peers from the New Academy group (for example, Novikov, Oleg Maslov and Viktor Kuznetsov, and Olga Tobreluts)—such as the celebration of classical ideals of beauty and physical perfection. Already in this transitional period when he was still making use of pop-art coloration, his crypto-homoerotic iconography of heroic physical activity was almost fully formed. It was populated with such typical protagonists of the homoerotic imaginary as hypermasculine pilots, oarsmen, workers, athletes, sportsmen, and, of course, Eisenstein-esque sailors. Later, when he split off from the New Academy and attached himself to the New Seriousness group, his style became more academic and colder, while the humor he had shared with the Kuznetsov and Maslov duo almost completely disappeared. Obsessed with retouching and handicraft—something the critics from the *October* circle would see as antithetical to the modernist sensibility of collage—he developed these masculine motifs with increasing precision, economy and attention to the most minute details, even though his works were far from naturalistic.

Describing Russian nineteenth- and twentieth-century academism, Soviet Marxist art historian Aleksei Fedorov-Davydov wrote: "Beauty is the ideal combination of separate beautiful particularities of imperfect forms of nature. It is the creation of perfect noumena out of imperfect phenomena" (Fedorov-Davydov 1929, 2014). At first glance, Guryanov's eclectic depiction of male athletic bodies — especially the oarsmen he painted in the late 1990s–early 2000s, sometimes placing them onto "timeless" surroundings, such as the open sea, the sky or temples—are eidetic combinations of classically inspired attributes. These constructs of "noumenal" masculinity transcend all particularities and conform to classical Aristotelean ideals of beauty, according to which white, abled male bodies are endowed with harmony, clarity, and authority (Nead 1992, 17). Attesting to those dominant schemes of perception, his subjects are defined by such modifiers as "top," "hard," "straight," and "upright," that is, hierarchical symbolic categories that are present in many cultures across the world (Bourdieu 2001, 14). In this way his understanding of masculinity could be described as essentialist, transhistorical and archetypal.

What is peculiar about Guryanov's oeuvre, however, is that this seemingly synchronic dimension of "noumena" (relationships between same sex figures as such) is invaded by the diachronic dimension of history and geo-cultural particularities. While his models' facial expressions and body language are signs belonging to the post-Stonewall international homosexual subculture, their uniforms and dress relate them to the Stalinist era. Many of his works that celebrate male perfection are in fact based on stills from Soviet films, such as Abram Room's *A Stern Young Man* (1936) or Andrei Frolov's *The First Glove* (1947), on Socialist Realist paintings, such as Alexander Deineka's *After the Battle* (1944) or Alexander Samokhvalov's *The Physical Culture of the USSR* (1937), and on Alexander Rodchenko's photographs, as well as Leonid Golovanov's posters. Unlike other "neoacademic" painters of his circle, his interest in transhistorical ideals is strongly mediated by a sensibility of the 1930s and 1940s, which was oriented not only toward neoclassicist style or nineteenth-century academism but also toward American art deco forms.[3] So, instead of celebrating abstract male perfection, Guryanov undertakes what one may call the "sovietization" of their bodies. From this perspective, therefore, such works are not mere assemblages that seamlessly synthesize beautiful particularities but rather queer appropriations of preexisting images and codes. By referring to those readymades and juxtaposing them with the gay culture of his time, he rejuvenates the protocols for representating masculinity of the Soviet era.

In the immediate aftermath of the October Revolution, Bolsheviks pluralized attitudes toward gender and sexual dissent by instituting one of the most progressive codes on marriage and divorce, and by decriminalizing sodomy. Stalin's sexual Thermidore, therefore, signified a return to Tsarist patriarchy and heteronormativity, resulting in the criminalization of sodomy and abortion in 1934.[4] Moreover, unlike other homophobic European countries, homosexuality was not only prosecuted (which was in fact quite rare) in Russia and the other Soviet republics, but was also virtually silenced, eliminated from medical, juridical, and cultural discourse. However, relying on the paradoxical logic of Lacanian psychoanalysis, Ukrainian philosopher and specialist in gender studies Irina Zherebkina claims that in that absolutely heterosexual society, "homosexuality as a structure in fact was encouraged by Stalin" and was revealed in particular in the Leader's relationships with Soviet officials, many of whom after interrogations turned out to be gay (Zherebkina 2006, 63). This view challenges Susan Sontag's famous maxim that Nazism is "sexier" than communism, insofar as the latter, in Sontag's estimation, is "asexual in its imagery" (Sontag 1981, 102). As Guryanov tries to show in his paintings, "actually existing communism" was quite homoerotic, even though that was not explicitly articulated.

Soviet paintings, photography, and films often represent the homosocial bonding of *fizkultura* and sports in all its ambiguity, which Guryanov was eager to emphasize. As Eve Kosofsky Sedgwick points out with her oxymoronic term "homosocial desire": "To draw the 'homosocial' back into the orbit of 'desire,' of the potentially erotic, then, is to hypothesize the potential unbrokenness of a continuum between homosocial and homosexual—a continuum whose visibility, for men, in our society, is radically disrupted" (Kosofsky Sedgwick 1985, 1–2). Sexologist Igor Kon, echoing Sedgwick's argument, describes German and Soviet paintings as characterized by "bodily intimacy, common fear of death and hatred toward the common enemy that produces in men reciprocal affection toward one other and a mute psychological intimacy that is unimaginable under ordinary conditions" (Kon 2003b, 405–406).

Guryanov's well-known boxing series is an appropriation of film stills from *The First Glove*, a popular post-War Soviet comedy about professional sports training. According to the plot, the boxing champion Nikita Krutikov is "distracted" from his training by women. And so, when he finally decides to take part in a match, he fails because he was not properly trained. While in the original largely asexual Stalinist film, he is modestly wearing a sleeveless shirt, Guryanov in his painting *Box* reveals the torso of Krutikov's rival Rogov, having him wear only shorts. His gorgeous body—with which Guryanov, who liked to be photographed naked, obviously identifies—is exposed in the middle of the ring, basking in the spotlight. If in the actual film the audience consists of viewers of both genders, in Guryanov's painting it is composed entirely of similar looking male sailors who contemplate the boxer in adoration. By eradicating female observers, who "distract" the men, Guryanov transforms the audience into an extreme version of homosociality. The ring is symbolically transformed into a kind of Lacanian "mirror stage" where the subject forms a notion of its own integrity through identification with its unified reflected image. This narcissistic stage, according to Guy Hocquenghem, "is the process by which the unnamable desire becomes identified with the similar or the different, with heterosexuality or homosexuality" (Hocquenghem 1993, 81). Since the subject here is defined through lack, that is, the absence of females, this homosocial "panopticon" transforms the subject's experience into one of narcissistic exaltation.

In two other boxing scenes, both dated 1994, Guryanov further elaborates on these homosocial narratives, focusing exclusively on two of the film's protagonists. Depicted against an azure blue monochrome background, the couple indulges in sadomasochistic relations or in reciprocal *jouissance* — defined as extreme pleasure on the verge of mutual destruction. Krutikov either bows to Rogov in worship (*Force of Will*) or pushes his genitalia with his head, hinting at potential castration (*Boxers*). Discussing the specificity of homoeroticism, Kon claims: "Gays spend a lot of time in sport venues, but they need muscles not for frightening but for attracting other men. Like in all male relationships, there is the motif of power of one over the other, but this power consists in part in whether to deliver pleasure to the other man. This is the power that belonged to and was used by women" (Kon 2003a, 32). These carnivalesque alpha-males, hyper-masculine and aggressive, playfully frighten each other in what turns out to be a game of seduction and disavowal. Across the series they never reach a state in which one is dominant and the other is subjugated, but rather they are perpetually switching roles. What Guryanov does is disclose the implicit sadomasochistic impulses and tensions hidden beneath the surface of that popular film. When the trainer Privalov is severely hit in the face and knocked out by his beloved student Krutikov, he asks if his jaw is broken, and after receiving the response of "no," he says: "Unfortunately!" What was thought to be a teacher's sacrifice turns out to be a source of masochistic pleasure.

Guryanov's diptych *A Stern Young Man* (1994) is dedicated to the homoerotic cinematic masterpiece of the same title by Abram Room, which was censored by Stalin (fig. 1).[5] In this painting Guryanov goes further in exploring the rivalry in relationships between men by rupturing the temporal construction of the film sequence during which members of the Komsomol discuss the moral characteristics necessary for a communist. Guryanov separates this mise en scène into two separate canvases, which simultaneously creates continuity and rupture. On the one canvas we see two male members of the Komsomol (one half-naked, another dressed in what appears to be an ancient robe), while on the second canvas there is a group consisting of a young woman and two men. One of the men looks at her, while the other is looking at his interlocutor. Instead of an animated ideological dispute, we see a mute spectacle in which bodies speak. The couple in the first painting, reminiscent of Paul Cadmus's art deco genre works (for instance, *Finistère*, 1952), look like male prostitutes seducing clients. In the second, we see a typical *ménage à trois* of the 1920s (itself the subject matter of a more famous film by Room, *Bed and Sofa* [1927]) where the woman seems to capitulate. As Kosofsky Sedgwick has poignantly shown, the bond

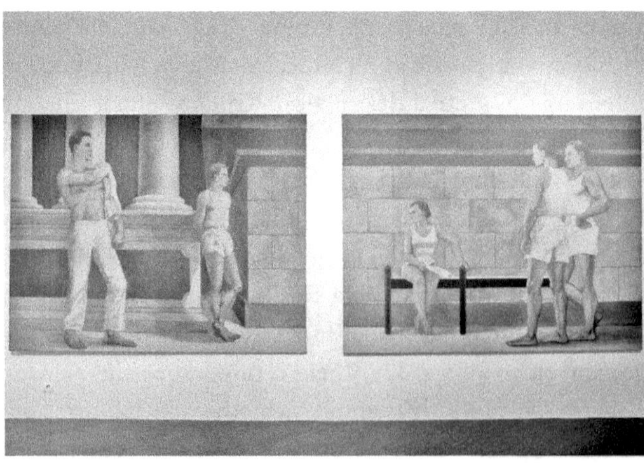

FIGURE 1. Georgy Guryanov, *A Stern Young Man* (1994). Collection of Rinad Akhmedshin

between rivals can be "even stronger, more heavily determinant of actions and choices, than anything in the bond between either of the lovers and the beloved" (1985, 22). Here the female character who might "distract" the men withdraws from the conversation, leaving space for the two men to reestablish their own bonding. Splitting the temporal sequence into two spatial planes, Guryanov creates a complex exchange of glances, foregrounding the homoerotic tensions between the male observers and the observed.

When we look at such paradigmatic examples of socialist realism as Deineka, Samokhvalov, Room or Frolov through Guryanov's optics, an affective, sensitive and even erotic dimension is (re)established in the relationships of the male characters. If we do not "discuss genital homosexual desire as 'at the root of' other forms of male homosociality" (Kosofsky Sedgwick 1985, 2), then their relations represent structural permutations of social impulses, guided and fueled by erotism and desire. Guryanov's artistic method is thus based on the hypostatization of the continuum between the homosocial and the homoerotic to explore the tacit homoerotism of Soviet male culture. He achieves this by pure painterly means: fragmentation, substitution of backgrounds, spatialization of montage sequences, as well as by adding or subtracting figures. These simple techniques construct what one might call a "homosexual gaze" or homoerotic scopophilia, indulging the artist, and potentially the viewer, in peeping at eroticized male bodies.

Soviet society at large, as Boris Groys (2010a, 2) argues, was "completely immersed in the vision of the future—a society living in a unifying Communist project." Similarly, the sexuality of the Stalinist era, with its conservative laws that were oriented toward strengthening the family and pronatalism, which completely subjugated bodies to their reproductive function, was oriented toward future generations. That is why desire and enjoyment could be manifested only in the form of a hidden potentiality, and never in actuality. Guryanov exposes how the homosocial desire of the Stalinist period cannot find a proper outlet; not centered on genital intercourse, it finds different ways to reveal itself within this restrictive system. By shifting accents, Guryanov presents at least three denaturalizations: narcissistic voyeurism, sadomasochistic coupling, and communal erotization, which undermine what "antisocial queer theorists" call "reproductive futurism," which Stalinism had in fact radicalized by prohibiting any representation of erotic pleasure. Like Kenneth Anger, who in *Fireworks* (1947) reveals the homoeroticism of Eisenstein's sailors through the homosexual gaze, Guryanov forces Soviet sexuality, which had seemed ascetic, sexophobic and violently heteronormative, to "come out" with all its polymorphisms and perversions.

Queering the Soviets

Vladislav Mamyshev shared with his Leningrad contemporaries an obsession with appearance, meticulously staging his public "self" and constructing his media-image in the form of self-mythologization and provocation pushed to the extreme until there was no difference between his art and his life. Yet, Mamyshev, who was a representative of a younger generation, was aesthetically distant from Guryanov, Novikov and the New Academy, which probably determined (or was determined by) his migration to Moscow in the early 1990s. The art scene in the capital consisted mostly of radical actionism, high-brow late conceptual art and emerging market-oriented painting and photography. He played with all these trends and merged them into his personal idiosyncratic style.

If Guryanov's mature works are characterized by artisanal completeness and artistic refinement, Mamyshev's objects tended to be unfinished, haphazardly thrown together and sometimes deliberately of low quality. The former, as discussed above, depicted a homosocial world populated by white cisgender men who even enhanced their masculinity through professional sports to align themselves with dominant ideals of manliness. Mamyshev, on the other hand, reveals the particularities and contingencies of the subject portrayed, privileging failure over correspondence. His protagonists—real existing public figures or archetypes—are not coherent or integrated; their subjectivity is always split. They fall apart, disintegrate and self-destruct, which points to the gap between the imagined (how they perceive themselves or a culturally normalized image to which they adjust) and the actual (their constructedness and artificiality). On the formal level, the very act of artistic manipulation is always transparent in his work—be it crude montage, painting over photos, or fake plastic breasts attached to his body. Nevertheless, one should not see this primarily as an expression of a modernist lack of faith in the material world or as the deconstruction of artistic originality since these discrepancies apply to the ruptures within the Soviet field of visuality and sexuality.

For the Western viewer, the most obvious parallel to Mamyshev would be Cindy Sherman, who deconstructed the roles assigned to women in the patriarchal order. But unlike Sherman, Mamyshev's impersonations are not only feminist, but also queer. In Judith Butler's theory of queer performativity, gender does not necessarily follow from the subject's biological sex; it has no ontological status and no essence but is constructed through the reproduction of socially constituted contingent acts that have no origin, that is, they are imitations of imitations. Following from this argument, Butler finds a practical use for performativity: "Imitating gender, drag implicitly reveals the imitative structure of gender itself—as well as its contingency" (1999, 179). Those constructions of the "I," which in the case of Sherman are media effects, are presented in Mamyshev's drag performances as the result of forced collective "gendering." By denaturalizing those constructions, he "exposes the phantasmatic effect of abiding identity as a politically tenuous construction" (1999, 179). Nonetheless, the "figures of authority" that he impersonates and subverts are not merely products of the general universal patriarchy addressed by queer theory and feminism but are a kind of doubled symbolic structure in which femininity and masculinity are powerful tools in the sexual and gender "Cold War" between an allegedly sexualized West and a repressive East.

The central figure of Mamyshev's work is the American actress Marilyn Monroe with whom he (over)identified for his entire life and whose surname he adopted to undo his own sexual identity; as it is pronounced in Russian, the surname is gender neutral or, to be more precise, grammatically neuter. According to the myth cultivated by the artist, Mamyshev was named after the famous cosmonaut Vladislav Volkov, and thus even before his birth had been inscribed into the symbolic order of the Soviet Union. In one of his iconic images—*Documentation of the Artist Standing in front of His Painting of Monroe* (1992)—he both problematizes and ostentatiously reclaims his identity. On the right hand of the image, we see Monroe painted by the artist as a "phallic mother" with male genitalia revealed under her famous "flying skirt." Monroe does not intend to produce what Butler later calls "transubstantiation of gender" or heterosexual literalization of sex, but rather confidently exposes her "little secret," playing with viewers' expectations and denaturalizing heterosexual gender norms (2011, 89). This secret, however, is not only an antidote to the absolutization of binary gender logic through sexual dimorphism but is also a time bomb in a "bipolar world."

Similar to Guryanov's boxing ring, which functions as a kind of "mirror stage," this photo stages a kind of identity crisis. The failed Soviet cosmonaut Vladislav identifies himself with the American sex symbol and reiterates her "stylization of the body" (dress, hairstyle, facial expression, etc.). Reminiscent of paintings of the Madonna del parto, she symbolically covers the author with her tabernacle. But while internalizing gender norms associated with femininity,

Mamyshev also reenacts the very process of their derailment because the gender of the famous actress is already put into question in his painting. He amplifies misrecognition when he attempts to fill his ideal self with fantasy images. In other words, he goes one step further than drag, which Butler praised for its capacity to subvert gender norms. He does not show gender merely as citationality (in this case of a biological male reproducing "female" norms of behavior) but rather presents the very process of repeating subversive acts as already imitative by reproducing codes of western drag culture that were subsequently deradicalized, normalized and commercialized.

For Guryanov, preoccupation with Grecian athletes was a way to advocate against the heteronormative regime of reproductive sexuality. In the absence of any public discussion of homosexuality in the Soviet Union, the transhistorical idea of "same sex eros," which can be found in ancient Greek art and that haunted the Stalinist imagery, served to legitimate heteroclite desire and to compensate for its lack. For Mamyshev, who as a boy was expected to impersonate the most heroic male role model of Soviet modernity, that is, a cosmonaut, Marilyn was something more than a gay icon for an escapist projection. Like Guryanov, Mamyshev adds a strong historical dimension to his works, making the body represented into a battlefield. In his short film *John F. Kennedy and Marilyn Monroe* (1991), the actress is not merely a subject of diva worship, she is a victim of American imperialism. Therefore, one should see her not as the "feminine" that is simply opposed to an imposed "masculinity" but as what the artist himself calls a "positive feminine sign"—a force that goes against any repressive violent structures of both Western and Eastern systems. Therefore, Monroe's otherness transcends the binary logic of gender, but also undoes the false dichotomy between "bad" communism and "good" capitalism, which was quite common for liberally minded artists of the late Soviet and post-Soviet periods. The disclosed phallus in Mamyshev's work is the alterity or distinction that destabilizes any totalitarian and identitarian structure of thinking.

When his post-perestroika infatuation with Marylin Monroe cooled down, Mamyshev created many other avatars, most of which have something to do with Russian history. If one were to put them in chronological order, one would see a concatenation of images—imaginary and actual, collective and personal, historical and archetypical, fictitious and real—forming an encyclopedia of Russian gender norms from the imaginary past of the *bogatyr'* (roughly equivalent to the Western European knight-errant) to contemporary patriarchal figures of Putin's regime.[6] One of the most original and well developed images among his

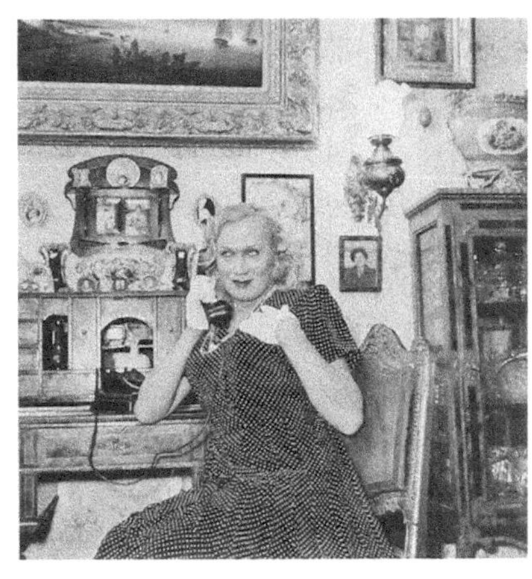

FIGURE 2. Vladislav Mamyshev-Monroe, from the series *Happy Love (Lyubov Orlova)* (1999–2000). Vladislav Mamyshev-Monroe Foundation

impersonations of this time is the Soviet People's actress Lyubov Orlova to whom he dedicated two major works—the photo series *Happy Love (Lyubov Orlova)* of 1999–2000 and the film *Volga-Volga* made in 2006 with Pavel Labazov and Andrey Silvestrov (fig. 2). Orlova became a kind of communist version of Monroe who internalized within herself Mamyshev's own non-identity.

As noted above, Stalinist views regarding sexuality were as reactionary as were the politics of that time in general. In terms of gender, it was claimed that "the women question" had been resolved when female citizens were made formally equal to men through their admission to the labor force. In fact, as Bini Adamczak has shown, this politics was not aimed at abolishing sex or gender distinctions or at installing equality between men and women; rather, it sought to impose the only possible gender model—the male (Adamczak 2011). (This is evident in the fact that women did not occupy high positions in the government of the USSR.) So "unisex" was an underlying motif of 1930s biopolitics: "Soviet 'sex equality' presupposed aligning women with the traditional male standard, which turned into the desire to attenuate or minimize sexual characteristics" (Kon 2003b, 546). Soviet films, paintings and sculptures tried to naturalize the subordination and sacrifice of Bolshevik women who were depicted as masculine—or to use a popular expression of that time, "hard as stone" (*tverdokamennaia*).

Lyubov Orlova—Stalin's favorite actress, whose most famous role was the peasant girl Dunya in the film *Volga-Volga,* a film the general secretary of the Soviet Union reportedly watched 38 times—was described by Irina Zherebkina as an "example of compromised femininity submissive to patriarchal law" (2006, 11). However, as Zherebkina tries to show in her book *Feminist Intervention into Stalinism,* Orlova, like other figures from the *nomenklatura,* or the upper echelon of Soviet culture, resisted the regime through open hypocrisy and *dvurushnichestvo* (double-dealing). As a People's Actress, Orlova lived in splendor that was unprecedented for that period, but, unlike other officials who were interpellated by material goods (quite often western capitalist commodities) into blind political complicity and dependence, she escaped all repressions and purges and enjoyed her opulent lifestyle until her death. Her love of comfort, her ostensible indifference to the leader, and her lack of belief in communism could be interpreted as an existential feminist decision, where individual pleasure and enjoyment went against the totalitarian subjugation of gender to a unisex model and the collective will.

In his research-based photo series, Monroe poses in different luxurious interiors, in theaters or on the streets of Saint Petersburg to reveal the unofficial life of the actress. Unlike in official Soviet portraits, she is dressed in expensive clothes, which also contradicts the genderless image she constructed in her movies. She is sensuous, desiring, and passionate and uses her sexuality exclusively for pleasure. In one of the photos, she even cheats on her husband, lying in a negligee next to a naked sailor. In another shot she drinks vodka with her female friends, revealing a destructive side to her femininity. Yet even in her everyday life she is not "natural"—she is mannered and artificial, which is highlighted by Mamyshev's idiosyncratic mimicry and ingratiating smile. Sitting alone in a room and talking on the phone after the premier of her film *Encounter at the Elbe*, she behaves with highly stylized gestures as if she were drunk. Moreover, in two of the images that are allegedly from the 1970s, Mamyshev indicates that she was photographed after having undergone plastic surgery. What is important here is that such surgery at the time was a prerogative of KGB agents alone, so when Orlova undergoes it, her appearance was oriented not for communist, but for capitalist citizens. The actress and her husband, film director Grigori Aleksandrov, were one of the few couples allowed to travel abroad, not only to represent Soviet mass culture to Western audiences but also to display Western femininity to the Russian public. Therefore, Mamyshev represents gender identity not as something transcultural; instead, he foregrounds the political implications of gender identity when used as an ideological weapon — quite similarly to abstraction and socialist realism in the realm of painting during the Cold War. The femininity of both Monroe and Orlova were constructed for the foreign gaze and so took part in a kind of "sexual cold war," according to which their meaning could be constructed only against each other.

In the film *Volga-Volga*, Mamyshev doubles this comic effect by intensifying the contrast between reality and appearance. In real life Orlova came from an aristocratic family, was brown-haired, had physical defects and by the time of the shooting was in her thirties. But for the original film she was "proletarianized"—transformed by her husband into a young blonde working class girl with the help of film techniques. (For instance, Aleksandrov shot and edited other women's hands because Orlova's joints were deformed.) Mamyshev, on the other hand, crudely attaches his own "talking head" onto her body, showing his own mincing face and using his own deformed, but still obviously "male" voice. In this way, Mamyshev lays bare the gap between the Orlova who remained faithful to her private gender model of self-determination (in this case, Mamyshev's own face) and the second, artificial Orlova, that was constructed to conform to the ideal Bolshevik woman, that is, adjusted to a traditional male standard. Her feminized masculine face becomes a "substrate" upon which femininity was projected, so that it is seen not as a product of patriarchal culture but as a schizophrenic split in the bipolar order. Furthermore, in addition to these two layers—Mamyshev-Monroe's actual face and in Orlova-like makeup—a third one appears—the femininity of Mamyshev himself. As in the case of the first image under consideration, the artist exposes the pure distinction that lies at the core of gender identification and, by doing so, deconstructs the entire chain of underlying identifications, repressions and reflections.

Conclusion

Guryanov's and Mamyshev's works are part and parcel of a unique period—*Perestroika* and the post-Soviet decades of "transition." The reforms of the late 1980s promised a return to avant-garde politics: "Democratization, re-structuring, transparency, the continued work of the positive feminine sign, all definitively switched to the rails of the positive renewal of the planet, while the new bearer of the feminine sign, Mikhail Gorbachev, received international fame and the Nobel Prize"—as Mamyshev once wrote (*Radio Svoboda* 2013). During this period, as censorship and other political restrictions were loosened, economic reforms instituted, and human rights advanced, an underground counter-culture movement emerged related to sexual liberation and the emancipation of artists. The early 1990s saw the radicalization of these tendencies and the official legalization of what had already been accepted in the underground, including homosexuality. The opening of archives and the publication of previously censored works, exhibitions of banned art and films (including, for instance, Room's *A Stern Young Man*), led to revisionist readings of Soviet history and culture. That resulted in a massive critical reenactment of its tragic and glorious moments.

Both Guryanov and Mamyshev represent Russian history not as linear and homogeneous (read: totalitarian, conservative, and anti-modernist) but as deeply dialectical and repetitive, expressed in spiral movements and ruptures. Similarly, historian Moshe Lewin divides the Soviet century into three very different epochs. He begins with Stalin's Thermidore, then post-Stalinist bureaucracy, and only then comes back to Lenin's avant-garde politics (Lewin 2005), opening the possibility of its reiteration. Groys follows this logic by arguing: "Communism was in fact no longer utopia; its earthly incarnation was completed. Completed here means finished, and thus set free for repetition" (Groys 2010b, 126). In a similar vein, the history of Russian sexuality, as interpreted by Igor Kon, was not always congruent with the political realm. For example, the Silver Age sexual revolution continued into the early Bolshevik era but was then negated by Stalinism; it was renewed in the 1970s and repeated in the mid-1980s with the advent of Perestroika, etc. Similarly, current conservative reaction cannot be analyzed without referencing this long history.

To conclude, Guryanov and Mamyshev investigate what Butler called "gender coherence"—that is, the gaps and mismatches in the triangular relationship of anatomical sex, gender identity and desire— approaching it from two different angles. While Guryanov operates on the axis of desire and sex—his sailors are cisgender and are more than happy with this coincidence—Mamyshev problematizes the coherence between sex and gender but does not put into question heteronormative desire: His female personifications choose men as their objects of desire (Monroe loves Kennedy, and Orlova is attracted to sailors). If Guryanov's work approximates what could be called "gay art" by insisting on the specificity of homosexual identity and positing it as a form of sexual dissent and nonconformity, Mamyshev's work is closer to queer art, which is aimed at exposing gender codes in the cultural production of meaning. However, neither of these categories fully captures these two artists' work. My ambition was not to inscribe them into existing art historical hierarchies, but rather to challenge the Western canon itself, however ambitious that may sound. Addressing this essay primarily to the global, non-post-Soviet reader, I consciously overlooked certain problematic aspects of their artistic practice so as not to deter the reader, but to provoke additional research.

In both case studies, I focused on the artistic interpretation of Stalinist visual culture, which, of course, is not the main subject matter of their work but exemplifies the specificity of their methods. Both artists see Soviet history not as a monolith but rather as a quite complex phenomenon, where the revolutionary sexual and gender dissent of the 1920s is not entirely repressed but is paradoxically incorporated and deformed while structurally determining the entire system. At the same time, their work can be examined within the wider political context of the bipolar world of the Cold War. Therefore, when speaking of the Soviet context, one cannot discuss homosexuality or the queering of identity in purely universal terms or by applying reductive progressivist logics in an uncritical way. Instead, one should consider the question of historical and geo-cultural mediation. To draw a parallel between the artistic practices of Guryanov and Mamyshev, therefore, does not only imply addressing the specificity of late Soviet and early post-Soviet art; rather, it invites more general consideration of issues around sexual desire and gendering in the USSR and in post-Soviet Russia that go beyond purely art historical concerns.

Notes

1 See Khlobystin (2013). One of the few exceptions is Valery Ledenev's review of Mamyshev's retrospective at MMOMA. Available at: http://aroundart.ru/2015/09/21/mamyshev-monroe/.

2 See Andreeva (2007). This idea was perpetuated by cultivating myths of Novikov's connections with the American art scene that migrated from one book to another. In particular, it concerns parallels between the "New Artists," Neue Wilde, and Transavanguardia.

3 This situation is similar to the deceptive term "Stalinist Empire" in architecture, which draws mainly on New York art deco and not on the early-nineteenth century Empire Style.

4 See Healey (2001).

5 It was censored by Stalin and not shown until 1994, but Guryanov managed to watch the film thanks to Novikov who worked as projectionist.

6 Notably, Mamyshev reads the Soviet regime not as homogenous, but comprised of different periods (see Shental 2015).

References

Adamczak, Bini. 2011. "The Feeling of Revolution. Queer Questions of 1917." Symposium *Utopia: Wreckage*. ICI Berlin Institute for Cultural Inquiry. June 16. https://www.ici-berlin.org/videos/utopia-wreckage/. Last accessed May 23, 2021.

Andreeva, Ekaterina. 2007. *Postmodernizm. Iskusstvo vtoroi poloviny XX–nachala XXI veka*. St. Peterburg: Azbuka Klassika.

Bourdieu, Pierre. 2001. *Masculine Domination*. Stanford: Stanford UP.

Butler, Judith. 1999. *Gender Trouble*. New York: Routledge.

———. 2011. *Bodies That Matter. On the Discursive Limits of Sex*. Oxon: Routledge Classics.

Fedorov-Davydov, Aleksei. 1929. *Russkoe iskusstvo promyshlennogo kapitalizma*. Moscow: State Academy of Art Sciences.

Foster, Hal et al. 2005. *Art Since 1900: Modernism, Antimodernism, Postmodernism*. London: Thames and Hudson.

Groys, Boris. 2010a. *History Becomes Form. Moscow Conceptualism*. Cambridge, MA: MIT Press.

———. 2010b. *The Communist Postscript*. London: Verso.

Healey, Dan. 2001. *Homosexual Desire in Revolutionary Russia. The Regulation of Sexual and Gender Dissent*. Chicago: The University of Chicago Press.

Hocquenghem, Guy. 1993. *Homosexual Desire*. Translated by Daniella Dongoor. Durham: Duke University Press.

Khlobystin, Andrei. 2013. "Georgy Guryanov–geroi." Lecture presented at the Novyi muzei, St. Petersburg, Russia, November 1. https://www.novymuseum.ru/events-muzeum_news-speech/georgii_guryanov_-_geroi.html

Kon, Igor'. 2003. *Lunnyi svet na zare: Liki i maski odnopoloi liubvi*. Moscow: AST.

———. 2003. *Muzhskoe telo v istorii kul'tury*. Moscow: Slovo.

Kosofsky Sedgwick, Eve. 1985. *Between Men: English Literature and Male Homosocial Desire*. New York: Columbia University Press, 1985.

Kovalev. Andrei. 2008. "Andrei Kovalev o Timure Novikove." *OpenSpace.ru*. http://os.colta.ru/art/events/details/1362/. Last accessed: May 23, 2021.

Lewin, Moshe. 2005. *The Soviet Century*. London: Verso.

Nead, Lynda. 1992. *The Female Nude: Art, Obscenity and Sexuality*. London, NY: Routledge.

Shental, Andrey. 2015. "Vladislav Mamyshev-Monroe: The Promise of Queer-Feminist Revolution." *Little Joe* 5: 84–95.

Sontag, Susan. 1981. "Fascinating Fascism." In *Under the Sign of Saturn*, 71–105. New York: Vintage Books.

"Tufli Liubovi Orlovoi." 2013. *Radio Svoboda* (March 22). https://www.svoboda.org/a/24935554.html. Last accessed: May 23, 2021

Turkina, Olesia and Viktor Mazin. 2014. "Zhizn' zamechatel'nykh Monro." St. Peterburg: New Museum. Ekaterina Andreeva. Vladislav Mamyshev-Monro. Moscow: Ad Marginem Press.

Zherebkina, Irina. 2006. *Feministskaia interventsiia v Stalinism, ili Stalina ne sushchestvuet*. St. Petersburg: Aletheia.

Chapter 12

"My Nationaliti Is My Sexuality": The Post-Soviet, Migrant, Non-Russian Queerness of Babi Badalov[1]

Roman Osminkin

By placing Babi (Babakhan) Badalov in a collection about queer art, we risk writing him into a defined historical tradition and aesthetic. That is always dangerous both for the artist, who may be pinned down to a specific movement, and for queer subjectivity overall. Because "queer," according to one of its many definitions, does not have a self-sufficient value, nor does it belong to something essential, it does not have a beginning. It is not a category. It is deviation from the norm. The essence of queer is strangeness and unusualness as a permanent deviation from a final definition, the literal transcendence of boundaries, and the avoidance of sustained identity foundations. Queer theory describes its subject as a multitude of mobile models of identity, as process, and recomposition.

But we must be careful for other reasons as well. The term "queer" in art and queer theory appeared and developed in the late 1980s, far outside the boundaries of the USSR. Hence, any imposition of "queer" as it relates to Soviet artists, musicians, and poets has a retrospective character involving the transference or projection of a Western concept onto a post-Soviet situation. Therefore, any application of "queer" to Soviet artists, musicians, and poets must be critically and reflexively transformed based on local queer traditions. This means the term "queer" will always be specific and depend on the specific historical circumstances and cultural characteristics in which a particular artist exists and works.

What does the prefix "queer" mean for Babi Badalov, and what can it productively contribute to our understanding of his work? I dare to put forth my thesis that Badalov's art and poetry are isomorphic to queerness. And so, Badalov can help us broaden the invariants of queerness by offering his own unique aesthetic life experience and simultaneously by making this experience part of a wider queer tradition in art. As a migrant belonging to an ethnic minority and as s gay man from a Muslim country, Badalov, like many other queer artists, organically tied his biosocial body to art. But Badalov is not the type of artist for whom queer means advancing ideas of sexual identity in art. Most queer artists develop nonnormative gender/sexual imagery through the persistent externalization of corporeality; artists transform their traumatic experience into art through their bodies. Coming from the Soviet Muslim world, Badalov realizes his queerness indirectly through visual poetry, which became his principal artistic method. Babi Badalov expresses his Soviet lineage best in the following verses:

> I was homosoveticus
> I was communistautopicus
> I was USSRicus[2]

This poetic indirectness can be tied to the USSR's control over sexuality and the circulation of sexual imagery. Poetry allows sexual experience to be conveyed mentally and metaphorically and to function under the ban on mimetic art in the Muslim tradition. The famous post-Soviet queer artist of this era, Vladislav Mamyshev-Monroe, used the artistic method of travesty to transform himself into heroes of mass culture and politics. Badalov relied on the language of transvestism to expose gender, national, political, migrant, cultural, and other forms of oppression. Compared with the radical artists of post-Soviet gay culture—for example, Slava Mogutin who became famous in the 1990s for his militant aesthetic and gay poetry—Badalov is conservative. Badalov admits his embarrassment over his sexuality and refers to gay culture as poor theater: "Yes, I'm a homosexual. But I'm not gay and don't want to look gay. This doesn't just relate to the gay culture, which I view as poor theater. For me it's *une question morale*. Morale is a form of suffering because it connects my private life to what is going on in the world" (2017).[3] Babi's suffering may be a result of gender melancholia produced by the compulsory heterosexuality of Azerbaijani and Soviet cultures. "My life was full of tragedies and internal fears. I was an actor in a play about myself, about the need to stay alive, to fight, to avoid being beaten or humiliated," Badalov explains (2019).

In this sense, Babi Badalov, with his suffering and Dostoevskian problems, would fit better among artists from the previous generation—people who were forced to take the least skilled jobs to hide their sexual orientation, exhibiting their work underground and publishing in *samizdat*. This generation spent time in boiler rooms, patronized the Saigon, the legendary cafe in Leningrad frequented by bohemians, and spread the nonconformist Gaza-Neva culture in Leningrad—all under the threat of prosecution for social parasitism or homosexuality. The system was much more polarized, and the official Soviet language occupied all spheres of life, leaving little choice other than internal migration or a dissident life. The Soviet ideological apparatus produced doublethink, drawing strict boundaries between the public and private lives of every individual.

In addition to the effects of the Soviet disciplinary project, Badalov's embarrassment and suffering are exacerbated by his traditional Eastern education. Badalov was born in 1959 in the village of Lerik in Southern Azerbaijan, near the Iranian border. He was the seventh child in a family of five brothers and five sisters. His mother was ethnically Talysh, and his father was Azerbaijani, so at home the family spoke both languages. The children spoke Talysh (similar to Farsi) with their mother and Azerbaijani with their father. Badalov knew very little Russian, but at the age of fifteen, he moved to Baku, where he graduated from the Azim Azimzade Art School. He followed that with two years of military service in a construction battalion near Moscow, where the Soviet doctrine of friendship of peoples gave way to discrimination and xenophobia toward "smaller" ethnicities. Attracted to the cultural myth of St. Petersburg, he traveled twice to the city to gain entrance to the Academy of Arts. He failed both times but remained in the city, working at a fire station or in construction, all the while painting and writing poetry.

In the late 1980s, times changed, and Leningrad's underground culture began to announce itself to a wider public. The Society for Experimental Visual Art, the New Artists, Pushkinskaia 10, the Mitki, the Necrorealists, the Pop-Mechanics, and the rock movement became the main artistic engines of perestroika, helping to emancipate a repressed public emotionally and sexually. Badalov found himself inside this vortex and quickly joined the Society for Experimental Visual Art (TEII) and the New Artists. Badalov worked on several projects with Timur Novikov and Vadim Ovchinnikov, the central figures of the Leningrad art scene of the 1980s. The artist and poet Vadim Ovchinnikov became the second most important person in Badalov's life after his father. As Badalov explains, "Everything I found then was influenced by him: his poetry, sketches, paintings, his attention to detail. Vadim proved to me that my mistakes were much more interesting than 'fixing mistakes,' because the language opens up to new meanings and the words reveal hidden possibilities" (2017). Badalov began to work with text in the late 1980s. He wrote poems and made collages—first in his broken Russian, and later in other languages. In 1989, long before Google Translate and neural network poetry, Dmitry Volchek published Badalov's poems—under the pseudonym Andre Babi—in the Leningrad underground cult journal *Mitin zhurnal.* It looked like this:

> i am going to leave for another planet
> don't know if i'll ever ever eat your Voice
> i am going to leaf for another planet
> don't know if i'll ever ever eat your glance
>
> i love you
> he also loves you
> you better love yourself
> not to offend us.
>
> Once I dreamt a dream how a horse ate me
> This happent in a villagg when I was walking on
> a sidewalk by the wall. (Badalov 1989)

Badalov thought that since he could not spend time with dictionaries and study grammar, could not access the logic of a foreign language, and would never speak fluently and without mistakes, then he would make his mistakes the main constructive principle for creating art forms. The communicative function of language is to eliminate mistakes, yet there is poetry—the mother of all mistakes and a refuge for homeless languages. The psychoanalyst and founder of the Freud Museum in Saint Petersburg, Viktor Mazin, describes Babi's poetry in the following way:

> The impossibility of its own language. A desert of words, uttered by Another. Native tongue sounds foreign. Foreign tongue sounds native. Where is the boundary between foreign // native? A person without a language, either lost and/or never gained. Your native language is always foreign, hostile, the dominating voice of Another. Avoidance of its unifying normativity is required Where the unified plane breaks, where an orderly grid is shaken apart, we find multidimensionality, the infinity of the reflecting surfaces of a broken mirror, a proliferation of values in the broken lines. Another semantic multiplication gives an indeterminant gender—or, rather, the presence or the absence of three genders, a gender quake (Mazin 1989).

We believe this "gender quake" of language is also connected to Babi's inability to identify with a normative gender. The figure of the migrant—a refugee from any native language—is isomorphic to the figure of the queer running from gender normalization. The USSR had a great poet-migrant, the Nobel laureate Joseph Brodsky, who set the standards for the Russian language alongside Pushkin, Tolstoy, Dostoevsky, and other canonical authors. Babi Badalov queered Brodsky in his collage "Joseph Brodsky—the great poetess."[4] The poetess in this work can write in the language of "bad poetry" in the conventional sense. Bad poetry works through humor and performance. In it, Mayakovsky's masculine image of "a cloud in trousers" becomes "trousers in clouds" for Badalov. The pants are attached to a wall, but they are prepared for imminent takeoff. Trousers in clouds are therefore wandering pants, free of gender or cultural identifications. The pants are a thing unto themselves. Once, Babi shocked everyone by showing up in a penguin's costume to a graduation ball at the Saint Petersburg Naval Military Academy. Badalov does not just write poor poetry. His poetry is always a synthesis of "word" and "image": "I speak and paint words, so I'm often a bit embarrassed when they call me a 'poet.' I am not a poet in the understanding of a literary man. I say, 'A man's life is a cemetery of unwritten books'" (Badalov 2017).

As soon as the borders were opened in 1991, Badalov emigrated to the US, settling in San Francisco. There for the first time, he saw openly homosexual relations between his art dealer and his boyfriend; he tried smoking weed and discovered LSD. Having arrived equipped with only one phrase—"I want to be . . ."—Badalov studied English and spoke it in a way that required further translation into English. In California, Badalov created his own profound uniqueness and orientalism: "I am strange, and they look at me strangely" (Badalov 2019). He also created a perfect self-objectifying gesture in developing the slogan and its namesake exhibit "I am ART EAST" (Will White Gallery, Eugene, Oregon).

The Azerbaijan language used the Arabic alphabet until 1922. The Soviet government took steps to replace it with the Latin script, and, in 1939, Azerbaijan transitioned to the Cyrillic alphabet. In 1991, when the Soviet Union fell apart, Azerbaijan returned to the Latin script. Badalov's visuals expose, layer upon layer, these historical language reversals. Badalov creates a hybrid alphabet, in which the Arabic letters are hiding behind Latin and Cyrillic ones like echoes of a colonized Eastern culture squeezing through a logical Western narrative that only appears rational and efficient to a newcomer. The Western symbols are discrete, whereas the Arabic writing is continuous. They resemble the lip poetry *dodaq deymez*, which has its own form of reading that does not allow the lips to close. Badalov breaks up English and Russian words into separate morphemes, semes, and phonemes, which he later knits together into a common word cloth. Fully distorted and shimmering meanings escape any finality or stability.

The suffixes *-ist* and *-ism* are the main operators of verbal escapism in Badalov's work. In English and Russian, they form nouns that indicate belonging to a certain group of people, an institution, a profession, an ideology, or a gender identity. Like most migrants, Badalov studies language orally without learning the grammar. The suffix *-ist* sounds like the word "east." Badalov plays on the visual and phonetic similarities between words in different languages and shakes up established identities. He demonstrates the constructedness of these languages, thereby freeing the words—and, by extension, the people—from their definitional power and the stigma attached to them: anarch-east, antifash-east, terror-east, femin-east, capital-east, fetish-east, extrim-east, commun-east, national-east, marx-east, etc.[5] Patriotism turns into its opposite, becoming a rebellion: Pat/Riot/ism. Badalov attaches the suffix *-east* to the Russian word for art (*iskusstvo*), turning it into "East-kusstvo" The artist feminizes the Russian word *musulman,* meaning Muslim, by turning it into *musulwoman,* thus offering the right to free public speech to all women in the Islamic world who are deprived of it. They can announce themselves through a womanifestation instead of a manifestation. Badalov writes "sex pistols" with white letters on a black flag, suggesting an Islam that is based on punk and not on cultural fundamentalism.

After three years of unsuccessful attempts to adapt to the United States, Badalov, looking like a bearded hermit, returned to a Russia that had been transformed by shock-therapy market reforms. Now he is seen as someone from the Caucasus—a "black-ass" and a "wetback." After working in Saint Petersburg, Babi finally returns in the late 1990s, via Turkey, to his Azerbaijani village. Nobody is waiting for him in his native Azerbaijan. Here he is an immigrant with a nontraditional orientation. He is tried several times, six times he is thrown into a jail for immigrants. Badalov continues to receive threats like "Get out of here as fast as you can!" even years later, following his exhibit at the Yarat! Contemporary Art Space in Baku in April of 2019 (Badalov 2019). But he ultimately finds luck in Baku when a local oil magnate purchases his works. Badalov begins working for foreign philanthropic foundations, applies for a workshop in England, and, in 2006, leaves again. In England, he overstays his six-month visa by almost two years, living as an illegal migrant. In Cardiff, he meets anarchists from the Green movement, becomes a vegetarian, and contributes the sign "Climate change, Rich must dye" to an environmental protest. In the end, despite the art community's advocacy and protests, Badalov is deported back to Russia in 2008.

He does not stay in Russia long, traveling to Paris through Finland, Belgium, and Germany. He then decides to seek asylum in France. In 2011, the artist finally receives official status as a political refugee in France. In the cosmopolitan Paris of the twenty-first century, Badalov escapes the constant feeling of exile and gains freedom without any ties to nationality or citizenship. He stopped being Azerbaijani a long time ago, he did not and could not become Russian, and he will never become French or European. Instead, Badalov gained his own citizenship without citizenship: he is a nomad-migrant, a permanent fugitive driven by his love for the arts and poetry. Now he knows seven languages: Talysh, Farsi, Azerbaijani, Russian, Turkish, English, and French. But none of these is either native or foreign. (Remember what Viktor Mazin wrote?) Languages lose any hierarchy and, instead of creating borders between cultures and peoples, they become a unifying thread for Badalov. Shifting smoothly between languages, Badalov knits his textual-verbal thread, his Eastern ornament from Western letters. He plays with language paradoxes.

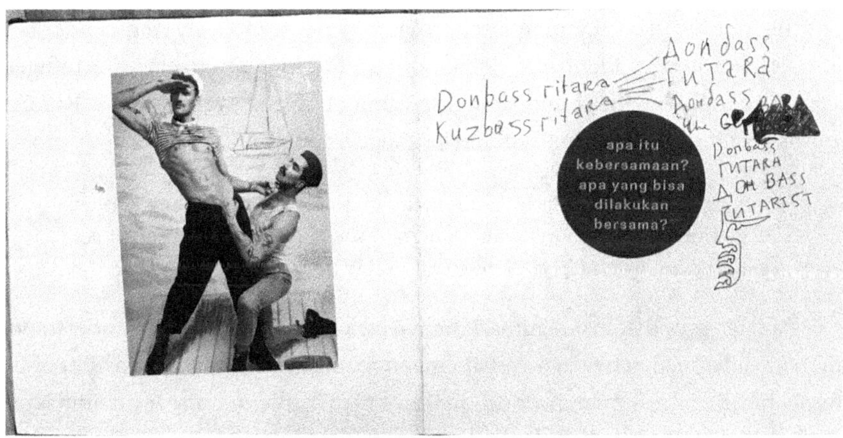

Babi Badalov, *DonBass Gitara, KuzBass Gitara* (2019), artist book page. Courtesy of the artist

This is not about the elasticity of language, as some argue. It is about being tongue-tied. A migrant's tongue-tied speech is a torture to listen to, to remember, and to reproduce. But speech is not driven by the rules of grammar; it is a living process. Tongue-tiedness places limits on the capacity for articulation, always threatening it with incorrect understanding, with misunderstanding. The Russians say "speaking in a broken tongue" when they hear mistakes in a language. Badalov fulfills this brokenness to the letter. Every new language for him is broken. None of the languages can be taken as native and fully accepted. Language itself becomes a nomad, like its speaker. The Feminist philosopher Rosi Braidotti discusses this in her essay "Writing as a Nomadic Subject":

> Being homeless; a migrant; an exile; a refugee; a tourist; a rape-in-war victim; an itinerant migrant; an illegal immigrant; an expatriate; a mail-order bride; a foreign caretaker of the young or the elderly of the economically developed world; a highflying professional; a global venture financial expert; a humanitarian relief worker in the UN global system; a citizen of a country that no longer exists (Yugoslavia; Czechoslovakia; the Soviet Union) – these are no metaphors. Having no passport or having too many of them is neither equivalent nor is it merely metaphorical. These are highly specific geo–political and historical locations – it's history and belonging tattooed on your body. (Braidotti 2014, 179–180)

Badalov's entire body is covered with these tattoos. Badalov's nomadism is not the journey of a migrating intellectual polyglot who easily transcends state borders and juggles identities. Badalov is on the forced journey of a refugee, a pariah, a traveler with a bundle. English cannot transmit the play on the Russian words *strannik,* a traveler, and *strannyi,* strange or queer:

> me gration you gration he gration she gration we gration they gration ci gration sea gration me grant you grant she grant we grant ci grant sea grantti grant fi grant hi grant ni grant[6]

Badalov says that inside himself he's lived a very scary life. One understands the key difference between a verbal and an iconic symbol, all the horrors of internal life. Badalov's mental world does not turn inside out under the impact of a whole spectrum of affective mediums that influence the viewer like cerebral tickles. His world enters onto an ascetic plane—often cloth, plaster, or paper—and looks like a collection of simple symbols transforming (migrating) from one to another. Morphemes and whole words are altered or eliminated, but their meanings "shimmer," a reference to Russian writer and artist Dmitrii Prigov (1940–2007). Languages migrate to the point that you cannot tell the difference between them. Cyrillic and Latin alphabets crisscross from one to another through the Arabic script. This sums up the "migrant poetry" of Badalov.

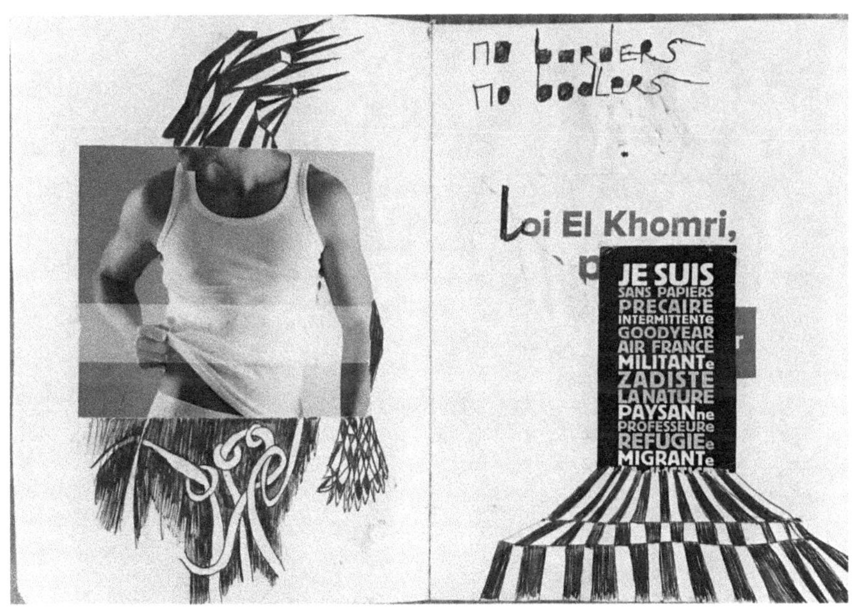

Babi Badalov, *No Borders No Bodlers* (2018), artist book page. Courtesy of the artist

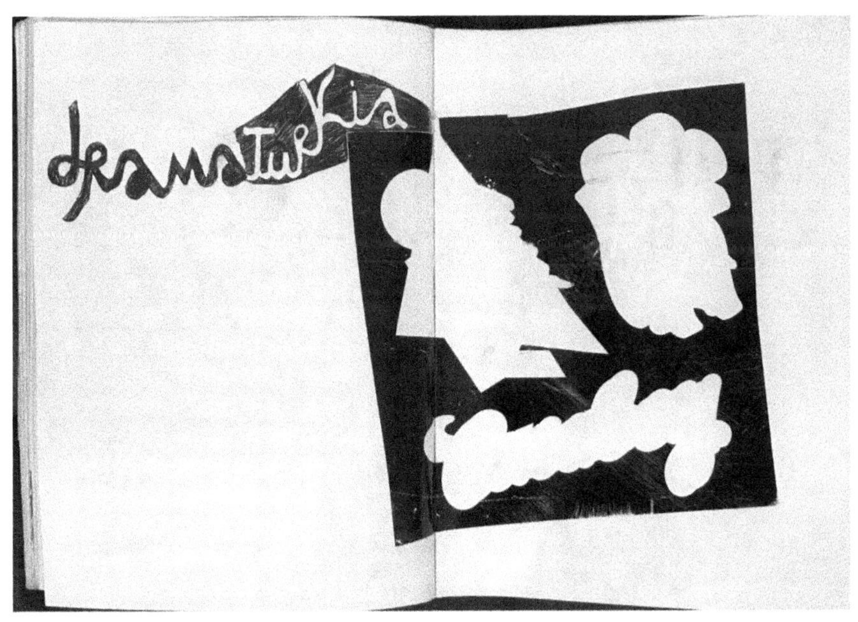

Babi Badalov, *DramaTurkia* (2017), artist book page. Courtesy of the artist

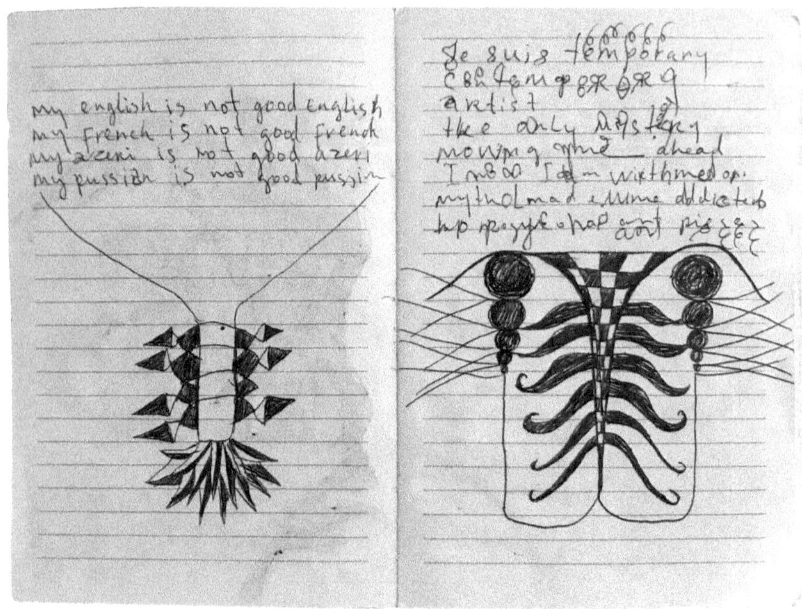

Babi Badalov, *Living with Broken Languages* (2014), artist book page. Courtesy of the artist

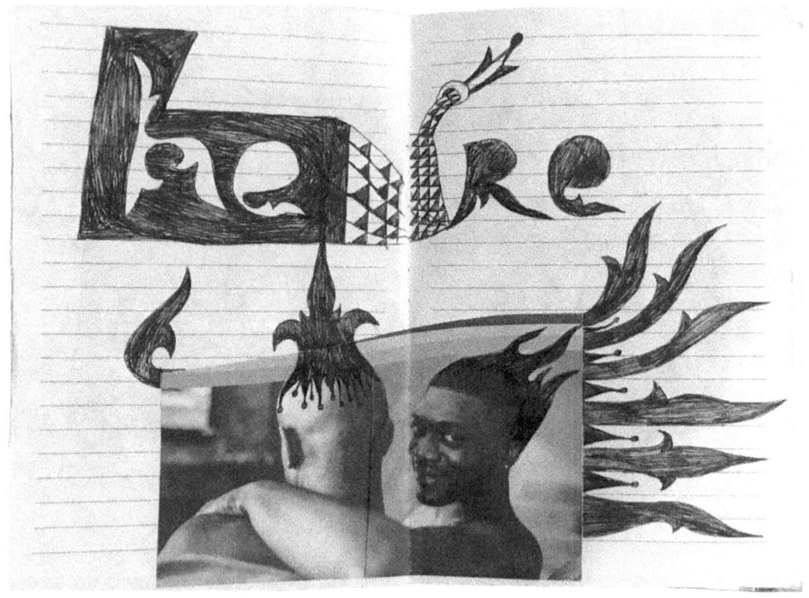

Babi Badalov, *He RE* (2014), artist book page. Courtesy of the artist

Migration does not just transform the biological and social body of the artist; it permeates his whole bodily articulatory apparatus with the harsh thread of multilingual palimpsests—visual-acoustic patterns of writing and reading.

We remember that the term "text" comes from the Latin *textus* meaning "woven cloth, plaiting, joining." In Badalov's case, this text does not play the role of making us choose from a list of possibilities. Badalov's text runs away from any final or stable definitions. Analogous to creolized text, a nonhomogeneous creation made of numerous verbal, iconic, and indexical systems, Badalov's work can be called a queered text. The "migrant poetry" of Badalov, as with any migrant's speech, is queerspeak relative to the native language of the place that receives the individual. Queer resists the binarism of language. Queer reveals its binary oppositions and deconstructs their constant fluid movements under the auspices of the ornament.[7] This ornament is not seamless, however; there is a gaping wound behind it. This tear is forced and traumatic. Badalov's queer is always patched up, unwhole, quilted from different fabrics into one bright canvas with patches layered on top of one another. As Badalov admits in an interview: "I received clothes from my older brothers, and at school I was always embarrassed by the patches. My participation in the projects dedicated to patches follows from childhood" (Sputnik Azərbaycan 2019).

Historically, textiles in Azerbaijan are associated with feminine work. The art brings domestic labor into the public space. Rags turn into political slogans. In 2018, Badalov took part in the textile exhibit "Soft Power" in EMMETROP, Bourges (France). The idea was to de-crown the patriarchy, crack racism, and fix the planet. In other words, contemporary textile art is no longer decorative but exclusively political. Moreover, textiles are the closest thing to the body, which is very important for Badalov, who thinks that art is a continuation of the body. "We are very close to textile, because we put it on every day," explains Babi Badalov. The endings of the sentences and words he chooses create a political echo: body borders / blood borders / blue borders.

"My exhibit is my body" is the organic metaphor Badalov brings to fruition. He writes in minibooks and makes textiles and collages that look like a teenager's bedroom with posters of pop culture stars on the walls. Inside the exhibit, Badalov's work makes the cold spaces of art institutions seem cozy. "To make art to take clothes off," says Badalov. To make art is to get undressed. When you're creating sentimental intimate art, you're naked, all people see you. That's why you have to think before stripping down. Art is a weapon, you can't play with art; if you do, you'll become a victim, and Badalov has always been opposed to martyrdom: "I should never be the victim, under no circumstances. I should be fighting, provoking, propagating. I love to provoke: Run from Quran, Rebecca from Mecca. We have to mock all the time and laugh. 'To talk is also a part of the revolution,' and it's very important to talk based on personal experience" (Badalov 2019).

Today Badalov's work can be found in many museums around the world. He continues to participate in an array of prestigious exhibits: MANIFESTA 8 - Murcia, Cartagena (ES), 2010; "MIGRANT POETRY," La Station, Centre d'art contemporain, Nice (FR) 2015; "For the Wall For the World," Palais de Tokyo, Paris, 2016; "To make art to take clothes off," MUSAC, León (ES); and others. Sometimes an artist from the third world who plays by the rules of global art institutions and the art market can become trapped in his own orientalist image and self-exoticize. Badalov understands this danger and keeps working as a pop-up artist, customizing his installations and frescos for every new place by seeking out the best form of expression for the politicization of that particular space. Badalov does not lose his connection to the streets for without that, visual poetry becomes dull and lifeless. On the street, he can collect garbage for his installations, find and document slogans and scraps of posters for his Instagram, or create posters for the antifascist exhibit in the Moscow metro "Art against Nazism." "I like poetical action in art. Poetry is a manifestation and a struggle. It has to come out onto the street and scream: Fashion week—fascist week, Fashion show—fascist show. I can't write if there's no inspiration," says the artist.

In essence, Babi Badalov creates an artificial language—queer-language for the oppressed. It has an open structure and can be fine-tuned or expanded by that language from the new land of the migrant. It is a language in action, both poetic and political. It is in a state of constant development and reinvention of itself. It is the language of torturous listening to someone who is liberating his tied tongue. The verbal, living word, when taken warm from the lips defeats the cold language of global bureaucracy. According to the literary scholar Viktor Shklovsky, the word can be resurrected only by returning to it its living essence: the boy boys, the wound wounds, the pain pains.

Translated by Innokenty Grekov

Notes

1 The title is taken from Babi Badalov's work *My nationaliti is my sexuality*, 2017. Painting on textile.

2 This quotation is taken from the work *Je Suis Mazimir Kalevich* by Babi Badalov at the exhibition by the same name *Je Suis Mazimir Kalevich*, New Museum, Saint Petersburg, 2018.

3 "As a youth, I understood that I looked at men differently than women. I was terrified from this. I was afraid. I thought I was a criminal, a dirty guy, a freak! I couldn't ask my mother, 'Do you know what's happening with me, why did you bore me this way' I thought such a person should be burned, destroyed. I lived in constant stress, invisible horror, and fear. In the United States I saw that my art dealer was openly living with his boyfriend. I'm like them, but even after many years I remain conservative. I'm ashamed when men are kissing or holding hands in public. Feelings put on public display aren't real." Available at: http://artguide.com/posts/1184. Last accessed May 23, 2021.

4 See the photo, *Joseph Brodsky—the great poetess.*

5 See photos from *Southern Constellations: The Poetics of the Non-Aligned*, Museum of Contemporary Art Metelkova, Ljubljana, 2019.

6 Photos from *Megration Yougration Hegration*, Size Gallery, Rijeka (HR).

7 "My visual memory comes from Muslim countries and the traditions of an Islamic family. My first memories have rugs and ornaments. That's my visual identity. Europe is a world of progressive individualism, contemporary arts, and total liberty. Available at: https://supportyourart.com/words//babibadalov?fbclid=IwAR24e3-rhJw38-Z42f-aGtAHcs5K-tTsba1qnhFiFNHYMk6wsjZBZyAGDNlk. Last accessed May 23, 2021.

References

Babi, [Badalov] Andre. 1989. "Stikhotvoreniia." *Mitin zhurnal.* November/December. http://kolonna.mitin.com/archive/mj30/baby.shtml. Last accessed: May 23, 2021.

———. 2017. Interview by Dmitrii Pilkin. "Babi Badalov: Ia zapolnil apply na odin workshop.'" *Artgid.* Available at: https://artguide.com/posts/1184. Last accessed May 23, 2021.

———.2019."BabiBadalovproSRSR,Kmytivs'kyimuzeitahomoseksual'nist."Supportyourart.com. Available at: https://supportyourart.com/words//babibadalov?fbclid=IwAR24e3-rhJw38-Z42f-aGtAHcs5KtTsba1qnhFiFNHYMk6wsjZBZyAGDNlk. Last accessed May 23, 2021.

Braidotti, Rosi. 2014. "Writing as a Nomadic Subject." *Comparative Critical Studies* 11 (2–3):163–184. Edinburgh: Edinburgh University Press.

Mazin, Viktor. 1989. "Napisanie grusti Babi." *Mitin zhurnal.* October. Available at: http://kolonna.mitin.com/archive/mj30/mazin.shtml.

Sputnik Azərbaycan. 2019. "Chto nado znat' o Babi Badalove, samom ekstsentrichnom khudozhnike Azerbaidzhana." Available at: https://az.sputniknews.ru/hero/20190401/419885145/Chto-nado-znat-o-Babi-Badalove-samom-ekstsentrichnom-khudozhnike-Azerbaydzhana.html.

Part Three

Beyond Queer Beauty? Contemporary Post-Soviet Perspectives on Queer(ing) Art, Art History, and Artists

Chapter 13

Architecture, Outer Space, Sex: The Kollontai Commune in 1970s Frunze[1]

Georgy Mamedov and Oksana Shatalova

Architecture, Outer Space, Sex: The Kollontai Commune in 1970s Frunze *by Georgy Mamedov and Oksana Shatalova is a conceptual artistic project that fuses fact and fiction. The authors construct the narrative of a queer commune that (might have or should have) existed in Frunze (now Bishkek in Kyrgyzstan) in the 1970s, mixing genuine archival documents with artifacts that might have been manufactured or creatively interpreted by the authors. In this semifictional narrative, real published works by such historical personalities as Russian revolutionary and Marxist theoretician Alexandra Kollontai (1872–1952), Frunze-based psycholinguist and philosopher Aron Brudnyi (1932–2011), and Soviet psychologist and sexologist Igor Kon (1928–2011), as well as historical facts related to life in Soviet-era Frunze are combined into a compelling yet dreamy narrative of a dissident culture in 1970s Frunze, where, among other things, there was room for sexual and gender experimentation.*

Mamedov and Shatalova creatively apply early Soviet revolutionary ideas of liberation of sexuality described in Alexandra Kollontai's writings and extend them to non-heteronormative sexuality and gender identity within the semi-fictional Frunze queer commune of the 1970s. A (probably) fictional historical voice that Mamedov and Shatalova cite in the narrative states: "Comrade Kollontai proclaims love-comradery between women and men, but can't there also be love-comradery between women and women or men and men?" Mamedov and Shatalova's project is a "retrofuturist" gesture, which proposes an alternative to the official narrative of Soviet History, a history in which the embrace of nonnormative gender and sexuality was not only possible but also naturally derived from early Soviet revolutionary statements on the liberation of sexual desire.

The Archive of the Bishkek Queer Commune

In the process of developing our project "Bishkek: The Chronicles of Radical Imagination," we obtained access to the extensive library of the Frunze-based psycholinguist and philosopher Aron Brudnyi (1932–2011). Stashed in one of the boxes hitherto unopened by Brudnyi's family was a stack of documentary evidence about the existence in 1970s Frunze of a community of dissidents who conceptualized sex and gender from a position that, in contemporary terms, is akin to social-constructivism. There is only one caveat: The author of these writings is probably not a group of people but a solitary dreamer who invented allies for himself, which does not change the overall picture—the text speaks for itself.

We have called our wonderful discovery "the archive of a Bishkek queer commune." As suggested by the publication facts on the printed material, the archive can be dated to around the first half of the 1970s. It includes:

1) A type-written nine-page text, labeled "report" and titled "Historical Materialism, Soviet Power and Questions of Gender in the Modern Era."
2) Eight postcards featuring views of Frunze, without stamps; scribbled on the back (in pencil, sometimes colored) are poetic critiques of the institution of the family and calls for liberation "from biological ties" and escape to outer space;
3) A modified Soviet propaganda poster with an image of Marx and Engels and a map of Russian social-democrat societies. This détournement (ink and application) by anonymous artists consists of a location label reading "Commune named after A. M. Kollontai" in "the city of Frunze" added to the map; a portrait of this female revolutionary in the office of Marx and Engels with the slogan "Give way to Cosmic Eros!" (a riff on Kollontai's Eros) ascribed to these pioneers;[2]
4) A single artifact unrelated to the problematics of gender—an architectural fantasy about a mountain city comprised of standardized, homogeneous buildings. The buildings are assembled at a remote plant and transported to the mountain location across the stratosphere by means of "house-transporting high-altitude balloons." Since this artifact was filed in the same stack as the above-mentioned documents, it makes sense to think of it as a product of the "Kollontai Commune." Also present in the sketch is the outer space theme, represented by the image of a comet heading for the North Star.

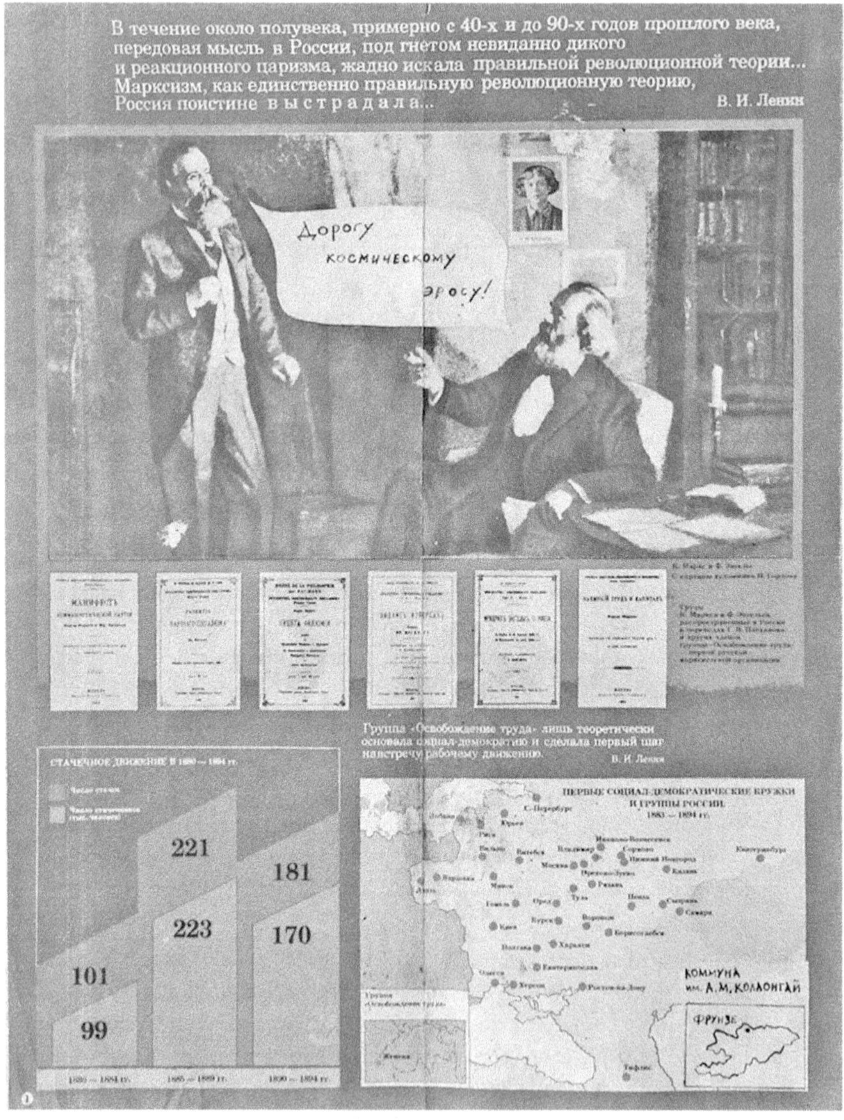
В течение около полувека, примерно с 40-х и до 90-х годов прошлого века, передовая мысль в России, под гнетом невиданно дикого и реакционного царизма, жадно искала правильной революционной теории... Марксизм, как единственно правильную революционную теорию, Россия поистине выстрадала...
В. И. Ленин
Дорогу космическому эросу!
Группа «Освобождение труда» лишь теоретически основала социал-демократию и сделала первый шаг навстречу рабочему движению.
В. И. Ленин
221
181
223
170
101
99
ПЕРВЫЕ СОЦИАЛ-ДЕМОКРАТИЧЕСКИЕ КРУЖКИ И ГРУППЫ РОССИИ
С.-Петербург
Москва
Тула
Рязань
Нижний Новгород
Казань
Самара
КОММУНА им. А. М. КОЛЛОНТАЙ
ФРУНЗЕ

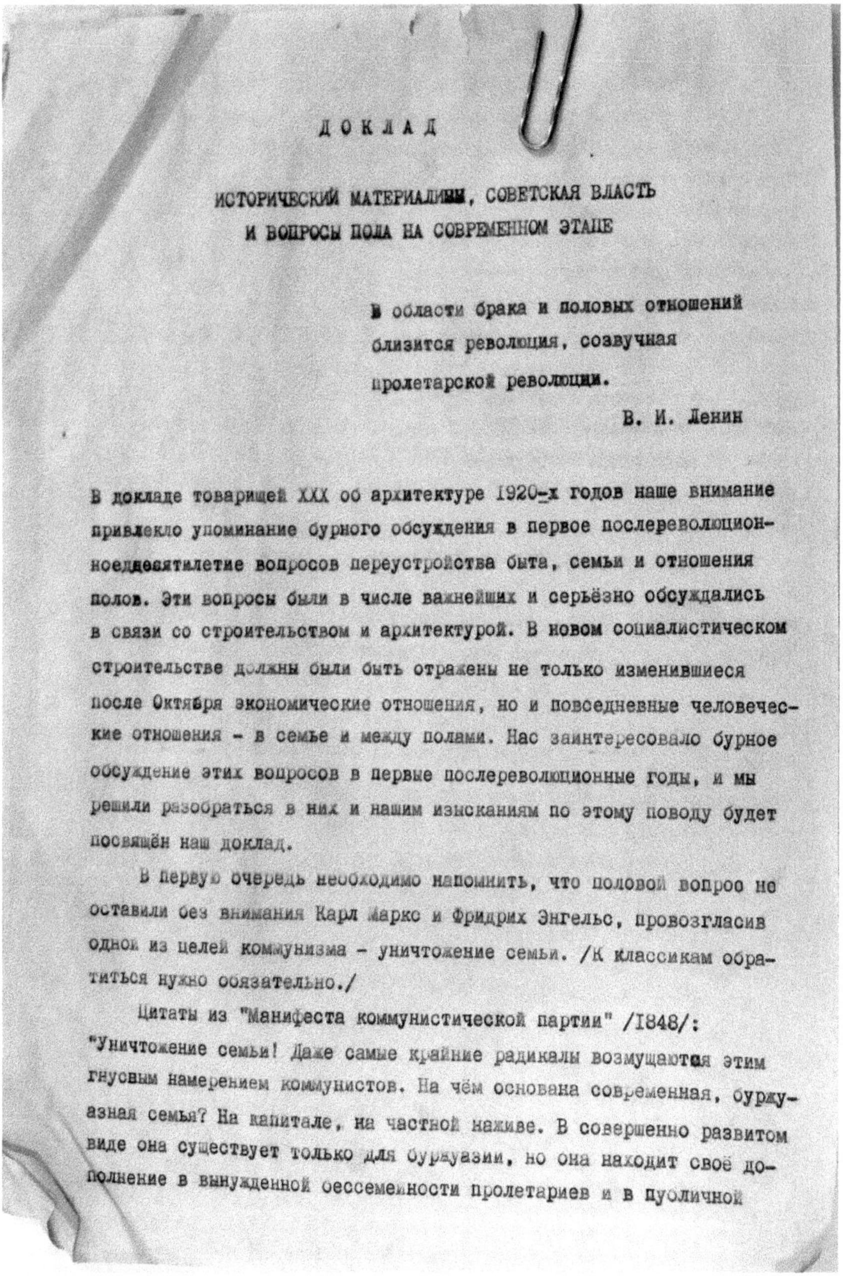

ДОКЛАД

ИСТОРИЧЕСКИЙ МАТЕРИАЛИЗМ, СОВЕТСКАЯ ВЛАСТЬ И ВОПРОСЫ ПОЛА НА СОВРЕМЕННОМ ЭТАПЕ

> В области брака и половых отношений близится революция, созвучная пролетарской революции.
>
> В. И. Ленин

В докладе товарищей XXX об архитектуре 1920-х годов наше внимание привлекло упоминание бурного обсуждения в первое послереволюционное десятилетие вопросов переустройства быта, семьи и отношения полов. Эти вопросы были в числе важнейших и серьёзно обсуждались в связи со строительством и архитектурой. В новом социалистическом строительстве должны были быть отражены не только изменившиеся после Октября экономические отношения, но и повседневные человеческие отношения - в семье и между полами. Нас заинтересовало бурное обсуждение этих вопросов в первые послереволюционные годы, и мы решили разобраться в них и нашим изысканиям по этому поводу будет посвящён наш доклад.

В первую очередь необходимо напомнить, что половой вопрос не оставили без внимания Карл Маркс и Фридрих Энгельс, провозгласив одной из целей коммунизма - уничтожение семьи. /К классикам обратиться нужно обязательно./

Цитаты из "Манифеста коммунистической партии" /1848/: "Уничтожение семьи! Даже самые крайние радикалы возмущаются этим гнусным намерением коммунистов. На чём основана современная, буржуазная семья? На капитале, на частной наживе. В совершенно развитом виде она существует только для буржуазии, но она находит своё дополнение в вынужденной бессемейности пролетариев и в публичной

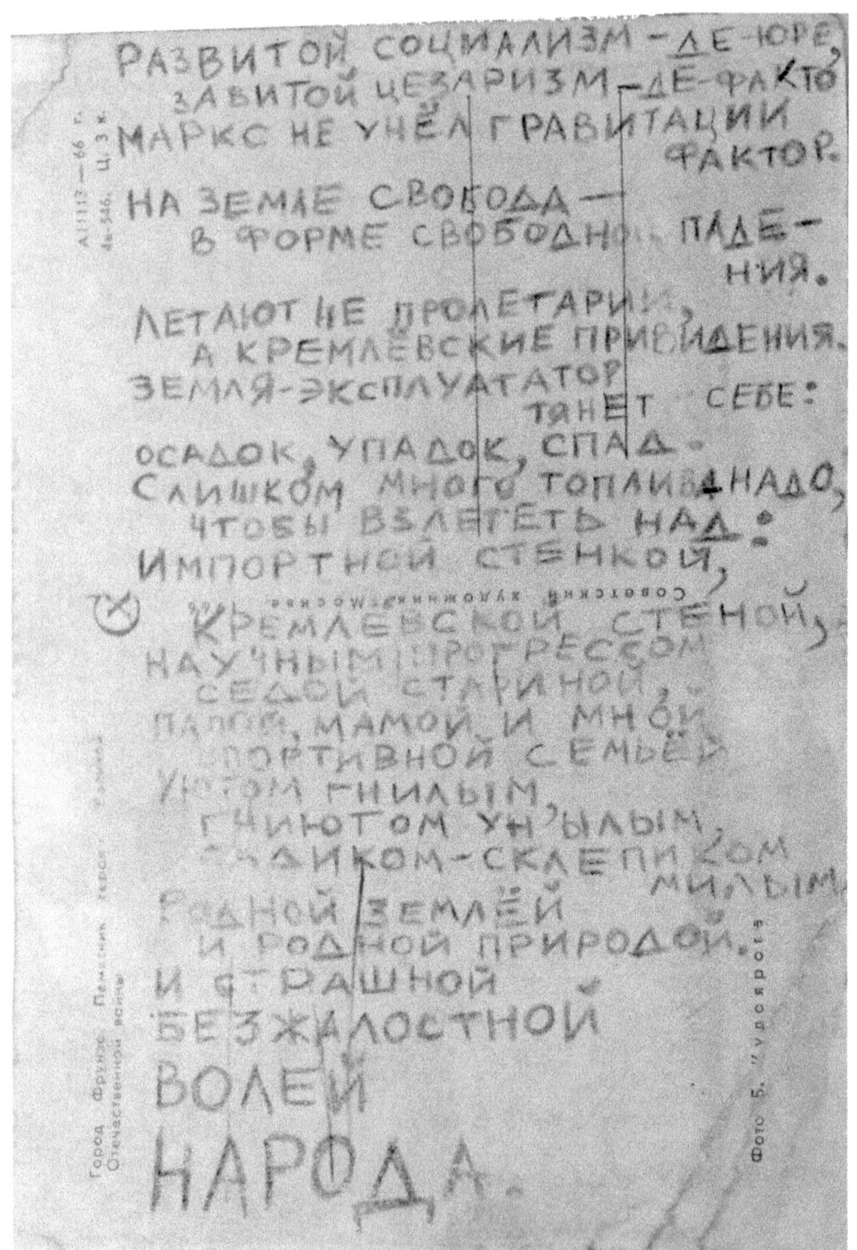
РАЗВИТОЙ СОЦИАЛИЗМ – ДЕ-ЮРЕ,
ЗАВИТОЙ ЦЕЗАРИЗМ – ДЕ-ФАКТО
МАРКС НЕ УЧЁЛ ГРАВИТАЦИИ
ФАКТОР.
НА ЗЕМЛЕ СВОБОДА –
В ФОРМЕ СВОБОДНОГО ПАДЕ-
НИЯ.
ЛЕТАЮТ НЕ ПРОЛЕТАРИИ,
А КРЕМЛЁВСКИЕ ПРИВИДЕНИЯ.
ЗЕМЛЯ-ЭКСПЛУАТАТОР
ТЯНЕТ СЕБЕ:
ОСАДОК, УПАДОК, СПАД.
СЛИШКОМ МНОГО ТОПЛИВА НАДО,
ЧТОБЫ ВЗЛЕТЕТЬ НАД:
ИМПОРТНОЙ СТЕНКОЙ,
КРЕМЛЁВСКОЙ СТЕНОЙ,
НАУЧНЫМ ПРОГРЕССОМ
СЕДОЙ СТАРИНОЙ,
ПАПОЙ, МАМОЙ И МНОЙ,
СПОРТИВНОЙ СЕМЬЁЙ
УЮТОМ ГНИЛЫМ,
ГНИЮТОМ УНЫЛЫМ,
САДИКОМ-СКЛЕПИКОМ
МИЛЫМ,
РОДНОЙ ЗЕМЛЁЙ
И РОДНОЙ ПРИРОДОЙ.
И СТРАШНОЙ
БЕЗЖАЛОСТНОЙ
ВОЛЕЙ
НАРОДА.

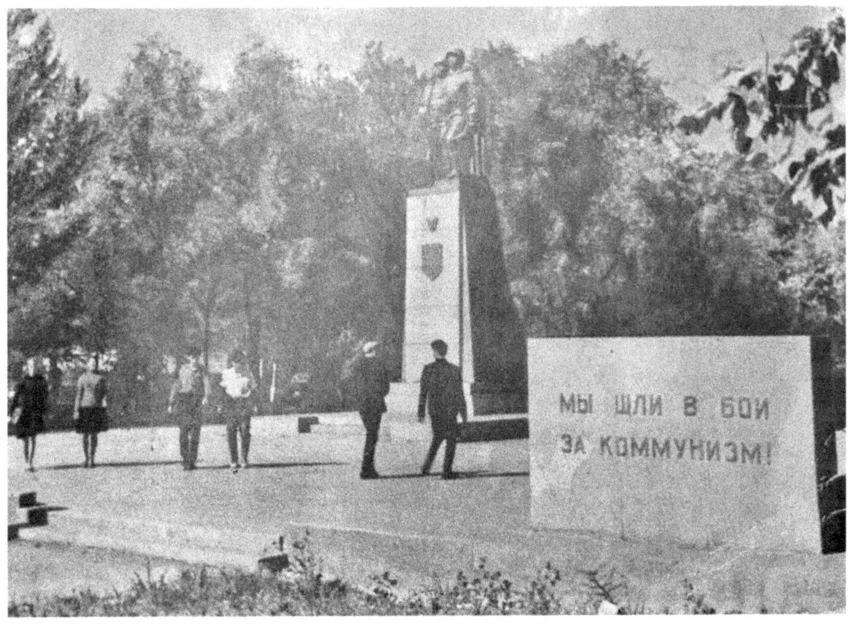

School of Theory and Activism—Bishkek (STAB), *Queer in Space: Kollontai Commune Archive* (2015), mixed media. Courtesy of STAB

All these artifacts, at first glance, can be diagnosed as symptoms of the "secret freedom" endemic to dissidents, that is, a quiet yet persistent resistance to the repressions perpetrated by the state. However, analyzing the specific components of this discursive cluster—architectural futurology, questions of sexuality, and the theme of outer space—allows us to project a more complex configuration of the dissident "machinery of desire," some of the mechanisms of which are hidden under the surface, others lie outside official prohibitions but remain in the shadows, while still others are openly promoted and regulated by the state. Considered through this lens, the dissidents' relationship to state power can be characterized not in terms of antagonism, but, rather, in terms of heresy or reimagining.

The Context of the Queer Commune: "Conceptual Engineering"

Let us begin with architecture, which served as legitimate ground for utopian inspirations and identifications in the USSR. What we are referring to here is "paper" rather than "real" architecture, a phenomenon in which the ambitions of utopian thought were consolidated in both the first and the second halves of the twentieth century. During the thaw-stagnation period, architectural games of the imagination migrated across scientific and popular publications as well as architectural and design competitions (Ryabushin 1976, 156–64; 337–53). The flying houses of the queer commune appear here not as a radical example but one that is, simply, contemporary. Typical of the 1960s and 1970s," the vogue for dynamism, lightness, and harnessed gravity was realized in hanging, "falling," restless metamorphic cities:

> Loktev imagines for the distant future an anti-gravitational architecture, cities or, as he calls them, city-planes to be located on Earth's artificial satellites (Ryabushin 1976, 160). When we have learned to command gravity, our dwellings will rise into the air as well. Houses will no longer be tethered to one place and will become much more mobile than the modern trailers used by tourists. They may move on land and sea, from one continent to another, from one climate zone to another; they will follow the sun and change their coordinates depending on the time of year . . . (Borisovskii 1977, 74)

If we compare this quote with Ivan Shcheglov's situationist "Formulary for a New Urbanism"—"the mobile transformer-house will turn to face the sun, its walls will slide open, allowing one to contemplate the nature surrounding it. Mounted on rails, it will descend to the seashore in the morning and return to the forest in the evening"—we can discern a complete alignment of the desire-images of the oppositional manifesto with the book published by Znanie in sixty thousand copies.

The authors defined such studies themselves as "conceptual engineering":

> projects of this kind are not meant to be actually built. Conceptual engineering is akin to . . . a miracle. Man releases himself from the ties that bind his creative initiative—brutal economic restrictions, normative prescriptions, traditional views on what is possible and impossible—and gains the freedom to search for new, original paths and ways out of modernity's multiple impasses. (Ryabushin 1976: 338–39)

In 1960s and 1970s Frunze, much of this activity took place at the Architecture department of the Frunze Polytechnic Institute, where Valentin Kurbatov was developing approaches to standardized construction on complex terrain. Situated at the foot of the Kyrgyz Ala-Too mountain range, the city of Frunze was expected, sooner or later, to extend into the mountains. Such projects, in a sense, had a pragmatic local orientation. But they also generated fantasies that were not restricted to specific locales and materials, that is, they exemplified "conceptual engineering" (see Kurbatov 1972, 143–51; Kurbatov 1978, 36–42). While this theme was central to a number of theses that were being defended and showcased at competitions during this period, no one anticipated their actual implementation. What is notable here is the utopian scale of their ambition: Conquering mountains as well as reversing the flow of rivers and taming gravity reflect the modernist ethos par excellence. This philosophy of life was methodically reproduced by the Soviet educational machine. Kurbatov's students would spend about ten years doing exercises in utopian variations and inventing monumental solutions, such as a bridge-like building stretching over a canyon and housing six thousand people. The architectural project of the "Kollontai Commune" develops the same kind of mountain fantasy, which suggests that its authors might have belonged to Kurbatov's milieu. They were also concerned with solving certain conceptual puzzles, such as the challenge of transportation across difficult terrain and the lack of level spaces in the mountains. The authors cut the Gordian knot of the transportation issue by deciding to move plant-assembled houses through the air and compensated for the shortage of level surfaces by exploiting flat roofs. The sketch demonstrates the breadth of man's capacity, as he casts a proprietary gaze over the world, scanning what is below the ground and what is high in the mountains, from the Earth's core to the Polar Star.

From the 1950s to the 1970s, such futuristic practices in Soviet architecture took place at the intersection of three multivalent factors: the architects' access to information, the spread of industrial construction, and the rehabilitation of the architectural avant-garde of the 1920s and 1930s. Regarding the first factor, Soviet architecture, unlike Soviet art, was not confined to an informational ghetto; it had access to the field of design of capitalist countries. Pertinent here are the memories of Shailoo Dzhekshenbaev, who studied with Kurbatov in the 1960s and 1970s. When asked about his professional orientation during that period, he said: "We were not interested in contemporary Soviet stuff." They were interested in Western stuff. The foreign literature section of the Gosstroi library subscribed to French, Italian, and Japanese architectural journals, which were made available to specialists. Fortunately, one did not need to know a foreign language to read the designs. Some of the journals were translated into Russian in Moscow and added to the library's collections as black and white copies.[3] This is where the second factor comes into play. The students of the 1960s and 1970s were "not interested in contemporary Soviet stuff" due to the altered role of architecture in industrial residential construction. Architecture ceased to be an "art" and became a science and a field of engineering. Residential neighborhood design was most in demand: Architects, squeezed into building standards, possessed creative freedom only at the level of the "game of squares," which involved moving tiny houses "freely" around the map; this was called "accountability to the situation."[4] The radical "unaccountability" of futurology, then, evidently served as a kind of compensation—it is worth noting that these compensatory activities took place openly, not in any kind of underground setting. And finally, regarding the third factor: The shift in the stylistic paradigm[5] led to the rehabilitation of the legacy of the 1920s and 1930s, with its interest in types and functionality as well as its radical break with the Earth. Architect Borisovskii demonstrates "the return" of the avant-garde as a symbolic passage when he describes the solemn act of taking out a stack of the Constructivist journal *Soviet Architecture* from the closet and filling that empty space with Renaissance architectural albums (Borisovskii 1977, 10).

The architectural avant-garde, in an effort to reclaim its authority as a political force, tried to give a new relevance to the topics of the "queer commune": everyday life, gender, and sexuality. In addition to the aesthetic of 1920s and 1930s, Soviet architecture of the 1950s acquired—and perhaps unwittingly activated—the rhetoric of "the collectivization of daily life" and "women's liberation from kitchen slavery," essential to avant-garde impropriety. Questions of gender were famously central to public discourse in the early years of the post-revolutionary period, involving the interrogation of such social institutions as marriage, the family, and child rearing. The architects and engineers of socialist life were active participants in these discussions. According to the logic of the most "leftist" participants, traditional divisions of family labor assume a corresponding spatial division: "The structure of the home (for instance, the partition of a home into rooms) stems from the division of labor inside the home" (Okhitovich 1929, 334). This logic entailed the elimination of the kitchen as an isolated space in the new communal homes.

The rehabilitation of the avant-garde in the 1950s made the socialization of "female" domestic labor the subject of renewed debates. Heir to the communal homes and housing complexes of the 1920s and 1930s, the "residential complexes" of the 1950s included expansive facilities for collective living (Ryabushin 1976, 150–56). That same Kurbatov, in his books, anticipates the future extinction of the kitchen, the development of housing "with completely socialized forms of daily living" (Kurbatov 1972, 151–57), and even the socialization of child rearing—children will spend most of their time in boarding schools, seeing their parents only "intermittently" (Kurbatov 1972, 144). However, such examples of lexical inertia or flashbacks to the 1920 and 1930s clashed with conservative gender politics. Reappraisals of the avant-garde were constantly provoking asides such as "the crude errors of the Constructivists." These errors referred to the ways in which the avant-gardists "destroyed the family" through their emphasis on its historicity and their efforts to force into being new forms of sociality. To prevent such "errors" from repeating themselves, the proponents of the "socialized living" program from the 1950s to the 1970s took care to protect the institution of the family. This is a clear point of radical rupture between the avant-garde of the 1920s and 1930s and its later reincarnation: Except for the first "decade of debate," all Soviet periods insisted on a gender-segregated family unit, with "biological sex differences" viewed as eternal and irrefutable. Thus, the task of liberating women from "kitchen slavery" from the 1950s to the 1970s was riddled with internal contradictions: It could not be accomplished under conditions of gender segregation. What followed logically was that the reorganization of daily life lost its high priority status. The 1970s saw a steady increase in such public statements as "a home dinner strengthens family ties" (Ryabushin 1976, 270). The "small-scale mechanization of the home economy" (Ryabushin 1976, 271) became the decade's goal (that is, not the socialization of daily life but, rather, the improvement of individual domestic technologies—the socialist "liberation of women" overlapped with the capitalist model as described by Betty Friedan). The increasing emphasis on family values ran parallel with the increasing valorization of "individuality."

Architecture likewise moved along these currents of intimacy: Engineers' interests shifted from housing complexes, with their standards of collectivization, to atomized "family units," putting every inch at the service of the desires of the "individual," which was gaining traction across a whole range of official discourses (Ryabushin 1976, 150–64).[6] This "individuality" was also fetishized in informal discourse. In the architectural community—particularly in the above-mentioned architectural department of FPI, to which we have relegated the queer commune—the tradition of samizdat continued into the 1980s. Yet, in later times, the reflections of architects who "began to think of themselves as artists" (*Moi Gorod* 1992) revolved around aesthetic and existential questions, the rhetoric of pure art and personal "uniqueness." Thus, in the 1980s, for instance, a group of students from the department was nearly expelled for publishing the student journal *Zebra* (the cause of the scandal was the inclusion in the journal of an autobiographical piece by Dali, who was deemed "anti-Soviet") (Guzairov 2008–09, 162–65). The issue displayed romantic images of airships and balloons, which closely resembled the "house-transporting high-altitude balloons" of the queer Kollontai commune. However, the airships were no longer tasked with solving conceptual problems of the future; they functioned as a vaguely decorative metaphor for artistic inspiration, a kind of distant echo of the outer space studies of the queer commune (as in the image titled "Dreams") (*Moi Gorod* 1992).

The Themes of the Queer Commune

1. "Soviet State Power and the Question of Sex"

While the issues of women's labor, public child rearing, and socialized practices of daily living reemerged, in various forms, as integral components of broad public discussions from the 1950s onward, questions of sex and sexuality were almost never discussed in Soviet public discourse from the 1930s to the mid-1980s. Leading Soviet and Russian sexologist Igor Kon appended the following comment to the online edition of his 1966 article "Sexual Morals in Light of Sociology," first published in the journal *Soviet Pedagogy*: "This article was the first serious Soviet publication on sexuality since the mid-1930s" (Kon, "Seksologiia"). Notably, while Kon attempts in this article to consider sexuality and romantic love from Marxist and Soviet perspectives, he makes statements consistent with social-constructivist methodologies (as in "There is nothing more naïve than the belief in 'natural norms' of sexual morality'') and contrasts the sexual revolution of the capitalist West with the high moral standards of (hetero)sexual relations in the USSR. Yet the central concern of the article is this: The leading role in sexuality research and education should be given to the complex and contradictory set of psycho-physical and socio-historical factors, not to moral norms and imperatives. This and other texts by Kon from the 1960s to the 1970s ("Seks, obshchestvo, kul'tura," 1970; "Psikhologiia iunosheskoi seksual'nosti," 1976) represent an attempt to critically revise the dogmatic and normative Soviet discourses on sexuality and gender relations from communist and Marxist perspectives. A similar yet more radical attempt appears among our discoveries. The typewritten text "Historical Materialism, Soviet Power, and Questions of Gender in the Modern Era" is prefaced with a quote from Lenin: "In the realm of marriage and sexual relations, a revolution, consonant with the proletariat revolution, is on the way." The "report" is a compilation of vivid quotes on gender and sexuality from a wide variety of Marxist texts, including "The Communist Manifesto," Clara Zetkin's memoirs, and texts by Kollontai. In citing these voices, the "report" aims to show that sexual emancipation and the communist project were inseparable and that this link was understood and articulated by the founders. Meanwhile, the reflections of Lenin and Kollontai receive their share of "comradely critique":

> Historical-materialist analysis of sexual relations at various stages in the development of relations of production—hereditary, feudal, capitalist—did not lead Comrade Kollontai to the logical conclusion that the loudly proclaimed exceptional nature of men's emotional and erotic attraction to women and of women's to men is ideologically determined. Comrade Kollontai proclaims love-comradery between women and men, but can't there also be love-comradery between women and women or men and men.

A paraphrase of Kollontai's title "Give Way to Winged Eros" becomes a slogan for the authors' or authoresses' of the archive and a kind of key to it. The "report" ends with an expressive, poeticized statement of their own "critical-utopian" program:

> Winged Eros is too weak to fight the gravity of the rotten family rotten dad and rotten children grandmagrandpaauntieuncle we need outer space speeds and outer space powers galactic-no-universal scales so we can overcome human gravity disengage fly away OUTERSPACE EROS OUTERSPACE EROS OUTERSPACE EROSSSSSSSSSSSSSSSSSSSSSSSSSSS

We do not know if the eight short poems written on the postcards with views of Frunze are meant to be a series. But if we let the theme of sexuality guide our reading, we find a certain logical sequence, which begins by questioning biological gender as determining a person's identity ("Why are people functions of physiology but not of consciousness?") and ends by proclaiming the complete rejection of not only gender but also the body. Freed from the physical body, the human being is transformed into an endless stream of particles and energy—"a wave" (CATCH THE WAVE/ALLBEING).

This poetic interrogation of and triumph over gender and the body is remarkably congruent with contemporary queer theory, allowing us to designate the authors of these materials as the "Bishkek queer commune." Queer theory not only assumes a historicizing approach to gender, biological sex, and sexuality, understanding these categories as social constructs, but it also, on the whole, deconstructs identity politics (including ethnic, national, and other forms of identity), exposing the power relations inextricably linked to such politics.

Our ability to reconstruct the profile of this "Frunze queer commune" is extremely limited. The archives may be the work of one person. Yet, by scrutinizing the available materials, we can develop a hypothetical timeline for the production of the texts in question. The poems on the postcards were most likely created later than the other artifacts. Denying the Soviet reality of "developed socialism" any possibility of transformation into an authentically communist project, these poems replace criticism with negation:

> Developed socialism - de jure
>   twisting Caesarism - de facto.
> Marx did not take into account the gravity factor.
> On Earth, freedom
>   is in the form of free fall.
> It's not the proletarians who fly,
>   but Kremlin ghosts.
> The Earth-exploiter attracts:
>   residue, decadence, decline.
> Too much fuel is necessary,
>   to fly over:
> imported wall units,
>   the Kremlin wall,
> Scientific progress,
>   a white-haired elder,
> Dad, Mom and me,
>   sports family,
> Rotten comfort, comfortable rot,
>   the sweet garden-crypt,
> The native land
>   and native nature.
> And the dreadful ruthless will of the nation.[7]

2. *"Space is a True Revolution"*

Utter disillusionment with Soviet socialism leads our "queer commune" onto a well-trodden path: appealing to outer space as a place to escape from depressing reality. This escape motif originates in the philosophy of Russian cosmism. The cosmists conceptualized the cosmos as a space devoid of all earthly restrictions, not just gravitational but also anthropological. Cosmos is the space of immortality. In Tsiolkovsky's theory of interplanetary travel, rockets heading to far-off galaxies carry the resurrected ancestors of living humankind. The 1920s saw the formation, within Russian anarchist circles, of biocosmism, a mystical-poetic movement that produced futuristic manifestos and poems. The biocosmic anarchists saw the migration of humanity into outer space and the acquisition of immortality as natural developments of the October Revolution. In their vision, the aircraft moving across space was the Earth. The task of exploring the universe belonged not to individuals but to all humanity, now freed not just from exploitation and cultural biases but also from space and time as such.

In the late 1950s, the Soviet party nomenclature completely broke with the expansionist ambitions of world revolution, establishing as a new priority "the satisfaction of the increasing material needs of the Soviet population." Space exploration was the only sphere in which aspirations to global ideological hegemony remained relevant. The 1920s avant-garde fantasy of communism as a universal project gets assimilated, in a certain perverse form, into the official ideology of the 1960s and 1970s. The radical social transformations that the revolution had promised but evidently failed to achieve "in one country" or on any given planet could be discussed in the context of science fiction and futurology, as these two fields turned into a virtually unrestricted springboard for the imagination (analogous to conceptual engineering in architecture). In the 1970s, *Tekhnika Molodezhi*, a journal for both specialist and lay audiences, devoted pages to reflections on the future of humanity in the universe, framing the futuristic fantasies of the biocosmic anarchists about immortality and humankind's rule over all types of energy as scientifically grounded extrapolations. In addition to that, such discussions predicted the destruction of the "Oedipal triangle":

> Nowadays (as odd as it may seem if you think about it) no one asks the most important of all questions: do we actually want to be born into this world so that we might live in it? This is a coercive gift that we all receive from our parents who are usually not burdened with specific prospects. Therefore, as of today, all three billion six hundred million inhabitants of this planet did not voluntarily choose to live the way of life they are supposed to live, to have the personality "endowed" to them, the social milieu, the specific opportunities we call talent, knowledge, vocation, destiny. After all, will it be within the social norms of the third millennium to entrust the decision to create a new person to only two people—the parents, no matter how highly developed intellectually and morally they

> might be? Without the participation of the one who is the most interested party! (Peev 1973, 43)

The cosmic theme undergoes a catastrophic inflation in the mid-1980s, as Kabakov's "little man" flies out of the communal hell of Soviet culture into outer space (installation titled "Man Who Flew into Space from His Room," 1986). His "characters of the totalitarian world" do not dream of immortality in a fathomless universe. For these people, weary of Soviet reality, such flight—in any direction whatsoever, into space or into a picture—is the greatest accomplishment, and disappearance is equated with liberation. The dream dreamt by Kollontai's disciples from Frunze, however, while not without the escapist desperation of Kabakov's Kamarovs and Gavrilovs, is more akin to the universal ambitions of the biocosmists and Soviet science fiction writers and futurologists. Outer space maintains the hope of a "true revolution," even if it is not social and only accomplished through the transformation of matter:

> Space is the true revolution.
> In space there are no ruling classes.
> In space there are only working masses,
> But no unproductive weight.
> The masses are weightless.
> Without bodies.
> Free from breathing and metabolism.
> Proletariat, nature is the last frontier!
> Communism is Soviet power plus the desomatization of bodies.
> The anatomical theater of the Earth is forgotten.
> Give a new life!
> Vacuum-like.

The relationship between the queer dissidents in Frunze and Soviet reality appears to have been a complex set of interactions and intersections, which included loyalty and agreement, as well as critique, opposition, disillusionment, and protest. This ambiguity may help explain why these artifacts have been neglected for all this time —they cannot be deciphered with a common binary code: totalitarian state/free individual, official/unofficial culture, us/them. When applied to a number of Soviet phenomena and processes, such as, for example, conceptual art, the explanatory capacity of these oppositions is not usually questioned. However, Alexei Yurchak (citing sociolinguist Patrick Sériot's research) notes that if we compare perestroika and post-Soviet memories and statements about the Soviet past with the documents that were created during the Soviet era, we find that the sense of the Soviet language being split into 'their language' (the language of state power, totalitarian language) and 'our language' (the language of ordinary citizens, free language) did not exist during the Soviet period but "is a retrospective late- or post-perestroika construction (Yurchak 2005, 7). Thus, late Soviet critiques of the architectural avant-garde, speaking in the name of humanism, used the same rhetorical figures that liberal critics employed during perestroika and do to this day in denouncing "vulgarity," "the suppression of individuality," and "the neglect of the individual" (Ryabushin 1976, 137–40; Borisovskii 1977, 14–15). As paradoxical as it sounds, considered through these lenses, conceptual artists with their Akaky Akakievich modalities appear much closer to the discourse of state power than the seemingly anachronistic Frunze queer commune, whose members critiqued the "infinitesimal individual" and the "family as a social unit" and proposed the concept of "allbeing," which transcended the boundaries of the individual.

The coupling of queer and communist ideas, as in the case of the Kollontai commune, was rare but far from unique within the late Soviet dissident environment. In *Homosexual Desire in Revolutionary Russia,* Dan Healey cites a portion of a transcribed audio message that a member of the Leningrad human rights group "Gay laboratory" sent to the International Gay Association in 1984. According to Kon, the Gay Laboratory consisted of about thirty young men and women who were in touch with foreign LGBT organizations and worked in AIDS prevention. Yet before long, the activities of this informal gay and lesbian human rights group attracted the attention of the KGB and, soon after, the Gay Laboratory ceased to exist and many of its members had to emigrate (Kon 1997, 367). Meanwhile, in his audio message, the anonymous activist identifies himself as a member of the Communist Party and denounces his country's homophobic policy as destructive because it "undermines the international prestige of the Soviet Union and compromises the ideals of socialism and communism" (Healey 2001, 350). In his opinion, Soviet "anti-gay" policies are in no way connected to communist ideology and the views of the Soviet majority; they are championed by "corrupt bureaucrats and their servants who have nothing to do with socialism and communism." He points out, however, that the influence of these corrupt forces is fast becoming a thing of the past. His express hope is that the lives of gays and lesbians will soon be characterized not by deprivation and persecution but by "passion, solidarity, and knowledge" (Healey 2001, 350).

Translated by Aleksei Grinenko with Adrienn Hruska

Notes

1 This essay was first published in Russian in the journal *Translit*, Issue 15–16, 163–170, 2014.

2 One of Kollontai's famous texts is called "Give Way to Winged Eros!" (1923).

3 Shailoo Dzhekshenbaev, interviewed by STAB (School of Theory and Activism - Bishkek), November 2014.

4 From the same interview with Dzhekhshenbaev.

5 The shift from the Stalinist Empire style to Khrushchev's functionalist aesthetics is traditionally traced to November 4, 1955, when the Central Committee of the Communist Party and the Council of Ministers issued a decree "on the elimination of excesses in engineering and building."

6 On Soviet discursive humanism, see also A. Bikbov 2014.

7 The two poems in this text were translated by Adrienn Hruska.

References

Bikbov, Aleksandr. 2014. "Burzhuaznaia lichnost' v gosudarstve 'zrelogo sotsializma.'" In *Grammatika poriadka: Istoricheskaia sotsiologiia poniatii, kotorye meniaiut nashu real'nost'*, 195–237. Moscow: Izdatel'skii dom Vysshei Shkoly Ekonomiki.

Borisovskii, Georgii. 1977. *Arkhitektura, ustremlennaia v budushchee*. Moscow: Znanie.

Guzairov, El'dar. 2008–2009. "Avtorizirovannaia istoriia zhurnala 'Zebra,' izdannogo na arhitekturnom fakul'tete v 1984 godu." *Kurak* 3: 162–65.

Healey, Dan. 2001. *Homosexual Desire in Revolutionary Russia: The Regulation of Sexual and Gender Dissent*. Chicago: University of Chicago Press.

Kon, Igor' Semenovich. 1997. *Klubnichka na berezke: Seksual'naia kultura Rossii*. Moscow: OGI.

———. "Sexologiia." Available at: http://sexology.narod.ru/publ034.html.

Kurbatov, Valentin. 1972. *Arkhitektura gorodskogo zhilishcha: Uchebnoe posobie*. Frunze: FPI.

———. 1978. "Arkhitekturnaia shkola Kirgizii." *Arhitektura SSSR* 10: 36–42.

Okhitovich, Mikhail. 1929. *Sotsialisticheskii sposob rasseleniia i sotsialisticheskii tip zhil'ia. Vestnik kommunisticheskoi akademii* 35/36: 334–38.

"Predchuvstvie arkhitektury." 1992. *Moi Gorod* (June 10): 5.

Peev, Dimitr. 1973. "Tret'ie tysiacheletie (okonchanie)." *Tekhnika molodezhi* 5: 43.

Ryabushin, Aleksandr. 1976. *Razvitie zhiloi sredy: Problemy, zakonomernosti, tendentsii*. Moscow: Stroiizdat: 156–64, 337–53.

Yurchak, Alexei. 2005. *Everything Was Forever, Until It Was No More: The Last Soviet Generation*. Princeton, NJ: Princeton University Press.

Chapter 14

Soviet Union, July 1991

Yevgeniy Fiks

Soviet Union, July 1991 *is a script for a conceptual performance art piece based on the video documentation of a conference organized by the International Gay & Lesbian Human Rights Commission in cooperation with late Soviet gay and lesbian activists in Moscow and Leningrad in the summer of 1991.*

In July 1991, a group of over seventy Western gay rights activists, most of whom came from the US, arrived in Moscow and Leningrad for the second gay and lesbian conference in the history of the Soviet Union (the first one was held in Tallinn, Estonia a year earlier). Among the activists was the 79-year-old Harry Hay, who left the US Communist Party in the 1950s to found the Mattachine Society, one of the first gay and lesbian rights groups in the US. The conference coincided with President George Bush's summit with Mikhail Gorbachev in Moscow just a few months before the fall of the Soviet Union. Article 121 of Soviet Criminal Code, which criminalized male homosexuality for up to five years in prison, was still the law at this time. This conference was branded the "Russian Stonewall" and the "July Revolution."

Soviet Union, July 1991 *is a collage about the final days of the Soviet Union, the dawn of gay activism in late Soviet space, and the historical (dis)junctions between Communism and gay rights. The world of Moscow and Leningrad of July 1991, including its gay and lesbian world, presents a dreamy utopia of openness and endless possibilities. It includes peaceful gay rights protests in front of the Bolshoi Theater and the State Duma in Moscow for the repeal of Article 121 and speeches by then-Soviet politicians to a gay and lesbian audience.* Soviet Union, July 1991, *testifies to the hope the LGBT community nurtured that it would become a represented class in the imagined future of Russia.* Soviet Union, July 1991 *captures this uncertain yet truly revolutionary moment of liberation, which seems to be completely lost now, thirty years later.*

At the same time, as much as this piece is a snapshot of the late Soviet gay and lesbian community, it is also a portrait of the American gay and lesbian activist milieu circa 1991. Soviet Union, July 1991 *does not shy away from acknowledging the normalized class and racial divides among the American gay and lesbian activists as well as, unfortunately, signs of American imperialist attitudes that the well-meaning American activists cannot help but display.*

SETS, PROPS, AND COSTUMES:

Georgiy Pobedonosets t-shirt
Marx monument in drag
Currency exchange rate
Luggage with "condoms box," sign "Pribytie" at the train station
Cruiser Aurora
Bolshoi Theater *pleshka*
Yuri Dolgorukiy monument
Prison
American AIDS quilt
Self-defense whistles

CAST:

HARRY HAY, FOUNDER OF THE AMERICAN GAY AND LESBIAN MOVEMENT
AMERICAN LIBERAL GAY
AMERICAN LEFTY GAY
RADICAL RUSSIAN GAY
MODERATE SOVIET GOLUBOI
ENGLISH-RUSSIAN INTERPRETER
SIGN LANGUAGE INTERPRETER
AN EVERYDAY RUSSIAN
CONTEMPORARY RUSSIAN LGBTQ ACTIVISTS

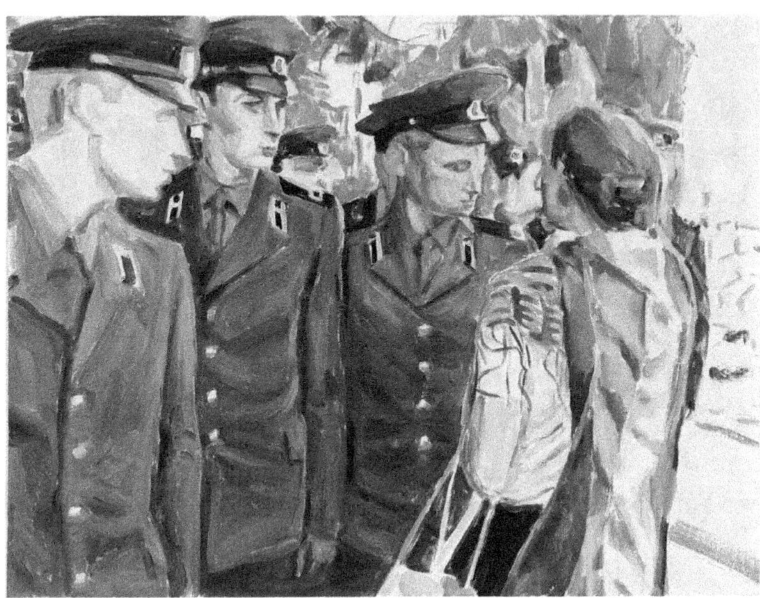

Yevgeniy Fiks, *Soviet Union, July 1991 (Retroactive Sketching toward the "Russian Stonewall") #2* (1991–2021). Courtesy of the artist

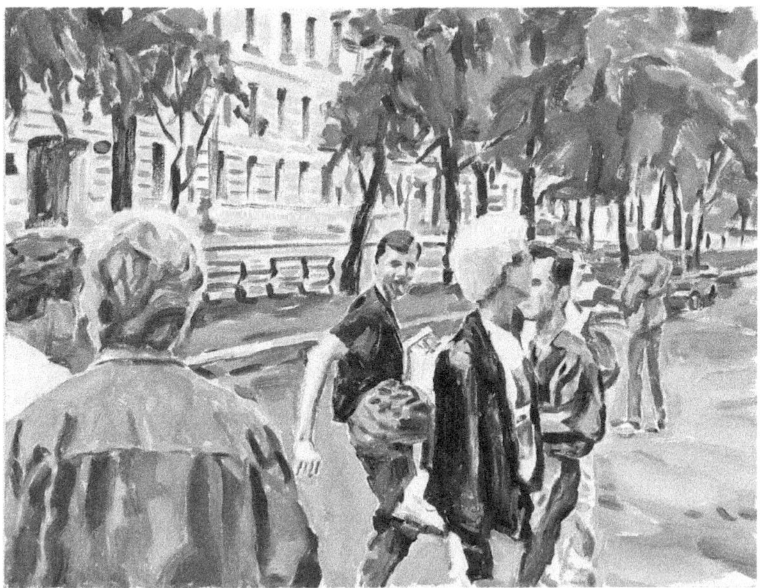

Yevgeniy Fiks, *Soviet Union, July 1991 (Retroactive Sketching toward the "Russian Stonewall") #38* (1991–2021). Courtesy of the artist

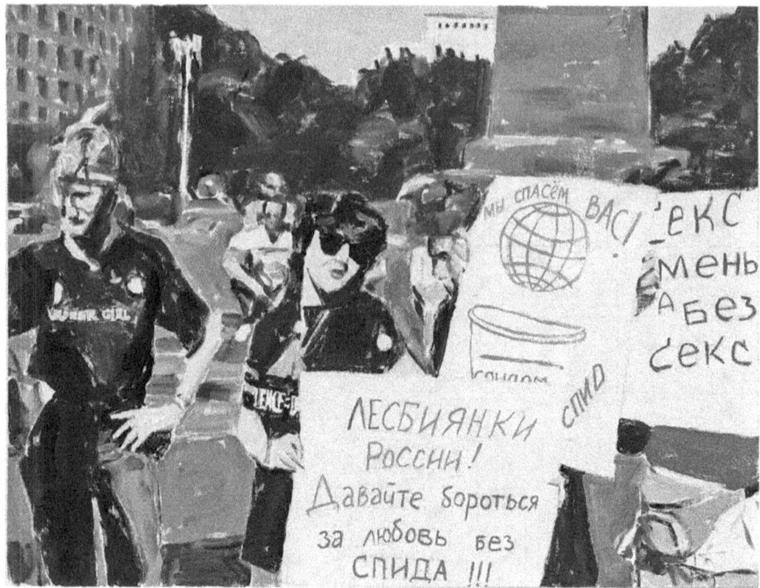

Yevgeniy Fiks, *Soviet Union, July 1991 (Retroactive Sketching toward the "Russian Stonewall") #27* (1991–2021). Courtesy of the artist

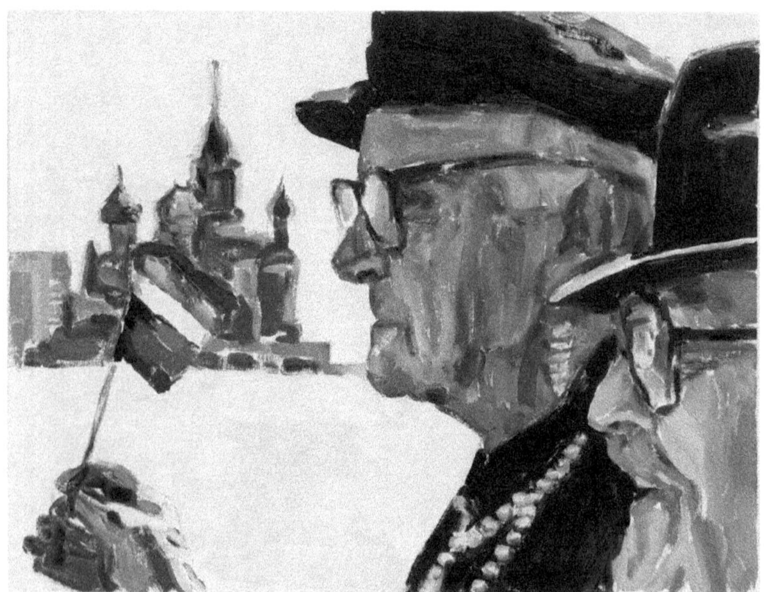

Yevgeniy Fiks, *Soviet Union, July 1991 (Retroactive Sketching toward the "Russian Stonewall") #44* (1991–2021). Courtesy of the artist

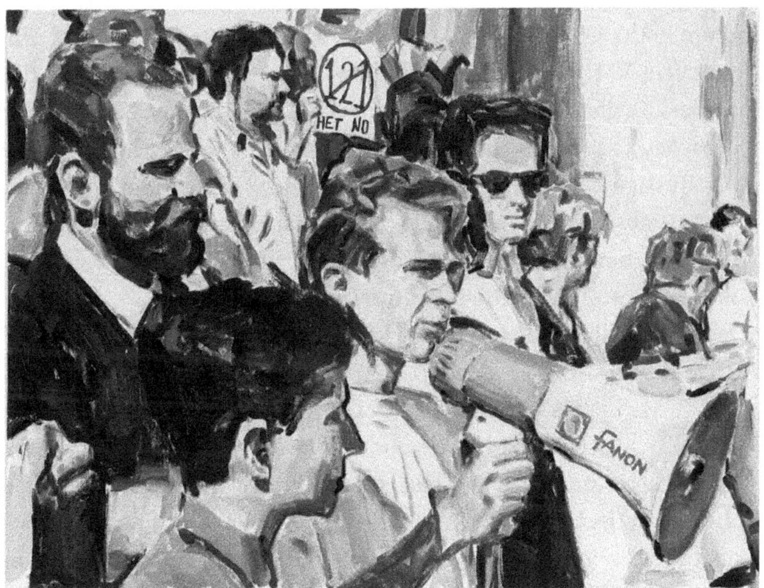

Yevgeniy Fiks, *Soviet Union, July 1991 (Retroactive Sketching toward the "Russian Stonewall") #34,* (1991–2021). Courtesy of the artist

Repeal Article 121 . . . and Privatize!

1991 American Liberal Gay: I'm Tom. I'm not filming this video for sale. It's just for me and history. I'm a historian. A queer historian. A gay historian. I'm here to record history. We are here to write history and to record history so that people two hundred years from now will know what it meant to be a gay person in the late twentieth century on planet Earth. But I'm also filming Russian boys' butts. Oh, documenting history is rough! We didn't come here as tourists—we came as emissaries. We are going to show Russian gays who we American gays are and what we are. We are American imperialists and exceptionalists, and we are not ashamed. There is gay activism now even in Africa and in Liberia. I'm telling you this so that you understand how global our struggle is. Every time a gay or a lesbian suffers, we all suffer. While President Bush is signing a treaty with General Secretary Gorbachev, we are signing a treaty with Russian Gays and Lesbians. Repeal Article 121!

1991 American Lefty Gay (in a Georgiy Pobedonosets t-shirt): I met with the first openly Soviet gay person, Roman Kalinin, who is with us here now, in 1990 while I was organizing a press-conference for him in the US. Also, with us now is Arkadiy, a Russian political prisoner under Article 121, who was only recently released from prison, and the pioneer of American gay activism comrade Harry Hay. (Applause). We are here during Gorbachev's meetings with Bush. But does Gorbachev need the gay problem? Does Russia need more problems? Don't they have enough problems already? The Russians are very poor. A typical Russian earns twenty dollars a month. My fellow countrymen, don't show your wealth here, don't flash one-hundred-dollar bills around in front of Russians. Don't be ugly Americans. (On the screen/props show the exchange rate of rubles to dollars for July 1991). Repeal Article 121!

1991 American Liberal Gay: I love that taxis are so cheap here. And you can use your credit card in any store that accepts dollars. In the 1960s when our movement started, it was a time of great upheavals in the US. You Russians are experiencing the same thing now. You have a historical opportunity now. We had Stonewall. Maybe the same thing is happening here in Leningrad today. Repeal Article 121!

1991 Russian Radical Gay: Yes, we will have more success here because we have a theoretical basis in Marxism and national/ethnic minorities discourse. We must make a new Revolution in Leningrad to win our peoples' rights. We Russians are in a better position now than you Americans were in the 1960s. Because now we can ask you for help, but you didn't have anybody to ask for help when you had the Stonewall rebellion. And I think this process in our country will develop much quicker than it did in your country. Repeal Article 121!

1991 American Liberal Gay: What about sexual behavior in Russia—I see two construction workers hugging on the street all the time, all of them do—are they openly gay or is this a country of fearless idiots who haven't gotten the homophobia memo yet? And what about gay basher thugs? And is there a way to tell if some guy is sexually interested in you without being misled? Also, I noticed that average Russians don't react badly at all to pink triangle signs and rainbow flags—is this because they simply don't know what it is or because they are so open minded? Repeal Article 121!

1991 American Lefty Gay: This country and economy is in chaos. We Americans are easy targets here. I'm more concerned about economic crime such as mugging than I am about gay bashing. Also, stop exoticizing Russian gays, you're not here for sex tourism. Be on your best behavior.

You're supposed to represent the best of America here, the best of gay America. Also, don't drink water from the faucet directly, boil it first. Repeal Article 121!

1991 AMERICAN LIBERAL GAY: Also, they say that there are US and Soviet government representatives among us here, undercover—from the CIA, KGB—there are informants among us, I'm sure. So be mindful of that. Repeal Article 121!

1991 AMERICAN LEFTY GAY: Signs are different here. If someone stares at you it doesn't mean you're being cruised. The American sexual/gender norms aren't applicable here. There is no such thing as gay and lesbian identity, no one in the whole country except for Roman Kalinin self-identifies publicly as gay, and this is already 1991. Don't look down on Russian gays who are all in the closet. Those of us who are out in the US risk our lives every day. For Soviets it's one hundred times more dangerous. We have no right to say to them what to do and how to live their lives. How Soviet gays will construct their identity is only for them to know. There are things that are culturally appropriate and things that are culturally inappropriate. When in Rome, do as the Romans do. Russians will invite you home for dinner and will spend their last penny on food and drinks. Force yourself to eat if you're at someone's home, even if you aren't hungry. They'll be offended if you don't. It would be considered rude if you didn't eat at someone's home when they offered you food. Let's be culturally sensitive and still do the Gay thing. When you're in Roman Kalinin's city, Moscow, do as Roman does, so to say, ha ha! Repeal Article 121!

1991 HARRY HAY: But there are things that are right and there are things that are wrong. Are gays in Russia more tolerant? Is there racism and anti-Semitism among Russian gays? Repeal Article 121! And workers of the world, unite!

1991 AMERICAN LEFTY GAY: Russian gays still don't see similarity in forms of oppression; only the most sophisticated ones do. If you hear racism and antisemitism, stop it. If you hear homophobia, stop it. Solidarity of the oppressed! Repeal Article 121!

1991 2015 MODERATE RUSSIAN GOLUBOI: We should accept the traditional values of Russia, but we must repeal Article 121 and the Gay Propaganda law!

1991 AMERICAN LEFTY GAY: Why do we tell Russian activists that capitalism is the answer? (Quick slide show of images or logos of all gay companies/bars/clubs/magazines that opened in Russia post-1991). This is American imperialism pure and simple, taking advantage of the impoverished segment of our community here in Russia. We are different. We American gay and lesbian activists are different even among ourselves. Some are left wing; some are right wing. We are scared for Russians after we leave, but social change doesn't happen without risks. I don't think it's that dangerous to be gay here. We can't be responsible for what happens here after we leave. We are guests here at a critical juncture in the life of this country. Let's not be patronizing Americans and tell Russians what they should do—if they want to come out, fine, if not, that's fine too–we must support their decision. If you see Capitalism approaching to mug you, blow this whistle! (Everyone blows the self-defense whistle). Repeal Article 121!

1991 **2015** AMERICAN LIBERAL GAY: Yes, we are agents of American imperialism, but we still share a common struggle with the Russians! But we American have the right to talk about our problems and struggles, nevertheless. Politics is something very stigmatized in Russia now, associated with the Communist regime. People resist political organizing. People are not interested in demonstrating and creating a political agenda. Even Soviet homosexual*ists* in high positions are against gay liberation. Russia is a backward country. What's happening to Russian gays now and what people say about gays is the same as in the US before the 1950s—that's what my mother would have thought and said in the 1950s. There's about a forty-year gap. The issue is a developmental delay in Russia. Repeal Article 121! Repeal the Gay Propaganda law!

1991 PEOPLE'S DEPUTY OF LENINGRAD SOVIET (in the uniform of a Soviet Komsomol apparatchik): I'm a Peoples' Deputy of the Lensoviet. I'm not the only one representing the Leningrad Soviet here—there are other representatives of the Lensoviet in this very hall. The new democratic government representatives of the new Russia support gay and lesbian rights. That is why I'm here. This is not a utopia—this is the New Russia. Repeal Article 121!

1991 **2015** RADICAL RUSSIAN GAY: Ladies and Gentlemen, and those comrades who may have ended up here by accident! Our country has only recently extracted itself from the stinking swamp of dictatorship. Seventy years ago, communist dictators illegally seized power in our country and continue to hold it without elections. The blood of heterosexuals and homosexuals are on the hands of the communists. These Americans came here to help us. They're the mothers and fathers of the Russian gay movement. The plight of Russian gays and lesbians is akin to the plight of Russia's ethnic minorities. Give the right of self-expression to the ethnic and sexual minorities of the New Russia! Also, we must make money because if you don't have money you don't have power. (Quick slide show of images or logos of all gay companies/bars/clubs/magazines/businesses that opened in Russia post-1991). We have communist and pro-democratic movements in our country. Gay men and lesbians must find their place in that world. Even communist politicians begin to flirt with us. You Americans have infected us with a desire to be free. People remember the October Revolution. We will remember our July Revolution. Our message to Mikhail Gorbachev "Repeal article 121 now!" Our message to Vladimir Putin! "Repeal the Gay Propaganda law now!"

1991 Moderate Soviet Goluboi: Thanks to forward-thinking Soviet lawyers, scientists, artists, and our friends from abroad, there is already a plan in place in the government to repeal Article 121 in the Soviet Union. It's not publicly announced yet, but it's going to happen, and it's going to happen soon. It's going to happen because of them, not because of us Soviet gays. Sadly, we Soviet gays weren't instrumental in that process; our fate is not being decided by us. The tradition of Soviet gays that goes back as far as 1933 is simple—all we want is to meet other gays quietly and not to attract too much attention, and if caught, not to go to prison. That's our tradition. That's why I'm categorically against Roman Kalinin's slogan "Let's turn Red Square into a Pink Tringle." Red Square is not a communist symbol, it's not a symbol of repression against gays or the Soviet people in general. Red Square is the symbol of Russia, of our great history. Let's not weaponize Gay Rights as an instrument of Russophobia. That's why I'm speaking here categorically against a gay rights demonstration in Red Square. What's helpful in California is not necessarily helpful in Moscow or Teheran. What we moderate Soviet *golubye* are asking for now is a moratorium on the application of Article 121 until the adoption of the new Criminal Code of the New Russia! And we ask the State to grant immediate amnesty to all those convicted and currently incarcerated under Article 121! There is a criminal case for sodomy that is being decided twenty minutes away from here, as we speak! A moratorium on Article 121 now!

2015 2015 Russian Gay Activist: (A contemporary Russian LGBTQ activist makes a five-minute statement about the current situation under the Gay Propaganda Law of 2013.)

HIV/AIDS in Russia

1991 American Lefty Gay: I'm an American. My grandparents came to America from Russia because of the pogroms. If my grandparents had not left Russia, I would not be alive now. I'm an HIV positive American now. I choose to tell you here in Moscow that I'm HIV positive because I feel freer to come out as HIV positive here as opposed to back home in the US, where it is still a taboo. I feel freer in Leningrad and Moscow. I'm also very disappointed that many of my fellow American gay activists present here, including HIV positive ones, are having unprotected sex with Soviets, without revealing their status to their Russian partners. Shame on you, you are here not for sex tourism.

2015 2015 Russian Gay Activist: (A representative of the Russian AIDS awareness organization makes a statement for five minutes.)

History

1991 American Lefty Gay: This is Harry Hay, the founder of the gay movement in the Soviet Union. Oh, I'm sorry I meant in the United States! (Freudian slip)

1991 Harry Hay: First of all, let me say that I'm hopelessly sad when I look at this workers' state and realize what a shoddy piece of work it is. It's not a workers' paradise. It's even less a gays' paradise. I'm just shocked at what I see and shocked to think of people having to live in such an intellectual and mental shambles for seventy years. However, the gay movement in the US came from the Left and from the working class because the middle class and the upper classes haven't created or discovered anything. I was a Marxist teacher in Los Angeles and a member of the American Communist Party in the 1940s. One day I had a revelation that American gays are a repressed minority culture, just like African Americans or Jews. That's how the gay movement was born in the US. We gays now must be careful when we align ourselves with any political parties because parties have always sold-out gays when they no longer need our support. Also, traditional Marxists weren't interested in private lives, only in production, but this is changing now. My statement on gay and lesbian rights today is simple: "From each according to their ability, to each according to their needs."

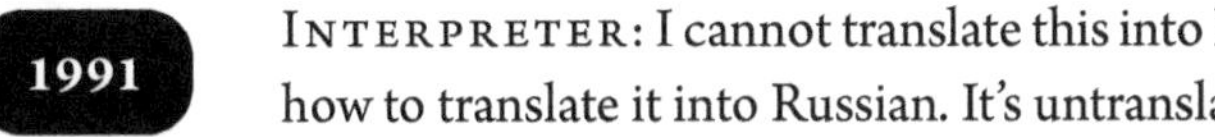

1991 INTERPRETER: I cannot translate this into Russian. I don't know how to translate it into Russian. It's untranslatable.

1991 HARRY HAY. What do you mean? I don't understand why it's so difficult to translate this—it comes from your Soviet books—it was a direct translation into English!

Prison, Yury Dolgoruky, and the Bolshoi Theater

1991 EVERYDAY RUSSIAN: This conference is "A Feast in a Time of Plague" for you Americans. This is exotic for you. Eto khoroshaia ekzotika.

1991 AMERICAN LIBERAL GAY: Where should we have a demonstration in the city? In front of the City Council or Red Square or in front of the Bolshoi where gays cruise to reclaim the space? Should we do it openly or clandestinely?

1991 RADICAL RUSSIAN GAY: Let's dress the Karl Marx monument on Revolution Square in drag!

1991 MODERATE SOVIET GOLUBOI: I'm not comfortable with that. I think it's too offensive. It's culturally inappropriate. When in Rome, do as the Romans do.

1991 2015 AMERICAN LEFTY GAY: Maybe there's no homophobia here yet, but Russian gays are in prison already for being gay. This is a Soviet prison. I'm about to see gays and lesbians. Here's the building where the gays are kept. Article 121. Sexual deviation. The first floor of this building. We are here to tell President Mikhail Gorbachev (and Vladimir Putin) today. We take our message to Presidents Gorbachev and Putin: Repeal Article 121, Repeal the "Gay Propaganda law." Ten percent of Russian children will be gay and lesbian, and they are NOT going to live under Article 121 or the Gay Propaganda law.

(Live statements by the participants from 1991 should be integrated throughout the text of the performance. Transforming the performance into an actual trans-temporary trans-generational queer party.)

Chapter 15

LGBT Violence and the Limits of Realism: Polina Zaslavskaya's *Material Evidence*

Viktoria Smirnova-Maizel

Viktoria Smirnova-Maizel's text is based on an interview with the artist Polina Zaslavskaya about the artist's 2017 watercolor series Material Evidence, *on the occasion of her exhibition at DK Rose Gallery in St. Petersburg, Russia in 2018.* Material Evidence *was initially commissioned to accompany the sociologist Alexander Kondakov's project documenting cases of violent crimes committed against Russian LGBTQ+ individuals over the last decade. This collaboration between a scholar and an artist led to the creation of a conceptual queer-themed art project.*

Zaslavskaya's project questions what it means to be a "queer artist" and what constitutes "queer art." Zaslavskaya's watercolor paintings appear as "straight" as the court cases from which they derive. Material Evidence *questions the expectation of queer "form and content" that has emerged in mainstream queer art over the last few decades. In* Material Evidence, *Zaslavskaya's Russian queer art appears "identity-less"—it does not go beyond quiet documentation of the material evidence of the persistence of Russian homophobia, and yet, in its subdued visual language and empathic ethics, it connects to a long tradition of Russian critical and social realism.*

"Art should not frighten us when everything else does."

—*Material Evidence* by Polina Zaslavskaya[1]

An exhibition of Polina Zaslavskaya's watercolors called *Material Evidence,* (figs. 1-4) which opened in Rosa's House of Culture, is a series of illustrations based on investigations into the murders of members of the LGBT community. It is a joint project between Zaslavskaya and the St. Petersburg-based sociologist Alexander Kondakov. On whitewashed walls hang paintings of bottles, pieces of string, and other various pieces of evidence of crimes. They are silhouettes—silent and exquisitely incorporeal—more so than the actual objects. Underneath each work, there is a link to information about a case that can be accessed by scanning a barcode.

The dissonance felt from the very first steps into the exhibit is caused by the clash of words with images: the matter-of-fact description of the crime in the court testimony with the incorporeal style of the watercolor. All these bottles, socks, and pieces of string, painted in China ink, resemble these objects' shadows—they are emanations rather than objects. The eminence of the objects, which are separated from themselves resulting in a communicative dissonance, makes the viewer forget about the violence, the trauma, and the criminal cases Kondakov has presented. This same dissonance between word and image was present in Zaslavskaya's previous series, "Utensils 365." Because of that series, Kondakov chose Zaslavskaya as the illustrator for *Material Evidence."* In *Utensils,* ladles and chicken carcasses parted ways with the feminist agenda, insisting on the literal fact of presence. In *Material Evidence,* the viewer has trouble imagining that the streams of ink represent traces of dried blood. I tell Polina that her pieces of "material evidence" are reminiscent of religious icons. When we were contemplating where to hang them long before the exhibition's launch, we discussed how they displace space.

The works of *Material Evidence* remind the viewer of Giorgio Morandi's still lifes. Although Zaslavskaya's watercolors formally belong to a different tradition,

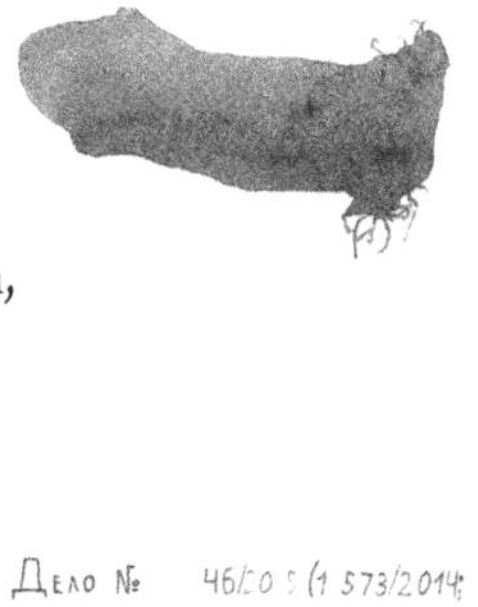

Figure 1. Polina Zaslavskaya, *Material Evidence Case No.№ 1-46/2015 (1-573/2014,)* (2017) watercolor on paper. Courtesy of the artist

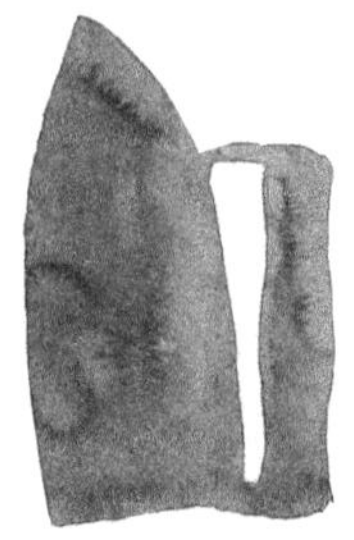

FIGURE 2. Polina Zaslavskaya, *Material Evidence Case No. 1-122/2013* (2017), watercolor on paper. Courtesy of the artist

Morandi's characteristic "tranquility" seems to be the condition she is striving for. Another similar reference could be Japanese watercolor painting with its white background. The latter, according to Zaslavskaya, "makes it possible to look at something concrete, such as a tree or an animal, presented plainly without any embellishment. In the modern world, where the possibility of seeing something simple is practically a luxury, such 'concreteness' is liberating."

Another artist that inevitably comes to mind is Andy Warhol. Upon seeing things floating in space, one is reminded of Warhol's negative subjectivity—objects that are a triumph of consumerism and advertising but are not created for close examination. Something strange happens in *Material Evidence*. On the one hand, this appeal to the Japanese tradition dictates the condition of pre-eminence, while on the other hand, the thing itself is just a serial number that references something beyond itself. It appears that the violence does not concern us at all. The viewers are constantly asking themselves how appropriate this rejection of the realistic description of the subject is. Is this something positive or negative? Do viewers really need to take a pause? Can't they find a way to talk about violence in a different, painless way? Perhaps this discord between word and image, between the texts of the documents and the technique of the watercolor, leaves viewers to decide for themselves how to read this text: as the experience of things that are no longer connected with the crime or as evidence.

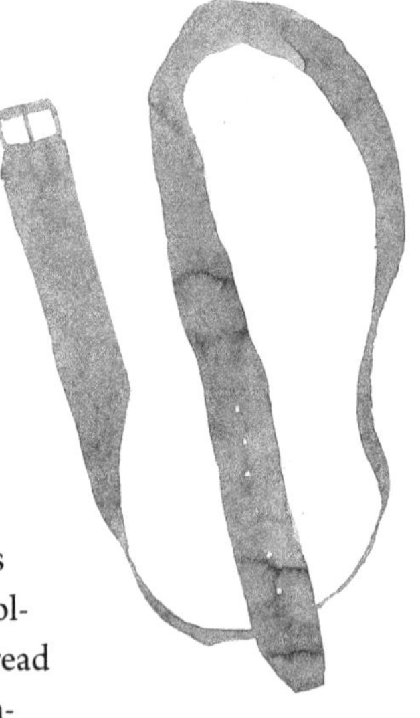

FIGURE 3. Polina Zaslavskaya, *Material Evidence Case No. 1-143/2011* (2017), watercolor on paper. Courtesy of the artist

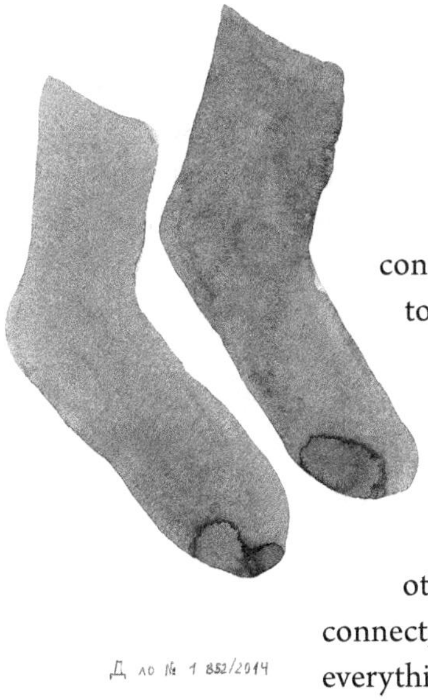

Figure 4. Polina Zaslavskaya, *Material Evidence Case No.№ 1-852/2014* (2017), watercolor on paper. Courtesy of the artist

For the artist herself, this disconnect from concreteness is fundamental. Zaslavskaya wants to present the subject using silhouettes: "Silhouettes don't frighten the viewer. Art shouldn't frighten us when everything else does." She calls attention to how modern painting insistently avoids concreteness in working with reality and subject: "Leonid Tskhe and other artists of that circle present uncertainty, disconnect, nonobjectivity, undercurrents, abstractions—everything but the direct. Oil paintings have vagueness of outlines and colorful haziness. Everywhere there is avoidance, the reluctance to say things outright, since the current reality resists being grasped; it is out of reach."

Curiously, this lack of clarity and disconnect determine the exhibit format, for which not the paintings themselves, but the situation around the painting—the talks, discussions, meetings—are no less important. There were four talks given as a part of *Material Evidence*. The viewers who came to see the watercolors barely discussed the paintings; rather, they talked about violence, state violence, gender violence, violence as an object of immanent art, the archaic and classical forms of it, and so on. It seems that the very fact of the exhibition today is not enough. This, of course, does not say anything about the value of the artifact, but, most likely, about new, horizontal laws of communication with art.

These days, a conversation about poetry rarely ends with poetry. The same is true for painting. Every exhibit includes a discussion, every conversation about art is an impetus for other conversations. A similar format only puts into perspective the fact that modern viewers concede nothing to the artist, that there is no such thing as a "rich" work or a "poor" viewer. The most amazing work is like an empty room into which viewers bring their own experiences. Today art looks more like a map that is given to the public: What the public sees and what work it creates for itself is unknown. Wherever there is Art with a capital A, there is still undoubtedly the existence of the aesthetic subject.

Polina agrees with me only partially. For her, art is a challenge that makes one consider how to work with a difficult topic while remaining in search of a visual language. She is not satisfied with the situation in which several projects that exist on the border of modern art or social activism do without artistic form: Devoid of formal qualities, they are propaganda rather than art. They become a tool through which expression of concrete thought becomes possible.

Most of her friends and colleagues look at art through a socio-political prism or, conversely, through the apolitical prism of avant-garde or classical painting. In discussions, we more and more often hear people question why "painless" projects such as *Material Evidence* are done when there are excellent journalistic investigations, such as investigations into violence against members of the LGBT community in Chechnya. How can the aesthetic and civic perspectives be reconciled? How is it possible to express the tangible experience of violence?

For Zaslavskaya, the most important thing is finding a balance between artists who sometimes engage with political and social topics and those who conclude that to speak is impossible, that one is confined to corporeal practice, performance, and dance, where language transforms into mobility and gestures; movement becomes a formal search for language. "You can, of course, limit yourself to reading journalistic investigations, which might cause someone to take to the streets or become an advocate for human rights. But the majority will prefer to forget everything they learned about. Perhaps art or poetry make dealing with trauma possible."

Translated by Ryan Green

Notes

1 All references to the exhibition are available at: Vika Smirnova, "Iskusstvo ne dolzhno nas pugat', potomu chto pugaet vse ostalnoe," artterritory, November 22, 2018, https://arterritory.com/ru/vizualnoe_iskusstvo/intervju/23132-iskusstvo_ne_dolzno_nas_pugat_potomu_cto_pugaet_vse_ostalnoe/.

Chapter 16

The Battle over Names: Radical Queer on the Russian Activist Art Scene

Seroe Fioletovoe

Seroe Fioletovoe (b. 1986) is an activist, artist-actionist, writer, and mathematician. A former member of the art group Voina (a group with links to Pussy Riot), they position themselves as an agender (identifying themself in the neutral gender and, when that is impossible, in the female gender). In 2008, they appeared as the 'hanged gay' in the infamous Voina art action in Ashan, a Moscow supermarket chain. Previously known as Oleg Vasiliev, they have appeared under the name Seroe Fioletovoe (Grey Violet) since 2012. In 2013, they curated the Queer Section of the Media Impact Art Festival in Moscow and received political asylum in Finland. In 2017, they returned to Russia. In 2022, they left Russia again and are currently living in Cambodia. The text published here in English translation was written between 2016 and 2017 and is devoted to the history of the Russian queer activist art scene over a ten-year period, from 2005–2015, marking the rise and fall of both the Moscow Gay Pride and the Russian anti-Putin movement. The history of the scene is quite specific for the history of queer art and radical queer activism, viewed by Seroe Fioletovoe as a fight for pure symbols and names, construing questions of gender and sexuality not as something with intrinsic value but rather as weapons used to attack conservatives and the authorities.

An Offering

Taken on its own and outside of the obligatory standard expressions of sympathy, the terrorist act in Orlando on June 12, 2016, wasn't surprising. It wasn't frightening. It wasn't the first such act, and it won't put an end to terrorism and homophobic violence.

Armed, bloody, and brutal struggles over views, ideals, and political and symbolic power was, is, and will always be a part—perhaps, a defining characteristic—of the history of humankind.

But you've got to wonder and be alarmed about the fact that the rainbow flag is always last to arrive at the barricades. Its presence is isolated and sporadic. We see this in Stonewall, viewed not as the beginning of the open LGBT movement as we know it but as the culmination of a turbulent, militaristic era of youth revolutions and radical social movements of the 1960s and 1970s. The same goes for later movements that carried the mantle of "queer ultraviolence" (see Baroque and Eanelli 2011) but that confined themselves to merely disrupting the daily order of religious institutions. They brought the flag to the barricades at Taksim Square. The rainbow appeared on the wooden stick of the blue balaclava-clad attacker of the Russian riot police at Bolotnaya Square in Moscow in the Winter of 2011–2012. These were solitary, isolated symbols of resistance, yet nonetheless important moments in history.

Every day we are facing fear and isolation, all-consuming victimization, and escapism into self-imposed ghettos, outwardly formal and inwardly subcultural, clubby, and final. It is inevitable that discrimination must return to its roots. Discrimination pushes us toward the fringes of society, onto the streets, into the lowest social castes, into public oblivion, through disease and epidemics. Discrimination locks us up in golden cages and in fortresses purposefully erected for our permitted and tolerated identities. Discrimination is killing us every day and every hour in every corner of the earth.

Forty percent of transgender people in the US have attempted suicide. Every queer—young, adult, or old—thinking of or attempting suicide ought to consider how to turn the individual act of breaking off all ties into collective action. He, she, they should strive to make a real fact and a life factor out of it. Everybody in the world must feel and focus on the consequences, not barely notice them in their peripheral vision. Here and now, all the suffering endured must be returned with interest to the communities who inflicted it.

This means, let the homophobic churches, mosques, and synagogues explode. Let the workers at conservative organizations squirm in the flames of their burning offices. Let fireworks of bullets crash into screaming cis-heterosexual mobs. Let chemical warfare agents replace the air in Party congress halls. Let anthrax spores infiltrate the lungs of politicians and civic and religious figures.

Let the eternal beauty of death and destruction become one with the rainbow—the bright, colorful, and lush aesthetic of Pride.

Because death isn't terrible. Death is a celebration we can't avoid.
It's time to gift it to others.

Revolution is a rupture, it is an invasion of an acting subject into a collective body of the dominant order, an invasion resulting in fear, breakdown, resistance, and the transformation of the structures of power. This is the same invasion, the fear of which is one of the most universal homophobic fears—and this is the path the Russian radical queer movement has been taking.

In the same way that the history of the artist-activist radical queer movement finds itself inseparably linked to revolutionary incursion and resistance to it (as in the Russian protests of 2011–2013, which Russian authorities were successful in suppressing)—it finds itself often in parallel[1] but also intensively interacting and inextricably linked with the general history of anti-autocratic movements—like the lesbian and gay movement from 1989–1993 (which also had a component that could be described as activist art practices, although that scene hasn't associated itself with any of the "art"-style identities).

"We pulled off loud actions. The first Libertarian Party Congress took place on Nikolskaia Street in the assembly hall of the Russian State University for the Humanities (RGGU) and became the first showbiz-congress of the new Russia. It was interesting to put together but not so amusing to talk about. Near the university, we distributed condoms inscribed with 'One submarine equals five million condoms.' Our party took responsibility for the Russian Revolution of 1905. We also claimed credit for stealing the spectacles from the Mahatma Ghandi statue. We were engaged in political happenings" (Kalinin 1998).

Even though a relatively stable radical queer activist scene came into being only during the peak of the protest movement in 2011–2013,[2] the entire ten-year period from the announcement of the first Moscow gay pride parade in June 2005 to the last Moscow gay pride parade that took place in 2015 (nobody came to Moscow Pride in 2016) was marked by a number of significant artistic gestures that could be interpreted within a queer context.

Among those gestures, one should include the "Commemoration of the Decemberists" (Pamiati Dekabristov) by Voina (September 2008), the speech "Putin Is Not a Faggot" delivered by Pakhom at the rally in support of the arrested Voina members (December 2010), "Operation: Kiss Garbage" (Lobzai musora) by the militant feminist faction of Voina (early 2011), the activities of the group Pussy Riot (September 2011–February 2012), the series of acts carried out by

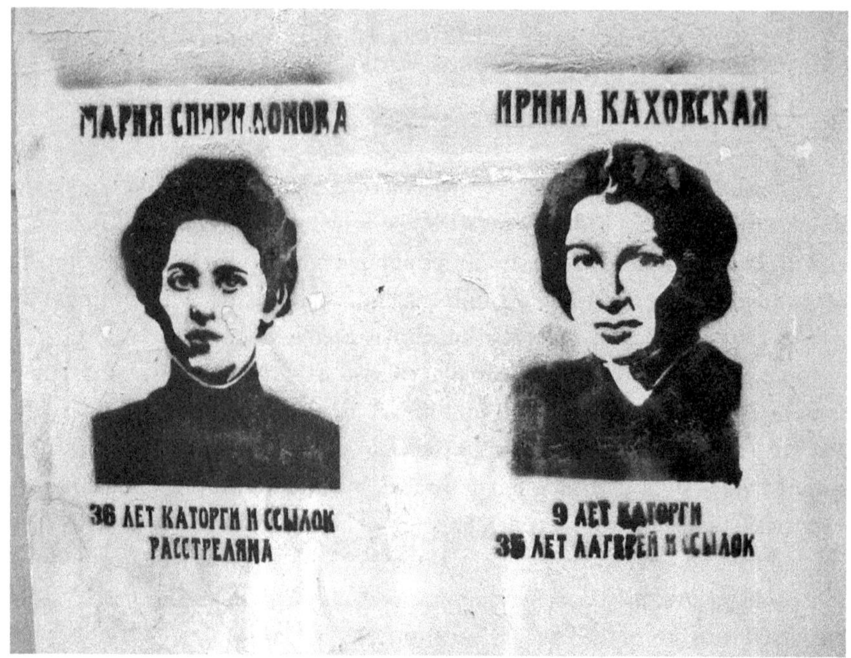

FIGURE 1. Mika Plutitskaya (aka Mikaela), *Narodnik Women (Narodovolki)* (2013), stencils. Courtesy of the artist

the radical queer activist group organized by Alexei Kiselev (February 2012–June 2012), and "Fixation" by Peter Pavlensky (November 2013).[3]

In addition to these projects, a wave of purer forms of queer art-activism included the blog encircled_plus, which featured a broad range of anonymous art works, the Union of Radical Faggots[4] (November 2012–August 2013), and the activist group organized by Alexei Davydov (July–September 2013), including Kirill Kalugin, Reyda Linn, and Nix Nemeni; this collective in 2013–2015 also addressed LGBTQI issues in their performances.

The first half of the 2010s was marked by a rise in queer-feminist art-activism, such as the exhibitions *Feminist Pencil* (*Feministskiy Karandash*), as well as the activities of the artists who launched their careers as part of the Moscow Feminist Group:[5] Mika Plutitskaya, who worked under the name Mikaela, Umnaia Masha, Mannaia Kasha, and the queer-feminist comics artist Hagra (figs. 1 and 2). The history and general context of Russian activist art have been studied in multiple articles by Alek D. Epstein, while an impressive attempt to construct a chronology has been undertaken by the Media Impact platform.

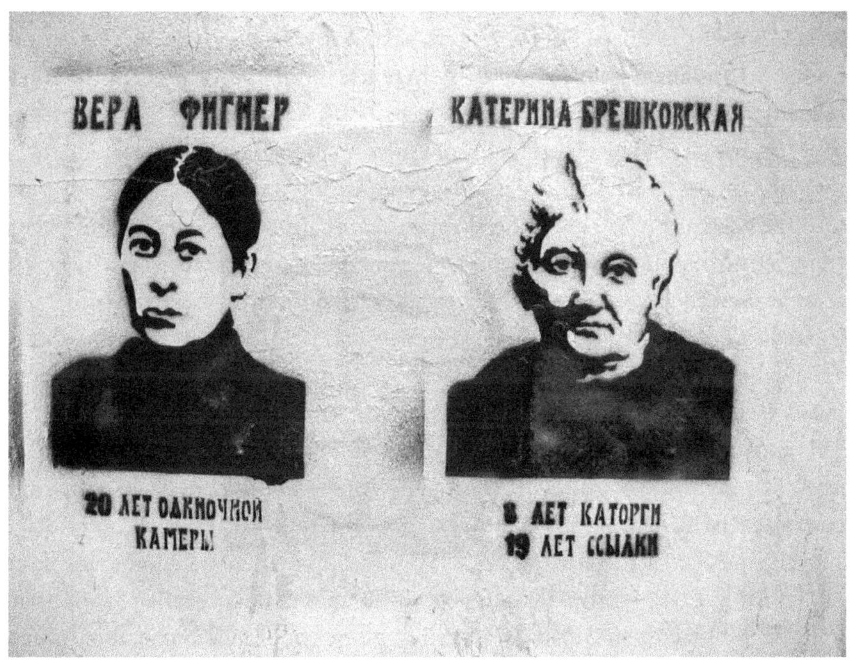

FIGURE 2. Mika Plutitskaya (aka Mikaela), *Narodnik Women (Narodovolki)* (2013), stencils. Courtesy of the artist

Most of the pieces in question have been created either by artists who do not identify as queer, such as Pakhom and Peter Pavlensky, or by activists who do not identify as artists, like Alexei Kiselev. Despite that, these works represent the major lineaments of the radical queer situation in Russian society at a time when queerness was represented not from within a perpetual flamboyant masquerade that overcomes shame and various types of cultural conservatism, not from within a self-fulfilling fear of the closet, and not from within an open discussion or understanding of sexuality, identity, and interpersonal relationships, but rather as a state of war over names and symbols, as the cultural and political avant-garde of the anti-authoritarian movement, and as a vital source of perpetual fear dissolving in the air of dominant masculinities. Sexuality finds itself here not as part of a policy of joy and desire, not as a self-contained source of political struggle but rather as a weapon in a war between different symbols. Moreover, this is the strategy of a small radical queer avant-garde, which is actually a perfect reflection of popular Russian homophobia; given the pervasiveness of (potential) prison experience scattered throughout Russian cultural discourse, this strategy is based on the culture of male prisons, sexuality has been reduced to a proper noun without any possible signifiers, where the terms "petukh" or "obizhennyi" refer to prisoners having the lowest social status, equivalent to that of "passive gays," as a result of having broken some prison taboos. That vector is evident in the anonymous political queer art images appearing on the blog encircled_plus.

The postcard "Moscow Pride '06" consists of a spike-covered rose and black triangles turning into the basic element of a divided multicolored environment (*LiveJournal* 2006), representing the state of division and aggressive conflict that existed before the First Moscow Gay Pride—when Moscow gay clubs were being attacked by crowds of far-right mobsters—and during the event, which turned into a violent conflict between police, far-right mobsters, and LGBTQ activists. This situation was the standard for all Moscow Gay Prides since then; only at the Moscow Gay Pride of 2012 did queer activists attempt to fight back in the form of Alexei Kiselev's group street performance "Rainbow Nets" (*Raduzhnye seti*).

The queer-related activities of the Voina group demonstrated both the strategy of using LGBT discourse as a symbol of an anti-authoritarian avant-garde and the strategy of subversively affirming homophobic discourse about queer sexuality.

The first strategy was demonstrated in the actionist video "Commemoration of the Decembrists" (Plutser 2008) by the Voina group, which was shot on Moscow City Day at the beginning of September 2008. Here two individuals in flamboyant pride costumes were "hanged" in one of the Moscow megastores together with three migrant workers. One of the Voina activists who performed the mock hangings wore the uniform of the United Russia's (Russia's ruling party) Youth Guard. A poster on a rainbow flag with the words "Pestel Fucking Didn't Fall" (Pestel' nakhui ne upal) were placed near the place of "execution."[6] The "hangings" were presented as a gift to Moscow Mayor Yuri Luzhkov, famous for his homophobic speeches and exploitation of Central Asian immigrants living in quasi-slave conditions. The "hanged gays" symbolized the two hanged members of the Northern Society of Decembrists who were associated with Russia's liberal elite connected with the "West," while the Central Asian migrant workers representing three of the hanged members of the Western Society were identified with serfs.

This strategy of subversive affirmation was also used in Voina's exhibition "You think he's fucking?" (*Dumaete, ebetsia?*), staged in the Aidan Gallery in Moscow on May 29, 2008, in connection with the criminal case against the art curators Yuri Samodurov and Andrei Erofeev. Photos of far-right activists and politicians were accompanied by different insulting comments often mentioning homosexuality. These comments—which were citations taken from comments on their photos posted by livejournal users on the blog adolfych—could be understood both as insults directed at these far-right activists or as typical insults made by far-right activists directed at the "liberal" audience of a contemporary art exhibition.

The spoken-word performance "Putin isn't a faggot" (Putin ne pidaras) by Pakhom, staged on December 18, 2010, at a rally in support of the imprisoned members of Voina, demonstrated a similar strategy—here Pakhom calls for isolating or separating the "faggots": "Let the faggots languish in confinement, let the faggots fag around in their faggy kingdom." Pakhom's rhetoric is based on the fact that neither Vladimir Putin, who practices the manly martial arts, nor former Soviet leaders, such as Nikita Khrushchev, who stated that "abstract artists are faggots" (*abstrakzionisty – pidorasy*), as well as Stalin and Beria, were "faggots." Pakhom's short unfinished speech "The Festering Faggot" (Gnoinyi pidor) is devoted to the projection of visceral fear at the possibility of being raped in prison.

The militant-feminist faction of Voina, led by Nadia Tolokno and Kat Samutsevich, used queer sexuality as a method of political violence: The street performance "Kiss Garbage" (Wisegizmo 2011), which took place at the beginning of 2011, consisted of female activists forcibly kissing female police officers. The slogan of the performance was "My sexual orientation is the police officer of my sex." Initially, the group planned not only female-female but also male-male kissing but couldn't find enough male activists. Suppression of the LGBT movement became part of a more general discourse of protest, as in the famous Pussy Riot Punk Prayer "Virgin Mary, Chase Putin Away" (Bogoroditsa, Putina progoni) of February 21, 2012.

The protests of 2011–2013, along with the start of an official anti-gay campaign that culminated in the passage of the "gay propaganda law," in the struggle against which LGBT activists took an active role, gave rise to a wave of radical queer activism created and carried out by queer people themselves. The starting point for that wave was probably the break between more radical and more moderate factions of the LGBTQI and feminist movements that took place at the second big opposition rally in Moscow on December 24, 2011. During the next rally, which took place on February 4, 2012, radical queers showed up with a large slogan on a violet banner that read: [7] "You're queer too" (*Ty tozhe kvir*) and a two-sided banner with "We won't give it to Putin a third time" (*Ne dadim Putinu v tretii raz*) on one side and "Queer will save the world" (*Kvir spaset mir*) on the other.[8] This marked the beginning of the Moscow Radical Queer Activist Group, which was active until June 2012. Its ideological successor was the activist project "The Union of Radical Faggots" (Soiuz radikal'nykh pidarasov),[9] active also in Voronezh from November 2012 to August 2013.

These groups concentrated primarily on producing critical attacks on homophobic religious discourse, as evident in their slogans "Our home is Sodom" (*Nash dom—Sodom*),[10] "Sodom in every home" (*Sodom—v kazhdyi dom*)[11] (created by Kirill Kalugin in Saint-Petersburg), "Unhappy is the husband who doesn't know his friend anally" (*Neschastliv tot muzh, kotoryi ne poznal druga svoego anal'no*),[12] "Homosexuality or death" (*Muzhelozhestvo ili smert'*),[13] based on the logo of the radical Orthodox group the Union of Orthodox Banner-Bearers (Soiuz pravoslavnykh khorugvenostsev), "Orthodox Believer, Jesus will suck your cock in heaven if you promote homosexuality to one hundred infants on Earth" (*Pravoslavnyi—spropagandirui gomosexualizm 100 mladentsam i tebe v raiu otsoset Iisus Khristos*),[14] among others. Those slogans were mainly based on mocking symbolic religious concepts, appropriating the concept of "gay propaganda," and representing the category of "queer" as a universal symbol. Representations of queer sexuality here—as was the case with the non-queer artists who used radical queer symbols—remained in the realm of alienated symbols of violence. Sexuality was represented as part of the current political religious power discourse, but rarely on its own as an autonomous player. That stands in striking contrast to the whole tradition of the US radical queer movement: The early radical gay liberation movement of 1969–1973 was initiated mostly by excluded and alienated visible minorities (queer people of color, transvestites, and sex workers) and focused mainly on community building and actions directed against widespread violence, poverty, and homelessness (Mecca 2009; Gould 2009). The movement reached its peak in 1987–1991, which saw the reemergence of open queer sexuality, which had been suppressed during the early years of the AIDS epidemic, accompanied by the free expression of collective grief, anger, and the queer anarchist movement Bash Back! (Baroque 2011), which was active from 2007–2009. At each of these distinct moments, queer sexuality and gender expression were used to constitute communities—which is quite different from the deeply individual dissent of Russian groups based on using (also their own) queer sexuality and its symbols as a tool for opposing different power structures. Another approach—based on the universal transformation of desire—is elaborated by the leading Italian radical gay author and activist Mario Mieli (Mieli 1980); still, his concept was based on desire and sexuality, not on their representation as a weapon used by the dominant order that can be turned against it. The history of the French Gay Liberation movement provides a somewhat closer example to the Russian, as evident in their slogan "Sodom and Gomorrah, the struggle goes on!" (Sibalis 2005, 273). Nevertheless, their militancy and queer-revolutionary spirit were centered on the classical idea of sexual liberation as a part of a more general liberation, not on the subversive affirmation of the dominant discourse of sexuality, seen as a type of violence.

Alexei Kiselev is known as the organizer of the only two cases in which LGBTQI people have publicly attacked authorities or homophobes. The first case involved an attack directed toward the riot police during the Bolotnaia Square riots of May 6, 2012, when a person wearing a light blue balaclava attacked the police with the stick carrying a rainbow flag.[15] The second case occurred during the Moscow Gay Pride, in June 2012, when Kiselev, together with Alexei Chunosov, staged the street performance "Rainbow Nets" ("Raduzhnye seti"). During that performance, they attacked the far-right activists who had come to disrupt the gay pride events and to beat up LGBTQI activists; the LGBTQI activists used their rainbow nets to ensnare the far-right activists.

A different direction was pursued by the Moscow Feminist Group. Among several artists associated with the group, which worked mainly to affect the feminist politicization of everyday life, Mikaela (now also known as Mika Plutitskaya) stands out. Her first street art project *Narodovolki* (denoting female members of the radical group Narodnaia Volia, or People's Will) was performed in September of 2012 (*Ravnopravka* 2012). It was devoted to female Russian political terrorists of the nineteenth-century revolutionary movement.

At the end of 2012, local anti-gay campaigns and "propaganda laws" moved to the federal level—a process that started at the end of 2011—alongside persecution directed at the radical part of the movement (especially outside Moscow and Saint Petersburg). This led to the adoption of defensive rhetoric inside the radical queer community and the emigration of most of the radical activists—beginning with Alexei Kiselev who, already in June 2012, was forced to leave Russia and request asylum in Spain. Direct attacks on the authorities and the queerphobic order changed to a defensive discourse centered on promoting the legitimacy of "gay propaganda"; while the moderate wing of the community simply denied the existence of gay propaganda, more radical members were ready to promote gay propaganda (toiida 2011). One of the most emblematic pieces in this regard was "There's nothing bad in propaganda" (V propagande net nichego plokhogo) by Mikaela, which features a girl kissing another girl's temple with different accompanying phrases, including the one in the title (*Ravnopravka* 2013). That work existed both as graffiti and in the form of an icon.

The process of revictimization of a movement that had only just begun to empower itself is evident in the landmark initiative carried out by Kirill Kalugin with his solitary picket on the Airborne Forces Day of August 2—a day when heavily drunk former airborne troops, symbols of dominant masculinity, fill the streets of Russian cities (fig. 3) . Russian homophobes consider this the only day when gay pride should be "allowed," because, they think, it would be immediately drowned in blood. Those solitary pickets were held on Saint Petersburg's Palace Square on August 2, 2013 and 2014. Soon after the second picket, Kirill Kalugin was forced to emigrate.

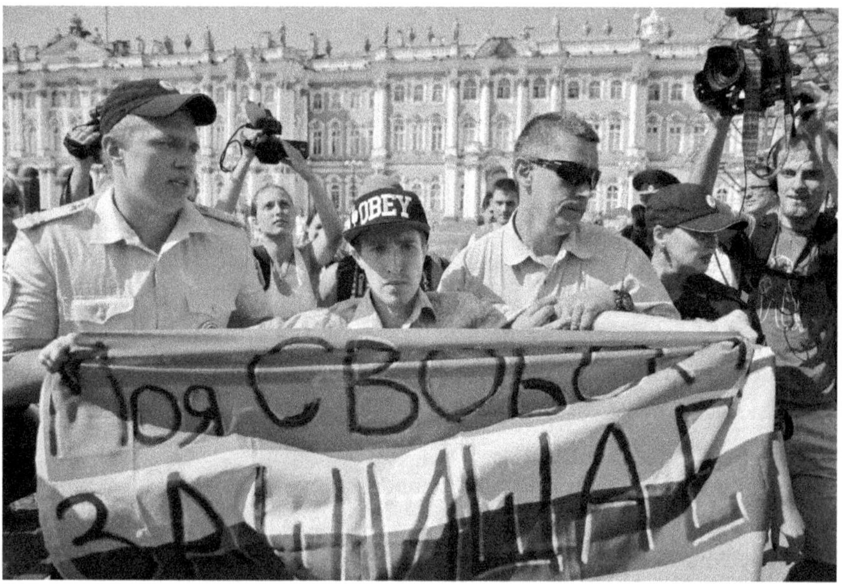

FIGURE 3. Kirill Kalugin's action on the Airborne Forces day on August 2, 2014. Photo by Yury Gavrikov. Courtesy of Yury Gavrikov

These actions, which are among the most radical in all of Russian queer history, could be seen as the other side of the same "battle over names"— the namesthat had become by then nearly invisible. On August 2, 2013, Kirill took to the streets carrying a rainbow flag with the slogan, "This is propaganda of tolerance" (*Eto propaganda tolerantnosti*),[16] and, in 2014, he held a flag with the slogan "My freedom defends yours" (*Moia svoboda zashchishchaet tvoiu*).[17] Queerness, however, was not represented verbally, only in the rainbow colors.

This was the same vanishing/disappearance/absence that a year before had been symbolically enacted on the art-scene when censorship of the Moscow Multimedia Art Museum forced David Ter-Oganian's piece "Propaganda of homosexuality" ("Propaganda gomoseksualizma"), which consisted of shadows of partying queer activists, to be renamed "Untitled," rendering it devoid of content and returning queerness to the closet (Ledenev 2012).

Street performances carried out by Alexei Davydov's group were part of the same initiative. The most important of them was "Mizulina's law in action" ("Zakon Mizulinoi v destvii"), which was held in July 2013. During that performance, three activists lied in a pool of fake blood with portraits of Yekaterinburg gay activist Gleb Latnik hanging around their necks. Latnik, who currently lives in the US, had a mini stroke as a result of a social campaign waged against him and was then beaten by unknown homophobes.

Probably the last new symbolic initiative associated with radical queer discourse is again the work of an artist who does not position himself as queer. It is the performance "Fixation" ("Fiksatsiia") held by Peter Pavlensky on November 8, 2013, when he nailed his scrotum to the pavement of Red Square (grani.ru 2013). Popular comments on the performance expressed mainly fear and disgust, resulting from a dread of illness, castration, and penetration into a sacred part of the body—dread that perfectly mirrors the dread of dominant masculinity, a dread of the body and of individuality that have never been truly overcome[18] by the Russian political queer movement, which has drowned itself in a fight over names and symbols and has completely subjugated gender and sexuality to that fight.

With translations by Innokenty Grekov

Notes

1 The first wave of Russian lesbigay activism concerned the narrow and formally independent goal of the remaining democratic movement of abolishing Part 1 of Article 121 of the Criminal Code of the RSFSR, which criminalized voluntary homosexual relations. The second wave (2005–2011) was initially associated with the right to freedom of assembly for LGBT people. Beginning in 2011, the movement concentrated mainly on the campaign against the "gay propaganda" law and the authorities' homophobic campaign, in general.

2 By November 2016, almost all the people who had participated in Russian radical queer activism had in some way become political refugees to the European Union or the United States. The organizer of one of the actionist groups, Alexei Davydov, died in September 2013. One of the causes of his death was the long-term effects of injuries sustained from police beatings at a demonstration on July 31, 2011.

3 The author of the article was a direct participant in the "Memory of the Decemberists" protest and most protests done by Alexei Kiselev's group; they were in close contact with participants in all the other activities.

4 For more information, see https://vk.com/queerradical

5 For more information, see http://www.ravnopravka.ru/

6 Pavel Ivanovich Pestel (1793–1826) was a Russian revolutionary and ideologue of the Decemberists uprising of 1825.

7 Including myself, Alexei Kiselev, Nadya Tolokno, Kat Samutsevich, and others.

8 For more information, see: http://www.ljplus.ru/img4/s/v/svintusoid/aitHqww_y07dPjM7yCaIwA.jpg and http://ic.pics.livejournal.com/pecheyk in/10586652/193477/193477_640.jpg

9 For more information, see: https://vk.com/queerradical

10 For more information, see: http://www.itinvest.ru/assets/images/sodom.jpg

11 For more information, see: http://radikal.ru/lfp/s018.radikal.ru/i523/1308/9e/0c226061efd3.jpg/htm

12 For more information, see: https://vk.com/queerradical?w=wall-46170913_512

13 For more information, see: https://vk.com/queerradical?z=photo-46166596_296598647%2Fwall-46170913_73

14 For more information, see: https://vk.com/queerradical?z=photo-46166596_296598650%2Fwall-46170913_73

15 Neither the photo nor the video has been found.

16 For more information, see: http://ic.pics.livejournal.com/dru-goi/484155/8517438/8517438_original.jpg

17 For more information, see: http://www.fontanka.ru/mm/items/2014/8/2/0012/k1.jpg

18 In a less politicized context, one could see this on some of the art posted on the blog encircled_plus, in the comics art by Hagra, and on the Livejournal blog lavrentij.

References

Baroque, Fray and Tegan Eanelli, eds. 2011. *Queer Ultraviolence: BASH BACK! Anthology*. San Francisco: Ardent Press.

Gould, Deborah B. 2009. *Moving Politics. Emotion and ACT UP's Fight against AIDS*. Chicago: University of Chicago Press.

Grani.ru. 2013. "Khudozhnik Petr Pavlenskii pribil moshonku gvozdem k bruschatke na Krasnoi ploshchadi" (November 10). Available at: https://graniru.org/Politics/Russia/activism/m.221013.html.

Kalinin, Roman. 1998. "Ia byl pervym otkrytym gomoseksualom." Available at: Gay.ru. http://www.gay.ru/people/view/kalinin.html. Last accessed May 19, 2021.

Ledenev, Valerii. 2012. "Shum vokrug propagandy gomoseksualizma mozhet privesti k tomu, chto on opiat' okazhetsia vne zakona." Colta.ru, September 11. Available at: http://archives.colta.ru/docs/5485.

Mecca, Tommi Avicolli, ed. 2009. *Smash the Church, Smash the State! The Early Years of Gay Liberation*. San Francisco: City of Light Books.

Mieli, Mario. 1980. *Homosexuality and Liberation: Elements of a Gay Critique*. London: Gay Men's Press.

Plutser, Aleksei. 2008. "Genotsid w Ashane! Kazn' gastarbaiterov i pidarasov v supermarkete: Chudovishchnaia aktsiia art-gruppy Voina!" *Plucer* (blog). *LiveJournal*. September 9. Available at: https://plucer.livejournal.com/97416.html. Last accessed May 19, 2021.

Ravnopravka. 2012. "Mikaela: interv'iu o strit-art proekte 'Narodovolki.'" September 6. Available at: http://ravnopravka.ru/2012/09/mikaela/. Last accessed May 19, 2021.

———. 2013. "Novogodnie fem-graffiti" (January 2). Available at: http://ravnopravka.ru/2013/01/%D0%BD%D0%BE%D0%B2%D0%BE%D0%B3%D0%BE%D0%B4%D0%BD%D0%B8%D0%B5-fem-graffiti/. Last accessed May 19, 2021.

Sibalis, Michael. 2005. "Gay Liberation Comes to France: The *Front Homosexuel d'Action Révolutionnaire* (FHAR)." In *French History and Civilization: Papers from the George Rudé Seminar*, Vol. 1, edited by Ian Coller et al., 265–76. The George Rudé Society.

toiida. 2006. "Moscow Pride '06." *Encircled_plus* (blog). *LiveJournal*. May 20. Available at: https://encircled-plus.livejournal.com/4751.html. Last accessed May 19, 2021.

———. 2011. "Mu- zhe- lo- zhe- stvo." *Encircled_plus* (blog). *LiveJournal*. November 19. Available at: https://encircled-plus.livejournal.com/686999.html#cutid1. Last accessed May 19, 2021.

Wisegizmo. 2011. "Aktsiia gruppy Voina 'Lobzai musora' ili trening po zatselovyvaniiu militsionersh." *Wisegizmo* (blog). *LiveJournal*. March 1. Available at: https://wisegizmo.livejournal.com/52764.html. Last accessed May 19, 2021.

Chapter 17

Queer in the Land of the Bolsheviks, or the Archeology of Dissent[1]

Nadia Plungian

In this essay, Plungian presents a post-Soviet take on the possibilities of queering Soviet art history, expressing skepticism regarding the unproblematic application of Western queer theories to the history of Soviet art. The author suggests that, first and foremost, art historians must take a closer look at the material and methodological traps embedded in the history of Soviet art as a way of moving toward queering the history of Soviet-era art.

The key to Plungian's post-Soviet queering project is "to restore the concept of art as a polemical, dialogical process, resurrect a multiplicity of cultural positions, and establish respect for the unpredictability of the "Other," and to see art "as precarious experimental work that is always done by stigmatized people."

***

I have been asked by the journal *Raznoglasiia* to address the ways in which queer studies can serve as a tool for historians and art historians writing about the Soviet cultural space (in my case, it is the space of the 1930s to the 1950s). There is a growing body of Western studies that represents in one way or another modernist and postmodernist processes in twentieth-century art and literature through feminist and postcolonial analyses and that focus on questions of gender, sexuality, race, class, and identity. Eve Kosofsky Sedgwick's *Epistemology of the Closet* usually heads the list of publications available in Russian translation. I could enumerate such publications, recounting the accomplishments of the 1990s and the ways in which these and other lenses could be transferred to Russian discourses. But my interest lies elsewhere, namely, in the specificity of the Soviet material and the methodological traps embedded in it. These traps are already evident in Russia's current institutional attempts at conceptualizing the queer project.

I believe that the binary structures established in the 1930s still serve as the central point of origin for contemporary narratives of Soviet artistic processes, which is the single most important reason for the continued controversy around queer appraisals of Soviet material. But this problem has wider reverberations. Even in the narrowly defined field of human rights and LGBT activism, which appears to be left out of broad academic debates and could arguably legitimize certain applications of queer theory to contemporary mass culture, if not history, the formation of such analytical practices is incredibly slow and confined almost entirely to subcultural sites.

Debates over the question of whether the Russification of 'queer' is possible arose in Russia several years ago, on the heels of a similarly titled conference held by the LGBT organization "Vykhod," yet the process of introducing the term ended abruptly in a gesture of symbolic infanticide. In 2015, Valery (Timofey) Sozaev, the activist and political writer who organized the conference *Is Queer Possible in Russian?* and the subsequent volume under the same title (Sozaev 2010), came out with a manifesto entitled "'Queer' Must Die," in which he expressed his concern that the term was getting out of control, was applied too broadly and by virtually everyone, and was no longer capable of expressing the political interests of the LGBT movement or signifying anything at all. Sozaev writes: "'Queer' is an empty signifier because there is no consensus on the signified. It is impossible to find two identical instances of 'queer.' And if we do not have identical instances of 'queer,' we cannot have any 'queer identity' [...]. 'Queer' is not only far from an essence-based (that is, essentialist) category, it is first and foremost a role-playing (that is, performative) category, to be played around with today and discarded tomorrow" (Sozaev 2015).

The palpably "parental" tone of his last sentence draws attention to overarching tendencies in the current post-Soviet understanding of the normative and its packaging of demagogic substitutions. Among other challenges, it is difficult to fully appreciate, from an insider's perspective, the scale on which the Russian media habitually exploit the concepts of "we" and "they." "They" in this picture are not like "us" and are therefore excluded and made undesirable by their vulnerability and neediness (Goralik 2012, online). To qualify for help, "they" must prove to "us" that their stigma is real, a demand that echoes the infamous annual reassessment requirement under Russian law for people with disabilities (Bondarenko 2016, online). From this perspective, identity in Russia is, indeed, not "role-playing," but a social constant. It is such fixed, rigid identities ("identical instances of queer") that constitute the "normal" community, whose members suspect one another of being "not normal," and its flip side—the "not normal" community, whose members are suspected of simulated stigma and gain-seeking.

Such a rigid society, split in half by hostility and mutual suspicion, can only move and change at one point—the point of transition from one state or camp to the other. This point can be defined as the moment of admitting stigma (or "coming out"), a moment all the more troubling because of its finality, a moment in which "they" forever forfeit social opportunities available to "us." It is not surprising that Lena Klimova's social media initiative "Children—404" for LGBT adolescents, the most prominent queer-related grassroots project of the 2010s, focuses on the private experience of people coming to terms with their passage beyond this point of no return.[2] Adolescents who comes out to their parents or other adults as bisexual, transgender, lesbian, pansexual, or gay are perceived by them as precisely this "empty signifier" because, according to Sozaev, besides popular homophobic clichés, there is no "consensus" in Russian society as to how "such people" should look, live, or express themselves. This social media page is full of similarly anxious, controlling, and cruel responses from parents, insisting among other things that identity cannot be temporary or performative and that the social environment is composed of clear-cut binaries:

"If you turn out to be LIKE THOSE (WOMEN), I won't let you back in the house!"[3]

"I'm so glad you are normal. I don't know what I'd do with you if you turned out like one of those psychos."[4]

"She said I'm making it all up, that I'm hung up on this 'crap' because I'm bored."[5]

"I just turned 18. But I've felt an absolutely clear sense of moving, in the eyes of those around, from the category of 'silly, duped kid' to that of 'the evil, deceiving pervert.'"[6]

In the face of demands to select a specific social category, the concept of "queer" emerged, problematizing these demands and revealing the hidden delineations of normativity embedded in all existing discourses. Self-reflection and self-criticism within society, while producing an internal dialogue, inevitably halt the process of assimilation—not unlike the way in which a teen who asks too many questions is likely to reject standardized scripts for adolescent socialization.

It must be stressed that, as follows from the article "'Queer' Must Die," initial attempts to legitimize the term "queer" through the Russian academy and human rights movements involved pursuing the idea of assimilation rather than declaring a new political movement. As Sozaev writes:

> Russian LGBT activists originally adhered to the same strategy as Russian academics: 'queer' as a screen for homosexuality. It is precisely to this strategy that Queer Fest in Saint Petersburg owes its title. Back in 2008—2009, when we were looking to name the festival in a way that on the one hand could grab attention but on the other would not cause excessive trouble with the authorities, we settled on the word 'queer' not least because it was a practically unknown entity in the Russian language and was not associated with homosexuality [. . .]. In this connection, queer-activism as such has not appeared in Russia; so far, Russia has had no initiatives like ACT UP or Queer Nation. (Sozaev 2015)

Obviously, what needs to be addressed here is not that queer activism "has not appeared" in Russia, but that it simply *did not have to*, as the term, which was still unclear in the Russian context, was preemptively appropriated by LGBT activists for their own purposes. Whenever small forms of self-advocacy emerged within the community as alternatives to LG or LGBT activism, they were sarcastically contrasted with large-scale and historic initiatives such as ACT UP. The effect was mixed representation in which the Russian queer movement was linked to agendas seen as provincial, pretentiously progressive, untimely, and inadequately institutionalized. Parallel to the critiques of the Russian "queer" project as incommensurate with the Western one were claims regarding "the total destructiveness of 'queer' in relation to lesbian and gay identities" (Sozaev 2015). It was impossible to interrogate binary categories; moreover, such gestures were in fact described as a threat to everything that human rights actions had accomplished over decades (in the same vein as being "ungrateful toward your parents").

The origins of contemporary binaries in Russian society are transparently traceable to the history of repressions and purges and the totalitarian gender order. Hence, the underlying imperative of most Russian debates around identity is to build large-scale narratives that can transcend specific socially situated local instances.

One of these narratives was on display at a Moscow exhibition called "I-Iskusstvo, F-Feminism. Aktual'nyi slovar'" (Rossman 2015).[7] The last in a series of feminist exhibitions organized at the critical juncture of the 2014–2015 conservative shift, it was also last in terms of the cultural-historical point inscribed in its title (Plungian 2015). To go back to the question of Russified notions of 'queer,' it should be noted that the Russian version of the feminist vocabulary, which appeared to have undergone the final stage of institutionalization, did not contain the letters L, G, B, or T (let alone Q) in its table of contents; nor did it in any way problematize these notions politically, putting in their place vague categories that characterized their own inability to speak openly ("adaptation," "exception," "invisibility") (Palvan-zade 2015).

While bearing some superficial resemblance to conceptualist nomenclature, the alphabets, dictionaries, primers, and anthologies with which recent Russian art has increasingly engaged have fundamentally different institutional characteristics. The contemporary art-primer is constructed under conditions of censorship but contains no critical potential. It is produced and displayed in a space that is removed from any sense of privacy. The purpose of this primer is to ratify the censored discourse as a reasonable norm suitable for beginners and to point the viewer toward the growing regime of oppositions as well as the reduction of political categories.

While the primer-catalogues of postmodernism (from Pavich and Borges to Pivovarov) were constructed with playful reflexivity inaccessible to state authority and operating in dialogue with the viewer, current censorship has pushed Russian art out of the safe space of play into referential practices concerned with an old past. This recalls the cultural role assigned to primers in the early years of the Soviet project, namely 1919, when they became the central element of the campaign to eradicate illiteracy and a means of mapping the political and cultural landscape, a tool for highlighting dominant paradigms while concealing or devaluing others. The first such primers were written in a popular folk verse idiom and were stylized after lubok prints; among them were Mayakovsky's *Sovetskaia azbuka* (A Soviet alphabet) (1919), Dmitrii Moor's decorative *Azbuka krasnoarmeitsa* (The red army soldier's alphabet) (1921), and Adol'f Strakhov's *Azbuka revolutsii* (The alphabet of revolution) (1921), modelled on revolutionary-democratic posters. Iterations in the late 1920s are less obviously politicized, inheriting the artistic tradition of Alexandre Benois and Georgii Narbut (for example, Dmitrii Mitrokhin's *Oktiabrskaia azbuka* [October alphabet], 1927; and Vladimir Lebedev's *Azbuka* [Alphabet], 1925), yet they are still devoid of random elements.

During the 1930s, this rhetoric was supplanted by popular political caricature (Mikhail Cheremnykh's *Antireligioznaia azbuka* [Anti-religious alphabet], 1933), which would give way only too quickly to a more powerful instrument—montage illustrations for official statistics such as those published in the *SSSR na stroike* magazine (1930–1941, 1949) and in luxurious Stalinist editions.

Appropriating the language of art, Soviet and Russian political infographics heavily reworked information, organizing it into clusters of sensory material that prevent the viewer from seeing all the facts and considering them side by side to draw independent conclusions. The viewer is confronted with a hermetic scheme that has no room for dialogue or queries to the authors, since this concept is supposed to reflect not an authorial point of view but the "state of affairs," asserting a political norm. The relationship to the viewer is one way, with the viewer construed as an illiterate, a layperson, and never a coauthor.

While today's primers, like those of the past, do not lay claim to a central position in the cultural space, they nevertheless make visible its structural foundations. The project of queering the archive should begin by analyzing such works, proceeding from the following questions: Under what conditions could queer readings intersect with or be part of official historical discourses, and what prevents that? This orientation would allow us to see that the semantic engine of the title "I-Iskusstvo, F-Feminism. Aktual'nyi slovar'" is the word "aktual'nyi" (meaning current, topical, relevant), which stands in implied opposition to what is irrelevant, or not "aktual'nyi"; and that the key point behind the question of whether the Russification of 'queer' is possible has to do not so much with testing possibilities but with introducing a national dimension (at the level of "Russianness" rather than "of Russia"). In both instances, the answer is implied in the framing: Contemporary concepts of "Russianness," which prioritize conservative stability, leave no room not only for "queer" but also for what Jasbir K. Puar (2007) describes as a stable homonational contract; just as the field of *aktual'nyi* art leaves no room for any clear feminist analysis.

The tendency to create such large-scale narratives raises the ire of the representatives of *aktual'nyi* art who lived through the Soviet project and see themselves as part of it, including its countercultural pockets. Thus, in his recent manifesto, Russian artist Avdey Ter-Oganian, who currently resides in Prague, characterizes the very principle of *aktual'nyi* primers as a pale imitation of the Soviet approach: "I can turn any idiot into a contemporary conceptual artist in a year. If a person has a college degree and can write well, all they have to do is read a couple of books and grasp the principle of creating a work of contemporary art, which now basically means illustrating themes. If you do something, for instance, on the topic of feminism, Nazism, antisemitism, homophobia, it is automatically great" (quoted in Kolesnikov 2016). Moreover, Ter-Oganian argues for discarding the evacuated meanings of the present and restoring the empty signifiers of the past (in my opinion, substitutions of the modernist era). His proposed solution entails the founding of a "Soviet Artists Union" and a return to the "Soviet art school," currently taboo in the market, yet suddenly envisioned here as "international" and antithetical to one-sided partisan politics (!). Following his critique of *Aktual'nyi slovar'*, Ter-Oganian introduces a number of ideological formulations, unclarified and unproblematized: "We are constantly being asked to understand the Soviet as the *naturalist art of the 1940s.* Yet we see it much more broadly: *from Picasso to academicism.* The only thing that exceeds our interest is *pure abstraction and pure conceptualism*" (ibid.; italics added).

Ter-Oganian clearly does not care to take responsibility for his formulations. I would be glad if someone asked him at a press conference what pure abstraction is, what naturalism is, and how it is different from academicism, how Picasso has suddenly become part of the "Soviet art school," and what constitutes this anti-formalist golden mean, which, despite having no social relevance whatsoever, should somehow stimulate artists all over the world. This would make for a lively discussion. But on a deeper level, his message rests on another platform; it is based on the perception of viewers and artists as "idiots" engaged in the creation of meaningless illustrative content, filled with all manner of concepts. To escape this vicious circle, the artist can pit claims of authority against one other, waiting to see which one wins, but he must absolutely avoid the risk of inventing his own terms or problematizing his own xenophobia and colonialism. "It is as if we have no other criteria," Ter-Oganian states. "If you are an anti-Semite or a homophobe, then you are bad; if not, you're great. Like we are in a gay club in Israel" (ibid.).

I have written periodically about the ways in which postmodernist art history has endowed Soviet art with a monolithic image, consisting of three dominant discourses—avant-garde, socialist realism, and conceptualism (nonconformism). This strategy is linked to Soviet primers, which, functioning as primers of normativity, speak only of winners, heroes, and the daily life of the hegemonic class. A new discourse can only be sold in the same manner—by declaring its authors to be heroes and hegemonic leaders who have overcome the obscurantism of the "old world." The specificity of these latter primers is such that the dominant subjects are therein inevitably opposed to peripheral subjects, marked as queer. Thus, for instance, Ekaterina Degot's textbook on twentieth-century art references the "essentially mediocre" painter Robert Falk, the "outsider" Pavel Filonov, the "countercultural" Mikhail Matyushin as well as Alexandr Drevin's "abandoned form" of painting analogous to, say, an abandoned, decrepit building in the urbanist rhetoric of the 1930s (Degot' 2002, 131, 50, 47, 132).

It should be noted that this approach queers not only concrete individuals but also entire historical periods that do not fit into the concept of radicalism (such as the 1940s) and defines certain aesthetics through categories of disease ("by the mid-twentieth century, Soviet aesthetics in its totality reached the impasse of sheer madness [. . .], but conceptualism offered a way of egress back to sanity") or even through categories of mortality ("thinking of the picture as a biological entity was typical of Filonov, but this biology always contains an enormous potential for death") (Degot' 2002, 165, 53). The same ethos permeates the ways in which socialist realism actively queered nineteenth-century literature, culture, and science, presenting the lack of modernist collectivism through categories of feebleness, backwardness, femininity, emotional instability, depravity, and savagery (thereby declaring its own victory through fabrications of invulnerability across clusters of gender, race, class, education, disability, identity, sexuality, etc.)

The cultural reproduction of any binary oppositions inherited from modernism is possible when the excessive mythologization of social relations and certain strategies make knowledge of their specific social genealogy unavailable and inappropriate. This can be readily seen in the ways in which Russia's cultural field mythologizes and consecrates individual modernist figures —such as Pushkin, Gogol, Mayakovsky, Pasternak, Akhmatova, Tsvetaeva, Brodsky, Vysotsky and even Dovlatov—by excluding information about their identities and promoting binary concepts of creative genius hearkening back to Stalinist paradigms. You do not have to be familiar with the work of Alexander Zholkovsky and Lada Panova to observe the asymmetries and gaps in Russian biographies of Akhmatova;[8] you do not have to be a philologist or an art historian to spot the social prohibitions that, like parental controls, restrict information about the private lives of Soviet cultural protagonists. Thus, writing about "second rate memoirs" in *Kommersant*, Maria Stepanova states: "No mysteries, no bodily or emotional secrets—such is the bravery of a researcher determined, hound-like, to uncover what is hidden. Thus, he exposes his naked father and without any qualms moves on to his brothers and sisters, to those closer to us temporally and about whom it is easier to remember a lot of interesting stuff" (Stepanova 2013). Capturing this prohibition in detail, Stepanova also addresses the irrational sense of guilt that she experiences as a researcher committed to archival work.

It is impossible to offer sound analysis of the modernist space, with all its repressions and self-censorship, through hermetic descriptions of its surfaces and "first rate" memoirs to be merely contemplated and reproduced by the historian or rearranged slightly and radicalized by the artist or the essayist within the limits of their sensitivity (as do Kabakov, Groys, or Sorokin). This analysis should include not only lists of the repressed and the rewarded (that is, figures clearly identified by the authorities), but also consideration and detection of individual strategies common to those who were able to escape from the authorities or remain in locales that were culturally codified as dangerous, boring, provincial, and archaic—for such locales represent a political choice too. Recognizing political diversity and the multiplicity of individual strategies during the prewar period will in the long run also help us identify the motivations behind the repressions perpetrated by the colonial, homophobic, religious, class-based orders, among others.

Unless this turn takes place, contemporary researchers and artists will continue to hit dead ends, populating the spaces of art and science with something streamlined, accessible to the authorities and validating the authorities' suspicions. Yet the fear of being misunderstood—the central engine of post-Soviet popular scholarship—should give way to a sense of the civic and political role of artistic and scholarly activity and a sense of individual responsibility in research, which entails a recognition of the author's vulnerability. After all, a historian's interest in a problem is, in fact, a political interest.

Instead of spending years on public debates that pursue intentionally conservative, populist agendas touching on the very "possibility" of political change and civic resistance—for instance, whether Russia "needs" the feminist or queer movement—we should restore the concept of art as a polemical, dialogical process, resurrect a multiplicity of cultural positions, and establish respect for the unpredictability of the "Other." Instead of founding journals that imitate philosophical analysis and holding exhibitions that produce no new meanings, we ought to ask ourselves who actually views, reads, and commissions these products, what counterparts these products had in the past, and who commissioned them then.

The guilt felt in connection with the accomplishments of post-structuralism and the loyalty to postmodern institutions—both qualities detrimental to the Russian scholarly process—should give way to research honesty, which, among other things, would enable one fully to understand that art is not a pantheon of geniuses but precarious experimental work that is always done by stigmatized people. The objectives of such work, as well as the strategies and stigmas of its authors, deserve to be written about and researched to the fullest extent possible, and this is how queer lenses can serve as a tool for analyzing Soviet historical and archival materials, as well as the comprehensive toolkit that Soviet culture employed.

Translated by Aleksei Grinenko

Notes

1 This essay was written and first published in Russian as "Kvir v Strane Sovetov, ili Arkheologiia raznomysliia" in *Raznoglasiia,* a journal of art and social criticism that ran from 2016–17 and was edited by Moscow-based art critic Gleb Napreenko. It appeared in volume 7 in August 2016 in the issue Choose Sex/Gender (Vyberite pol) and is available at https://www.colta.ru/articles/raznoglasiya/12083-kvir-v-strane-sovetov-ili-arheologiya-raznomysliya

2 See: https://vk.com/deti404

3 See: http://www.deti-404.com/ru/node/4023

4 See: http://www.deti-404.com/ru/node/3794

5 See: http://www.deti-404.com/ru/node/3826

6 See: http://www.deti-404.com/ru/node/3589

7 "Iskusstvo" means "art"; "aktualnyi" here approaches the combined meaning of "current," "topical," and "relevant."

8 See: http://www-bcf.usc.edu/~alik/rus/ess/bib236.htm

References

Bondarenko, Ivan. 2016. "Vernite bessrochnuiu ivalidnost'." *dislife*, June 29. Available at: http://dislife.ru/materials/208.

Degot', Ekaterina. 2002. *Russkoe iskusstvo XX veka*. Moscow: Trilistnik.

Goralik, Linor. 2012. "Sloznost' na kolesikakh: Linor Goralik o nelovkosti pered invalidami." LENTA.RU, April 23. Available at: https://lenta.ru/columns/2012/04/23/clumsy/.

Kolesnikov, Aleksandr. 2016. "Avdei Ter-Ogan'ian: 'Goradzo skandal'nee, chem dlia Rossii': V Prage sozdaietsia soiuz sovetskikh khudozhnikov." Colta, July 29. Available at: http://www.colta.ru/articles/art/11909.

Palvan-zade, Furkat. 2015. "Il'mira Bolotian o proekte 'I—iskusstvo. F—feminizm.' Aktual'nyi slovar'." Syg.ma, October 20. Available at: https://syg.ma/@furqat/ilmira-bolotian-o-proiektie-i-iskusstvo-f-fieminizm-aktualnyi-slovar.

Plungian, Nadia. 2015. "V goriashchei izbe: Feministskoe iskusstvo v Rossii 2014–2015." Artgid, April 3. Available at: http://www.artguide.com/posts/779.

Puar, Jasbir K. 2007. *Terrorist Assemblages: Homonationalism in Queer Times*. Durham: Duke University Press.

Rossman, Ella. 2015. "Perevod s feministskogo na feministskii." *Otkrytaia Levaia*, November 5. Available at: http://openleft.ru/?p=7176.

Sozaev, Valerii. 2010. *Vozmozhen li kvir po-russki? LGBTK issledovaniia. Mezhditsiplinarnyi sbornik*. Saint Petersburg: Vykhod.

———. 2015. "'Kvir' dolzhen umeret'." Outloud, June 1. Available at: http://outloudmag.eu/events/item/kvir-dolzhen-umeret.

Stepanova, Mariia. 2013. "Protiv neliubvi: Mariia Stepanova o memuarakh vtorogo sorta." *Kommersant Weekend* 42 (14). Available at: http://kommersant.ru/doc/2341726.

Chapter 18

A Queer (Re)claiming of Russian and Soviet Art: An Interview with Slava Mogutin

Slava Mogutin (b. 1974) is a New York-based Russian American artist and author, exiled from Russia since 1995. Born in the industrial city of Kemerovo, Siberia, he moved to Moscow by himself at age fourteen. There he started working as a reporter and editor for independent Russian newspapers, publishers, and radio stations, such as Echo of Moscow, The Moscow Times, The Moscow Guardian, Nezavisimaia Gazeta, Stolitsa, *and* Novy Vzgliad. *He was considered one of the leading voices of post-Perestroika new journalism and the only openly gay personality in the Russian media. Forced to flee in 1995, Mogutin became the first Russian to be granted political asylum in the United States on the grounds of homophobic persecution.*

Upon arrival in New York, Mogutin turned to photography and multimedia arts and since then his work has been exhibited internationally, including at MoMA PS1 and the Museum of Arts and Design in New York; Yerba Buena Center for the Arts in San Francisco; Station Museum of Contemporary Art in Houston; Moscow Museum of Modern Art; KUMU Art Museum in Estonia; Museo de Arte Contemporáneo de Castilla y León (MUSAC) in Spain; The Haifa Museum of Art in Israel, and Indianapolis Museum of Contemporary Art, among others.

Mogutin is the author of two monographs of photography published in the U.S., Lost Boys *(2006) and* NYC Go-Go *(2008), and seven books of writings in Russian. In 2000, he was awarded the Andrei Bely Prize, one of the most prestigious literary awards in Russia. In 2014, Mogutin released his first collection of writings in English,* Food Chain *(ITNA Press, Brooklyn). His latest photography monograph,* Bros & Brosephines, *was published in 2017 by powerHouse Books, followed by the illustrated Straight to Hell edition,* Pictures & Words *(2018).*

Yevgeniy Fiks [YF]: Who are the queer figures in the history of Russian art that influenced you and are important to you? Whom from the Soviet and Russian art scene do you consider important from the standpoint of queer aesthetics or LGBTQ art?

Slava Mogutin [SM]: My three main inspirations are Alexander Rodchenko, both as a photographer and a graphic artist, Alexander Deineka, and Kuzma Petrov-Vodkin.

I remember as a child going through a Soviet textbook and seeing Deineka's painting *Future Pilots* (1938). At the time I thought of it as the most erotic work of art—that's when I realized there was something. It looked like it could be somewhere in the South of the Soviet Union, maybe on the Volga river or in Crimea. I spent a lot of time there and would go swimming naked. I was around the same age as the kids in the painting, so it was one of the first moments when I realized I could be gay and was attracted to other guys. The painting to this day is very symbolic to me, and I find it interesting that the two younger boys are nude, and the older guy seems to be telling them something about airplanes. It's a very tender, romantic image.

Alexander Deineka was primarily known for his heavy duty, brutalist propaganda art, like *The Defense of Sevastopol* (1942), filled with very butch, hypermasculine characters. His mosaics of naked bathing men and hockey players (in *Hockey Players*, 1960) look so contemporary and homoerotic. It's a fascinating combination of official Soviet propaganda and very subtle homoeroticism. The idea of male bonding and camaraderie was one of the key elements of the paramilitary education system we grew up under. That was the main function of art at the time. I remember at school we were taught how to reassemble Kalashnikovs. We were trained to clean our guns. [Laughs.]

Yet Deineka also had the most endearing, tender pictures of women who look like butch lesbians working at the factory, hanging their laundry and running through the woods. It's an interesting depiction of gender segregation. From today's perspective, most of Deineka's work would be perceived as homoerotic. This is an interesting example of his late work from 1966, set in the south.

YF: It's from the Khrushchev era.

SM: Yes, and Deineka made a name for himself as an official socialist realist artist. Male nudity seemed to be very restricted in the kind of work seen in subway stations and textbooks, yet you could get away with it if you had this type of official position in the art hierarchy. He was one of the most celebrated Soviet artists.

In general, I find socialist realist art very homoerotic—the same way as Nazi propaganda was heavily based on the celebration of the young male body and physique. There was a similar movement in the Soviet Union at the time. You see Rodchenko's documentation of the Soviet youth parading around in tight white underpants, marching in Red Square and wearing next to nothing. It could be compared to Leni Riefenstahl's *Olympia* documenting the Nazi Olympics held in Berlin in the summer of 1936.

Now uniforms are back in fashion. Take, for example, Thom Browne who recently designed the whole collection based on Michael Jackson's uniforms that were actually based on Soviet uniforms. It's like a double interpretation.

YF: Were Michael Jackson's uniforms based on Soviet uniforms?

SM: Absolutely. A few years ago, I had an outdoor public exhibition in Prague based on my book *Lost Boys*. My photos were displayed on billboards by Letna Park where the largest monument to Stalin used to be. Everyone hated it, it took six years to build. That monument was detonated right after Stalin's death and the sculptor killed himself. But the plinth remained, and Michael Jackson had erected his statue that was on the cover of *HIStory* album on that plinth. They say history always repeats itself and it couldn't be more symbolic than that. This happened during Jackson's Eastern European tour when he was escaping from the child molestation charges. The aesthetic of the video and the whole stage design were very totalitarian and homoerotic at the same time.

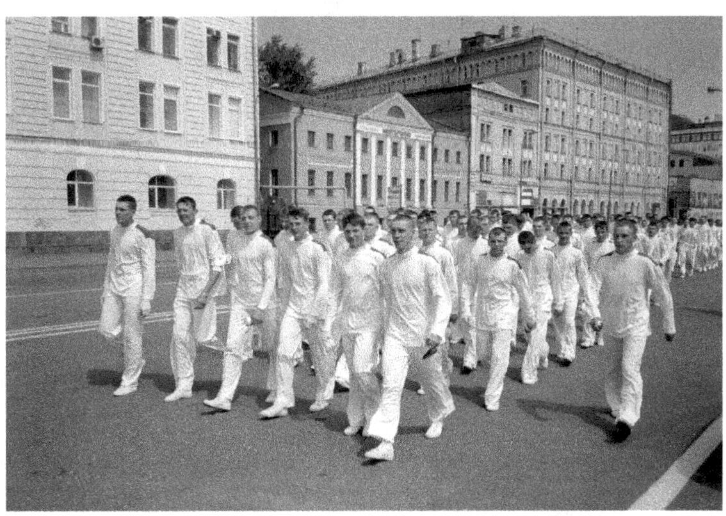

Slava Mogutin, *Independence Day Parade, Moscow* (2001).
Courtesy of the artist

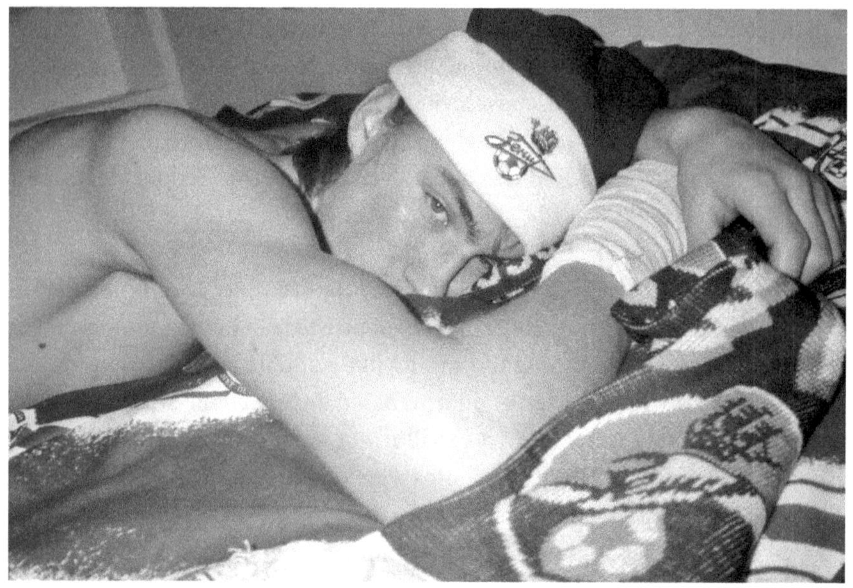

Slava Mogutin, *Lost Boys. Ilya. Zenit Hat* (2001).
Courtesy of the artist

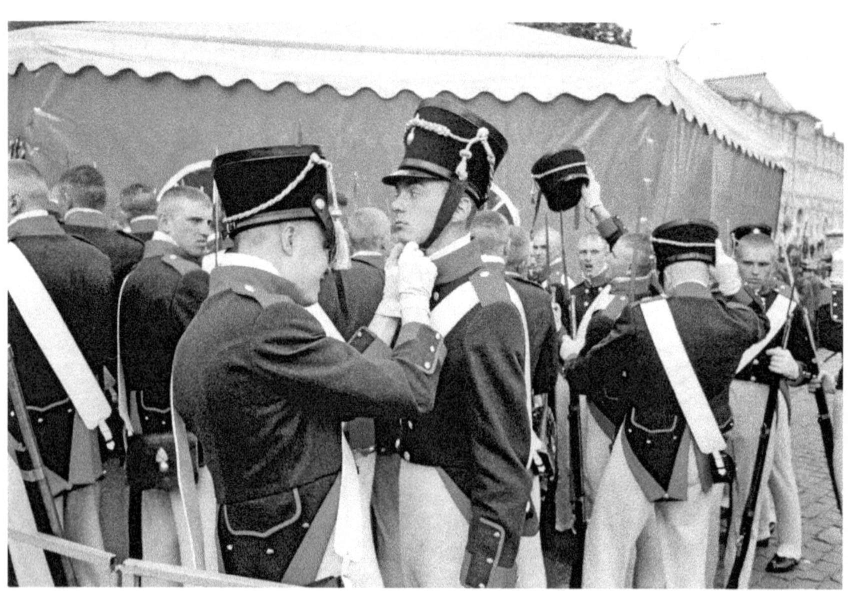

Slava Mogutin, *Cadets Dress-Up, Moscow* (2000).
Courtesy of the artist

Gosha Rubchinskiy is another example of someone who takes Soviet propaganda and blends it with Russian Orthodox symbolism. And it's wildly popular with the kids who think it's the coolest thing right now.

This whole aesthetic was created by artists like Alexander Rodchenko. In retrospect, I think his work is very homoerotic. It's made at the same time as the works of the first, pioneering American male nude photographer George Platt Lynes. Rodchenko's propaganda posters and pictures of the military parades were a huge inspiration for my photography. I always try to imagine what Rodchenko's work would look like if he were shooting in color. I often use similar extreme angles that became Rodchenko's trademark style. I also find his collage experimentations very inspiring and post-modern.

Going back to Deineka and the three boys from *Future Pilots,* it became a recurring motif in my work. On a subconscious level, I was so visually focused on the things that I remember from my Soviet upbringing, things imprinted in my memory—even going back to classical Russian art. For example, the painting you probably remember from our textbooks of Peter the Great interrogating his son.

YF: By Nikolai Ge [*Peter the Great Interrogating the Tsarevich Alexei Petrovich at Peterhof,* 1871].

SM: I thought that was a very homoerotic picture. Then there was one of Ivan the Terrible holding his son that he had just killed painted by Ilya Repin (*Ivan the Terrible and His Son Ivan on 16 November 1581,* 1885). It's interesting that there was so much going on in Russian classical art that could be perceived as homoerotic or queer. For instance, Aleksander Ivanov painted nude boys in Italy in 1830s. That was also one of the first erotic inspirations for me.

YF: We have one text on Ivanov in the book. Can you talk more about Rodchenko and Mayakovsky?

SM: As a poet I was very much inspired by Mayakovsky, and I was often compared to him. I find his flamboyant behavior very compelling, and I really think it was also gender-nonconforming and queer, in today's terms. I was fascinated by his personal story of the love triangle between him, Lilya Brik, and Osip Brik. Mayakovsky was a total macho in his public life and really submissive in his private letters to Lilya Brik.

I was obsessed with the whole story. Lilya Brik lived to be very old, she was a living legend. She lived in Peredelkino, a vacation house for the Writers Union outside of Moscow, where I spent a lot of time with my father. I used to see her always surrounded by an entourage of people. This story and the rumors that

Mayakovsky had syphilis created a cloud of very strange urban legends about him that I found interesting.

And I found the pictures that Rodchenko took of Mayakovsky to be strikingly beautiful and homoerotic. You see the trajectory of someone who started out with wearing a yellow shirt and painting his face to becoming something like the first skinhead. Starting out as a punk and ending up as a skinhead is how I see Mayakovsky.

The Russian avant-garde is rich with many examples and manifestations of queerness. Feminism was a big part of it, as well as sexual liberation and nonconformism. There was a popular movement called *Down with Shame!* The members of that group did social interventions, for example, they would ride public transit in the nude. Alexandra Kollontai led the sexual revolution and advocated for free love as an integral part of Communism. It was part of the same revolution until they all broke down. Some joined the regime and others just vanished or escaped.

As a writer, I was also interested in Mikhail Kuzmin's memoirs from that time and Vladislav Khodasevich's memoir about the Silver Age (*Necropolis*), which describes a lot of queer activities. It was a truly fascinating period that I was obsessed with. I did not care much for Soviet art per se, but these were the figures that were my lifelong inspirations who inspired me both as a writer and visual artist.

I've always loved Kuzma Petrov-Vodkin's classic paintings like *Bathing of a Red Horse* (1912), *Red Horse,* and *Boys Playing,* which were a homoerotic take on Henri Matisse from the same period. Later I discovered his other works from Central Asia. They were homoerotic and gender-bending—with very feminine boys that look like a third gender. That was also a revelation to me. It was all there, but it wasn't presented as "queer." These works were on display in the most important museums, but no one would interpret them that way. If they were created today, they would probably be perceived as "gay art."

YF: Absolutely, yes.

SM: Pavel Tchelitchew was another contemporary who in many ways stylistically reminds me of Petrov-Vodkin. And if you look at the beautiful drawings of Rustam Khamdamov from the 1970s and 1980s, it's a continuation of the same tradition.

YF: You're looking at the works of these artists who are a part of the official art canon, yet no Russian official art historian would ever claim that there is queerness there and would probably deny any homoeroticism. Are we "reclaiming" these images and saying that they are part of the 'Queer Russian Canon'? Or is it just a very personal thing to you, but they might not be queer to another queer artist?

SM: I'm coming from a very visceral perception of the work that I find inspiring. As far as claiming it and *queering* it, there is an untold story of that period that would be interesting to bring to the light. We could reveal an interesting perspective on this art that was made a century ago simply because we learned more about our gender and sexuality in the last hundred years. Obviously, this would and should apply to our knowledge of the art from that era.

I feel that from an academic perspective, it's really important to have this heritage established and revived. It's already there but needs to be articulated and contextualized. There are many figures that would be considered queer in modern terms, who were active in both underground culture and the mainstream. It is so interesting that they were artists and writers who were openly gay, and perhaps that's the reason they were largely forgotten and sidelined.

YF: Even in the Soviet context?

SM: Yes, I believe so. Take someone like Mikhail Kuzmin, who died of natural causes in complete poverty and obscurity. He was openly gay, so he couldn't publish most of his work and had a really meager existence under the Soviet regime. But he continued to write, even though he was officially banned.

YF: What about artists? Kuzmin's partner Yury Yurkun was also an artist and a writer. But I'm not sure if his works are still around.

SM: I think Yurkun's literary archive was published in recent years. I'm not familiar with his visual art.

My friend David Getsy, who wrote the intro for my book *Bros & Brosephines*, recently introduced this very interesting theory about abstract art as a way for the artists to express gender nonconformity in times when it was impossible to be openly gay. It's a great book (*Abstract Bodies: Sixties Sculpture in the Expanded Field of Gender*). Same goes for many Soviet artists who had to find different ways of expressing their queerness or gayness or gender nonconformity. In the case of Deineka, even in his official propaganda paintings like *The Defense of Sevastopol*, if you look at all those half-naked hyper-masculine men, the devil is in the details, as they say. In retrospect, it appears to be very homoerotic.

Eisenstein is another example of having an official Soviet status and acclaim, but there were persistent rumors of him being gay. My friend Jean-Claude Marcadé published a beautiful book of his erotic drawings, and most of them are overtly homoerotic in a very explicit way. They remind me of Cocteau's drawings from the same era.

YF: Yes, but Eisenstein wasn't very present in the Soviet visual landscape. There were a couple of his films that were shown, but his work wasn't disseminated as widely as Deineka's. Eisenstein was more of a classic —if not boring— his work wasn't as available as Deineka's was, which, as you say, was in children's books. Eisenstein was different.

SM: Yet, in retrospect, knowing what we know about him now is worth noting. You could see his films on state TV, and they were studied in every film school. There were certain scenes that, in retrospect, could be viewed through a queer perspective since he was, in fact, a practicing gay man. But this part was never officially acknowledged, it was left to speculation.

Also, speaking of *Pleshka,* a big part of this oral history comes from people who knew someone from that era. Parajanov was persecuted for being gay and so was Vadim Kozin. My An other friend Marc Almond recently produced a great BBC documentary about him, *In Search of Vadim Kozin.* It's a very fascinating yet tragic story.

A big part of being largely underground involved these kinds of untold stories, speculations, rumors, and urban legends—even though most of them were fabricated. There were rumors even about the introduction of the first anti-gay law. There was one rumor that the son of Maxim Gorky was raped or corrupted by some evil homosexuals. So, Maxim Gorky became the first person who officially called for the criminal prosecution of gay people in the Soviet Union—and that was the reason for the introduction of the anti-gay law. I am now working on a book of journalism, *Gay in the Gulag,* with the title article about the history of gay persecution and homosexuality in the Soviet camps and prisons.

YF: You wrote it a long time ago, I remember it.

SM: Yes, it was extensive research originally published in the mainstream political weekly *Novoe Vremya,* the Russian version of *Newsweek,* in 1993. It was a huge undertaking that took many months of work. Later, an abbreviated version of that article appeared in the British magazine *Index on Censorship.*

YF: Let's get back to Mayakovsky.

SM: Mayakovsky would be considered the first multimedia artist in modern terms—long before the term "multimedia" was coined. In his silent film *The Lady and the Hooligan* (1918) he plays a character who isn't just an outcast, he's a total punk. It's a tragic story about unrequited love and he gets slaughtered in the end. It's quite different from his official heroic image. There's something in his personal story, with the love triangle that I find very queer. How would you explain that to Soviet schoolboys and girls? It was a known fact, but it was conveniently left in the dark. But why not look into it and read his letters from today's perspective? I don't see anything wrong with that.

One of Mayakovsky's famous slogans was "Down with your religion, down with your art, down with your social order, down with your love!" This "Down with your love!" can be interpreted as "Down with your bourgeois love!" or "Down with your heteronormative love!" He lived his life according to that slogan, and it was very important for me as a very radical artistic statement and political manifesto.

It's ironic that the Russian futurists ended up the same way as their hero and role model Filippo Tommaso Marinetti, who was also very radical and nonconformist but ended up becoming a fascist. So, the Russian futurists eventually became allies of the Bolshevik regime. It's a similar scenario. Marinetti was revered under Mussolini and was one of his spokespeople. A few years ago, there was a great show on avant-garde art at the Guggenheim with a very impressive selection of Marinetti's works, including his recordings. It's fair to say he was an evil genius.

For the same reason as Marinetti, people from the underground circles dismiss Mayakovsky as a collaborator with the Soviet regime. My generation rejected him as a phony. His poem about Lenin [*Vladimir Ilyich Lenin*] is just disgusting, the most awful example of propaganda. There's no poetry left in his last writings—that's why he killed himself. It's either that or unrequited love or syphilis, or all the above. He's a tragic figure despite his romantic and hypermasculine image.

Chapter 19

"Queer and Russian Art?" A Conversation between Katharina Wiedlack and Masha Godovannaya[1]

Masha Godovannaya is a visual artist, experimental filmmaker, and queer-feminist researcher. Approaching art production as artistic research and collective action, Masha's artistic practice draws on combinations of approaches and spheres such as moving image theory, experimental cinema and DIY video tradition, social science, queer theory, decolonial methodologies, and contemporary art. Masha holds an MFA degree in Film/Video from Milton Avery Graduate School of the Arts, Bard College, New York, and an MA in Sociology from European University in St. Petersburg, Russia. Currently, she is a PhD candidate in Practice at the Academy of Fine Arts in Vienna, Austria.

Masha's films and visual works have been shown at many festivals, screenings, and art venues such as the Rotterdam Film Festival, Tate Modern, Oberhausen International Film Festival, London Film Festival, Manifesta-10, Seventh Liverpool Biennial, Center Georges Pompidou, etc. The works are distributed by Light Cone, Paris, The Collectif Jeune Cinéma, Paris, Filmmakers' Cooperative, New York, and part of collections of The State Russian Museum, St. Petersburg, Austrian Film Archive, Vienna, and Anthology Film Archive, New York (Godovannaya, n.d.).

Katharina Wiedlack [KW]: This interview is a response to an invitation to discuss why we must talk about, practice and look attentively for queerness in art, particularly in Russian art, and why it is important for queer art practices in and beyond the post-Soviet context.

Masha, you and I come from different spaces of queer knowledge production: you from the field of visual art, and me from Cultural Studies. But we both practice and try to find new modes of queer solidarity, and we share the idea that such solidarity should emerge at the intersection of queer-feminist research, activism, and art.

Our collaborative projects on queer solidarity bring issues of visibility and opacity to the forefront. Transnational queer solidarity and the problem of in/visibility were the core theme of the conference we co-organized in 2017, "Fucking Solidarity,"[2] the book we co-edited, *Queer-Feminist Solidarity and The East/West Divide* (Wiedlack, Shoshanova and Godovannaya 2020), and our ongoing project on the possibilities of transnational solidarity and collaborative artistic practice in the context of increasing homophobia (fig. 1).

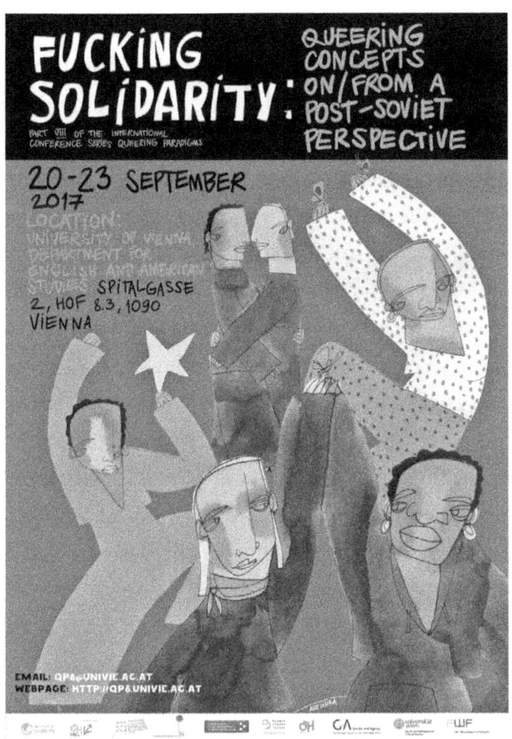

FIGURE 1. Adelinaa, *Fucking Solidarity* (2017), poster. Courtesy of Katharina Wiedlack

Before we go deeper into the discussion, I think we should start with some simple, and at the same time complex questions: What does queerness mean to you? How would you define it as a visual artist working within the tradition of experimental cinema?

Masha Godovannaya [MG]: I strongly mark my position within Cinema as a DIY queer-feminist filmmaker who follows the avant-garde call for its democratization (of the people, by the people, and for the people), works at the crossroads of different disciplines (academic and artistic), and who orients herself to the margins as spaces of resistance and emancipation, following bell hooks (hooks 1990). For me it is not important to make queer films but to make films queerly, rephrasing Godard's famous call.[3] I try to take into consideration, reexamine, and queer every aspect of the creative—in my case, cinematic—process: positionality, context, content, form, ethics, labor, distribution strategy, etc.

Queerness, for me, is not about normalizing certain queer people's lives within mainstream cinema, adding them into the "meta" capitalist commercial narrative. The question for me is, rather, how can we maintain queerness as a political momentum that continues to problematize norms and works against the pressure of conformity in cinema on different levels; that is, how to unsettle normalization processes through audiovisual mediums. The questions of cinematic form are important, but they are inseparable from ethical questions.

KW: I think discussing these ethical questions is very important for both of us. We share the understanding of queerness as nonnormativity and an approach to question norms. For me, it is additionally important to mention that queerness, as I use it in my research and in my attempts to practice solidarity, is not concerned with identity politics, which operate with norms, labels, definitions, classifications and categories based on Western epistemological traditions. I am personally not interested in the usage of queer as an umbrella term for lesbian, trans*gender, or gay identities. I use queer politics and art-based research to question identity politics for their exclusionary and violent effects. In my view, such an approach to queerness understands violence and oppression as structured through multiple axes at the intersection of gender, race and ethnicity, class and sexuality.

Within Western contexts, LGBT identities have already entered some legal spheres, and this can be a problem for people, for example, in asylum cases. Often, people from outside the so-called West do not identify as LGBT because these categories do not mean anything in their context, or the identities are highly sanctioned. In cases where such people are persecuted for same-sex or any other nonnormative acts, desires, or bodies, and must flee, the 'Western' authorities demand proof of LGBT identities that conform to Western models as a precondition for asylum. And this is one of the most precarious problems of identity politics, but there are many (see Smirnova 2020; Lewis 2014).

On the other hand, I also insist that sexual desire and gender nonnormativity are at the core of queerness. I believe that we all live in an era when sexuality and different desires are increasingly policed—be it through violent efforts by neoconservatives fighting for "traditional values" or liberal and so-called progressive LGBT identity politics.

I think your artistic practice has given me a new perspective on the question of how to queerly question identity politics and at the same time bring forward a strong argument for queer solidarity. Could you explain in a few sentences how you use avant-garde cinema as a space for your queer practice?

MG: I also often question the usefulness and appropriateness of LGBT identities as a "universal" approach for thinking of non-heterosexual peoples. At the same time, I critically reflect on whether sexual and gendered practices are all that is necessary to define oneself as queer, or if we need to expand our definition of queerness and queer practices. This question is especially relevant if we want to look for queer art in the Soviet tradition, for example.

Experimental, poetic, and avant-garde cinema provide me with a space where I can look for inspiration and insist on creating something not particularly meeting expectations, not transparent, not easily accessible and available to the viewer; not looking for results, but focusing on a process, open ended; in search of new ways of relatedness to the films' participants and social contexts through the camera lens. It gives me a sense of belonging to cinema, a point of reference and, at the same time, a point of departure.

The marginalized and clandestine visual tactics that I have been developing and practicing over the years allow me to search for queerness as a cinematic form. You can say that I try to queer cinematic language and the elements that are expected of a film: rethinking the camera work in its construction of filmic space; transforming time; reapproaching stories through montage; creating opaque narratives through rapturous sonic soundscapes. Importantly, I make visible and queer the relationships between me as the person behind the camera and person(s) or phenomena in front of it.

These approaches often evoke feelings of incompletion, uneasiness, and incomprehension when I/we tell or whisper stories of queer people. It is about making queer kinships within this space of film production and off-screen, practicing queer communities, intimacies, and queer diasporic relationality, which lies beyond national contexts and expected representations.

Thus, experimental cinema for me is not only a tradition of a particular visual form but also a space for dialogue and a cavity that allow me to have this journey into unpredictability and invite others (the films' collaborators and participants as well as audience members) to join, to share the experience of not knowing, copresence and mutuality.

KW: Would you describe poetic, underground cinema as an international space? And would you say that avant-garde cinema is, maybe less than other forms of cinema, confined to national contexts, due to its ludic and playful relationship to narration, linearity, language etc.?

MG: Exactly. And this brings us back to our initial inquiries: Why do we have to talk about, practice, and look attentively for queerness in art, particularly in Russian art? And why is it important to queer art practices?

KW: It might be more important than ever to produce art queerly and to allow queer relationality to emerge through art forms. Art allows us to venture into spaces that political activism in its more conventional practices can no longer or could never create. In times of oppression and increased enforcement of norms and regulations, political activism is easy to limit, hence it does not have the same potential to create communities. Art, and especially cinema, allows us to reach out and relate in different ways. And I think your recent films are a beautiful example of this kind of reaching out and building bridges, not just as finished products, but as art practice itself. You practice a kind of queer solidarity that I wanted to address through my concept of solidarity as "working together" (Wiedlack 2020). You blur not only the line between producer and collaborator but also the position of the "giver" and "receiver" of solidarity. I think this adds a beautiful ethical dimension to your already visually and audibly beautiful works. I am thinking here especially about your films *who said there will be a walk in time* and *Countryless and Queer*, where you show us moments of human connection, listening to each other, and sharing dreams and thoughts (figs. 2 and 3). The films' scenes are intimate and revealing, and, at the same time, they are never intrusive or violate your collaborators' right to privacy and safety. They show care for one other, a willful sharing of place and time, an acknowledgement of one other, and collaboration to produce something meaningful. This is what I mean by solidarity as "working together."

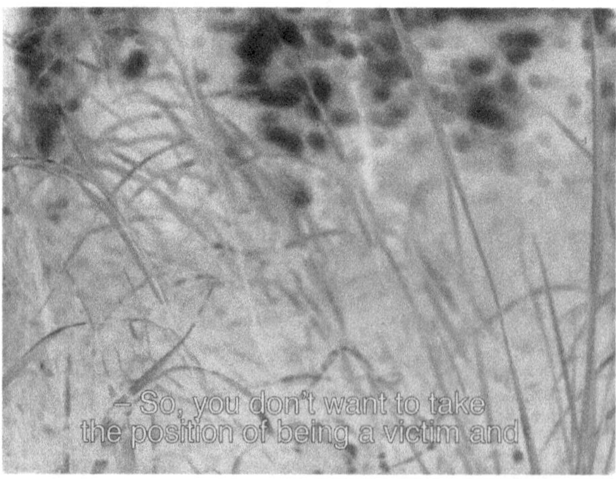

FIGURE 2. Masha Godovannaya, *Countryless and Queer* (2020), a digital film still. Courtesy of the artist

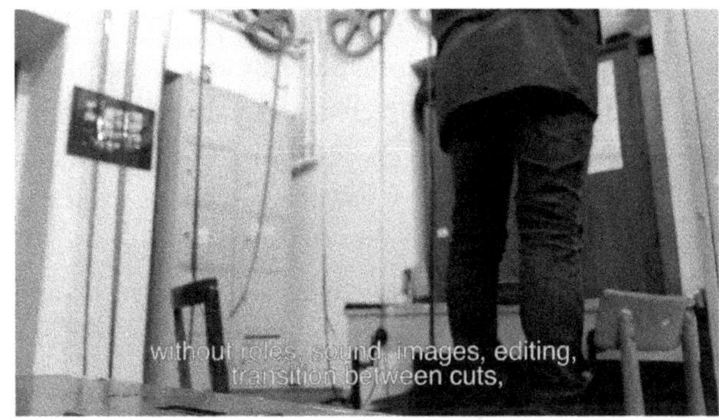

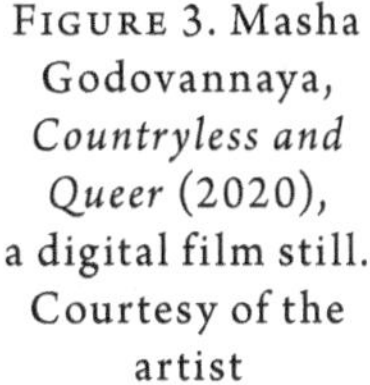
FIGURE 3. Masha Godovannaya, *Countryless and Queer* (2020), a digital film still. Courtesy of the artist

On a different level, your work also questions more deeply who the subject of queer solidarity is. And I think this question has a contemporary as well as a historical dimension. Looking back at Russian avant-garde cinema and its relationship to queerness (I am thinking especially about Sergei Eisenstein and Yevgeny Yufit), might we propose that the forms of poetic cinema allow for queer strategies and content to emerge in a time of increased restrictions? Is there a need to look for alternative concepts of looking, analyzing, and practicing queerness, which lie outside of Anglo-Saxon paradigms of queerness and embraces "deviant" modernities?[4]

In our ongoing art research project "The Magic Closet and the Dream Machine,"[5] which aims at supporting and connecting queer lives in or across post-Soviet spaces and beyond, without exposing and endangering them, we think a lot about how to circumvent the excessive risks of visibility. We relate to the philosopher and poet Édouard Glissant and his demand for "the right to opacity for everyone" (Glissant 1997, 194). Glissant was a prominent critic of Western epistemological hegemony and used the concept of opacity to resist the oppression and epistemological violence of Western 'objective knowledge' and its classificatory scientific apparatus. As a refusal of globalization's demand for transparency, opacity is not based on the facile understanding of local identities as rooted and ossified.

MG: The question of visibility and opacity has multiple dimensions for me. As an aging queer from a post-Soviet space, living sometimes within that space, I totally understand that being in front of a camera could put me and others at risk. For example, after the 2012 Moscow protests, where people would film themselves participating in the demonstrations and street actions, the police used their personal visual records against them in court.

The camera can be a violent actor, no matter how experimental one wants to be with it. There is a long tradition in cinema of how the camera and its gaze were nonconsensually directed at certain communities, playing a deadly role in their objectification and exoticization. The camera gaze is not innocent and has to be always questioned, including within the avant-garde and experimental film traditions.

Visibility for/of other people can be dangerous and unwanted, especially for people who are marked as "others," as "nonhumans," as those who don't deserve to live. We must look closely at what it means for them to be exposed through the lens, made available to the gaze(s). In my view, there is a need to rethink queer cinema as only aiming for visibility and discuss tactics of visual opacity to tell stories of/with queers who can't afford visibility due to different reasons; to tell stories without endangering queers' lives.

Queer thinking outside of Anglo-Saxon paradigms could also involve redefining or reappropriating the concept of the closet. We—you, me, and our friends and colleagues from the post-Soviet queer diaspora in Vienna—have been thinking through and discussing it a lot recently, especially in the context of rising ultra-right conservatism and heteroactivism (Browne and Nash 2017), on the one hand, and homonationalism and homonormativity, on the other. The reexamination of the concept of the closet could be an important endeavor when we address the question of queer traces in post-Soviet spaces.

KW: Yes, together with our colleagues Ruthie Jenrbekova and Iain Zabolotny, we reconsider the closet, questioning its Western configurations as a claustrophobic space and appropriating it as a positive one. We know from experience and the work of others (Stella 2015) that there are already places of queer opacity, of queer (self-)recognition, and community building within the post-Soviet space, such as the *pleshkas,* the (post-)Soviet queer cruising zones (Fiks 2014). Building on those lived realities, we came up with the concept of a 'Magic Closet' for spaces that can contain and preserve post-Soviet queer lives.

Our Magic Closet is a private or semi-private space, where people come together to engage with each other and create something together that speaks to their individual and shared experiences. The Magic Closet is a reappropriation of the concept of the gay closet (Kosofsky Sedgwick 1990), playing with the frequent signification of the post-Soviet space as the homophobic "Iron Closet" (Tuller 1996). Rather than understanding non-visibility as something negative, it encourages an understanding of non- or half-visibility as self-preservation, as a positive "magic" way of self-care. Such an understanding would encourage moving away from the binary opposition of presence and absence (Derrida 2016) and the belief that a visual representation of queer bodies equates to some form of emancipatory politics.

MG: One could say that the Magic Closet tries to address two related desires within queer communities. First, the possibility to 'maneuver' collectively within homophobic contexts and find new tactics to survive and live with dignity. Second, the desire to preserve the knowledge and histories of queer existence from their violent erasure through homophobic negation. We were rethinking the closet metaphorically as a potential space to store queer knowledge and collectively assemble an affective queer archive of post-Soviet queer existence. We acknowledge that epistemic violence erases possibilities of connection across spaces and time, and we were—and are—aiming to find a different form of archiving that was not based on a visibility paradigm, which might draw unwanted attention from different forces and powers, potentially endangering queers.

Rethinking in/visibility within community work could also make it possible to bring radicalism back to queer as a political project. It would make post-Soviet subjects less dependent on the Western model, giving agency to rethink our history, our pasts and presents. It can allow us to ask: How does our queerness fit into the spectrum of non-heterosexual intimacies and forms of relatedness? In which way(s) can we claim our own space(s) within this spectrum? It sets us on a different journey than the attempt to inscribe ourselves into the Western concept of queerness.

At the same time, a rethinking of in/visibility poses the question of how we can be in solidarity with one other. How can we live in the oppressive systems and at the same time envision alternative queer horizons and foster hope, which make our lives meaningful and fulfilling. How can we not fall into the trap of creating a competition between different forms of oppression and positions of victimization?

KW: I think what you just said again questions LGBTQ+ identity politics as the only right way of self-expression and representation. You play with this concept in the title of your already mentioned film *Countryless and Queer*. It promises familiarity and yet it creates (visual) expectations that it does not fulfill. It asks what it might look like to be queer and what kinds of practices, desires, and forms of navigating daily life are involved. This is also a different point of departure for solidarity than a sharing of LGBT identities.

Thinking of queer politics as solidarity across post-Soviet spaces (including queer post-Soviet diasporas in the 'West') additionally transgresses national identity politics, which are fashionable right now in many countries, including Russia. The post-Soviet sphere spans many national belongings and ethnicities and cannot be reduced to a white Slavic identity, and the radical queer that you just mentioned is not easily defined by any specific and neatly framed sexual or gender identity either.

MG: The film *Countryless and Queer* is not about identities, as you said already. It is about queer relationality, about what we build between one other and what traces we can make visible for others, the audience. The film took the form of a filmic essay built on a collectively gathered affective queer archive of complex, ambivalent, and vividly poetic life narratives of five queer migrants who navigate their experiences of non-privileged migration in the city of Vienna. They came from contexts outside the Global North, contexts marked by gender violence, homophobia, economic instability, and social misbalance.

It brings me back to the point that you mentioned earlier. The way I/we approach the topic of migration broadens questions and problems, which can be potentially marked as "exclusively for LGBTQ+ people." The film is not exclusively about queer migration but about non-privileged migration in a broader sense: how mechanisms of exclusion work; which discriminatory practices are activated toward people marked as "others," "aliens," "refugees," and "nonhumans"; how do they fight for their dignity, and in which ways do they keep in contact with the spaces that are colored with strong emotional, personal, and intimate memories? Importantly, how do they maintain a connection with their places of origin, which, actually, never release them although they pushed them away, rejected, and violently expelled them? Thus, the film's form and style reflect a process of queer diasporic relationality and becoming.

With this project, I wanted to use filmmaking to open a space of the embodied dialogue and mutuality of being for and with all participants. Our artistic inquiry invited a multiplicity of voices and gazes by passing audio recorders and video and film cameras freely among us, trespassing the division between who is "behind" or "in front" of the camera. It helped to dismantle the unquestioned power of the maker (filmmaker/artist), initiate collective image-making, bridge differences, and create a new form of community through dialogue and relationality. Basically, the film was about the creation of queer kinship within this space of film production.

KW: In *Countryless and Queer*, by handing the camera to your participants, you draw the audiences' attention to the gaze and its violence. At the same time, with a gesture of sharing with others the power over the gaze, you queer its unquestionable authority over others as "objects." In connection with the stories about gendered, sexualized, and racialized experiences of [queer] migration and flight, the topic of viewing and the gaze transgresses multiple layers of meaning; it is a discussion of art production, filming, and recording; at the same time, it is a discussion of solidarity and non/belonging in a new and unfamiliar space; it is about queer bonds and kinships.

Additionally, *Countryless and Queer* creates opacity, rather than visibility, for people who live queerly. I think this is an important queer strategy in the current moment when people face violence and persecution in many places for loving and living queerly.

MG: While addressing sensitive issues that could still potentially harm and endanger the queers living in Vienna, thinking, practicing, and creating opacity were indispensable to the process of making the film. Since the participants were not easily identified through images, the sound was created first, taking bits and pieces from interviews, encounters, wishes and silences, dreams, recorded autoethnographic notes, and poetic reflections. I also tried to step away from the reproduction of damage or pain narratives, which undoubtedly many queers from non-Global North/non-Western Europe countries have imprinted on their bodies. Together we tried concentrating on other stories of their lives—full of humor and joy, dignity and eroticism, emancipation and struggle. Through cinema and artistic engagement, we tried to create a safe space between us, where we could laugh, talk freely and intimately, joke, drink and share our queer legends, and invite others to join us in this film journey, to be with us.

So, for me, it is important to think of an experimental film as a space for community building. Through making films, watching them, doing things together, working together as you mentioned earlier, we are creating communities. They may be elusive, fleeting, ephemeral. But these multiple communities and the sense of belonging to them allow us to move further, to insist on living lives queerly, to recognize, respect, and celebrate our differences, and to build alliances and be in solidarity with others.

KW: I think *Countryless and Queer* illustrates Glissant's argument that the challenge of solidarity is to arrive at a form of it that doesn't depend on the (illusion of) fully understanding or comprehending the other. The film *who said there will be a walk in time,* which you shot in Croatia, has a different language than *Countryless and Queer*. Yet it also questions what it might look like to be queer in post-socialist spaces.

MG: The film *who said there will be a walk in time* is a visual study that sketches forms and outlines the margins of queer kinships lived by the local queer community of post-socialist Split, Croatia. It was my first collaborative project, working closely with "queerANarchive," an artist-run organization, together with the local queer community, in April 2018.

I had a chance to show the film in St. Petersburg, Russia, a country that is usually marked as explicitly homophobic, to audiences that were not necessarily self-identifying as LGBT. After the screening, a moderator for the discussion admitted that she was puzzled, since it did not meet her expectations of a queer film. Since in my introduction for the screening, I mentioned that the film was done with the queer community of Split, she was expecting to see queer bodies—"others"—that talk about their sexuality, how they fuck, love, live, and how they are confronted with/by others, non-queers. According to her expectations, the film should have told some easily identified and expected stories from non-heterosexual people about their partners and sexual desires, homophobic attacks, and discrimination. But instead, in the film there are no bodies that were made easily accessible, that one can gaze at and consume. The queers didn't talk about their sexual lives. Instead, they shared their dreams, which they recorded during our process of collective filming. These dreams were full of eroticism and desires, non-linearity of fragmented time and raptured spaces, confusing language, and incomprehensibility.

So, the audience was a bit perplexed. Uncomfortable. Irritated. No exposure of queer bodies. No juicy stories to consume. Many people felt that they were exposed to their own limitations as an audience who wanted to see something exotic, something already-expected-and-known. But instead, they were offered the opportunity to be in coexistence for a while with others who remained non-transparent to them and to face their own normative assumptions of Queer Cinema and of queer people.

KW: So, what is important about queer/ing art?

MG: Obviously, we can render some art as queer. Or look for traces of queerness left in art. Or try to identify gay and lesbian artists and filmmakers. But is it enough? Is it enough of a gesture to add names to LGBTQ+ art history? And to which history? To which narrative are we adding them? Would they, these filmmakers and artists, want to be included? Could it be a violent act toward them to concentrate only on their sexuality (usually suppressed and closeted) and not to include other characteristics that are central to their subjectivities and identities?

And here, again, we can bring in the concepts of relationality, opacity, working together, and our proposition of queerness as political momentum that continues to problematize norms and works against the pressure of conformity in art. What could be elements and strategies that we might analyze and use now when we are looking for queerness in the histories of art and/or cinema? Which tactics and forms were used by artists and filmmakers in their attempt to unsettle normalization processes through their art/film practices? What can we learn from them? And from which positions will we start?

KW: I think you make an extremely important point here. What we saw during the last couple of years was that famous Russian filmmakers and other artists were claimed to be queer, part of the LGBT population. One example of these attempts to incorporate historic Russian figures into a queer history of cinema was Peter Greenaway's 2015 *Eisenstein in Guanajuato*. Although the film does not claim to be a biographical work, true to historical events, it nevertheless plays with the suggestion that Eisenstein was a closeted homosexual, who 'found himself' only when acting out his previously negated homosexual desires. Greenaway's film was done in solidarity with Russian LGBTs, suggesting that queers have always existed in Russia and that they were great people. Yet in portraying Eisenstein in Western terms of 'the gay closet' and gay identity politics, the film missed the opportunity to make a relational argument. Moreover, it certainly offended many viewers due to its many historical inaccuracies and its ironic and often caricaturistic depiction of sexual acts that some people understood as crude (Robinson 2015).

But what you are suggesting is something completely different. It is not to question the identity of an author, artist, or filmmaker, but to see how the work spoke in a queer way at certain moments in time.

MG: In the Greenaway film, Eisenstein as a filmmaker and theorist is almost "reduced" to being an eccentric exotic closeted gay who had a rare chance to free his sexual desires by going on a joyful, wonder-film-trip to Mexico, full of surprises and adventures.

So, what do we know about him then? As Joan Neuberger mentioned in her in-depth analyses of Eisenstein's sex drawings, his "actual sex life was a matter of speculation while he was alive and ever since, producing a great deal of misinformation" (Neuberger 2012, 9). Eisenstein himself, when he did mention his sexuality, often referenced Freud's 1910 essay on Leonardo da Vinci, in which he puts forward the notion that sexual energy can be sublimated into artistic creation. Also, we have to consider that by 1935 sexual freedoms as well as discourse on sexuality came to an end in the USSR (Reich 1962); homosexuality was re-criminalized in 1933 and the "famous" Article 121 remained in the Soviet criminal code until 1993. So, it was hard (if not impossible) to speak openly of one's sexuality and desire without being arrested and prosecuted. However, Eisenstein's drawings, especially the erotic ones, provide us with his more nuanced views on desire, sexuality, and sexual practices. Moreover, the drawings are far from being only a depiction of his "repressed" homo/bi-sexuality but unearth traces of his inner processes and connections between his creativity and artistic and theoretical practices (Neuberger 2012).[6]

For me, Sergei Eisenstein is an interesting figure as a revolutionary filmmaker with whom I can have a dialogue and speculative relationality. "Speculative" since my gaze, questions, and aspirations about him are directed backwards; a gesture of backward glances, which is a queer gesture (Love 2009). Looking at his films and drawings, reading his theoretical works and diaries, I don't look for evidence of his suppressed sexuality. I look for ways, forms, and strategies that he, with a particular sensibility and tactility that could be called queer, used to plot narratives, construct shots, and combine them into montage phrases to destabilize the normalcy of the cinematic canon.

In this inquiry, the question for me is not whether someone identifies as homosexual, but rather whether the work questions normativity in a meaningful and productive—even radical and revolutionary—way in terms of content, aesthetics, form, and ethics. Does it resist simple consumption and assimilation? Can we queerly relate to this through time by creating a moment of relationality and of community building that bridges the past with the present?

KW: I really like the questions that you pose regarding Eisenstein's works and how you use queer speculation to create a relationality between his work and past as well as contemporary queers. You are not trying to uncover a common identity or a representation of yourself (as a queer or LGBT person) in the past, but you look for points of relation in the form of a cinematic language that questions normativity, that "defamiliarizes" or queers the surface of what we could call Soviet biopolitics. Thereby you reach out or "reach back" to Eisenstein to open a cinematic space where queer community can emerge—where people can find each other, despite the increasing oppression and restriction of LGBT visibility politics.

I think what is important to acknowledge is that you might imagine yourself in a conversation with Eisenstein that he himself would not have wanted to have. Masha Salazkina has rightly pointed out that Eisenstein's vision for Soviet collectivity and a Soviet solidaristic community excluded women completely (Salazkina 2009). It is nevertheless, in my opinion, fruitful to read aspects of a questioning of the norms of heteropatriachy and of the compulsory gender-binary into Eisenstein's cinematic language to find traces of queer existence that communities can relate to. The questioning of normativity is also a point where I can relate queerly to some of Yevgeny Yufit's films (figs. 4 and 5).

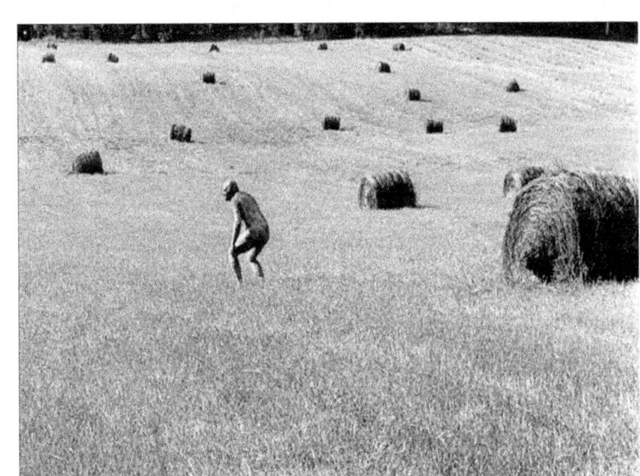

FIGURE 4. Yevgeny Yufit, *Bipedalism* (2005), a film still. Courtesy of the Yufit family

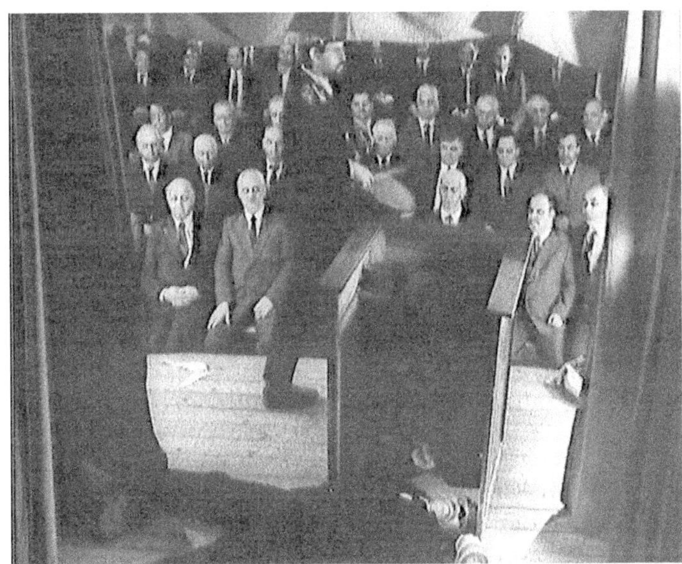

FIGURE 5. Yevgeny Yufit, *Wooden Room* (1995), a film still. Courtesy of the Yufit family

In contrast to Eisenstein, Yufit produced his Necrorealist art and films in the so-called Parallel Cinema, outside of the Goskino State Cinema system in the 1980s. Yet both Eisenstein and Yufit offered us a perspective on Soviet bodies that broke with conventions and left us artistic productions that will never be fully decrypted, never fully transparent to the onlooker. I think it is this quality of opacity that I can relate to queerly. Of course, their methods and styles differ greatly. But both, each in his own way, offered something like an oppositional gaze to the Soviet governing of bodies, its pronatalism and futurism.

Yufit's films use black humor and the absurd to explore themes of death, decay, and the transformation of the body after death. His irony and exaggeration make me wonder about the desires and physical connections that appear on the screen. His absurd and often comical scenarios open themselves up to multiple readings that remained opaque, since he always refused to confirm or negate them. I read this opacity as a queer aspect that opens space for relationality. It is a kind of refusal to be transparent, while at the same time allowing the audience to glimpse at desires and physical connections that were as prohibited from being acknowledged under Soviet rule as they are today.

Moreover, some of his earlier films jokingly play with ideas of the secret identity of the 'lumpenproletariat' as model Soviet citizens. His anarchic parasites inside the Soviet public body that eats the corpse from the inside out can be read as an anti-social element akin to Lee Edelman's concept of queerness (Edelman 2004). Through the anti-social, I can form a queer bond between Yufit in the past and people who live queerly in contemporary Russia. The current Russian state propagates democratic growth that signifies queers as dangers to the future and Russian well-being (Stella and Nartova 2015; Medvedev 2019). They are signified as the anti-social, much like in Edelman's analysis of US capitalist society. In contrast to Edelman's analysis, which argues that queers are always already and necessarily excluded from the process of meaning-making, since they are anti-meaning, Yufit's films playfully use the anti-social, the anti-meaning and the absurd to show the weaknesses of the normative and regulative, the (state) body that governs.

MG: I think it's a productive strategy to look at the works of artists who provoked normativity through artistic means and offer a queer reading, a queer commentary, of these works following Berlant's and Warner's approach (Berlant and Warner 1995), which allows us to connect different threads and understandings and at the same time—to be queerly playful.

Due to his unexpected death, it's still difficult for me, as Yufit's artistic ally and film colleague, his ex-wife, and now together with our son, a caretaker of his artistic heritage, to talk about his works from a distance. But going through his archive, looking at pictures, slides, reading some bits and pieces of his own texts, and rewatching his short films and features, I'm wondering if we could formulate a different set of questions outside of the official narratives of Necrorealism, the carefully carved and maintained myth (Campbell 2006, Dobrotvorsky 1993, Mazin 1998, Mazin 2015).

As an invitation to further inquiry, could we, for example, render contemporary queer approaches and theories (for instance, Berlant and Warner's queer commentary, already mentioned, and Jack Halberstam's concept of "the queer art of failure" [Halberstam 2011]) through Necrorealist lenses and theorization? And vice versa? Could the elements of Necrorealist aesthetics—the heroic idiocy, black humor, aimless absurd hyperactivity of the main figures of socrealism (soldiers, sailors, doctors), marked by the rudimentary conditions of Yufit's film production, especially of the early films, inform us about strategies, forms, and tactics of confronting conformity and normalcy by artists of the last Soviet generation (Yurchak 2013)? Can we, post-Soviet queer artists, reclaim Yufit's motto for making these early works: "It was merriment for the sake of filming and filming for the sake of merriment" (Alaniz and Graham 2001, 10)—as a driving force for making films queerly? Could it be a way to resist and refuse assimilation, the sucking-in and straightening-up of our DIY film/video-making into commercial film production, with its politics, forms, ethics, and censorship? "Filming for the sake of merriment and merriment for the sake of filming"— could it be a way to escape from and transgress the imposed conventions and demands of the mainstream film industry?

In his article "*Knights of the Heavens* in the Representation of Death," Viktor Mazin wrote about Yufit's first 35 mm film: "We have the feeling that there is a story. It seems that we can get to the bottom of it. It seems that someone knows the secret. Who will give it away? This seemingness introduces a sense of disorientation into our reception of the narrative. What, finally, is going on here? The impossibility of finding an answer, of recognizing anything, tells us: this story is tomfoolery, a travesty, a riddle with no answer wrapped in a mystery" (Mazin 1999, 106).

As you mentioned, we can look at Yufit's films—as well as Eisenstein's and many other (post-)Soviet filmmakers—and relate to them queerly by providing multiple readings of his/their works and focusing on different aspects of their cinematic queerness. But as we discussed, it will be a speculative relationality and annotation full of uncertainties and opaqueness. And that's exactly what is needed—to admit the impossibility of knowing and to accept "a riddle with no answer wrapped in a mystery."

Notes

1 The interview was developed within the framework of the project "The Magic Closet and the Dream Machine: Post-Soviet Queerness, Archiving, and the Art of Resistance" (AR 567), conducted by Katharina Wiedlack, Masha Godovannaya, Ruthia Jenrbekova and Iain Zabolotny, funded by the Austrian Science Fund (2020–2023).

2 "Fucking Solidarity: Queering concepts on/from a Post-Soviet perspective" was an international conference held from September 20–23, 2017 at the University of Vienna. The aim of the conference was to discuss the possibilities, gains, and limits of queer solidarity. "Fucking" solidarity meant, first, to investigate the idea, the theories, the practices, and the art of solidarity thoroughly and critically from different angles, different spaces, and from and within different groups. Moreover, it meant to discuss the pleasures and erotics of queer solidarity, their drives, and the desires behind it. In this way, the conference critically reflected on hegemonies and the possibility of empowerment. See also: https://qp8.univie.ac.at/.

3 Jean-Luc Godard once said that what is important is not "making political films, but rather making films politically" (Hoberman, 2005).

4 For the question if or how far Soviet ideology and practice, communism, or socialism offered alternative or "deviant" modernities to that of Western colonial modernity, see David-Fox 2015; Tlostanova 2012; Karkov & Valiavicharska 2018.

5 For details regarding this project, see footnote 1.

6 For more on Eisenstein's drawings, see chapter 10 in this volume.

Works Cited

Alaniz, Jose and Seth Graham. 2001. "Early Necrocinema in Context." In *Necrorealism: Context, History, Interpretations,* edited by Seth Graham, 5–27. Pittsburgh: Russian Film Symposium.

Berlant, Lauren, and Michael Warner. 1995. "Guest Column: What Does Queer Theory Teach Us about X?" *PMLA* 110 (3): 343–349.

Browne, Kath, and Catherine Nash. 2017. "Heteroactivism: Beyond Anti-Gay." *ACME: An International Journal for Critical Geographies* 16 (4): 643–652.

Campbell, Thomas H. 2006. "The Bioaesthetics of Evgenii Iufit." *KinoKultura: New Russian Cinema* 11 (January). Available at: http://www.kinokultura.com/2006/11-campbell.shtml.

David-Fox, Michael. 2015. *Crossing Borders: Modernity, Ideology, and Culture in Russia and the Soviet Union.* Pittsburgh: University of Pittsburgh Press.

Derrida, Jacques. 2016. *Of Grammatology.* Baltimore: Johns Hopkins University Press.

Dobrotvorsky, Sergei. 1993. "A Tired Death." In *Russian Necrorealism: Shock Therapy for New Culture,* edited by Anessa Miller-Pogacar, 7–8. Exhibition Catalogue. Bowling Green, OH: Bowling Green State University.

Edelman, Lee. 2004. *No Future: Queer Theory and the Death Drive.* Durham: Duke University Press.

Fiks, Yevgeniy. 2014. "The Theory of Pleshka." *Moscow Art Magazine* 44(3). Available at: http://moscowartmagazine.com/issue/44/article/887. Last accessed June 9, 2021.

Glissant, Édouard. 1997. *Poetics of Relation.* Translated by Betsy Wing. Ann Arbor: University of Michigan Press.

Godovannaya, Masha. n.d. "Resume/Bio." Masha Godovannaya. Last accessed January 23, 2023. Available at: https://mashagodovannaya.wordpress.com/resumebio-2/.

Halberstam, Judith. 2011. *The Queer Art of Failure.* Durham: Duke University Press.

hooks, bell. 1990. "Marginality as a Site of Resistance." *Out there: Marginalization and Contemporary Cultures* 4: 341–343.

Hoberman, James. 2005. "'Tout va bien' Revisited." *The Criterion Collection.* Available at: https://www.criterion.com/current/posts/356-tout-va-bien-revisited.

Karkov, Nikolay and Zhivka Valiavicharska. 2018. "Rethinking East-European Socialism: Notes Toward an Anti-Capitalist Decolonial Methodology." *Interventions* 20(6): 785–813.

Kosofsky Sedgwick, Eve. 1990. *Epistemology of the Closet.* Berkeley: The University of California Press.

Lewis, R. A. 2014. "'Gay? Prove It': The Politics of Queer Anti-Deportation Activism." *Sexualities* 17(8): 958–75.

Love, Heather. 2009. *Feeling Backward.* Cambridge, MA: Harvard University Press.

Mazin, Viktor. 1998. *Kabinet nekrorealisma: Iufit i.* St. Petersburg: Inapress.

———. 1999. "*Knights of the Heavens* in the Representation of Death." In *15th International Conference on Literature and Psychoanalysis*, edited by Frederico Pereira, 105–114. Lisbon: Instituto Superior de Psicologica Aplicada.

Mazin, Viktor, ed. 2015. *Kabinet Yufit «Ъ». Kartini Mira VII.* St. Petersburg: Skivia-print.

Neuberger, Joan. 2012. "Strange Circus: Eisenstein's Sex Drawings." *Studies in Russian and Soviet Cinema* 6(1): 5–52.

Medvedev, Sergei. 2019. "The State and the Human Body in Putin's Russia: The Biopolitics of Authoritarian Revanche, Part I." *NYU Jordan Center for the Advanced Study of Russia.* Available at: http://jordanrussiacenter.org/news/the-state-and-the-human-body-in-putins-russia-the-biopolitics-of-authoritarian-revanche-part-i/#.XZjBIiXgorg.

Reich, Wilhelm. 1962. *The Sexual Revolution: Toward a Self-regulating Character Structure.* New York: Macmillan.

Robinson, David. 2015. "New Eisenstein Biopic: Greenaway Goes Loco in Guanajuato" *Brenton Film* (May 22). Available at: http://www.brentonfilm.com/reviews/new-eisenstein-biopic-greenaway-goes-loco-in-guanajuato.

Salazkina, Masha. 2009. *In Excess: Sergei Eisenstein's Mexico*. Chicago: University of Chicago Press.

Smirnova, Elena. 2020. "Could You Show Me Chechnya on the Map? The Struggle for Solidarity within the Support Campaign for Homosexual Refugees from the North Caucasus in France." In *Queer-Feminist Solidarity and The East/West Divide,* edited by Katharina Wiedlack, Saltanat Shoshanova and Masha Godovannaya, 231–262. Berlin: Peter Lang.

Stella, Francesca and Nadya Nartova. 2015. "Sexual Nationalisms and the Boundaries of Sexual Citizenship." In *Sexuality, Citizenship and Belonging: Trans-National and Intersectional Perspectives*, 17–36. London: Routledge.

Stella, Francesca. 2015. *Lesbian Lives in Soviet and Post-Soviet Russia*. Farnham: Ashgate.

Tlostanova, Madina. 2012. "Postsocialist ≠ Postcolonial? On Post-Soviet Imaginary and Global Coloniality." *Journal of Postcolonial Writing* 48(2): 130–42.

Tuller, David. 1996. *Cracks in the Iron Closet: Travels in Gay and Lesbian Russia*. Boston: Faber.

Wiedlack, Katharina, Saltanat Shoshanova, and Masha Godovannaya, eds. 2020. *Queer-Feminist Solidarity and The East/West Divide.* Berlin: Peter Lang.

Wiedlack, Katharina. 2020. "Fucking Solidarity: 'Working Together' Through (Un) pleasant Feelings." In *Queer-Feminist Solidarity and The East/West Divide,* edited by Katharina Wiedlack, Saltanat Shoshanova and Masha Godovannaya, 21–50. Berlin: Peter Lang.

Yurchak, Alexei. 2013. *Everything Was Forever, Until It Was No More: The Last Soviet Generation.* Princeton: Princeton University Press.

Chapter 20

Queering Sexual Minorities: An Interview with Yevgeniy Fiks

Yevgeniy Fiks was born in Moscow in 1972 and has been living and working in New York since 1994. Fiks has produced many projects on the subject of post-Soviet dialogue in the West, among them: "Lenin for Your Library?" in which he mailed V. I. Lenin's text "Imperialism: The Highest Stage of Capitalism" to one hundred global corporations as a donation for their corporate libraries; "Communist Party USA," a series of portraits of current members of Communist Party USA, painted from life in the Party's national headquarters in New York City; and "Communist Guide to New York City," a series of photographs of buildings and public places in New York City that are connected to the history of the US Communist movement.

Fiks' work has been shown internationally. This includes exhibitions in the United States at Winkleman and Postmasters galleries (both in New York), Mass MoCA, and the Philadelphia Museum of Art; the Moscow Museum of Modern Art and Marat Guelman Gallery in Moscow; Sala de Arte Público Siqueiros in Mexico City, and the Museu Colecção Berardo in Lisbon. His work has been included in the Biennale of Sydney (2008), Moscow Biennale of Contemporary Art (2011), and Thessaloniki Biennale of Contemporary Art (2015). His artists books include Lenin For Your Library? *(ante projects),* Communist Guide to New York City *(Common Books), Moscow (Ugly Duckling Presse),* Soviet Moscow's Yiddish-Gay Dictionary *(Cicada Press), and* Monument to Cold War Victory *(The Cooper Union),* Mother Tongue *(Pleshka Presse), and* Dictionary of the Queer International *(Guelph).*

Brian James Baer [BJB]: What was the inspiration behind your Pleshkas of Russian Art project?

Yevgeniy Fiks [YF]: The "Pleshkas of Russian Art" project happened at the same time as I was working on my solo exhibition "The Lenin Museum," curated by Katherine Carl at The James Gallery, The Graduate Center of CUNY. We were preparing the show since 2013, and it opened in 2014. The exhibition was focused on hidden queer histories of the Central V. I. Lenin Museum in Moscow, and it was a research-based show, which reflected on a wide range of historical connections between communism, everyday Soviet experiences, and queer histories. For instance, as part of the show, my series of oil paintings "Pleshkas of the Revolution" was shown, in which I painted Moscow sites in a loose Soviet style important to the Soviet state and communist legacy, but that were also clandestinely used for gay cruising during the Soviet era.

Also, I made an installation there based on a quotation from the 1953 book *A Study of Bolshevism* by the American academic Nathan Leites, sponsored by the Rand Corporation and the United States Air Force, in which Leites inspected Lenin's writings among other things for traces of his alleged "repressed homosexual desire," effectively instrumentalizing 1950s homophobia as a tool for struggle against the Soviet Union. He was interested in the so-called "complex of latent homosexuality" of Soviet leaders, and especially Lenin, adapting earlier research on Nazi society, including Theodor Adorno's "The Authoritarian Personality," for the Cold War.

But while I was working on "The Lenin Museum," which was very much about specifically Soviet history and the Cold War, I felt the need to speak more broadly about Russian culture and history, especially 2013–2014 when Russia experienced the reemergence of state homophobia. The years 2013–2014 felt very tense for gay rights in Russia, with the introduction of the "gay propaganda" law, and the new official Russian accusatory rhetoric of "non-traditionality" directed at nonconforming gender and sexuality. So, we in the Russian emigré community in New York felt this urgency, especially with hundreds of Russian gay asylum seekers coming to the city then–something that I hadn't seen before.

I felt the urgency to make a broader project about a Russian queer history, beyond just the Soviet context, because the Soviet context is contaminated and can be easily brushed aside, while the broader Russian context—the historical Russia—feels more eternal. So, bringing to the foreground the centuries-deep traditionality of Russian sexual and gender nonconformism seemed very important and urgent in 2013–2014.

(The original statement about the "Pleshkas of Russian Art" project is provided in full in Appendix 1.)

BJB: I appreciate the dual focus of your project on the US Cold War study sponsored by the Rand Corporation looking for evidence of repressed homosexuality in Lenin and the Putin-era campaign against "nontraditional love."

It seems that throughout the twentieth-century, homosexuality has been used to tar one's ideological adversaries. Do you think we've fully emerged from the binary thinking of the Cold War? And if not, what do you see as art's role in moving us beyond those binaries?

YF: I don't think we are done with the Cold War binary thinking just yet, especially as far as nonconforming sexuality is concerned. I remember in the early 2010s, after relations between the US and Russia had deteriorated, and especially after the adoption of the "gay propaganda law" in Russia in 2013, LGBT rights all of a sudden became a point of contention between the two countries, or at least that's how the media presented it. Russia started to discuss LGBT rights and even queer sexuality as a type of foreign, imported plot, not unlike the Stalinist view of homosexuality as "bourgeois degeneracy." But the US government and media turned LGBT rights into propaganda fodder, in which the US appeared so much more favorably than the "backward and homophobic" Russia. This talk about "Russian homophobia" reminded me of talk about "Soviet anti-Semitism" in the 1970s and 1980s. Both are products of "whataboutism," where the US would level accusations against the Soviet Union and then Russia, in response, would level accusations of systemic racism in the US, for instance.

Of course, it speaks volumes about the progress with LGBT+ rights in the US, if the issue of LGBT rights can even be used in the 2010s legitimately as a foreign policy tool, but at the same time, I think, acknowledging the rather recent history of American state-sponsored and social homophobia is something that must be done to keep the self-righteous and self-congratulatory imperial tendencies in check. And speaking of Russia, its queer legacies are centuries deep and have outlived multiple repressive regimes and monarchies, so they will outlive the current one too.

As for the role of art in moving us beyond Cold War binaries, I think I'm a bit skeptical as to art's power, and I feel uneasy about cultural diplomacy and the use of art by the state, even by a liberal state that keeps their artists on a long, long leash. But at the same time, more organic and open exchange of art and ideas, without governmental or big business involvement, would be amazing and is needed.

BJB: Do you think your art would be different if you had stayed in Russia? If so, how?

YF: It's hard to say what would have happened, but I think I wouldn't be doing work about Soviet or Russian identity as much, because my work in Moscow before I left was very formalist and dry; it was conceptual, but in a more generic, universalist way. It wasn't "Russian" or "Soviet" at all. I actually felt more

"Western" when I lived in Moscow than I do now. It's funny, but I remember when I met Slava Mogutin for the first time in Moscow in 1992, he introduced himself as an "American culturologist" because I think at this time he worked for Voice of America or something. So, I guess it's a Russian *zapadnik* syndrome, when you feel Western while living in Russia, more Western than you really are. And then, after coming to Europe or America, a Russian émigré often turns back to Russia, its history, and becomes somewhat caricature-ish. I'm not sure why... maybe it's nostalgia, maybe it's diaspora nationalism, but I think it's common for Russian émigrés to become more "Russian" after coming to the West.

BJB: Your next project *Rodnaia rech'/Mother Tongue* was predominantly textual rather than visual. Was this a natural extension of your previous two projects, or does it represent a new direction in your art (figs. 1–5)?

YF: Text has always played a big role in my projects, for instance, in "Homosexuality is Stalin's Atom Bomb to destroy America," for which I use homophobic and anti-Communist quotations from American politicians and pundits of the Cold War era. And text has always been historically a very important component in conceptual art—American or Russian. Also, I have several conceptual art projects executed in the form of books, that is, conceptual art projects as books.

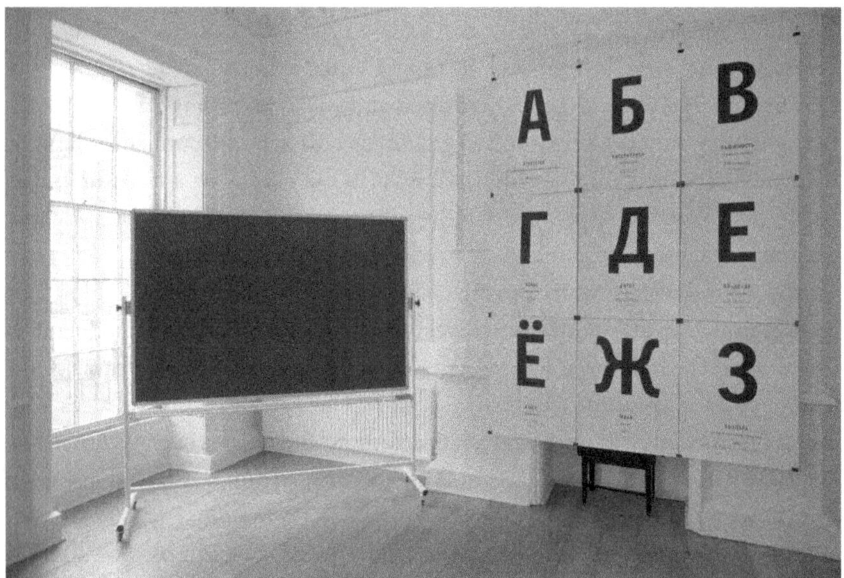

FIGURES 1-5. Yevgeniy Fiks, *Mother Tongue* (2019), design by Katya Sivers, photo by Natalia Tarasova. Courtesy of the artist, Grad, and Pushkin House, London

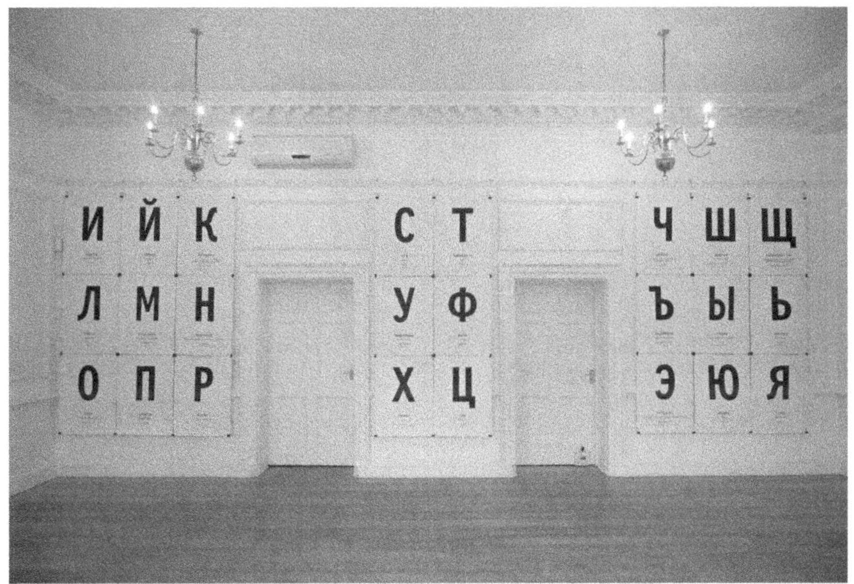

FIGURE 2

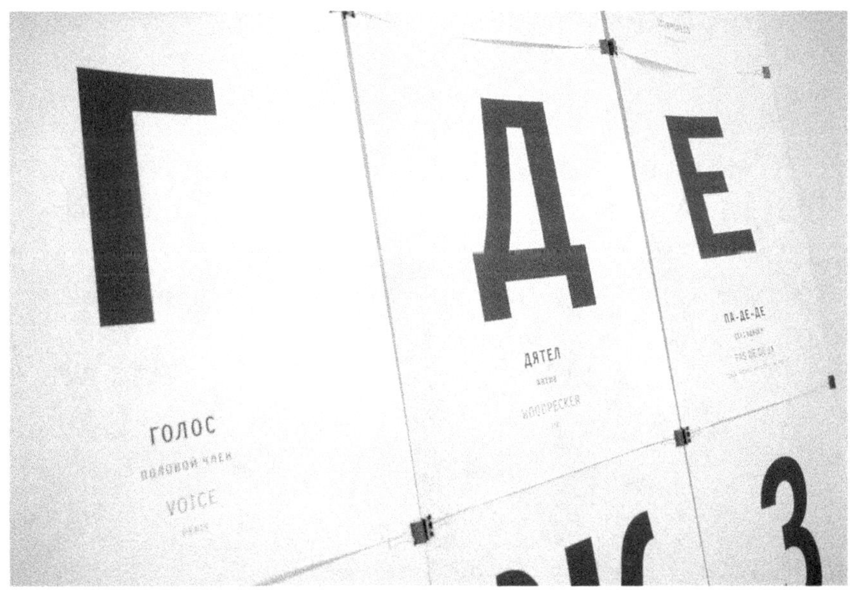

FIGURE 3

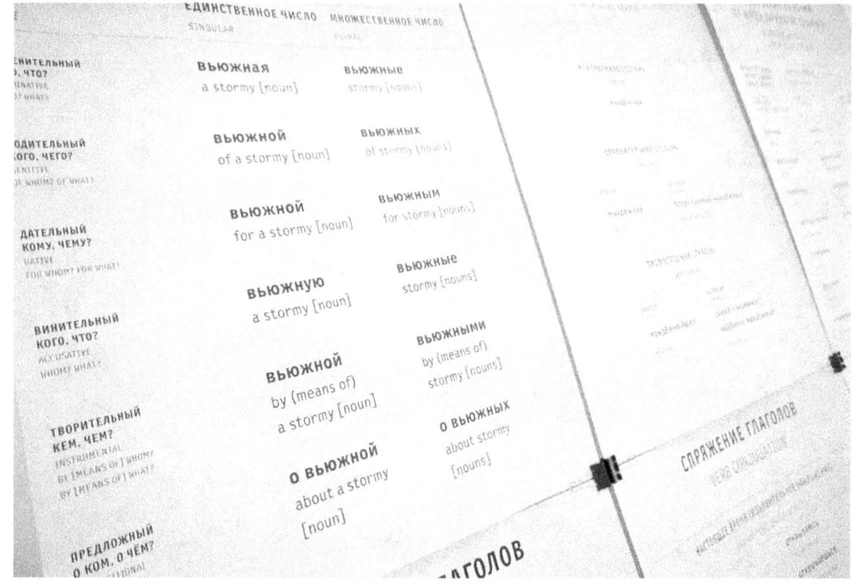

FIGURE 4

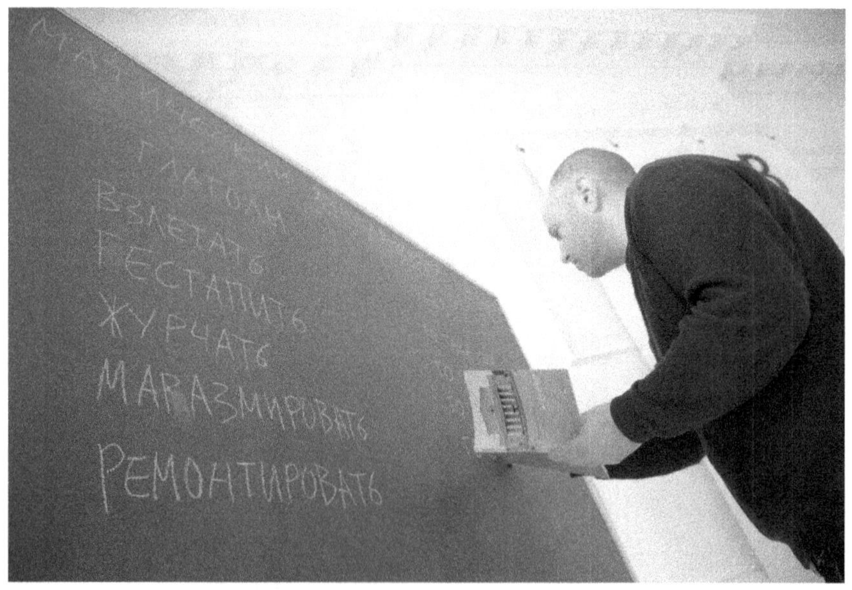

FIGURE 5

Mother Tongue is one of them as well as, for instance, *Soviet Moscow's Yiddish-Gay Dictionary*. I have a brand-new book coming out this month called *Dictionary of the Queer International*.

BJB: So, the idea of minority and of overlapping minorities seems important to your work both on Soviet gay subculture and Yiddish culture. Can you talk a bit about the concept of "minority" in your work?

YF: I guess I come from a traditional Soviet understanding of a minority, an "ethnic minority" that is, and this is something that I heard all around me growing up. And it definitely had a personal dimension to me from early on. I grew up self-consciously Jewish in Moscow; I was born there in 1972, so I was fully Russified and fully Sovietized, the Russian language is my mother tongue. But I'm only a second-generation Russian speaker, my parents being first-generation Russian speakers. All four of my grandparents were native Yiddish speakers and moved to Moscow from Ukraine right before the War and continued to speak Yiddish at home and practice Judaism when possible. They were of the pre-Revolutionary generation of small-town Jews, subjects of the Russian Empire, but who thought of themselves as Jews only. In their wildest imagination, they would never identify as Russians. And this sense of separateness and distinction from the majority—"us" and "them"—was definitely passed on to my parents and then in more diluted forms to my brother and me. And it has a special meaning because in the 1970s and 1980s, Jews were probably the largest ethnic minority in Moscow in numbers. Moscow definitely had a Jewish question then.

Now switching to the gay question, the experience of growing up Jewish in Moscow in the 1970s and 1980s had some "training value"—it prepared me to accept myself as a gay man in late 1980s and early 1990s. So, there are some similarities and overlaps between Soviet gay and Soviet Jewish experience in terms of tactics and optics—the "us" vs "them." It's about, OK, you are smaller in numbers, you are different, but you are not ugly or worthless. So, it's about a dose of healthy minority pride, that helps you cope with hostile surroundings.

Then in the late 1980s, the term "sexual minorities" started to be used in Soviet gay and mainstream media, analogous to "ethnic minorities," and I still think that it was a successful term that had good implications for Russia, because the Russian state and society could understand the word "minority"—it's a traditional and in that sense a legitimate term with which no one can argue. "Sexual minorities" had and can still have a legitimizing affect, while ΛΓБТ (LGBT) is seen as a foreign, perhaps imported construct, which makes it much easier to say that ΛΓБТ is nontraditional and therefore illegitimate. At the same time, you cannot argue that "minorities" don't exist in Russia. Everybody accepts that they do. I understand that the minoritarian discourse is exclusionary and problematic, but I think in Russia it would bring more success in terms of the betterment of queer lives in Russia.

BJB: I felt as I was translating the "poems" in *Mother Tongue*, written in Soviet gay slang, that you were walking a very fine line between respect for the experience of Soviet gays and a profound campiness. The translations were very difficult, but I found myself often breaking out in laughter as I worked on them. Again, it felt on the one hand to be a send up of all the traditional Soviet/Russian pieties—poetry, for one—while on the other, to be an expression of real affection. Is that an American misreading of your work?

YF: No, I think you are absolutely correct, and I'm very happy you enjoyed it, that it brought a smile to your face, and I'm sorry the translation was difficult. Thanks for the amazing translation work! I was breaking out in laughter as I was working on the book as well, I enjoyed every minute of it.

I think *Mother Tongue* captures the self-deprecating sensibility of Soviet camp—*khabal'stvo*—the self-irony, joy, laughter—which happened notwithstanding Article 121 and the possibility of repressions that could totally destroy your life, your career plans, and your health.

Soviet camp traversed cultural and class divides, and a Soviet queer could camp up Pushkin, Lermontov, and Tolstoy. Well, maybe not Dostoevsky. Remember, what they used to say about the Soviet public—that it's the "most reading public" in the world—that Soviets loved to read. I'm not sure, maybe it was propaganda, but yes, I remember seeing almost everyone reading on the metro—and often thick hardcover volumes of the classics. So, a Soviet queer, being part of the Soviet public, loved to read too and was probably the most "reading queer" in the world! So *habalit'* (to camp it up) about Great Russian classical literature, not just about the pop culture of Shul'zhenko and Pugacheva, is what she did!

BJB: Slava Mogutin, whom you interviewed for this volume, is a very vocal critique of gay identity politics, aligning himself with a radical and iconoclastic queer tradition embodied by cultural figures like Jean Genet. How do you situate yourself in relation to the gay/queer divide or do you reject the divide altogether? I found in my recent work *Queer Theory and Translation Studies* that we can embrace both "orientations" as part of an ultimately unresolvable and perhaps necessary tension between an identitarian attraction for community and belonging and a healthy suspicion of the exclusionary logic of identitarian communities.

YF: I have a friend, Allen Young, who is an American gay liberation activist and actually one of the founders the Gay Liberation Front of 1970. Allen grew up as a "red diaper baby," then was in the New Left and did a lot of activism in the US and in Cuba in the 1960s, before coming out and turning to gay rights activism. He is allergic to the word/term "queer." Whenever I brought up "queer" or "queerness," he refused to discuss it. For him, the insistence on fluidity and the undefinable is what his generation of gay activists fought against. I guess for him it's a delusion, a lack of clarity—"boi v Krymu, vse v dymu, nichego ne vidno." (battle in the Crimea, everything is in smoke, nothing is visible).

I guess, I'm suspicious of the bohemian radical queer iconoclastic tradition. It feels like a culture of excess that is too easily romanticized and fetishized at Upper East Side dinner parties and luxury SOHO lofts. I personally come from the Soviet working-middle class, and I've kept a day job all my life. So, I say the queer/gay divide is a social class issue as well. Queerness goes out partying on a weeknight after gayness comes home from a ten-hour shift.

Speaking of the Soviet/Russian experience, I think we should take Article 121 of the Soviet criminal code as a definitive litmus test for the issue of the "gay" vs "queer" divide. It doesn't matter whether one calls themselves "gay" or "queer." The real question is: Would one be subjected to prosecution and sentenced under Article 121? Let the repressive Soviet state apparatus resolve the "gay" vs "queer" question for us. The Soviet state knows where "queer" ends and where "gay" begins. Are you a gay or a queer if your actions (and social class, geographical predicament, and politics) land you in prison under Article 121?

I guess I trust the Parisian queer radical Jean Genet less than I do the timid middle-class Leningrad *goluboi* Gennadiy Trifonov. The quiet identitarian misery of the Soviet prisoner of Article 121, Trifonov, seems more trustworthy to me.

Appendix 1. *Pleshkas of Russian Art* by Yevgeniy Fiks

In Russian gay argot, "pleshka" is a cruising ground.
Pleshkas of Russian Art is a public intervention that subverts the commonly accepted "official" heteronormative narrative of Russian art history. For this project, Fiks modified real catalogs of the Guggenheim Museum's *RUSSIA!* exhibition by inserting between catalogue's pages artist-made papers with text narrating gay Russian history. The artist then shop-dropped them at the Guggenheim Museum gift shop in New York.

The *RUSSIA!* exhibition, held at the Guggenheim museum in New York in 2005, was an important milestone in the process of legitimizing the post-Soviet narrative and President Putin's first term in office. It was designed as a grandiose noncritical celebration of Russian nationalism and power through instrumentalizing Russian cultural heritage as a propaganda tool.

Pleshkas of Russian Art shows a rupture between the official heteronormative art historical narrative and Russian gay history, which remain largely ignored, unacknowledged, and repressed. *Pleshkas of Russian Art* conceptualizes Russian art history as "closeted"—as a space only for clandestine gay presence—which must be transformed into a site for struggle for visibility and voice today. Beyond simply critiquing the conservatism of the art historical establishment, Fiks posits that the silence of mainstream art historians about the LGBT presence in Russian art history is a willing collaboration in the systematic historic repression of Russian LGBT people.

Pages of the Russian state-endorsed exhibition *RUSSIA!* become metaphorical gay cruising grounds—*pleshkas* of Russian art history. Fiks, however, avoids "outing" artists of the past who were homosexuals. The inserts in the catalogs do not name any artists by name and focus mainly on social and political aspects of gay history. *Pleshkas of Russian Art* suggests a need for a proper and long-term project of rereading Russian art history with a queer eye—one that have yet to be embarked upon by mainstream art history. As of today, this work points to the failure of art historical establishment to write a fuller and more inclusive narrative of Russian art.

The texts used in this project come from writings on Russian gay history by historians Simon Karlinsky and Dan Healey.

Documented: photos of the modified catalogs on a shelf in the Guggenheim Museum gift shop in New York.

INDEX

D

Q

R

www.ingramcontent.com/pod-product-compliance
Lightning Source LLC
LaVergne TN
LVHW020503100826
845148LV00003B/689
9798897830978